MAKING EDUCATION WORK FOR THE POOR

Making Education Work for the Poor

THE POTENTIAL OF CHILDREN'S SAVINGS ACCOUNTS

William Elliott and Melinda Lewis

OXFORD
UNIVERSITY PRESS

Oxford University Press is a department of the University of Oxford. It furthers
the University's objective of excellence in research, scholarship, and education
by publishing worldwide. Oxford is a registered trade mark of Oxford University
Press in the UK and certain other countries.

Published in the United States of America by Oxford University Press
198 Madison Avenue, New York, NY 10016, United States of America.

CIP data is on file at the Library of Congress
ISBN 978–0–19–086684–6 (pbk.)
ISBN 978–0–19–062156–8 (hbk.)

9 8 7 6 5 4 3 2 1

Paperback printed by Webcom Inc., Canada
Hardback printed by Bridgeport National Bindery, Inc., United States of America

Contents

Preface

Research with a Clear Public Purpose

It is our contention in this book—and our conviction—that wealth inequality and inequality of opportunity are related but distinct concepts. Specifically, wealth inequality undermines equal opportunity. Inequality of opportunity funnels Americans into diverging institutional relationships that then lead to wealth gaps. In turn, the resulting wealth inequality contributes to inequality of opportunity, as wealthy individuals use their resources to secure better chances—including within the institution of education—for themselves and their children. However, these circular connections do not mean that the same policy responses will effectively address both wealth inequality and inequality of opportunity, nor that both injustices demand the same level of redress. Specifically, while to fully eliminate wealth inequality, everyone would have to be given the same *amount* of wealth, eliminating inequality of opportunity requires only that everyone have the same *opportunity* for building wealth.

Another way of putting this is that eliminating opportunity gaps starts with examining whether there are enough institutional resources available to a person in order to ensure that it is her effort and ability that actually determine her position on the economic ladder. If so, she may not end up with the same wealth as her peers, but it will not be because she lacked a fair chance to do so. This framing, which centers on opportunities more than outcomes, has real significance when we think of the types of policies to pursue. The focus turns to the institutional resources needed to make effort and ability the deciding factors in determining one's success. Importantly, the connection between opportunity and inequality may also matter politically, as evidence suggests that Americans are more concerned with the threats that a given dimension of inequality poses to equitable opportunities than with a particular level of inequality, per se.[1]

From our perspective, wealth inequality and opportunity inequality—and the policies needed to counter them—are complementary. Research and policy development can—and should—proceed on both fronts, examining ways to disrupt the link between wealth gaps and the opportunity divide. However, the prospects of change may vary substantially, depending on whether the emphasis is placed on equalizing opportunities or equalizing wealth. Specifically, while we see talking about eradicating the opportunity gap as aligned with American values, the policies required to ensure completely equal asset holdings would be less likely to resonate with the American ideal that effort and ability should determine winners and losers.

If our interests with this book were only to explore evidence and advance theory, we may be agnostic as to how inequality is framed. Indeed, there is an academic tradition that touts the idea that research should be "value free," without a "clear public purpose."[2] Significantly, however, this commitment is not equally-held by those arrayed at different points along the ideological spectrum. As a result, while the success of some conservatives in framing research and policy in ways that resonate with American values has reshaped policy preferences across many domains,[2] many liberal-leaning academics have eschewed such considerations as undermining intellectual purity. In recoiling from perceived "bias," these scholars have failed to make efforts to connect their research to relevant policy debates or even to talk about findings and their implications in ways that invite public engagement.

From the perspective of many academics, particularly adherents to liberal intellectual traditions, research is supposed to challenge assertions on empirical grounds but make no attempt to connect with people's values. Adopting a value-free approach to research means that researchers do not have to consider how to talk about their analyses in ways that fit with Americans' beliefs. They do not have to think about how to translate research findings into tangible policy implications. Of course, consigning research to the purely theoretical and empirical planes makes irrelevance a possible, even likely, outcome.[3] Directly pertinent to the subject of this book, there is no chance of a meaningful conversation about reducing wealth inequality in order to close the opportunity divide if wealth transfers are not put on the table. However, winning wealth transfer policy is currently seen as impossible; further, much academic inquiry does little to alter this calculus, often gravitating to the poles of total avoidance of even the word "transfer" or, conversely, dispassionate analysis that may alienate. This example underscores that academics who want to see their research transform the landscape cannot afford to ignore the process of helping people understand how research findings and implications fit with American values.

In an attempt to avoid irrelevance and to instead contribute to conversations about what might be possible in American policymaking, here we adopt a clear public purpose for our scholarship. We reject as a false dichotomy the presumed conflict between academic integrity and attachment to core values. We acknowledge that we all have a set of beliefs about the world and how it works. Indeed, shared values animate collective identity and help people to interpret events. As researchers, we carry our values with us when choosing the questions we ask, conducting analysis, and interpreting findings. That is, researchers—ourselves included—do not stop being human when we approach inquiry. This is different than saying that a researcher cannot achieve objectivity when confronted with facts that do not support his/her hypotheses. While the definition of "good" science as value-free has provided an opening to label facts with which we do not agree as merely ideological and thus invalid, if we acknowledge that merely having values does not make one incapable of objectivity, perhaps we can move forward with a more honest conversation about the problems we face. Only then do we have a real chance to arrive at the solutions that may have the best chance of working. Objectivity requires following the facts regardless of where they take you. We have observed that this is a feat most easily done with a clear public purpose. That is, researchers are able to achieve objectivity best when their public purpose is the guidepost they follow, overriding even their value predispositions.

Our public purpose is to generate a meaningful conversation about opportunity and the institutions charged with facilitating it. We are transparent about our objective: to foster change by making our research transformative. Toward this aim, we frame the challenge we face: eradicating the opportunity gap. This will require eliminating persistent patterns of wealth inequality. However, it does not necessarily mean that the wealth divide must entirely close, or even that it must be shrunk to a predetermined size. America is built on the idea that competition is key for creating prosperity. Most Americans believe that people need to be motivated to work and, further, that motivation comes from competition. These beliefs matter, whether research upholds them as factual or not. While providing everyone with an equal amount of wealth is in direct contradiction to an aim of fostering an environment where competition thrives, most Americans would acknowledge that competition does not motivate when the game is clearly rigged to favor some and not others. Therefore, we contend that making competition fair by closing the opportunity gap is not out of sync with American values. Instead, creating institutions that give everyone an equal shot at winning reinforces Americans' ways of seeing ourselves and our chances. America is at its best when effort and ability are truly the factors that decide why one person or group succeeds and another does not. The converse, then, has to also be true; America is its worst when effort and ability do not explain why one person or group succeeds and another does not. That, however, is precisely the case today. We situate the research findings and policy proposal presented in this book within this value context so that we can ask what role children's assets might play in bringing Americans' realities in line with their value preferences.

While eradicating the opportunity gap should be the main goal of American policy, we do not see that this can be accomplished without attending to wealth inequality. The most vivid example of the imperative to address wealth inequality directly is the case of the racial wealth gap.[4-6] As discussed in chapter 2, the racial wealth gap is the result of a long history of policies and practices that have provided White Americans a huge asset advantage over, in particular, African Americans and Latinos.[7] Adequately addressing the racial wealth gap, itself an assault on fair competition, requires building into an opportunity agenda an additional level of progressivity targeted specifically at people of color[8] to undo the damage caused by unfair policies, an approach some have called "targeted universalism."[9]

In large part, the need for additional redress is compelled by continuing racial discrimination. That is, racial discrimination is an added barrier that people of color face in their pursuit of equal opportunities. As a result, with two poor people, one Black and the other White, even with similar levels of assets, the Black person would be at a greater disadvantage. In 2004, Tom Shapiro calculated this additional disadvantage and arrived at a "cost" of being African American of $136,174.[5] Alarmingly, this inequality appears to have survived substantial changes in US financial and labor markets and to persist even at higher levels of prosperity. For example, Shapiro, Meschede, and Osoro found that a $1.00 increase in income later translates to a $5.00 increase in wealth for Whites but only a $0.70 increase for Blacks.[10] Importantly, they also found that even when Blacks start off with similar levels of assets, they have a return of $4.03 for each dollar increase in income, less than the $5.00 increase Whites realize. These gaps largely reflect differences in the opportunities afforded by crucial wealth-building institutions. These findings suggest that while universal policies can greatly reduce the racial wealth gap, if we want to ensure that all Americans have a level foundation on which to pursue their dreams, we must not ignore the particular case of how race closes doors to equal chances.

We would never presume nor pretend to have all of the answers about how the United States should approach narrowing wealth divides as part of a concerted quest to equalize opportunity in ways aligned with our American dream. We do believe, however, that looking at what ails the dream today through a lens of wealth inequality offers particular promise for correctly diagnosing the disease, particularly at the bottleneck of its greatest conduit—the education system. This is the public purpose for our scholarship, and we endeavor to approach it rooted in values that we hope can catalyze collective action. Only then, by leveraging the potency of American beliefs in fair chances, can we construct a policy "cure," before it is too late.

Acknowledgments

William Elliott

Over the years there have been many people who have helped shape my thinking about how to make effort and ability the real reason why people succeed and fail in America and not where they are born or the color of their skin. And while I cannot mention them all here, I do want to thank Michael Sherraden and his wife Margret Sherraden who introduced me to Children's Savings Accounts, helped me develop as a PhD student, and challenged me to understand how even small-dollar accounts could improve the lives of poor children. I would also like to thank Bob Friedman, Andrea Levere, Justin King, Ray Boshara, and Reid Cramer; they have done so much to make sure the work I have done has made it into the hands of practitioners, the media, researchers, and the general public. I would also like to thank the people on the ground running the programs such as Clint Kugler, Colleen Quint, Ona Porter, and Jose Cisneros. They have challenged me to go beyond theory and research to think about the realities of implementing CSAs in communities like theirs. This work would not be possible without funding. Three funders in particular did more than provide funding, however, as they have shared their thoughts and ideas about where the field should go. They are Benita Melton, Kilolo Kijakazi, and Frank DeGiovanni. But most of all I want to thank my family—both my parents and my sister, who helped shaped me as a person, as well as my wife, Amy, and my three children (Jordan, Michelle, and Michael) who put up with the long hours required to write this book.

Melinda Lewis

This book is inspired by the Children's Savings Account champions whose visions of early children's asset investments are sowing hope and expanding opportunity across the country. Our analysis has been informed by impressive scholarship in the fields of education and wealth inequality, as well as by insights generously shared by CSA participants. However, my greatest gratitude is to my husband and kids, who share my conviction that policy must provide fair chances to all American children, and whose resolve toward this end sustained them through everything required to bring the book to fruition.

Introduction

THIS BOOK EXAMINES the American education system through a lens of wealth inequality. From a perspective centered on wealth, education is revealed as one of the largest investments America makes in providing equitable opportunities. For the poor, education is supposed to be the way to climb the proverbial economic ladder. The level playing field that the education system is purported to provide is what is perceived as legitimizing the idea of the American dream. While it may take somewhat different forms for its millions of adherents—an ownership stake, surpassing one's parents, liberty to pursue one's own path[1]— here we broadly construe the American dream as fair chances to secure a "good life," through hard work and application of innate talent. Education is central to most individuals' perception of their chances to achieve the American dream.[2] As wealth researchers, then, our interest in the education system is not as much about acquisition of knowledge as an end in itself as about the power of educational attainment to equalize life chances and, in turn, to reduce wealth inequality. That does not mean we do not value education. Rather, we assume that America has historically invested in education not merely because policymakers and the populace want an educated citizenry for its own sake but primarily because Americans believe education is a path to individual prosperity, a tool for increasing overall productivity, and an engine of the economic growth on which our collective fortunes depend.

Our critiques of the weaknesses in the opportunity pipeline that runs through the US education system should not be construed, then, as negating the importance of education. There is evidence to suggest that educational attainment pays real dividends to individual students and to the larger society. For example, Rothwell finds that college graduates contribute, on average, $278,000 more than high school graduates to their local economies over their lifetimes.[3] Further, education serves a rhetorical purpose beyond this economic utility. American investments in education can be seen as a way of reconciling our shared belief in equitable opportunities with the undeniable reality of considerable inequality.

Indeed, the inequality that concerns us most is that which is seen as undermining equitable opportunity.[4] It is the education system that is supposed to be the level playing field on which individual merit is fairly evaluated, unfair advantage counteracted, and authentic accomplishments justly rewarded. Perhaps counterintuitively, then, we see hope in today's growing attention to Americans' declining mobility prospects. It is when pessimism about our chances to get ahead surges that the American public musters the greatest energy to address inequality.[4] As evidence mounts to suggest that wealth inequality is closing doors to fair chances in our education system—the kind of inequality that American public opinion is most consistently and strongly against—Americans are demanding that their dream be salvaged.

As we outline the wealth perspective around which this book is organized, we emphasize that we are intentionally referring to ourselves as *wealth* researchers and not *poverty* researchers. Poverty research has largely been concerned with income-based programs designed to reduce the negative effects associated with being in poverty (e.g., "welfare"). The emphasis is on programs that aim to provide poor people with some minimum amount of goods or their substitutes, in order to guarantee subsistence. However, as wealth researchers, we are shifting the focus from attempting to find the minimum that poor people require to survive to instead analyzing what is required to equip them with equitable life chances. Clearly there has to be a floor from which people can launch themselves upward, but a floor is insufficient. Further, we argue that a myopic attention to policies of survival may even be a barrier to upward mobility, if this foundation is not constructed with takeoff in mind.

If the goal of policies for the poor is framed as providing them with some minimal amount of goods and services, as it mostly has been, it becomes acceptable to include policy features that force people to choose between receiving valuable government assistance and leveraging resources for the purpose of upward mobility. Policy that aims only at survival, in other words, seldom even attempts to facilitate advancement.[5] This means that anti-poverty policy may include compromises such as means tests that drastically limit asset accumulation and explicitly make it harder for those in and near poverty to climb through the same systems that encourage asset accumulation and upward mobility for others. This framework and the outcomes it perpetuates stand in stark contrast to policy aimed at those who are already economically-advantaged. Perhaps even more importantly, this policy apparatus stands apart from the investments and mechanisms that undergird the American dream, serving to separate entire populations from the promises the dream extends—and policy subsidizes—for others.

In contrast, for rich Americans, institutional arrangements explicitly aim to facilitate asset growth. Policies aimed at those equipped with a strong wealth position set expectations that people should leverage institutions for growth and upward mobility. For example, as Shapiro highlights, when rich people save for their children's college educations, this practice is seen as a marker of good parenting to be rewarded through the tax code, while low-income parents attempting the same feat may be punished.[5] The practical consequences of these counter-approaches include stalled mobility prospects and a harsh daily accounting that trades future growth for current maintenance. The rhetorical implications send a clear message that the American dream of upward mobility—including through education—is not for all, at least not equitably.

In these ways, government benefit and policy support structures chart divergent futures for Americans, depending on their wealth. This means that the rising fortunes of the already wealthy and the stagnant futures of the imperiled-poor are not incidental outcomes, but anticipated results of deliberate policy structures. This dual paradigm, with survival policies for the poor and growth policies for the rich, ensures there will be little mobility in America. At least, there will be little relative mobility of the sort captured in the American dream narrative of climbing from "rags to riches." Instead, movement will mostly consist of the poor standing still or sliding down and the well-off advancing further up the ladder. Even when absolute mobility enables Americans to do better than their parents, the greater distance between the rungs on the economic ladder ensures that this progress will be insufficient to vault people to a higher relative standard of living.[6] Significantly, the diverging streams of growth and subsistence policies not only contribute to today's widening inequality but also betray American ideals that suggest that everyone should have a fair opportunity to achieve the American dream, regardless of their starting point. That is the story of America we tell our children, one of equal life chances. Making it more than a fable will require policy change. Achieving that shift begins with altering how we see the institutions that are supposed to catalyze the kind of mobility we mean—the kind poor Americans need, and the kind all

Americans want to believe is still possible. In this book, we begin with the central opportunity engine of today's United States: the education system.

Responsibility for Poverty Shared across the Ideological Spectrum

Policymakers and pundits of all ideological persuasions are largely locked into a perspective that mostly ignores the role of wealth in charting Americans' trajectories and determining the outcomes they can wring from institutions. Many of the policies that have driven the subsistence and growth approaches in diverging directions, including welfare policy for the poor and tax-code subsidies for wealth building, have attracted substantial bipartisan support. Therefore, we do not see today's growing wealth inequality as an exclusively conservative creation. Indeed, many liberal researchers and policymakers have embraced the idea that policies for the poor should be survival policies and that only after the basic needs of the poor are met should attention shift to growth. Importantly, this can perpetuate narratives of the poor as being present-time oriented or even incapable of truly thriving, which serve to further obscure the institutional dynamics that drive behavior and subsequent outcomes. Unsurprisingly, because the poor largely remain poor, it never seems like a good time to consider policies that would facilitate their wealth building.

The poor are further trapped in their position when, in the process of political compromise, survival policies collide with conservative "small government" ideologies. The result seldom provides any means for moving up the economic ladder. Locked out of institutions that build wealth for the privileged and relegated to structures that prevent their climb, poor people are virtually guaranteed to hover around the "survival" threshold. Specifically, people in poverty are often penalized for trying to accumulate any assets while receiving assistance, while wealth-building incentives delivered through the tax code offer no value to those who do not earn enough to owe tax liability. What our analysis highlights is this: when moving up the economic ladder is facilitated by institutions, it is equally true that staying at the bottom or falling farther down is also facilitated by institutions. While ideologies may dispute whether institutions or behavior matter more for determining outcomes, we should be able to agree that each plays a role. Therefore, each should do its part to make the American dream meaningfully possible for all.

In the initial chapters of this book, we use our own life stories, particularly as they intersect with elements of the US education system, to illustrate how wealth inequality influences experiences and respective outcomes. Here, too, in the diverging effects of growth and survival policies, we see reflections of our own lives. For example, Medicaid allows Willie's dad to receive care in an assisted living facility. However, Medicaid rules require Willie's elderly mother, who cares for his disabled sister, to keep her income low in order to qualify for this essential assistance. She is not even allowed to receive gifts from family that would raise her income above the required limit. Further, she can have few assets in her name. As a result, in order to secure the care her husband vitally needs, she is consigned to living in poverty.

Similarly, Willie's sister has degenerative rheumatoid arthritis, which confines her to a wheelchair and limits her ability to work. While there are times that the medication is working and she could work more, if she earns too much or works too many hours, she will lose her disability benefits. Moreover, because she is very frugal, she could scrimp to save more, but that is not allowed. In these ways, the nature of survival policies similarly dooms her to poverty. Of course, it is not only the elderly and those with disabilities who are limited by the survival paradigm. The wealth-building prospects of all low-income Americans are constrained by the impossible choices compelled by this inequitable system. These rules encourage the poor to adopt behaviors that will prevent asset building and force them to sell off the very assets they would need to vault out of poverty—through pursuing additional education, moving to a mobility-enhancing locale, or making some other productive investment in their well-being. As such, policy makes it more likely that people in poverty will remain there.[7]

Redeeming the American dream will require transcending these narrow and inherently unfair approaches. Legislatively, that demands the kind of true political compromises only possible with strong champions from both liberal and conservative perspectives who share an underlying commitment that facilitating mobility should be a core policy aim, even if there remains some disagreement about what type of mobility matters most or the types of policies that will deliver it.[8,9] Instead, negotiations today often begin as a "compromise" between survival policies for the poor and wealth creation for the rich. This is a cycle of deal-making that the poor can never win. Because liberals spend their time proposing and defending the survival policies that can contribute to widening inequality, conservatives and the elites whose interests they often serve never really stand to lose anything. Their worst-case scenario is usually that policies are adopted that may help to maintain the status quo. Notably, when they win, the resulting increase in their economic power often positions them to more successfully angle for advantage in the next round.[10] And so, conservatives have learned that they can "lose" any number of policy battles; as long as they secure a few victories, over time, these accumulate to drastically tilt the landscape in their direction.

Illustrating this dynamic are the tax cuts enacted in the George W. Bush administration, which Democrats largely came to support, fearing that their repeal would raise taxes for the middle class and risk the anger of this important political constituency. This position required that Democratic leaders argue in favor of tax policy that included provisions that primarily benefit wealthy individuals, such as lower taxes on capital gains and lower rates on the first $250,000 of income for even the richest Americans.[11] The net result of this kind of deal is that the most advantaged Americans profit more, in order to preserve more modest gains for those less privileged. Especially when the truly disadvantaged are excluded nearly entirely, these are not the kind of "compromises" that should count.

BIG GOVERNMENT FALLACY

Survival and growth policies can be distinguished not just by their outcomes but also by the means by which they pursue their respective aims. In particular, because survival policies for the poor require direct appropriations and, often, considerable bureaucracy (to determine eligibility and oversee compliance), they have come to be equated with the "big government" that conservatives loathe and of which Americans are generally somewhat skeptical.[12] This framing then creates openings to penalize poor people for using government programs or to eliminate programs altogether, in the name of small government. While growth supports for the rich (particularly social insurance and tax-based incentives for wealth building) represent larger governmental investments, liberal emphasis on survival policies contributes to the relative invisibility of government investments in wealth building.[13,14] With the decisive role of policy and institutional supports in facilitating economic prosperity for only some Americans thus obscured, there is relatively little demand to equitably include poor people in wealth-building structures, even though doing so could result in greater aggregate prosperity and stronger prospects for upward mobility. Public ambivalence about survival policies has also led some to conclude that Americans are not that concerned about inequality. In reality, evidence suggests considerable appetite for mechanisms for creating and distributing opportunity; however, this receptivity does not extend to policies taking a subsistence approach.[4]

Government action is not the only possible response to wealth inequality's threat to the American dream. At the same time, looking at policy from a perspective of wealth inequality reveals the extent to which government already intervenes to enhance the standing of some Americans. This analysis, in other words, gives lie to the idea of "getting government out" of people's lives. Americans have always believed in government intervention and have historically supported institutions they perceive as capable of improving their lives. Opinion polls have consistently found a strong majority agreeing that the United States should do what is necessary to give all Americans an equal opportunity to get ahead.[4] Our government is one of America's greatest strengths. The questions remain and have always been when, how, and for whom government should provide assistance and to what ends. Therefore, from our perspective, a more productive form of conservatism would focus on eliminating unproductive programs, while focusing policy goals on fostering equitable chances for asset growth, in forms both financial and social. A more constructive form of liberalism would transcend subsistence to insist on equitable inclusion in the full promise of America. Champions from both perspectives would accept only compromises that advance toward this central aim of fair growth. The focus on asset building as the end goal of policy is the ideological framework behind an opportunity agenda. It is neither liberal nor conservative. Creating equal opportunity for all, regardless of the starting point, is the quintessentially *American* idea.

Opportunity Pipeline

In the United States, it is commonly agreed that education is one of the most powerful tools we have for leveling the playing field and equalizing opportunity. The term "education pipeline" is often used to refer to the idea that children progress on a continuum from early childhood through postsecondary education. While the education pipeline is the largest investment America makes in providing everyone with the opportunity to achieve the American dream, we suggest that in the 21st century, we need something more. We have termed this conduit of equitable chances for success the "opportunity pipeline." The opportunity pipeline extends what has traditionally been called the education pipeline in both directions, including families' early investments in children's well-being, on the front end, and post-college financial health, at the other. It takes the focus off education as *the* goal and places it squarely on the opportunities education should afford children to reach the American dream.

Beginning in chapter 1, we make the case that the US education system is not the "great equalizer" it is purported to be. Nowhere is this clearer than at the point of college completion, when disadvantaged students who have managed to make it all the way to and through college do not realize the same returns on that achievement as those who started from privilege.[15,16] In chapter 6, we introduce Opportunity Investment Accounts (OIAs) as a starting point for creating an opportunity agenda for America. OIAs are an extension of the intervention known as Children's Savings Accounts (CSAs). CSAs are accounts typically opened at birth or kindergarten that leverage families' investments with a small-dollar initial deposit (from $25 to $1,000) and savings matches, usually on a 1:1 ratio. As we outline them, OIAs are CSAs combined with a significant ($10,000 or more) progressive initial deposit. They are grounded in evidence that suggests that early educational assets can transform children's lives and are informed by our research that reveals that poor families will need substantial institutional support if they are to accrue these assets.

While, as we explain in the final chapter, OIAs must be complemented by other policies, as part of the comprehensive wealth-building agenda Americans need and deserve, they represent the aspect of the study of wealth inequality and its consequenceswith which we have the most experience. We see the articulation of the opportunity pipeline as the encapsulation of the next important step for the research agenda that aims to make the case for an alternative, wealth-building approach to anti-poverty policy: Can the fact that poor children had assets from the beginning mean that they arrive at a similar place as those whose journeys were propelled by economic privilege? In other words, can countering wealth inequality through "advance asset accumulation"[17] in the domain of education arrest the erosion of equitable opportunity? An evidence base is emerging that suggests this may be the case. Specifically, our understanding of the research examining how assets affect children during the stages along the opportunity pipeline leads us to believe that assets' effects on children's academic preparation, educational expectations, and early achievement can help to close achievement gaps. Disadvantaged students may select and qualify for more elite institutions when they start to orient toward college from birth. The supportive structures provided by CSA programs may forge social networks that lead to better job opportunities. Changes in teachers' expectations about what children will achieve after high school may cultivate stronger relationships and provide students with crucial mentors as they navigate opportunities.

Even with these gains, however, wealth inequality matters.[18] The American dream requires not only greater opportunities but also more equitable rewards. This makes CSAs' direct effects on children's wealth holdings a crucial dimension of their capacity to equalize overall life chances. While a constellation of interventions that help American children travel through the opportunity pipeline may close gaps in college degree attainment, only addressing the effects of wealth inequality at their source can make education a truly equalizing force. As described in more detail in chapter 4, CSAs are the only institutions in the financial aid landscape designed to facilitate students' *financial well-being* in addition to their *educational success*. CSAs have the potential to integrate young people into wealth-building systems. Further, they may reduce reliance on student debt.[19] As our own stories will illustrate, countering student debt's corrosion of return on degree will go a long way toward equalizing the gains conferred by education. Additionally, college graduates who paid for their degrees from assets rather than debt will be better-positioned to engage strategically with other institutions that confer wealth, including housing and investment markets. When their wealth positions have been enhanced over their lifetimes rather than compromised by reliance on survival policies, disadvantaged college graduates will face fewer of the financial pressures that erode their ability to capitalize on their hard-earned credentials.[20] While we do not yet have the samples and research designs that will allow us to study it in the field, the evidence base that makes the case for children's assets points to real promise that policies such as OIAs may help to equalize children's chances in the institutions where their American dreams are pursued.

Educational attainment facilitates economic mobility and catalyzes wealth.[21,22] However, education can only be the conduit to the American dream that Americans expect when outcomes all along a child's trajectory through school to economic success are determined, at every stage, by her own merits, not the lingering legacies of inequality. Education can only constitute a true opportunity pipeline when equivalent accomplishments bear equitable fruits. This is the promise of policies that universally gird children with assets for their journeys. It is far from today's reality. Instead, as Willie's own life underscores, even when disadvantaged students earn degrees—even elite credentials—this accomplishment does not result in the same prosperity enjoyed by those who start out ahead.

Like Willie, poor strivers may command the higher salaries that would position them for wealth building but see their asset accumulation constrained by the drain of student debt. Lacking experience in making financial systems work to their advantage, they may struggle to optimize the institutions that more privileged college graduates use to jumpstart their wealth building. Their asset poverty denies them equitable access to many of the actions and arenas where social capital is accumulated and makes it harder for them to leverage their educational attainment.[23,24] They lack the asset empowerment that facilitates productive risk-taking and are unlikely to be able to turn to their parents for infusions of assets at critical moments in their early careers.[25–27] Indeed, racial gaps in return on degree may be partially explained by differences in the direction of family financial supports; college-educated Black households provide financial support to parents three times more often than Whites, who are more likely to receive than give help.[20] In these ways, from a wealth perspective, education operates on a parallel plane to welfare policy, helping advantaged Americans build and wield assets, while simultaneously delivering inequitable returns for those seeking to use education to climb. Particularly unfairly, better outcomes are often taken as evidence of superior accomplishments, even though the contest resembles a relay—where some start considerably ahead—more than a race.[17]

As wealth researchers who have particularly focused on children's assets, our "end game" is not the advancement of the CSA field, per se, or certainly the exultation of a particular CSA model. What we hope comes of the laborious work conducted by researchers in a variety of institutions and disciplines and of our effort to weave together a cohesive analysis, is a meaningful improvement in the life chances of disadvantaged children. We want an opportunity pipeline capable of carrying children to what we see as the real destination: not just greater educational attainment, but a meaningful opportunity to live into their American dreams. We believe this is the true potential of investing in children's assets as a cornerstone of an equitable wealth-building agenda. In this book, we lay out our understanding of why this is the most important challenge we face. In what we hope will be the beginning of a robust public conversation, we share our vision for how the promise of children's assets could be operationalized into policy.

Summary of Book Chapters

CHAPTER 1

We begin where the story of many Americans starts: with the idea that education is supposed to be the great equalizer and the playing field on which children's life chances unfold. In chapter 1, we trace our own journeys to illustrate the ways in which the American education system today fails to live up to that ideal, instead serving to solidify the privilege of the advantaged while routinely dashing the hopes and squandering the potential of the poor. We use our own lives to illustrate the diverging outcomes of American students not because we think they are perfectly representative but as a reminder that people's real lives animate the statistics to which we sometimes become immune, such as how high-performing low-income children complete college at roughly the same rates as their lower-achieving, high-income peers.[28] At every point along the opportunity pipeline, our experiences differed, often dramatically. So, too, do the experiences of other American children—the poor and the privileged. We describe how Melinda's college-educated parents invested in her early academic preparation, how the school system amplified that head start, and how she leveraged these accumulated advantages to bargain successfully with higher education and financial institutions.

In contrast, Willie tells his story of growing up in a close but perpetually poor family. Hindered by the pernicious effects of poverty and struggling to overcome initial disadvantage, the virtuous cycle that fueled Melinda's success worked against him. While Willie's exertions carried him all the way to a PhD from an elite university, such an outcome is rare for a student facing his odds. The first chapter documents the harsh realities of our two-tiered higher education system and debt-dependent financial aid. Circling back to the equalizing role education is supposed to play in the United States, we conclude our retelling of our journeys—which belie the American aspiration of equal chances for equitable outcomes—with a warning. It is our contention that inequities in American education are not merely unfortunate or unfair but existential threats to the American dream. We further assert that equalizing distribution of the spoils the education system confers will require not mere reforms but a fundamental recalibration of the bargaining power children and their families bring to the institutions that determine who gets to climb.

CHAPTER 2

This chapter assigns culpability for inequities in life chances to what we see as the primary force determining how well people do today: wealth inequality. We continue our stories post-college, explaining how student debt eroded Willie's ability to profit from his advanced education, while Melinda's family's assets allowed her to avoid student loans and build a stronger financial foundation. Chapter 2 documents the wide gaps in wealth holdings by race, gender, age, and geography, but we do more than compile these bleak statistics. We identify financial assets as a lever particularly amenable to policy manipulation and one that deserves far greater attention in discussions of how to improve educational outcomes. US policy offers many examples of how governmental action helps people build wealth through retirement, college savings, and homeownership. However, the *rights* to own property, conferred by our capitalist economy, do not mean that everyone has the *capacity* to build wealth. Instead, as described earlier, there are few policy attempts to use assets as a lever of upward mobility for those in poverty and, conversely, many examples of policies that perpetuate divides by amplifying existing wealth.

After recounting evidence of the existence of wealth inequality, chapter 2 introduces theories that explain how wealth shapes life chances and then how individuals' perceptions of what will be possible for them become internalized through the cultivation of expectations. Further, we peel back the curtain to reveal how strategic actors design life chances in ways that preserve their own advantage, sometimes codified into law and sometimes less explicitly incorporated into our embedded thought processes. This discussion lays the foundation for the principal rationale for our articulated policy proposal: because wealth inequality is undermining the equalizing function of education, the United States needs to directly counter it, at the source. Further, this intervention must come before wealth inequality can distort children's understanding of what education can do for them—and what they can do through education.

CHAPTER 3

In this chapter, as part of our pursuit of redemption of the ideals of the American dream, we introduce a 21st-century version. Where the American dream calculus has held that effort and ability should lead to fair outcomes, we name what many Americans already sense: effort, while still valuable, is no longer enough. Americans have built powerful tools that give decisive advantage to those who wield them. As a result, success today requires institutions that can amplify individuals' efforts and create the conditions in which their abilities are fairly rewarded. However, Americans' understanding of the dream has not traditionally incorporated a role for institutions. Indeed, we do not even really have language with which to speak about how institutions help to determine success. This is more than a rhetorical failing. Because belief in the American dream motivates the striving that fuels American capitalism, eroding Americans' confidence that their efforts will pay off could end in disaster: the collapse of our whole economic system.

In chapter 3, we move from these dire threats to outline an opportunity framework that could rescue the American dream by integrating institutional efficacy into how Americans see their life chances. Institutional efficacy builds on the concept of self-efficacy to frame success as an end realized with institutional augmentation of individual efforts. When individuals have reason to believe that institutions will help their efforts to pay off equitably, their faith in a new, updated, American dream equation is restored. They develop cognitive expectations that envision their future selves (including as college graduates), and these expectations, in turn, become automatic responses. In this way, wealth literally redefines how children come to see themselves and what they can become. Our life stories illustrate the unequal distribution of the potent tools US society has built—not just technology but also financial aid, instructional innovations, and investment instruments. We have witnessed how these disparities have influenced our lives. The United States will not have equitable outcomes for children who start out disadvantaged until we create policies that (a) construct institutions capable of facilitating their success and (b) distribute access to these institutions so that children come to depend on their support. We will not get that system until we reckon with the undeniable accounting of how wealth inequality tips the scales today.

CHAPTER 4

This chapter pivots to our introduction, explanation, and credentialing of CSAs, the intervention that has inspired our foundation of an equitable opportunity pipeline. First, we provide an admittedly brief overview of current financial aid policy, including an indictment of its inadequacy, complexity, and inequity. We include this analysis to draw clear distinctions between CSAs, which work at multiple points along a child's travel through the opportunity pipeline, and financial aid policies such as postsecondary education tax benefits, student loans, and even need-based assistance such as Pell Grants. Chapter 4 is positioned between the backdrop of the first three chapters, where we place wealth inequality at the center of the threats to Americans' upward mobility, and our articulation of the promise of asset-based financial aid to turn the US education system into an equitable opportunity pipeline. At this juxtaposition, the failure of current financial aid to even attempt to address the wealth gap is glaring.

Chapter 4 also details CSAs' origins and rapid proliferation, as evidence of the growing demand for institutional responses to the opportunity divide. Today, there are CSAs operating in San Francisco, California; rural Indiana; St. Louis, Missouri; the entire state of Maine; and many places in between. While design parameters vary, all CSAs provide some initial seed deposit to facilitate wealth building and jumpstart families' saving. Most incorporate matches for saving or reaching particular benchmarks, features that shift the distributional consequences of existing wealth-building institutions in ways that may particularly benefit disadvantaged families. Some CSAs are administered through state-supported 529 college savings plans, while others offer accounts through local financial institutions. Increasingly, CSA initiatives bypass processes that require parents to sign up for accounts, in favor of universal and automatic enrollment that more closely resembles an "institution" of the type we believe children need. Considered from a wealth perspective, CSAs help children build tangible assets and begin to close wealth divides. They also may reduce the influence of wealth inequality on children's outcomes, specifically through the cultivation of college-saver identities. As briefly explained in chapter 4, by helping children to hold onto not only an expectation that college is in their futures, but also a real strategy for how they will get there, college-saver identities encourage behavior consistent with college-bound possible selves and, not incidentally, with improved educational outcomes.

CHAPTER 5

This chapter draws on the mounting body of CSA research to map the opportunity pipeline, highlighting the four stages along that trajectory where research suggests CSAs can make the greatest difference: early childhood, academic achievement during the school years, college access and completion, and post-college financial health. Findings from CSA research, including the rigorous randomized control trial conducted in the SEED for Oklahoma Kids (SEED OK) program, have demonstrated that children provided with a CSA at birth display stronger social and emotional competency,[29] a crucial precursor to success in school. SEED OK research has further explored the dynamics believed to explain these effects, citing reductions in mothers' depressive symptoms and mitigation of the effects of material hardship on children's social and emotional well-being.[30,31] Crucially, it appears that equipping families with assets for their children's education may interrupt the effects of poverty on development, from the beginning.

Children's academic achievement is supported by this stronger early preparation. Additionally, early children's assets appear to catalyze improved performance on key measures of academic performance, such as reading and math scores, likely through the medium of greater college expectations. Again, these expectations shape how children see their chances and can embed in their thought processes, leading to greater engagement in school. Chapter 5 includes a review of earlier research linking educational assets and achievement, as well as recent analysis of math and reading among accountholders in the Promise Indiana CSA.[32]

CSAs can increase enrollment in college by (a) facilitating successful progress through schooling and (b) helping families to overcome the financial hurdles that can otherwise derail the transition to higher education. Crucially, CSAs may also increase the college graduation rate of disadvantaged students, thereby closing a gap that is particularly imperative to reducing inequity in American education. In this chapter, we include Willie's research that helped to attract the attention of policymakers and program administrators to the CSA concept, including his finding that a dedicated education savings account with as little as $500 can increase the chance that a low- or moderate-income student makes it to and through college as much as threefold.[33]

Finally, notable among the distinctions between children's assets and the constellation of other proposals aimed at helping poor children in school is their potential to strengthen return on degree and equip college graduates with a stronger financial foundation. Chapter 5 concludes with research that finds that those who save as children are more likely to continue to save as adults and to do so in increasingly sophisticated products with greater wealth-building potential.[34,35] This realization of education's aims to galvanize *prosperity*, not just attainment of knowledge, is what makes children's assets central to an essential opportunity pipeline, not just a path to learning.

CHAPTER 6

This chapter lays out our proposal for OIAs as conduits for meaningful and transformative wealth transfers and, essentially, the "fuel" for a 21st-century American opportunity pipeline. We outline the core principles that should inform the development of such a policy. We also include a reminder that the American dream has long rested on a policy infrastructure, including public schools themselves and availability of property ownership. Additionally, there is precedent for the explicit redistribution of the opportunities these institutions extend, as in the GI Bill and the Homestead Act. OIAs incorporate individual effort, in school and in saving, to construct a uniquely American investment in equal opportunity. The policy proposed here would connect all American children, at birth, to the types of financial institutions that facilitate wealth accumulation among the privileged today.

OIAs would provide a seed deposit sufficient to ensure that children graduate high school with enough money to finance debt-free public higher education. This policy would also serve as a platform for local and state efforts to cultivate college-saver identities and align children's realistic outcome expectations with their aspirations for success in college and in life. As explained in chapter 6, the United States can do this for less than we spend today on student debt forgiveness alone. In the process, we would construct an institution worthy of incorporation into a revised and reinvigorated American dream, one that intervenes at all points where we systematically fail poor children today. Our discussion of OIAs draws on CSA evidence to inform policy decisions about how to structure, finance, and deliver what we see as our best chance to strike at the heart of what is ailing the American dream—wealth inequality—and to make education really work for the poor.

CHAPTER 7

In the final chapter, we position OIAs within a broader opportunity agenda, one that begins by reducing wealth inequality in order to close the opportunity gap that threatens the hopes of millions and erodes the viability of our shared American dream. While we see OIAs as a cornerstone of an opportunity agenda, children's assets are not the only investment needed to equalize oppor-tunities. Education is not the only institutional arena where wealth distorts people's life chances. And our reading of children's asset research in the United States and around the globe—including our own findings from new, original CSA research—suggests that policy such as OIAs will be bolstered by attending to the threats to families' finances posed by insufficient incomes, unanticipated and unwelcome income shocks, and disparate outcomes in other wealth-build-ing systems such as housing markets and employer benefits. We conclude the book, then, with a beginning, by briefly outlining some of what we see as nec-essary policy changes in order to reduce wealth inequality, position people to leverage institutions, and provide every American with a real opportunity to have their effort and ability determine where they arrive. The conclusion high-lights policy areas that complement OIAs and can help to develop growth poli-cies for the poor, as part of the American opportunity agenda essential to keep the dream from dying.

1 Going to School in Unequal America

In the United States, Education Is Our "Great Equalizer," Charged with Providing All Children Opportunity for Upward Mobility

In the United States, the education system is more than just a mechanism for transmitting knowledge. It is the nation's most powerful tool for creating economic opportunities and helping individuals secure a good quality of life and parents' primary plan for securing the well-being of their children. As such, educational attainment is often touted as the proverbial "key to the kingdom" that puts those who hold it on the path to prosperity. This link between economic mobility and education sets the United States apart from much of the rest of the developed world, where most countries have strong welfare systems that allow individuals to succeed routinely without postsecondary education. This international contrast provides an important framework for understanding how the role of education aligns with how Americans see themselves and their futures. More specifically, Americans vest their hopes in education as a means of getting ahead instead of relying on a generous welfare state that ensures that "nobody is in need"—the predominant view, for example, among Europeans.[1]

Crucially, the institution of education is supposed to work equally for all Americans, regardless of their starting point. This belief in education as a force for equity as well as opportunity was ensconced in its foundations, as articulated by Horace Mann in 1848,[2] "Education then, beyond all other devices of human origin, is a great equalizer of the conditions of men—the balance wheel of the social machinery."[3] It persists, extolled by Arne Duncan, US Secretary of Education in the Obama Administration, "In America, education is still the great equalizer" and National Education Association President Dennis Van Roekel, "Education is the great equalizer . . . opening doors of opportunity for all."[3,4] However, there are signs that Americans increasingly doubt the viability of these egalitarian ideals and question whether education can truly realize the promise of a better future. In 2014, only 64% of Americans reported that they still believe in the American dream.[5] Belief in this promise is particularly low among young adults, as seen in a recent survey that suggests that half of young adults are ready to concede that the American dream is dead.[6] And when Americans confront the clash between their hopes and their unfair realities, they have a place to focus their anxieties: the education system they were told would deliver them to the good life.[7] People are frustrated with the high cost of tuition and the low return on their degree. In 2014, a national poll found that only 44% of Americans viewed higher education as "very important" for success, down from 77% only four years earlier.[8,9] New America's most recent annual higher education survey found that only a quarter of Americans think the US higher education system is "functioning just fine the way it is."[10]

Research confirms what many Americans feel: our opportunity structures deliver remarkably little chance that children's future standing transcends their origins.[11] Studies have highlighted greater chances of upward mobility in Canada and much of Europe than in the United States.[12,13] While a child's chance of long-distance mobility from the bottom to the top of the income distribution multiplies fourfold with a college degree, a growing number of studies demonstrate that today's young adults will have fewer opportunities than their parents.[14] For instance, an American child born in 1980 has far less of a chance to surpass her parents than one born in 1940.[15] Average incomes for today's young adult workers are lower than in 1975, in adjusted figures, even though young people today are better educated.[16] Even when young adults out-earn their parents, their wealth accumulation and overall economic well-being often lag behind, in large part because of the financial strain of pursuing the college education they needed to secure the futures they wanted.[17] These facts collide with the American concept of studying one's way to the top.

These realities create a real conundrum for most American parents, as they consider how to talk with their children about college, their futures, and the promise of the American dream, and as they attempt to chart routes through narrow opportunity structures. Education is essential to upward mobility, but wealth is increasingly important as a determinant of children's educational outcomes.[18-21] And millions of children are coming of age in households locked out of wealth accumulation—by loans parents took out to try to get an education themselves or dependence on government assistance or because their parents' parents' economic status could not get them to a degree. As these forces collide, it is hard to imagine looking into our collective children's eyes and really *meaning it* when we tell them that how far they go just depends on how smart they are and hard they try.

Privilege Confers Educational Advantages That Accumulate over Time

Rhetorical commitment to the ideal of egalitarian educational opportunity notwithstanding, inequity is woven into every aspect of the American education system, from early childhood through the post-college payoff. These gaps widen as children move through the education system and disadvantages accumulate. Young children who enter kindergarten with smaller vocabularies and weaker social and emotional skills are perceived by their teachers as being less "ready" to learn, and these perceptions—even when flawed—can influence later achievement.[22] Instead of compensating for early disadvantages, the classrooms of poor children are comparatively poor themselves, while higher-income children are further bolstered by schools that spend more.[23]

Lower-income students rarely catch up to their higher-income peers. In the onramp to college, lower-income students are unprepared academically and fare poorly in the college admissions game as well as the merit aid marketplace.[24,25] While some of these students are ill-prepared for college because they assumed they would never go and then failed to get ready for it, achievement differences cannot explain all of the gaps.[26] College completion rates for the academically strongest poor children match those of mediocre-scoring students from richer families.[27] And even when poor children get to and through college, usually through some combination of extraordinary individual initiative and fortuitous circumstance, their educations do not reap the same rewards as those of their privileged peers.[28] At all points along the journey, educational outcomes highlight unequal chances for success, even among students equally talented and hard-working.

Rather than attempt to trace the full scope of unequal educational opportunity for already disadvantaged children, as others have done, or exhaustively analyze how schooling conceals mechanisms of social reproduction, we use the stories of our own respective routes to and through higher education to bring to life how inequity in the education system drives disparate outcomes.[29,30] In this way, we aim to set the stage for consideration of how changing how we finance college— seemingly, only a small part of this overall picture—could catalyze fundamental changes throughout. We use our narratives also to avoid a frequent failing of discussions of inequality in education, which tend to focus narrowly on those who fall behind, as if our unequal system produces only losers.[31] Instead, the juxtaposition of our own stories represents how some benefit from unequally distributed resources.[32] Evidence of the injustice of the US education system today is seen not only in the dilapidated classrooms to which low-income children are relegated but just as surely in the sleek environments that educate the privileged.[33-35] The differences in our paths—and the outcomes they secured—illustrate this divide.

As others have emphasized, the gap that separates poor children's educational experiences from those of the rich is neither natural nor inevitable but instead the result of actions by those who seek advantages for their children in order to help them succeed.[36] Advantages are pursued through informal social networks, legislation, and litigation.[37-40] Advantages can also be purchased when families leverage their assets to (a) secure spots in particular school districts, (b) invest in enrichment, (c) wield influence to access top-flight postsecondary institutions or secure prestigious internships, or (d) underwrite adult children's further human capital accumulation.[36,41-45] While our own lives provide evidence of only some of these dynamics, the US education system is rife with examples. At every step, those who start out ahead reap the fruits of the best the system has to offer.[46]

You Don't Have to Be "Rich" for Your Kids to Gain an Advantage

Melinda was born into a family of college-goers. Her parents have three college degrees between them, and most of her relatives and many of her parents' friends are college graduates as well. Her older sister left for college before Melinda finished elementary school. Melinda's own college attendance seemed almost preordained.[a] To redouble the advantages conferred by their social network, Melinda's family invested heavily in her intellectual development. In nearly all of the domains research suggests can make a difference in ultimate outcomes, the inputs she received were designed to induce academic success: early exposure to learning and preparation for school, selection of a high-performing school by virtue of residential neighborhood, school stability facilitated by parental homeownership, participation in extracurricular activities, and assistance navigating postsecondary options.[48-55]

Melinda went to a fairly unremarkable suburban elementary school that nonetheless offered access to a selective gifted program and free transportation to get there. She spent most afternoons reading from the hundreds of books her family owned or the thousands more available from the nearby public library. When she took trips with her family every spring and summer break to visit museums and national parks, she got further ahead of her peers even when school was not in session. Her mom drove her to piano lessons, acting classes, writing workshops, and volunteer commitments, of the sort that fill the résumés of high-income children.[56,57] Her dad once took a day off from his managerial job to drive her to the next state to hear Mikhail Gorbachev speak. When she expressed interest in photojournalism, her parents bought her a camera and enrolled her in photography class, actions that mirror other privileged parents' educational investments.[58]

The advantages Melinda received as a child paved the way for a successful college career. As do many privileged students, she received college entrance exam coaching and took the Preliminary Scholastic Aptitude Test (PSAT) as a freshman in high school.[42,57] This gave her a leg up in the contest for a National Merit Scholarship. She also had the benefit of earning college credit from her high school honors classes so that she could enter college with sophomore status. The University of Kansas (KU) offered her a full scholarship as a National Merit Scholar, even though her family earned too much to qualify for need-based financial aid. Combined with other awards, she had enough aid left over to pay for a summer in Europe and trips to Latin America to study Spanish. She did not work for pay during her first year at KU, focusing instead on unpaid internships that helped to define her career direction and informed a compelling Truman Scholarship application.[59] Although Melinda's family was not extraordinarily wealthy, they made investments in her education that are common for those in the middle class but elusive for most of those in disadvantaged America: high-performing public schools, ample enrichment, and opportunities to live into a college-bound future from an early age. These actions made a difference. Crucially, they not only helped to determine her later outcomes. They also inadvertently hindered those who could not match her family's pace.

Using Privilege to Gain an Advantage for Our Kids Is Human Nature

Conditioned to believe that schools are meritocratic institutions, Americans readily explain many observed educational inequalities as stemming from justifiable differences in aptitudes or preferences.[55] Closer analysis, however, reveals how inequity is baked into the system. Informed by his own early experiences, Willie's observations as a parent have underscored the entrenched and pernicious inequities of the US education system. Willie's children's journeys through school have paralleled Melinda's more than his own. For example, his middle daughter Michelle was placed into fifth-grade math while she was in fourth grade. At the time, her scores on state assessments were only slightly higher than her peers'. However, Michelle's teachers, with a lot of prodding by her parents, eventually placed her in advanced math, positioning her to achieve more. This is apparently a common practice among privileged families in her school district and undoubtedly others as well. Not surprisingly, at the end of the year, her scores increased considerably.[60] They were based on the averages of fourth-graders taking the test, and, while most of her classmates were learning fourth-grade math, she was learning fifth-grade skills. As a result, her slim advantage at the start of fourth grade widened significantly. In sixth grade, Michelle took seventh and eighth grade math and far outperformed her grade-level peers. Fueled by these early advantages and their compounding nature, Michelle is likely to attend college and to benefit from merit aid when she gets there. By that time, it will be hard to discern that her achievement is not solely reflective of her own effort and ability but also a product of opportunities she was given—that others were not. These influential chances, in turn, were only realized because her parents knew what it meant to get her into advanced math early, when the gap between her classmates and her was barely discernible.

In contrast to the cycles of disadvantage that often trap children who start out behind, Michelle's story represents the beginning of a cycle of educational advantage. It is the mundane and often invisible nature of these nonetheless determinant inputs that helps to explain how an education system that is supposed to equalize opportunity has instead become a tool with which those who enjoy elevated status end up preserving and reproducing it.[61] Wide gaps in educational attainment can be understood as natural consequences of the sum of millions of almost-imperceptible decisions about where families live, how children spend their time, what teachers reward, and who gets what financial aid.[62,63] Analysis of the household budgets of wealthy and poor families further highlights the difference money makes in children's futures; while poor families must dedicate much of their spending to things that keep them alive (food, health care, housing), rich parents can focus their spending on things that help their families thrive (investments and, especially, education).[64]

High-income parents increased their spending on enrichment by 151% between 1972 and 2006, while low-income parents, in an effort to keep up, could only increase their investments by 57%.[43] These expenses are not confined to purely academic realms; similarly, privileged parents pay considerable sums for their children's participation in athletic and artistic pursuits as well, activities that some research suggests can contribute to improved educational outcomes.[53,65] Willie's family will spend $10,340 this year—on fees, equipment, coaches, and travel—for his three children to participate in extracurricular wrestling, gymnastics, track, and volleyball. This figure does not even account for the costs in disrupted work schedules and mental energy to manage these commitments. These costs are obviously out of the reach of many American families and therefore figure prominently into the growing "engagement gap" that some blame for at least some of the thwarted social mobility of lower-income youth.[56] The hard math of relative mobility means that some at the top will have to fall if others are to rise.[66] Therefore, as families wield privileges in the educational arena in order to tilt the playing field to advantage their own children, their actions often block the talented but less advantaged.[67] And, because education is the principal way that those who get ahead manage to do so, every action that prevents this rise is potentially significant, even if the trajectory is not always evident at the time.

Advantage Gained through Privilege Translates into Higher Odds of Educational Success

The academic advantage that economic privilege buys is not inconsequential. Students from the highest-income households are more than twice as likely to earn bachelor's degrees than those from the bottom income quartile—59% versus 26%.[68] As securing postsecondary educational attainment becomes the principal objective of many privileged parents, low-income students are even less likely to keep up.[67,69] In 2013, high-income 24-year-olds were eight times more likely to have received a bachelor's degree than those from low-income families, a gap even wider than in 1970, when relatively fewer wealthy young people completed college.[68] Indeed, comparing the postsecondary outcomes of students with equivalent achievement but different household resources suggests that a financial "leg up" is apparently sufficient to overcome some students' liabilities. The lowest-achieving high-income children graduate college at roughly the same rate as the highest-achieving children from low-income families.[27,70,71] In short, then, while we like to tell ourselves that college completion drives family socioeconomic status, data suggest that this relationship is actually reversed.[21,72] Evidently, especially once students make it to college, money matters at least as much as academic ability in determining who gets a diploma.

Recent years have seen an increase in inequality in college outcomes, even as high school graduation rates increase.[73,74] For example, the SAT score gap between high- and low-income students was about 90 points in the 1980s, compared to more than 125 points today.[75] For at least a few decades, then, rich children have been pulling away from their poorer peers. These trends seem to have only accelerated in the Great Recession, when the postsecondary prospects of lower-income students suffered acutely. While college enrollment rates fell somewhat across the board from

2008 to 2013, the decline was much more dramatic for lower-income students (from 55.9% in 2008 to 45.5% in 2013) than for those in the top 20% of earners (from 81.9% in 2008 to 78.5% in 2013).[74] As the financial downturn battered already struggling families, college enrollment rates of low-income high-school completers fell from a high of 58.4% in 2007 to 50.9% in 2012, equal to middle-income students' enrollment rate in the 1980s.[76] When it comes to ensuring that students have truly equitable chances of academic success, we are moving in the wrong direction.

Importantly, income is only one dimension of privilege. Other advantages may be even more determinant of children's outcomes. In particular, wealth can be used strategically to optimize children's chances.[77] Separate even from income, family net worth predicts children's early test scores and helps to determine each level of educational attainment.[78–83] As the privileged work multiple levers to improve their children's chances, the divide widens. Analysis by Fabian Pfeffer finds that family wealth plays an outsized role in determining one's chance of college completion.[21]

Educational inequality is even starker when we also consider parental educational attainment and race. Children whose parents did not complete college are far less likely to enroll in college themselves, particularly right after high school.[84] Even when they make it to college, first-generation students are less likely to graduate. Six years after enrollment, only 50.2% of first-generation students had completed their degrees, compared to more than 64% of their peers whose parents went to college.[85] As a result, only 9% of low-income students whose parents do not have college degrees obtain a bachelor's degree by age 26, compared to 68% of students with college-educated, higher-earning parents.[86] Additionally, the significance of race in determining how children fare in the education system cannot be understated. Although postsecondary attainment by students of color has increased, progress for other groups has been faster, resulting in a growing gap. In 2013, the Black/White college graduation rate gap was 20.4 points, compared to 17.2 points in 2003.[87] Even while running fast on their own tracks, disadvantaged students cannot "catch up" with privileged youth operating on a different plane.

Overwhelmingly, then, the fault line between the educated and upwardly mobile, and those struggling to capitalize on the presumed relationship between education and economic well-being, is demarcated by family socioeconomic status. The factors that limit the achievements of lower-income students run throughout the education system, particularly at the postsecondary level. The divide is particularly dramatic at the most elite institutions, where nearly three-quarters of students are from the top quartile of socioeconomic status and 61% have parents with bachelor's degrees.[24,88] In the Ivy League, there are more students from the top 1% of households by income than from the bottom 20%.[89] However, this is not just a problem for the marquee colleges long considered the relatively exclusive domain of the privileged. Even schools designed as refuges of affordability have often moved beyond the reach of lower-income families. As is the case in other dimensions of inequality, this is far from an accidental outcome. Many attribute the trend of rising tuition to reductions in state funding for public institutions that have shifted costs to students and parents and led colleges to consider applicants' financial as well as intellectual capacities in admissions decisions.[25,90–93] As a result of these compounding forces, the deck is increasingly stacked in the favor of those who have wealth.

It's an Uphill Climb for Poor Students

The path to and through college is an uphill climb for poor students. As a result, the very children who could benefit most from receiving a college degree are least likely to get one.[94] There are some poor students, like Willie, who have succeeded despite the odds against them. When these triumphs occur, they are seen as evidence that the system still "works," instead of what they really are: anomalies.[95] And because we miss the lessons we should learn about how to build systems that generate different outcomes on a large scale, with disadvantaged children succeeding routinely rather than rarely, stories like Willie's stay exceptional.

Willie shares his story to illustrate how a fairer system could have smoothed his path—and how this could matter for millions of American children whose futures could be transformed. Willie's family was poor—as he tells it, not just "we wish we had more" poor but so poor that there were months when they did not have running water or a secure place to sleep. His parents worked hard at low-paying and unreliable jobs and were often laid off. While he was always certain of his parents' love, Willie was indelibly affected by this persistent strain. Indeed, science suggests that poverty can alter young children's brain development.[96] By nine months of age, low-income infants' cognitive and social-emotional development lag behind their high-income peers', a divide that doubles by age two.[97]

While it is difficult to precisely trace the legacy of deprivation in Willie's life today, he recognizes early deficits against which he still struggles. When he was studying philosophy at Geneva College, the students in his classes had better grammar and writing skills than he did. Because Willie missed a lot of school from fourth through seventh grades, when his family was living in homes that sometimes lacked utilities, he missed out on learning some basic skills. This led college classmates to mock his writing, although Dr. Bitar, his philosophy instructor, recognized Willie's ability to think logically and the obstacles he was attempting to overcome. Willie has often had to work harder than his peers to compensate—looking up words he did not recognize, reading important texts to which he had not already been exposed, going to writing labs, and spending more time reviewing concepts. His success has been complicated, even slowed, by the accumulation of initial disadvantages.

If Melinda was almost certainly destined for college, Willie—as a child of color living in poverty—was a much less likely prospect. Research finds strong relationships between parents' educational and economic standings and their children's outcomes, particularly in postsecondary education.[83,81, 98–100] Pfeffer found that the gap in college graduation between the highest and lowest quantiles of net worth was almost 20% greater than the gap in high school graduation rates (43% versus 25%).[21] In addition, studies have found that a parent's educational level when her child is eight determines the child's occupational success 40 years later.[101] In other words, it is not just how hard one works. It also matters—a lot—who one's parents are and what they have.

Willie grew up knowing that his parents wanted the best for him. Nonetheless, his family background placed him at a disadvantage when it came to preparing for college. His father had an eighth-grade education and did not learn to read until he was in his 20s, while his mom had a high school diploma. His parents' education level was an important input shaping his own chances. Some evidence suggests that parents' influence on their children's development, including their role in shepherding children through the education system, is so critical that *their* childhood environmental context may matter even more than the child's.[102] In this case, Willie's dad's upbringing was even more deprived than his own. This meant that Willie started even further behind than his own initial condition would suggest, an accounting that brings his journey into sharper relief.

Even beyond his immediate family, the challenges in Willie's former steel town placed him at a disadvantage. To start, Willie's school district was more impoverished than Melinda's. Although the district is certainly not the poorest in the country, today more than 77% of its students are eligible for free or reduced-price lunch, compared to only 38% in the district Melinda attended.[103,104] Willie was also a Black student in a nation that has made only sporadic and anemic progress in closing racial achievement gaps and reducing school segregation.[105–107] Apart from the obstacles he faced because of race and place, Willie's school attendance was impacted by his family's frequent moves and his need to go to work to make money to buy shoes and school supplies. As described earlier, this left many holes in his knowledge.

Even if he had been in school consistently, Willie may not have gained as much as those in more privileged settings. Some evidence suggests that disadvantaged children, particularly students of color, get *more behind* as they advance through each grade.[108] The Black/White achievement gap, for example, grows during elementary school.[109] Racial achievement gaps in math and reading are larger at age 17 than age 9, a particularly stark finding given the greater incidence of dropout among students of color, which disproportionately affects the sample size of non-White students in later grades.[110] While it is not entirely clear how schools contribute to these divides, dramatic inequities in per pupil funding and teacher biases[23,111,112]—both factors in Willie's educational experiences—likely play important parts. Despite his obvious intellectual abilities, Willie's teachers and administrators focused more on his prowess on the football field than on his learning. Their expectations for his future centered on athletics rather than academics. As such, they became currents against which he had to swim, rather than encouragement for his development.[113–116]

As is the case for many low-income students of color, Willie was not tracked into college-preparatory classes nor encouraged to take Advanced Placement courses.[55,117–120] Nationally, research has found that intellectual merit explains less than 40% of the variance in track placement.[121] In contrast to Willie's daughter Michelle, kids in poverty with less-educated parents are often left to languish below their true abilities. Subsequently, low assessment scores are interpreted as ability deficits and used to justify transfer of resources away from underperforming students. As is also common, Willie had little access to guidance regarding critical decisions about his future. He neither had classes to prepare him for college entrance exams nor would have been able to afford such classes if they had been available.[122,123] Against this backdrop, the fact that Willie made it to and through college is a testament to his drive and a credit to the example his parents set to never quit. At the same time, the fact that many of Willie's classmates never attended college says a lot about the odds they faced and how hard it is to overcome them, despite innate abilities.[124]

Inequality Extends Beyond High School Halls to Campus Quads

Inequities are woven into the educational experiences of every American child from the first moments of comprehension. It should come as no surprise, then, that they carry over in the transition to college. Indeed, the postsecondary education system is arguably even more unfair than high schools, coming as it does at the culmination of a student's education, when accumulated disadvantages have multiplied.[125–127] The stakes are perhaps never greater than in higher education, too, given the gatekeeping function college degrees serve in the American labor market.[128] As the economy increasingly demands higher educational attainment, college has become central to upward mobility.[14,129–131] Nonetheless, many people never have the chance to reap the benefits of higher education. The system was working against them before they were even born. Remarkably, this bleak accounting was forecast even at the apex of American upward mobility. President Harry Truman said in 1947, "If the ladder of educational opportunity rises high at the doors of some youth and scarcely rises at the doors of others, while at the same time formal education is made a prerequisite to occupational and social advance, then education may become the means, not of eliminating race and class distinctions, but of deepening and solidifying them." In 2017, there can no longer be a question of "if."[132]

American parents overwhelmingly hope that their children will go to college.[133,134] However, this nearly universal aspiration is virtually the only point when the experiences of rich and poor students converge. While more Americans are making it to and through college than in previous generations, the needle disadvantaged students must thread is still narrow, while privileged children usually follow a paved path. While low-income high school graduates' postsecondary enrollment rates increased from 31% in 1975 to 46% in 2013, they lag behind high-income students, for whom college is almost a foregone conclusion.[74,135] In 2012, 89% of high-income high school graduates continued on to college.[68]

Further, the divide is not just between those who go to college and those who do not. There are also substantial differences in the types of institutions students attend, with commensurate implications for later life chances.[136,137] Chetty and colleagues have found that students from similar postsecondary institutions have similar labor market earnings, despite differences in starting conditions.[89] However, institutional selection depends more on family resources than any intrinsic factor or student preference, and the force of family finances on postsecondary options may be growing. Pressured to generate both revenues and rankings, selective private and flagship public institutions enroll smaller shares of low-income students than in the past. As a result, lower-income students are funneled toward for-profit or two-year colleges with outcomes that lag behind those of more selective schools.[138] First-generation college students, too, are increasingly moving toward schools with lower graduation rates, because they are also low-income, because they lack help navigating postsecondary options, or both.[139] For the most part, the postsecondary institutions disadvantaged students attend offer something less than a straight shot to the "good life," a fact that makes highly inequitable enrollment patterns a direct threat to the education path to the American dream.

We both completed college and even went on to graduate school. In some ways, then, our stories are not representative of the disparate outcomes that typically characterize the postsecondary experiences of poor students and their privileged peers. However, on the cusp of college and while pursuing our degrees, we experienced pressures and supports characteristic of our respective economic positions. In Willie's case, these dynamics could have easily derailed his degree pursuit, and, indeed, did delay it; he started college older than a traditional student. As we discuss later, even with a PhD, he continues to carry some of the toll—financial and otherwise—exacted along the way.

After dropping out of high school during his senior year, completing his GED, and starting a Christian mission at age 19, Willie's postsecondary education career began at Geneva College when he was 21. Geneva is a Christian liberal arts college in his hometown of Beaver Falls, Pennsylvania. While many low-income students select institutions similarly close to home, Willie's decision to go to a private, four-year school rather than a less expensive two-year option[140]—such as the community college 10 miles away—defied national trends. However, Willie's faith drew him to Geneva, and his work and ministry experiences made the school willing to admit him despite his poor academic preparation, although they might have rejected a similar student. Additionally, one of Willie's older friends from high school who had attended a Historically-Black college and returned to work in admissions at Geneva put in a good word for him. Willie's decision was also encouraged by another friend who was playing football at Geneva and whose mother worked as a secretary there. Without these developments, Willie's only option, like many other low-income students of color, might have been a two-year college. If he had received any counseling about higher education, that almost surely would have been the recommendation.

Selective Institutions Afford Better Chance of Completion and Fuller Opportunities

Although Willie did not know it at the time, going to a private four-year college likely gave him a greater chance of success. College completion rates are 61.2% for students at four-year public institutions and 71.5% at private nonprofit schools like the one Willie chose, while only 39% of students at two-year, public community colleges graduate within six years.[141] Hindered by limitations in his preparation, Willie had to start Geneva on probation and take remedial classes until he met academic requirements. These factors probably precluded his admission to a highly-selective school where almost all students complete bachelor's degrees within six years, even though research suggests that students "on the bubble"[142]—who just barely make it into more selective schools—benefit from these institutions' advantages and mostly overcome initial deficits.[143-145] Indeed, there is no evidence to support the idea that disadvantaged students should choose open-access institutions to avoid being academically overwhelmed.[146] Instead, as was Willie's experience, low-income students seem to mostly prosper in the environments of more selective institutions. While not an elite school, Geneva College provided Willie with valuable opportunities. He was exposed to dedicated faculty and small classes and surrounded by students who had significantly better academic preparation than he did. It was a world apart from his previous educational experiences, and it gave him what he needed to thrive.

Willie opted to live on campus and buy a meal card despite the fact that his parents lived in town. This was also a somewhat unusual decision. Low-income students often live at home to save money, even though financial aid formulas can mean that this cost-cutting does not significantly lessen their budget strain.[147,148] While living on campus raised the cost of attendance and Willie's student debt, it also made it much more likely he would graduate.[149] At the time, his parents lived in a rental house—from which they would later be evicted—that had no gas heat or flushable toilets. His first year at Geneva, then, was the first time he had a truly supportive learning environment, with not only reliable food and shelter but also exposure to people and ideas that challenged his mind. This context made previously unimagined options possible, including the notion of graduate school. Many of his classmates talked about graduate school as a logical next step. Prior to attending Geneva, however, Willie could not recall even *hearing* about graduate school, let alone aspiring to attend.

Changes in College Financing Have Further Tilted Bargaining Power in the Financial Aid Marketplace in Favor of the Privileged

Melinda's route to and through higher education was notable primarily for its financing. For most Americans, contemplation of college begins with consideration of how to finance it.[150] In recent years, the cost of college attendance to the average student has risen dramatically.[151] While the average net price (the difference between the publicized sticker price and available financial aid) is often lower for low-income families than wealthier ones, due to tuition subsidies, college costs nonetheless consume an almost inconceivable share of the family incomes of those in and near poverty: 82% in 2012.[68,152] Analysis by the Institute for Higher Education Policy has found that, for many low-income students, fewer than 5% of US postsecondary institutions can be considered "affordable," even with some family savings and regular part-time work while in school.[153] Such figures may divert some students altogether.[154,155]

Privileged families are not immune from the reality of tuition increases. When Melinda was considering her options, the cost of attending a public university had risen dramatically from the tuition her sister had paid seven years earlier. However, Melinda's family had ample resources to cover these additional expenses, so rising tuition had no effect on her decision-making. The fact that Melinda's family's savings and relative economic security allowed her to consider colleges based on her interests and their offerings, rather than sheer affordability, made her experience unusual. Even though her college career did not depend on it, she also benefitted from the trend toward merit scholarships rather than those based on financial need.

Trend Toward Merit Aid, Away from Need-Based Aid

While the definition of "merit" is fluid and contested, for our purposes, "merit" aid means college financial assistance that does not hinge on demonstrated need and is not progressive in design or effect.[130] Such merit awards exert growing force in the US financial aid system today. In the 1995–1996 school year, financial aid based on family economic need accounted for 13% of aid awarded by higher education institutions, while merit aid made up just 8%. However, by 2007–2008, merit aid had surpassed need-based aid, making up 18% of institutional aid while need-based aid accounted for just 16%.[25] Nor are schools alone in tilting toward merit aid. In 2012, more than 25 states used public dollars to award merit scholarships.[156] In 15 states, less than half of taxpayer-funded financial aid takes need into account, while in some states, more than 85% of publicly financed scholarship dollars are given without regard to financial need.[156,157] Crucially, this is not just a case of moving money from one column to another. These policy shifts directly affect who does and does not receive financial aid.[158] On the one hand, the proportion of merit aid recipients in the highest family income quartile rose from 23% in 1995–1996 to 28% in 2007–2008, meaning that they are overrepresented. On the other hand, the proportion of merit aid recipients in the lowest quartile, also at 23% in 1995–1996, fell to 20% in 2007–2008, making them underrepresented.[159]

As aid increasingly comes to hinge on merit, individual students' chances of receiving financial assistance have changed. Between 1999–2000 and 2011–2012, the percentage of the lowest-income independent students receiving nonfederal grant aid decreased from 37% to 31%, while the percentage of dependent students from the highest-earning households receiving financial assistance increased by a comparable margin, from 31% to 40%.[160] This means that poor students trying to pay their own way through college are now less likely to receive financial aid from their states or institutions than high-income students whose parents are helping them. Such shifts in financial aid subsequently reshape cohorts, taking students' prospects along with them. Today, the proportion of merit aid recipients exceeds need-based recipients at four-year public and private nonprofit institutions, while students receiving need-based aid are increasingly funneled into for-profit and two-year schools that offer less chance of upward mobility.[159]

Many aspects of merit aid programs may undermine the educational attainment of disadvantaged students. Some set parameters so stringent they exclude precisely those students most dependent on and responsive to financial aid.[160] Others leave troubling gaps and fail to support students to degree completion.[161] For example, after diverting funds to the more prestigious Zell Miller scholarships that predominantly benefit middle- and upper-income students, Georgia's merit-based HOPE scholarship now only covers approximately 65% of mandatory tuition and fees.[162] This can force low-income students to borrow, as the state has no need-based financial aid.[162] In sum, the shift to merit aid has reduced financial aid's ability to facilitate educational attainment among the students who most need assistance.[163] At face value, merit aid sounds like a very American idea: effort and talent should determine who gets the fruits of the systems we construct. However, this assumes that those with the best qualifications received them solely as a result of their initiative, rather than due to inequities in the systems that shape them. This is not the case. Merit aid also ignores the ways that wealth inequality can hinder the achievements of disadvantaged students and squeezes the bottleneck of college entrance so tightly that the window of opportunity is nearly closed.[164]

Unequal Bargaining Power in the Financial Aid Marketplace

With the shift toward merit aid, institutions of higher education use dollars to compete for desirable students rather than to expand opportunities for those who might otherwise find their path to college blocked.[25] In what some have called the institutional "arms race," colleges and universities[25]—not just the most elite but also those aspiring to greater prestige[165,166]—leverage their institutional aid to lure students who offer one or both of the most-sought attributes: pockets from which to pay rising tuition dollars and/or academic achievement that can drive the outcomes schools covet, such as on-time graduation rates.[167] This practice is not new. Almost a generation ago, McPherson and Shapiro lamented that

> universities, beset by their own fiscal problems and by intense competition for highly qualified, fee-paying students, have ceased to think of their financial aid efforts principally as a noble charitable opportunity and have instead

come to focus on the financial aid operation as a key strategic weapon both in recruiting students and in maximizing institutional revenues.[168]

In the years since, this financial aid model has grown in popularity. In many cases, such angling comes at the explicit expense of disadvantaged students.[169,170] Some schools deliberately offer underfunded financial aid packages to discourage low-income students from enrolling.[25,171,172] Others give affluent students a leg up by discounting their tuition, awarding legacy preferences, and/or keeping criteria flexible enough to allow rewarding of donors.[25,44] In other words, family financial resources improve students' chances not only by equipping them with stronger preparation and endowing them with résumés that stack up well in the quest for merit aid. They can also literally help to "buy" a seat in a freshman class.

While Melinda's receipt of aid was not explicitly predicated on her family's financial standing, her financial privilege was just as surely a factor in her journey to a merit aid package. KU offered Melinda a merit scholarship to entice her to stay in her home state. At a special reception for the state's National Merit Scholars, KU's Chancellor made a direct pitch to Melinda's father: she can get her bachelor's degree for free and you can save your money to send her to graduate school at an elite institution. Her dad was sold, and Melinda was convinced by the prospect of spending those college savings on the study abroad experiences she craved. Importantly for her later outcomes, although some of Melinda's closest friends chose schools like Harvard University, her choice of a state university was not a case of "undermatching." Common among disadvantaged students influenced by financial or other constraints, undermatching occurs when a student selects a college with standards well below his credentials.[173] In many cases, disadvantaged students' chances are then curtailed by these unfortunate selections. Instead, in Melinda's case, her parents' advice helped her optimize opportunities within the education system. At KU, she took all honors classes her freshman year and was matched with a faculty mentor through a special program for National Merit Scholars. For privileged students and the schools that want them, this is the consummate "win/win."

In contrast, Willie's financial aid story bears many of the signs of a student unprepared to bargain at the financial aid table. Unlike Melinda, Willie had no one to counsel him about what a good financial aid package looked like. Further, he had what appeared to be limited prospects, with a GED, no savings, and parents without higher education. Melinda, on the other hand, came to the bargaining table from a position of power that ensured she got the best deal. Here, our two stories reveal that rather than equalizing opportunity, higher education and, in particular, the way it is financed, often multiplies inequities.

In light of his subsequent student debt burden, some observers might fault Willie's selection of a private college, judging that he should have instead selected an more affordable school such as a two-year community college.[140, 174] Indeed, this is the route many low-income students follow, even if they find relatively few affordable options of any kind today. Between 2008 and 2013, state expenditures for higher education declined from $7,400 to $6,000 per full-time equivalent student.[175] This trend has put pressure on public institutions to pursue business models that more closely resemble private colleges.[176] Very few claim to be "need-blind," awarding admission without regard to ability to pay; even fewer are among the only 62 institutions reporting in 2014 that they met 100% of demonstrated financial need.[177] Instead, as a result of rising prices and diversion of aid to entice coveted students, many low-income students find themselves priced out of schools that are supposed to be within reach.[153] Even where tuition remains affordable, other costs—for books, fees, and room and board—intrude.[178] An Urban Institute study found that room and board costs have doubled since 1980, adjusted for inflation, and represent a large portion of the cost increase at most four-year institutions.[179] In the 2011–2012 school year, 90% of the lowest-income independent students in community colleges had a gap between their education costs and their financial aid.[180] In relation to Willie's story, he could certainly have reduced his immediate assumption of student loans by going to a college with a cheaper sticker price than Geneva College. However, evidence suggests that he would likely have paid a very real price for those short-term savings.

Elite Schools Offer Different Experiences, Opportunities, and Outcomes

Educational experiences and outcomes are starkly different between America's open-access institutions and the campuses of the most elite schools. Including those who transfer to other institutions, only 39% of community college students receive associate's degrees; 15.1% complete a four-year degree within six years of starting at a community college.[141,181] In open-access schools, low-income students have far lower graduation rates than their wealthier peers—56% compared to 83%—but this division is almost erased at the most selective institutions.[182] Even for those who graduate, returns on degrees are similarly unequal. Hersch, for instance, finds that a male with a postgraduate degree from an institution with at least fairly selective admissions can expect to earn approximately $50,000 more per year than a similar graduate from an open-access school.[183] At least some of this divide is likely attributable to stark differences in institutional resources. Using expenditures per student as a metric, students at the least competitive institutions receive $5,359 in annual inputs, compared to $27,000 each at the most selective schools.[173] Crucially, this is not only a case of wealthy students getting what they (or their families) pay for; analysis reveals that tax exemptions essentially subsidize greater expenditures at elite private schools.[184] For example, in 2013, Princeton students each received approximately $100,000 in taxpayer subsidies (exemptions on endowments and property holdings), compared to only $2,400 at New Jersey's Essex Community College.[184] On average, the public subsidy at elite private institutions is roughly three times that of the flagship public university in the same state, another example of how the rules and investments that undergird the education system advance the interests of the relatively privileged at the expense of the disadvantaged.

The inequity of the US' two-tiered postsecondary education system is not found only in the ways in which it diverts resources from the many to the few, but also in how institutional practices and policies block talented students from fair chances to access the places that would give them the best opportunity to succeed. A growing body of evidence recognizes that elite institutions are particularly valuable to students like Willie who enter them at a disadvantage.[185–188] While it is impossible to precisely articulate the counterfactual, Willie's chance of journeying from an undergraduate on academic probation to a PhD graduate from one of the nation's most prestigious universities may have been even more remote had he been on a different institutional track. Stohl and Carnevale estimate that 73% of the more than 111,000 high-scoring college students of color who do not achieve a degree within eight years would have graduated if they had been at a top school.[189]

Sorting Students by Status

Students are sorted into their respective postsecondary tiers primarily on their ability to pay, not their academic achievements.[190] Many disadvantaged students who signal an intention to pursue higher education are encouraged to consider affordability in making institutional selections. Even those who set their sights on elite schools often quickly confront an admissions and recruitment process stacked against them. The admissions criteria of many selective schools weigh factors where low-income students are systematically disadvantaged. These factors include (a) the strength of high school curriculum,[191] (b) grades in college-preparatory courses,[120] (c) entrance exam scores,[b,192] and even (d) visits to campus.[c] As evidence of the cumulative effects of these interlocking factors, even disadvantaged students with high academic qualifications are dramatically underrepresented at top-tier schools and more likely to study in two-year or unselective four-year schools than elite colleges.[24,86] In 2013, Pell Grant recipients accounted for 17% of first-time, full-time students at the 193 postsecondary institutions with the most competitive admissions, virtually unchanged from 2000, despite efforts by many schools to lower (or eliminate) tuition for low-income students. These trends are observed along dimensions of disadvantage other than income as well; more than 30% of African American and Latino students with grade point averages over 3.5 enroll in two-year community colleges, compared to only 22% of similar White students.[24,193]

The Financial Aid Marketplace Leaves Disadvantaged Students with Few Options Other than Debt

After a childhood of poverty, Willie had to study hard, make smart choices, and commit himself fully to what was an unlikely dream in order to position himself to climb through the postsecondary education system. This pursuit required more than his talent and efforts, however. It also required him to borrow against his future. This is the case for many low-income students, to whom US financial aid policy extends not a hand up but a pen out, awaiting signature on the promissory note that is their only hope. Even after receiving a financial aid package from Geneva, Willie grappled with "unmet need," or the gap between the help he could get and the money he really needed.[195] As is the case for many low-income students who struggle with prohibitive non-tuition expenses and paid employment that distracts from school work, the constant stress made it hard for Willie to focus on school.[196–200] In the end, financial pressures were the cause of his departure from Akron University's law school, where not even a generous scholarship could make up for the strains of a daily three-hour commute to avoid room and board expenses or the guilt of not being able to subsidize his family, particularly when they were evicted at the end of his first year. This marked the beginning of his career in the military, which he joined laden with $40,000 in student debt.

Unfortunately, the challenges Willie faced have only become more common. In particular, the Pell Grants he received have lost purchasing power as tuition has increased.[201] As a result, researchers estimate that disadvantaged students' unmet need doubled between 1990 and 2012, to more than $8,000 per year for those in the bottom income quartile.[68] These financial strains can alter educational trajectories. Where privileged students often have some "cushion" that allows them to take steps such as dropping or adding classes, purchasing additional materials, or even paying for tutoring, low-income students cannot afford these risks.

Later, we describe how Willie's dependence on student debt and Melinda's avoidance of it has affected our balance sheets and post-college financial futures. Here we review literature on how student loans impact educational outcomes and note other ways student loans and their absence shaped our educations. Willie initially viewed student loans positively, as his only chance to access higher education. Looking back, he is not entirely sure why the prospect of borrowing more money than he had ever seen did not deter him from pursuing college, as it does some disadvantaged students.[202,203] Certainly he had peers whose college careers were stopped short by these financial pressures, stories consistent with research that finds that student debt, at least above certain dollar thresholds, may reduce the likelihood of college completion or graduate.[204–209] Willie got through his studies without letting student debt determine his institutional selection or distort his major or career choices.[210–212] However, as he moved to and through graduate school, his experience with student debt took on many of the characteristics pervasive among borrowers today.

A variety of forces buffeted Willie's journey from college graduation to enrollment in the master of social work (MSW) program at Washington University (WashU) in St. Louis, including the unforeseen convergence of global conflict (which prevented his exit from the military) and state budget cuts (which ended his promised job as a prison inspector). When he arrived at WashU, he encountered not only what he expected—one of the top social work programs in the country—but also what he did not fully understand: WashU was also noteworthy for failing to provide adequate financial support to low-income students. While the finances work somewhat differently for graduate students, analysis by *The New York Times* found that only about 6% of WashU's recent freshman classes were eligible for Pell Grants, even though, as one of the country's 25 richest colleges on a per-student basis, the institution could afford to provide generous assistance to low-income students.[213]

While the knowledge and connections he gained at WashU were invaluable aids to his academic career, Willie borrowed heavily for the privilege of attending. He raced through the program in order to minimize his borrowing, sacrificed sleep and time with his family, and left with a PhD and more than $100,000 in student debt. Even today, he identifies with research documenting how student debt burdens compromise life satisfaction and overall well-being.[214–216] While now an accomplished professor, he still often feels very much like a "student debtor." If student debt were truly a universal experience that every student equally relied on and which equally shaped every student's postsecondary educational experience, Willie's story would be lamentable, perhaps, but not inequitable. The dramatic increase in student borrowing observed in recent years would not necessarily threaten the American vision of economic mobility through educational attainment.[217] But it is not. Instead, largely as a result of the distortions of debt dependence, students disadvantaged by race and class cannot educate themselves to wealth parity with those who start out ahead.[218]

Melinda also earned her MSW at WashU. She also benefitted from the top-notch social work library, career counseling, award-winning professors, and talented peers. Her MSW was free, though, because the partial merit scholarship that WashU provided was complemented by the merit-based Truman scholarship her mentor had coached her to apply for while at KU. The combination left her not with unmet need but enough money to buy a computer before she moved to St. Louis and spend another summer studying Spanish in Guatemala. Critically, however, her decision to go to WashU was made before she even knew she would receive the Truman. Her parents and grandparents were ready to pay for graduate school, as they had done for her older sister. Indeed, higher-income parents send their children to college—the best ones possible—whether or not they receive financial assistance.[219] Far more common for Whites than Blacks, such parent-to-adult child transfers help to ensure the perpetuation of social standing among the privileged.[72,220] With valuable family contributions assured, what financial aid did for Melinda was allow her to finish her graduate studies without dipping much into the money her parents had originally saved for college. That proved decisive later in her life, positioning her to take a relatively low-paying job with strong career potential right out of graduate school. All things considered, the plan the KU Chancellor outlined when he initially recruited Melinda worked out even better than he could have imagined.

On the surface, we had remarkably similar educational journeys. We just missed each other at WashU, met at KU, and worked together to build the Center on Assets, Education, and Inclusion into a research hub studying the effects of assets on educational outcomes and the implications of debt-dependent financial aid. However, this apparent equivalency of final destination belies tremendous disparities along the way. Where Willie encountered disadvantage at every turn, requiring him to surmount huge obstacles and pay disproportionately for his educational gains, Melinda's way (and now that of Willie's children) was paved by layers of advantage, as her family's privilege was compounded by institutional policies that propelled her forward. This is the opposite of what disadvantaged children deserve and what we should expect from a system that is allegedly the "great equalizer." Critically, this inequity is more than just an unfortunate development. As we outline in the coming chapters, it is a huge and harsh obstacle to the economic mobility prospects of generations of Americans. At this point, there is no widely-viable alternative route to the American dream other than through educational attainment. Instead, having cast our die and told generations that education is the key to their success, it is now imperative that we make good on this promise.

Conclusion

At every point where we look for evidence of higher education as a catalyst of equitable opportunity, children's outcomes instead depend on how financially equipped they are to navigate an inequitable landscape. This bleak reality is reflected in the disparate educational experiences of American students today, even after several years of policies aimed at increasing attainment and closing, including proposals to: increase institutional accountability, augment Pell Grants, reform student lending, and invest in "upstream" efforts such as expanded preschool and K-12 reform.[221] If enacted, policy proposals under the Trump administration may further deepen these divides. Planned spending cuts by the current administration will fall disproportionately on low-income families and communities, while tax cuts will primarily benefit the wealthy, affording them additional leverage in service of their children's chances.[222,223] Michigan's past two decades of experience with the "school choice" policies championed by Education Secretary Betsy DeVos portend escalating inequality as well. There, overall achievement has lagged behind other states', while proliferation of charter schools has weakened public school finances, exposed poor communities to for-profit operators, and failed to translate into meaningful options for those most marginalized.[34,224]

Policy changes that perpetuate inequalities may do long-term damage to children's prospects. Analysis by Sharkey reveals that two consecutive generations in a poor neighborhood reduce children's cognitive skills commensurate with missing two to four years of school.[102] There is evidence that children in poverty display more than a two-grade gap in reading mastery by the time they are in fourth grade, and these divides appear to be widening.[225,226] Achievement gaps by income are 30% to 40% larger among children born in 2001 than among children born in 1976, even as aggregate educational attainment rises.[109] These gaps matter; some analysis has attributed much of the racial difference in adults' upward and downward mobility to gaps in test scores in adolescence.[227]

Collectively, these findings and the patterns they reveal underscore that making education work—really—for the poor is not a challenge suited to tweaks around the edges nor a case where rising tides will lift all boats. Absent intentional pursuit of equal opportunity, raising the bar for everyone does not close the gap.[228] Unless we change the very workings of our educational structures, how a child does will continue to depend more on who her parents are than how smart she is or how hard she tries.[86] And while education is certainly not the nation's only inequitable arena, it is education alone that has been explicitly vested with equalizing opportunity in our uniquely capitalistic society, which is designed to thrive only when it provides a reasonably level playing field for all.[229]

Capitalism supposes that those who emerge as victors have done so after a fair contest. Instead, today's education system serves more to "launder" the privilege of the children of the wealthy—wrapping it in the mantle of merit—than to truly test and fairly reward the mettle of American young people. This matters not just rhetorically but also functionally. Inequities in the education system undermine capitalism's foundation at precisely the place where it is presumed to excel—free competition. Because education—particularly at the postsecondary level—is supposed to facilitate pursuit of the prosperity this nation has to offer, the corrosive force of wealth inequality threatens to pull out the very rungs of the ladder Americans are told to climb. This means that setting disadvantaged and privileged students on inherently disparate tracks is not merely unfortunate or even simply unfair. It is an existential threat to the American dream.

Notes

a. Analysis suggests that the question of who will earn a bachelor's degree by age 24 is largely determined by birth.[47]

b. Even the College Board acknowledges that college entrance exams are often unfairly bolstered for the privileged.[194]

c. Trips to campus are prohibitively expensive for low-income students.[24] This may give the impression that they are "less committed" to an institution than someone who travels to check out the campus.

2 The Battle to Define Life Chances and the Distributional Consequences of the Current Education and Economic Systems in America

OUR STORIES SERVE to illustrate that divergent experiences are not primarily the result of different choices or preferences. Willie's route to and through higher education was often perilous and frustrating because he lacked the resources with which to maneuver and bend institutions in order to meet his needs. In contrast, Melinda's college aspirations were encouraged and rewarded by the same institutions because she had the resources to make them work for her. As stark as these different routes were, if the gap in our families' wealth had ceased to matter once we got our degrees, some might still argue that higher education is "working" as a leveler. Sure, Willie had to try harder, wait longer, and forego many opportunities, but isn't it where you end up that really matters? Our stories suggest that the answer to this question is a resounding "No." Instead, our lives continue to be marked by the effects of wealth inequality and by the substantial differences in how the education system treats those who start with money and those working to get it. This is the thesis of this chapter: that wealth inequality is not just another manifestation of unfairness in US society but instead a primary force determining how people fare, including in the institutions that are supposed to catalyze equitable opportunities.

Our lives reveal how assets chart one's course not only at the beginning of a college career but also well into a college graduate's future. In Willie's case, even though it has been more than nine years since he graduated from his PhD program, student debt still compromises his ability to leverage his relatively high salary to secure sound financial footing. His lingering financial instability is rooted in the economic disadvantages of his family of origin, but, critically, it was not erased when he graduated. Instead, his imperative to confront his six-figure student debt deficit ensured that the effects of wealth inequality would persist, *despite* his educational successes. Conversely, Melinda's consistent ability to rely on her family's assets through college and beyond placed her in a much better financial position than Willie, even though she has less education. In addition to graduating without any student debt, Melinda's continued access to her family's resources during her young adulthood meant that events like buying a new vehicle to accommodate the arrival of her twins or coming up with a down payment sufficient to avoid costly mortgage insurance were mere bumps in the road instead of substantial detours from a strong financial future. She was able to leverage her family's resources to advance her husband's upward mobility trajectory too, including when money from her grandparents helped to pay for some of his graduate degree. This is the role that inheritances and in vivo family transfers play in the lives of many privileged Americans, and it matters, influencing how much wealth people can generate from their own efforts.[1,2] Before she turned 40, Melinda's family had resources to cushion them from future shocks, productive assets that grew each year, and bank balances that represented promises to their children. This relative advantage looks particularly dramatic when viewed in contrast to those who had to sign on for debt before they could sit down in a college classroom.

In order for the education system to serve as the platform for equitable opportunity and upward mobility that Americans envision, the outcomes it delivers must hinge on the effort and ability—the inputs—inserted. In other words, for education to work in the United States as we hope it will and sometimes imagine it does, a student's chance of success has to depend almost entirely on her own initiative, rather than her starting point. However, as Willie's journey underscores, hard work and raw talent are only sporadically sufficient to lift a disadvantaged student to and through college. Just 9% of the poorest students graduate from college.[3] Even high-achieving low-income students struggle to match the educational attainment of their privileged peers. There is a more than 30% gap in the college graduation rates of the highest-scoring students, by family income.[4]

Gaps in initial conditions—in particular, parental educational attainment and household resources for schooling—compound as children pass through unequal school systems. At the primary and secondary school levels, school finance formulas that hinge on property valuations lead to gross inequities that deprive the poorest students of the public investment they need to catch up to and keep pace with their privileged peers, even where states attempt to counteract the imbalance.[5,6]

These gaps are then legitimized by the conferring of institutional credentials that are presumed to be meritocratic rather than inherited. In other words, the US education system allows those who start out ahead to cloak their privilege in the trappings of "achievement," so that it appears entirely earned. Peeling back the curtains, as we have tried to do through our own life stories, it becomes clear that who one is and where one begins can alter the benefits the education system bestows. In a nation where education is supposed to be an equalizing force, this is a fatal flaw that compels reckoning.

Inequities in the education system become even more pronounced when examining outcomes beyond mere degree attainment. Differences in institutional selection, career pursuit, and social networks create profoundly stratified trajectories, such that "postsecondary education" means many different things and secures very different returns. Some institutions add far greater value for their graduates than others.[7] This accounting underscores the significance of support to navigate institutional options and optimize choices, help that is less often available to poorer students.[8] Recent analysis has contributed nuance to the growing sense that "college no longer pays off," suggesting that it may instead be the case that the greatest spoils of American postsecondary education are inequitably concentrated, for the benefit of a few. For example, students from the lowest quintile of household earnings are only 3.6% of the student body at Stanford but, if they graduate from that institution, they have an 18.5% chance of reaching the top 1% of earners.[9] At the aggregate level, the payoff gap between two- and four-year degrees is greater than the gap between a high school diploma and an associate's degree.[10] In total, the route through the education system to a lifetime of prosperity is a circuitous and uncertain one, with many places where the outcomes of privileged and disadvantaged students can diverge.

If financial aid dollars were truly created equal, two students who earned degrees in the same field from the same institution should realize similar returns. This is the "effort plus ability equals outcomes" equation that animates the American understanding of how the education system should work. It is not, however, how our lives have unfolded. It is not what millions of American college graduates realize, as they accept both their diplomas and the stark truth that credentials do not "pay off" for everyone equally. While we both graduated from the George Warren Brown (GWB) School of Social Work at Washington University—Willie with the terminal degree of our profession, the PhD, and Melinda with a master of social work (MSW)—the financial fruits of our credentials differ sharply. The effects of student debt and its absence continue to shape our economic prospects and our overall well-being.

Where Melinda's education was paid for through a combination of merit-based scholarships and her family's savings, the merit aid package GWB offered to Willie was not enough to meet his full financial need. As described previously, his unmet need is not surprising or rare; the stipends that are available to students are often insufficient. Willie bridged the resulting gap with student loans, tore rapidly through his doctoral studies, and graduated with a promising career ahead of him—and approximately $100,000 in student debt.

In contrast, Melinda finished her MSW with money left in the account that her parents had originally opened for her education. She married someone who also had a college degree, in a pattern of increasingly common "assortative mating" that contributes to today's economic inequality.[11,12] Melinda's debt-free higher education made a difference in her husband's financial future too. She used her leftover college savings to pay off her husband's undergraduate loan. Without student debt repayment to divert their income, Melinda and her husband could focus on current consumption and crucial future asset accumulation. They bought a home before they celebrated their first anniversary. They could even continue to save for retirement, albeit modestly, when her husband returned to graduate school himself. They financed his degree from their stored assets, which were themselves seeded with transfers from Melinda's family. They lived fairly frugally, particularly during the years when the Great Recession forced furloughs and Melinda was home part-time with their children. They handled home repairs themselves, always bought clothes at discount, and never stopped for lattes. They started college savings accounts for all four children before the youngest was even born and asked relatives to give contributions instead of presents for their children's milestones. They worked hard to secure jobs that, particularly in her husband's case, offered high salaries and promising advancement opportunities. Still, replicating that same frugality and advance planning would not have yielded the same returns for a couple who depended on student loans to finance their educations or lacked the financial foundation Melinda's family's support provided. Indeed, Willie's route demonstrates that it did not.

In some respects, Willie's story is the archetype of upward mobility. From a childhood spent entirely in or near poverty to his current standing as a well-regarded scholar, he has undeniably ascended. His children enjoy a standard of living far higher than his own at that age. They go to better-performing schools, live in a nicer home, and have a clearer path to their own future careers. Willie has worked hard to get to where he is now. Those efforts have paid off, securing him a place among the reported 1.7% of Americans aged 25 and older who possess a doctoral degree.[13] At the same time, all of this exertion has still not garnered true financial security. Years of student loan deferment and forbearance mean that he will still face five-figure student debt when he turns 50. He struggles to figure out how to save enough for his three children's educations when his own debts feel daunting. Even living in an affordable Midwestern city and eschewing many luxuries, he has financial anxieties he never imagined professors would carry.

Certainly we both could have attended a less expensive social work program than GWB. Indeed, that is exactly what many admissions counselors and financial planners would have advised Willie to do, as a low-income student. However, we believe parallels in our paths make our stories useful illustrations of the ways that wealth inequality erodes education's equalizing potential. We both selected the same graduate school. We both worked hard and, we believe, wrung the most value possible out of that vaunted institution. We both have distinguished ourselves as successful instructors and respected researchers. All of these similarities notwithstanding, our balance sheets are highly divergent. Contemplating the resulting gaps—far too large to be explained by the minor differences in our respective actions—we are left with the conclusion that where we stand today must be strongly influenced by where we started and by the ways in which institutions amplified, rather than mitigated, those inequities.

Wealth Inequality Largely Ignored in Policy Discussions About How to Improve Our Education System

In this book we focus on financial assets, the most tangible and influential component of what we understand as "wealth." In part, this focus on wealth is pragmatic, as it is a lever that can be readily manipulated in pursuit of dramatic social change. As Michael Sherraden states in his seminal book on the centrality of assets to human welfare, "focusing on financial assets is what social policy can do best and with the least bureaucracy."[14] Outcomes from existing policies demonstrate the potency of government action to catalyze wealth creation. For example, legislative and regulatory changes in the housing market and tax code contributed to the dramatic increase in homeownership and accumulated housing equity in the postwar period.[15-18] Similarly, the construction of tax-advantaged 529 state college savings plans and provision of generous tax benefits for contributions to these accounts have resulted in a 100-fold increase in the assets families hold in these accounts, to more than $250 billion in 2016.[19] Tax policy to encourage retirement saving in employer 401(k) and individual retirement accounts have fueled growth in retirement holdings among middle-class Americans, from 38% of annual incomes in 1970 to 210% in 2014.[20]

Unequally distributed and inequitably incentivized, these policies have contributed to the widening racial wealth gap.[21] These patterns underscore that the hurdles to broader wealth distribution are primarily political, not technical. Unlike technically complex problems that involve completely reworking integral parts of our culture and society (e.g., pivoting away from fossil fuels or combatting obesity), policies to extend wealth accumulation to all Americans can be pursued right now. They admittedly require the political will to enact major legislation, but they are nonetheless feasible. The United States has used policy to turn Americans into wealth-builders on a grand scale before. We can do it again.

Our emphasis on wealth is not merely pragmatic, however. It is also the case that wealth has an outsized importance in Americans' lives and, we assert, explains much of the persistent inequity we see. As technological advances in public health, information, and energy have smoothed out some of the differences in the experiences of Americans on either side of the "have" and "have not" divide, wealth has taken on increasing significance as a determinant of relative position. Wealthy Americans understand that assets are integral to financial well-being. They have therefore adopted practices that increase their holdings. As a result, among the top 1% of households, only 39% of personal income is derived from labor income while 53% is capital income (e.g., business profits, dividends, net capital gains, taxable interest, and tax-exempt interest), a shift that will be increasingly important as jobs continue to be replaced by automation.[22] In addition to having a diverse and robust range of income sources beyond labor, the wealthy are also highly influential when it comes to creating and advancing policies that preserve their wealth advantage.[23,24] In a nation where, today, few Americans die from inadequate sanitation and even the poorest can access knowledge that was unimaginable in centuries past, the concentration of wealth in the hands of a few is particularly anomalous. It is also acutely destructive—not merely an economic problem but a threat to the foundations of liberty and opportunity on which our republic stands.[25]

Although the wealthy rightly understand assets as essential tools for their upward mobility, this recognition does not translate to broad recognition of the utility of assets for combating the pervasive financial insecurity that afflicts most of the nation.[26] Disturbingly, when it comes to asset building, most contemporary policies ignore the plight of lower-income Americans and instead work[27]— overtly and covertly—to subsidize the wealth building of those who already start out ahead.[28] Unfortunately, these "oversights" in policy extend well beyond the chambers in which our laws are made, permeating the priorities of the very people who such policies could truly help. One example of this is that we often see those who are at or near poverty make demands for higher wages and more adequate benefits, but it is rare to hear those same voices protesting poorer access to wealth-building institutions.[29,30]

Even though Americans at nearly every income level express a desire for stronger financial security, the policies that would facilitate such an aim are largely invisible to lower-income families.[31] In part, this is because they typically only have experience with wages; numerically, few Americans have enough wealth to care much about the institutions that could help them amass it.[1] More than half of households with incomes less than $30,000 per year have no savings at all.[32] Nine million American households were unbanked in 2015, and evidence suggests they are mostly low-income; 57% of unbanked households cited lack of money to keep in an account as the reason they do not have one.[33] These households have few interactions with mainstream financial institutions and no opportunity to see their paychecks augmented by capital earnings. Instead, earned income from labor is often the sum total of their economic well-being. This is not just myopia on the part of low-income Americans. It also reflects the psychology of scarcity, the relative complexity of the tax policies and financial instruments that wealthy people use to their advantage, and an astute recognition of wealth-building institutions' limited relevance to their current financial realities.[34] Even the rhetoric of economic mobility in the United States obscures the role of wealth creation in fueling ascent. After all, it is a story of "*working* one's way up," not of saving up for the climb. How well one does is described as being primarily a function of how much one earns, even if that is not really the way that most people get ahead—today or in our likely future.

While individuals with limited exposure to financial institutions and only rudimentary knowledge of financial mechanisms may experience "choice paralysis" when confronted with complicated investment options, even the savviest low-income investors fare relatively poorly in America's wealth-generating systems.[35] Close examination of these institutions reveals ways that they unfairly reward the already wealthy. For example, the top 10% of taxpayers receive 86% of the benefit of the mortgage interest deduction, while homeowners who do not itemize their taxes receive nothing.[36] The institutions that are supposed to help Americans build wealth were not designed with low-income Americans in mind, and it shows.

If low-income Americans and their advocates seldom have policies to build financial assets on their radar, such initiatives are even less represented on the agendas of policymakers—even those committed to reducing poverty and closing gaps. In a 2013 speech, then-President Obama described inequality as the "defining challenge of our time" but focused his attention on *income* inequality, mentioning wealth inequality only once.[37] When wealth is part of the conversation about how disadvantaged households are doing, it is usually in the context of explaining why low-income people cannot or even should not build wealth. In particular, some conservative policymakers take the position that lower-income families are unable to build assets because they lack the necessary character. According to this analysis, the culprit is neither inadequate access to wealth-building institutions nor regressive incentive structures. Instead, the problem is that low-income families have not exerted the required effort or, perhaps, lack the innate ability to accumulate assets (e.g., are not smart enough or financially undisciplined). These diagnoses often serve to excuse policies that exclude the poor from the engines of wealth building.

While policymakers are not unique in their frequently-flawed assumptions about lower-income families, their mistaken views are particularly high-profile. More specifically, some of the most powerful policymakers of our age have expressed beliefs that those who lack assets are lazy or present-time oriented, and that it is these qualities that make them fail at upward mobility. For instance, when John Boehner was Speaker of the House, he blamed unemployment on those who would "rather just sit around."[38] Similarly, Senate Majority Leader Mitch McConnell claimed that businesses have "a hard time finding people to do the work because they're doing too good with food stamps, Social Security and all the rest."[39] Speaker of the House Paul Ryan divided the country between those who rely on public assistance and those who "want the American dream," seeming to cast the economically disadvantaged outside of mainstream American values altogether.[40] Out of the national spotlight, some elected officials' statements about the moral conduct and inherent worth of people living in poverty are even more inflammatory. Former South Carolina Lieutenant Governor Andre Bauer argued against government assistance to low-income people by equating such help to "feeding stray animals . . . they will reproduce."[41]

This is not to suggest that conservative policymakers are of monolithic opinion about the dubious prospects for wealth building among the poor. Indeed, many tenets of asset-based approaches to facilitating economic mobility align with conservative ideals, at least in theory. President George W. Bush championed the notion of an "ownership society," starting with the contention that asset ownership "benefits individual families by building stability and long-term financial security."[42] Speaking in 2004, Bush sounded themes that mirror scholarship examining asset effects on attitudes and behavior[43]: "If you own something, you have a vital stake in the future of our country. The more ownership there is in America, the more vitality there is in America."

More recently, during his 2016 presidential campaign, Republican Senator Marco Rubio (FL) alluded to the need for asset-based complements to income supports:

> We need to address the fact that we have 40-some odd million people who feel trapped in poverty and do not feel like they have an equal opportunity

to get ahead. As far as the war on poverty is concerned, its programs have utility—they do help alleviate the consequences of poverty—but they don't help people to emerge from that poverty. . . . I think we have to take the next step, which is to help people trapped with inequality of opportunity to have the opportunity to build for themselves a better life.[44]

Some policymakers are exploring ways to create opportunities for equitable and inclusive wealth building. With Democrat Ron Wyden (OR), Republican Senator Jerry Moran (KS) co-founded the bipartisan Senate Economic Mobility Caucus "to discuss the policies Washington needs to pursue to make certain our children and grandchildren can live in an America that allows them to dream big and pursue those dreams."[45]

To date, however, there have been few champions on the political right for policies that would distribute assets as platforms of upward mobility. Nor are conservatives alone in mostly eschewing assets as a tool to lift disadvantaged Americans. Some liberal policymakers and researchers take the position that encouraging low-income families to save would harm them by diverting already inadequate income away from meeting basic needs. Others argue from a similar position of scarcity but on a macroeconomic scale. They take the stance that there is a limited fiscal pie and, therefore, shifting money designated for safety-net programs toward investments in asset building will lead to detrimental cuts in programs such as Temporary Assistance for Needy Families (TANF) or Supplemental Nutrition Assistance Program (SNAP). In the United States and other developed nations, some have criticized social investment approaches, including asset-based welfare, as entrenching in social policy what they see as harmful neoliberal ideas.[46,47] Specifically when aimed at children, some have criticized investments in human capital as reducing children to future workers, rather than rooting poverty eradication in a human rights framework.[48] And some lament any policy that pivots away from pure entitlement to introduce risk as well as return[49]—what some high-profile liberals in the United States have derided as "market-based solutions."[50]

From neither end of the ideological spectrum, then, are the needs and aspirations of lower-income families well-represented in wealth building. As a result, current wealth creation policies focus heavily—and almost exclusively—on bolstering higher-income Americans' climbs up the economic ladder, particularly in the arenas of retirement saving, homeownership, and college saving. These policies reward the efforts of higher-income Americans, particularly through the tax code, and reduce the exertion required to realize results.[51] At the same time, current wealth-building policies make it harder, if not impossible, for lower-income families to build assets by forbidding those who depend on public assistance from accumulating any wealth.[27] This two-tier system stacks the odds against lower-income families and positions them in a continuous cycle of poverty.[52] And, because assets beget assets, initial wealth disparities compound. Considering how this dynamic unfolds by race, analysis by the Institute for Assets and Social Policy shows that White families do not just own more wealth than Blacks; they also *accumulate* wealth at three times the rate.[53] Specifically, White families started the period of observation with $29,000 more wealth than Black families but ended $119,000 ahead. This is wealth inequality fueled by institutional inequity. It runs directly contrary to the ideal of the American dream.

The Landscape of Wealth Inequality in America
RACE, CLASS, AND WEALTH INEQUALITY

Wealth inequality in the United States is intensifying dramatically.[54–56] Although average wealth has increased over the past 50 years, not all groups have benefitted. Instead, wealth inequality has increased continuously since 1978, such that, by 2012, the share owned by the top 0.1% was three times higher than in the late 1980s.[55] Between 1963 and 2013, while families near the bottom of the wealth distribution lost ground, those in the middle roughly doubled their wealth, particularly before 1983, and families near the top saw their wealth quadruple.[21] Families of color are disproportionately overrepresented among those in the lower rungs of the wealth distribution. In 2013, the average wealth of White families was $500,000 higher than the average wealth of Black and Latino families.[21] In other words, White families had, on average, seven times the wealth of Black families and six times the wealth of Latino families.[a,21]

Of course, differences in income partially explain racial wealth divides. Income inequality means that White Americans, on average, have more money to devote to wealth accumulation than Blacks. And income inequality today is unprecedented in American history. Unbelievably, some analysis has concluded that the United States was more economically unequal in 2012 than in 1774, even counting the abomination of slavery.[57] Crucially, however, the racial wealth gap persists even among families at the same income levels, and increases in income do not result in equal wealth gains for everyone.[58] This is primarily because families of color have limited access to wealth-building structures. For example, in the third quarter of 2016, the homeownership rate for households headed by non-Hispanic Whites was 71.9%, compared to 41.3% for Black households and 47% for households identified as Hispanic or Latino.[59]

As in other domains, even when Americans of color achieve a given milestone, such as homeownership, they seldom realize the same outcomes as Whites. Black homeowners fared worse in the Great Recession than White homeowners, largely due to discriminatory lending practices.[60,61] Today, Black homeowners are more than twice as likely as White homeowners to have negative equity—owing more than their homes are worth.[62] Families of color experience starkly poorer outcomes in other financial markets, as well. In 2013, White families had over $100,000 more in average liquid retirement savings than Black and Hispanic families, a disparity that has quadrupled in sheer dollar terms over the past 25 years.[21] As our own stories have illustrated, even higher education, supposed to be the "great equalizer," is far from equal in terms of wealth generation. Researchers at the Institute on Assets and Social Policy have documented how White, but not Black, college-educated households amass wealth, fueled at least in part by Whites' greater likelihood of receipt of parental transfers to fund their education.[63] The divergent wealth-building patterns of White and Black college graduates contribute to overall widening of racial wealth disparities.[63] When even the very same accomplishment does not realize the same outcomes, institutions are clearly implicated in inequity.

As we see in our own lives, baseline differences in wealth widen as gaps in the critical early-career period multiply. Melinda started saving for retirement before she graduated college, when her dad convinced her to set aside funds from her college savings account. This $1,500, invested at age 21, will matter more at retirement than the contributions Willie makes later in his career. Such disparities manifest in national data, as well. Whites have three times the wealth of Blacks in their 30s and 11 times as much wealth by the time they are in their 60s.[21] Of course, these gaps do not magically materialize in young adulthood. Instead, differences in what people receive from their families as they grow up set them on different tracks as they launch adulthood. As was the case for Melinda, White young adults are five times more likely than Blacks to receive financial gifts or inheritances, transfers that may finance debt-free college education and fuel wealth-building investments such as home purchase or business development.[64,65] Indeed, analysis has traced much of the racial inheritance gap to discriminatory US housing policies, which facilitated wealth building by previous generations of Whites, while denying these opportunities to their Black peers.[61]

In these and other ways, Blacks' experiences with US institutional power are fraught with unparalleled exploitation and oppression. However, acknowledging the severity and entrenched roots of the White/Black wealth gap must not obscure the real struggles that many White families face. Otherwise, framing wealth inequality as a "Black problem" can incorrectly and unwisely cast policies designed to reduce wealth inequality as aimed narrowly at only Americans of color. This would likely result in flawed policies that fail to address the economic distress plaguing many White families. Additionally, the US policy and economic landscapes provide evidence for the unfortunate conclusion: when economically disadvantaged Blacks and Whites are divided on the issue of wealth inequality, the wealth gap widens and those who benefit from unfair rules are virtually unchallenged in their ability to continue to craft them.

WEALTH INEQUALITIES BEYOND RACE AND CLASS

Wealth inequality extends beyond race to manifest along other demographic lines within American society. While White women own more assets than men and women of color, they accumulate less wealth than White men, as their unequal positions in the labor market translate into less asset-building potential and as inequities in public systems and in private-sector practices constrain women's wealth building.[66–68] The gender wealth gap is even greater than the earnings divide. In a study of single men and women, Chang finds while women earn about 79 cents on the dollar compared to men, they own only 32 cents.[66] Similarly, while never-married women working full time earn 95% of the earnings of never-married men, they own only 16% of the wealth of never-married men. Median wealth for single women is $3,210, compared to $10,150 for single men.[66]

Women's wealth positions provide evidence of the influence of institutional access and rewards on asset holdings. The gender retirement savings gap is threatens women's financial well-being throughout their working years and beyond.[69] Illustrating the compounding effects of inequities in wealth-building systems, the gender gap in median wealth grows with greater education, as women experience difficulties leveraging their educational credentials. Specifically, while the gap between men and women's wealth is negligible for those with less than high school diplomas, American men with graduate degrees own almost twice as much wealth as equivalently educated women.[66] Crucially, with women taking financial responsibility for a growing percentage of US households, gender disparities in wealth threaten the economic security and mobility prospects of millions of Americans.

Besides gendered wealth inequality, some geographic regions saw disproportionate wealth losses during the Great Recession.[70] These regions continue to grapple with higher poverty and fewer opportunities to advance economically. For the most part, these are also communities with concentrations of adults without college degrees who struggle to accumulate wealth and often find themselves economically insecure.[71] Indeed, the wealth divide between those with advanced degrees and those with less education continues to widen. Between 1989 and 2013, the median wealth of those with advanced degrees rose 45%, compared to only 3% for those with two- or four-year degrees and net worth *declines* for those with less education, an outcome reflective of the overall worsening position of Americans without education beyond high school.[72,73] Evidently, many Americans have some reason to believe that they are falling behind others and behind their own aspirations of the American dream.

Finally, there are apparent temporal aspects to wealth inequality; young people today have poorer prospects for building wealth than if they had been born decades ago.[74] Young adults suffered the greatest job losses during the Great Recession, constraining their early-career earning and wealth-building prospects.[75] There is evidence that these adverse economic conditions not only delayed the financial independence of Generation X and Millennial Americans but also affected their perception of what is truly possible for their futures by eroding confidence in the institutions that are supposed to deliver the American dream.[75,76]

THE GREAT RECESSION AND WEALTH INEQUALITY

Young adults' balance sheets were not the only casualties of the Great Recession. This nearly-unprecedented economic collapse harmed the middle class and intensified wealth inequalities between the middle and upper classes. During this time, Americans in the middle class lost much of their wealth as well as some of their earning power.[77-79] The Great Recession was particularly brutal for Americans of color; researchers at Pew estimate that African Americans lost 50% of their wealth and Hispanics 66%.[80] Additionally, across racial groups, the increasing polarization in economic standing is the most striking feature of post-Recession distributions. Only Black Americans are just as likely to be middle class in 2015 as in 1971, while Asians, Whites, and Hispanics are more likely to be either low- or high-income.[77] Further, those who managed to stay in the middle class have seen their relative share of wealth decrease. Researchers at Pew found that in 1983, upper-class households had three times the wealth of middle-class households, while, by 2013, the wealth gap between upper- and middle-class households had risen to seven-fold.[77] This sheds light on a dramatic change in the economic fortunes of Americans who had previously considered themselves evidence of the fundamental soundness of the American dream and of the vitality of the institutions that deliver it. Zakaria explains:

> The United States is going through a great power shift. Working-class whites don't think of themselves as an elite group. But, in a sense, they have been, certainly compared with Blacks, Hispanics, Native Americans and most immigrants. They were central to America's economy, its society, indeed its very identity. They are not anymore.[81]

While analyses of the 2016 election continue to dispute its meaning, the shrinking of the middle class, and, maybe even more potently, fears of its shadow, may have led some Whites to seek the power they once had by seeking allies in the political system who they believe will favor their interests.[82,83] It has not led, at least yet, to broad demands for policies that would more equitably distribute wealth-building opportunities among all Americans.

Recovery from the recession has been at least as uneven as experiences in its depths.[84] As is usually the case in a racially unjust society, households of color were particularly hard-hit by the economic downturn. Analysis suggests that Black wealth levels have been slow to rebound, a disparity that may exact a severe and long-lasting cost. Specifically, by 2031, a typical Black family's median wealth will be almost $98,000 (or 40%) lower than it would have been without the devastating downturn.[85] While wealthy Americans have rebounded to greater prosperity than prior to the recession, poorer households continue to struggle through the fallout of what some have characterized as "an enormous transfer of wealth from the middle class and poor to the wealthy."[86] It is then not a coincidence that attention to the depth and consequence of economic inequality has escalated in post-recession America. Wealth inequality deepens divides between the winners and losers in the American economic system and contributes to a growing sense that the game is rigged against those trying to move up. It is a threat to all Americans who, despite their best efforts, are unable to secure equitable access to the resources that institutions can provide because they are blocked by wealth inequality that constrains their options and thwarts real opportunity.

WEALTH INEQUALITY LIMITS MOBILITY IN AMERICA AND
WEAKENS BELIEF IN THE AMERICAN DREAM

The dramatic wealth divide is a conundrum that contributes to Americans' sense of malaise in a climate fraught with insecurity. According to a 2013 poll, 53% of Americans in the middle class perceive that they will either remain there or slip backwards in the coming years.[87] Research has found that such pessimism about upward mobility is the best predictor of concern about inequality.[88] There is good reason for the alarm. Inequality in income and wealth is not only bad theoretically, as an injury to American ideals of egalitarianism, broadly shared prosperity, and meaningful opportunity. Economic disparities may actually be making it harder for Americans to climb.

Current research suggests that young adults today may not have the same economic opportunities as their parents. Using longitudinal data, Chetty and colleagues quantified the growing "stickiness" of the rungs on the US economic ladder.[89] They found that an American born in 1980 has only about a 50% chance of out-earning her parents, which is far less than an American born in 1940.[89] Even more concerning, some regions of the country seem to be trending toward downward mobility, giving young people in these communities little chance at the American dream.[89] Significantly, this research does not just document the fact that those who are born at the top or bottom are more likely to stay at either pole but also seeks to explain why this is so. Here, the analysis attributed most of the decrease in mobility to increased inequality, finding that holding economic inequality to its 1970 level would give today's 36-year-olds an 80% chance of surpassing their parents. In contrast, when researchers instead modeled greater economic growth within today's unchecked inequality, they found less improvement in mobility rates.[89] It seems, then, that the American dream is best realized through equitably sharing the fruits of US economic growth—the opposite of current policies and resulting economic trends.

With this examination of wealth inequality as the central force shaping Americans' outcomes and, we contend, imperiling American values of equal opportunity and meritocratic advancement, we intend more than an overview of the wealth divide. Our aim is not to merely trace the landscape but to contribute to its transformation. Toward this end, we pivot from a description of the backdrop of wealth inequality and its manifestation in patterns crushing yet predictable, to next consider how individuals' actions unfold within what are overtly unfair institutions. Further, we examine how individual exertion interplays with wealth and its power to determine how people do and how they explain where they end up.

The Law Provides Everyone with the *Right* to Own Capital, But Systems Do Not Equip Everyone with the *Capacity* to Build Wealth

For capitalism to be practically functional and morally defensible, all individuals must have the ability to take advantage of its institutional capabilities. Today's societal arrangements diverge significantly from these ideals. We see this gulf between rhetoric and reality vividly when it comes to postsecondary education. Americans are given the empty assurance that "everyone can go to college," when the truth is that not everyone has the money to pay for it or has received equitable preparation to equip them to succeed there. Even more concerning, this hollow focus on one's theoretical "right" to attend college transcends platitudes and is enshrined in contemporary financial aid policies, which overwhelmingly focus on facilitating mere *access* to college. Such a narrow view has backed the US financial aid system into a corner dominated by student debt, and taken students along with it. When all that matters is giving people a chance, at least on paper, to get in the door, there is little attention to the consequences on the back end. In other words, the US financial aid system is presumed to be adequate if it helps students pay tuition when it comes due, even if it completely fails when these same students confront what could be a lifetime of paying off student debt. Instead, in order to truly live up to the practical and moral ideals of our society—and broker the fair competition on which capitalism is predicated—our policies must place students with and without family wealth on a level playing field before, during, and *after* college.

When it comes to paying for college, not all dollars are created equal. Instead, as Melinda's story illustrated, individuals who possess resources are endowed with not only money with which to pay the bills but, more significantly, greater bargaining power from which to approach the institution. In this way, wealth inequality distorts the higher education process, perhaps not in terms of knowledge acquisition in the classroom but in the dimension Americans value most: the ability to secure returns. This is a crucial point. The indictment of wealth inequality is not that one person has four houses while another has none. While owning four houses might be questionable from a standpoint of energy efficiency or ethical conduct, it is not necessarily *the problem* that wealth inequality creates in the marketplace. Instead, the problem is that the person with assets is in a better position to leverage key institutions than the person without assets. He is therefore better able to secure the benefits that institutions confer. This is anathema to American values. When the rules of the game—institutional arrangements in the tax code, financial aid policy, higher education admissions, and other spheres—reward some people's exertions more than others', based on their starting conditions, the contest cannot justly be called anything like fair.

College saving presents a pertinent example of how people can have "access" to an institution but not the position or wealth needed to take advantage of it. Authorized in the Internal Revenue Code since 2001 and named after the section of the tax code that created them, 529 plans are tax-preferred vehicles for postsecondary education saving. These plans are administered by states, usually through contractual agreements with private financial institutions.[90,91] Although theoretically anyone can use them, state 529 plans are an example of an asset-building policy where true access is largely for those with wealth.

Since households taxed at a higher rate receive greater benefits for every dollar invested, tax benefits for saving in 529 plans disproportionately favor higher-income families.[92,93] Adelman explains, "For high-income households, the tax advantages of financing college expenses through 529 plans can amount to as much as a 39% advantage over traditional taxable savings accounts. For middle-income families, the advantage was 35%, but for low-income families, it was only

22%."[92] In addition to inequitable tax treatment, many 529s have features that pose barriers to low-income households. For example, some have high initial balance requirements. Most do not allow cash deposits and therefore effectively require that individuals already have a bank account before they can make transfers to the 529 account. Few 529 plans have retail banking presences but, instead, often use investment firms that are culturally and often physically distant from low-income participants.[94]

There is considerable evidence that this nominal "access" to 529 college savings plans is inadequate to facilitate equitable outcomes. In 2010, while only 11% of dependent college students had family incomes over $150,000, almost half of those saving in 529 accounts did.[95] Similarly, the Government Accountability Office found that families with 529 college savings accounts have three times the median income and 25 times the median assets of those without accounts.[96] Even after efforts to reform 529s to distribute their benefits more broadly, enrollment continues to skew toward those households already economically advantaged.[97] This amounts to inequitable institutional facilitation of the postsecondary education journeys of only some Americans.

The consequences of using state 529 college savings plan systems—or not—can be substantial. Supported by tax-based subsidies, those saving for college in this system have more assets set aside for their children's college educations, with average balances of $7,534, compared to $6,043 for those saving in general bank accounts.[98] As an example of how privileged individuals will seek to protect even inequitable institutional rewards, when then-President Obama proposed ending the federal tax benefits associated with 529 plans as part of a plan for "middle-class economics," vociferous resistance from parents and policymakers of both parties forced him to relent.[99,100]

INSTITUTIONS PLAY AN IMPORTANT ROLE IN DETERMINING WHO BUILDS ASSETS

A big part of what asset researchers like Michael Sherraden have suggested is that, in addition to one's effort and ability, accumulating assets requires access to the capabilities institutions provide.[14] More recent analysis has quantified the percentage of the wealth gap attributable to individual initiative and concluded that only fundamental institutional change can equalize outcomes.[101] Individual behavioral adjustments alone are resoundingly insufficient.[102] In American society, the primary way people gain access to institutions is through social policies. Historic examples of institutions that facilitate—and block—access to asset accumulation include the policies of the Federal Housing Administration (FHA) during the 1960s.

These FHA policies changed the rules for buying a home by lowering the amount of a down payment from 90% of the price to 10%.[103] However, explicit policy decisions made this change only helpful only to some, mostly in White neighborhoods.[61] Another policy that helped to change the rules of the game was the GI Bill, which made mortgages available to World War II veterans with no down payment.[103] Once again, this policy helped some, but others who should have benefitted were left by the wayside.[102] Specifically, non-Whites could seldom buy houses in the mostly White neighborhoods that bank mortgage underwriters considered prudent risks.[104]

With regard to education, while increased access to financial aid did fuel college degree attainment by Black men, GI Bill education benefits also widened the educational gap between Whites and Blacks.[105] Black veterans were restricted to a limited number of postsecondary institutions, mostly segregated and often overcrowded, which further constrained the GI Bill's equalizing effects. Importantly, these historical examples are not meant to convey that policies that inequitably determine access to institutional benefits are a thing of the past.[105] There are many contemporary social policies that do the same thing. For instance, more recent tax and labor policies have fueled the shift from defined-benefit pension plans (where the employer promises a specified payment on retirement) to defined-contribution plans (an individual investment account is established and the employer or employee [or both] makes contributions on a regular schedule) for retirement saving. The result is facilitation of asset-building only by those with access to employer-provided retirement accounts and the resources to invest in them, which has, in turn, contributed to widening inequality.[106–109]

American institutions have shaped individual fortunes in ways that, through the lens of the American dream, then become seen as rightly rewarding the effort and ability of the deserving while penalizing the underserving. For example, after changes in financial aid and mortgage lending policy expanded opportunities, owning a home and going to college became central avenues through which Americans advantaged by race and income strove toward the American dream. Similarly, saving for retirement has become the only way most Americans can secure a decent standard of living in later life. As such, is considered a mark of an individual's financial responsibility. While some lower-income individuals are also able to take advantage of these policies—buying a house in a neighborhood at least somewhat upwardly mobile, finding an employer with a generous benefit package, or becoming the first in their families to go to college—those exceptions around the edges do not change the accounting of the ways in which these institutional arrangements concentrate privilege.

There is no question that institutions augment some Americans' efforts to accumulate assets while hampering the efforts of others. These diverging policy forces create new gaps and widen small ones. In this way, it can be said that American institutions have helped to shape behaviors into patterns that become self-reinforcing, forging identities as "asset builders" by force of policy incentive.[14] By choosing winners and losers and widening the distance between them, it might even be suggested that social policy actually carved out the American middle class from what was an upper class and a lower class.[103]

Certainly America, through its social policies, has a long history of helping some families build wealth, while others are denied the benefit of such assistance.[61,103,110] These investments are often sizable in sheer dollar value. They loom even larger when viewed against a backdrop of emerging evidence revealing the extent to which wealth drives not only economic standing but also the educational attainment that largely determines people's later outcomes. In this context, it is no wonder that children from low-income families languish in school districts hampered by low property values, miss out on the opportunities facilitated by the 529 system, end up in low-paying jobs that do not offer retirement savings, and have fewer resources to pass onto their own children. To a significant extent, those are the outcomes these institutional arrangements deliver.

US tax policy has been an especially popular tool to manipulate institutions to the advantage of those who seek to improve their positions.[111] Tax policies adopted in the mid-1980s significantly reduced the wealth of low- and moderate-income families while greatly boosting the wealth of the most affluent.[56] This trend of using the tax code, not to level the playing field but to redouble the advantages of the privileged, continues. According to Black, the fiscal year 2015 federal budget allocated about $573 billion for pro-savings and asset-building investments (e.g., retirement security, homeownership, postsecondary education, and entrepreneurship) in the form of tax expenditures that largely benefit higher-income families.[112] While spending on survival-focused programs for low-income Americans (e.g., Medicaid, SNAP, and Supplemental Security Income) that same year was greater—$848 billion[113]—the disparate outcomes of these different types of assistance make them incomparable. We have not seen the peak of tax policy manipulation to serve elites' interests. Most of the benefits of recent tax policy changes are expected to flow to the wealthy.[114] Presumably, these "savings" will further add to the wealth of those already at the top of the economic order.

Tax policy is not the only tool at the disposal of privileged Americans, however, nor the only domain in which the interests of the poor are pitted against the distributional preferences of the rich. President Trump's proposed budgets would slash many government programs on which low-income Americans depend, including for housing, energy assistance, health care, nutrition, and affordable financial services, while undermining public education and harming disadvantaged children.[115,116]

These cuts would further imperil poor households' financial well-being, making the prospect of asset-building esoteric at best. These prognoses underscore that taking stock of the gap between the wealthy and the poor in the United States does not mean just measuring the difference between these groups. It also requires accounting for the extent to which US policy pushes one up while holding the other down.

Two characteristics distinguish the two very disparate approaches to policy for the wealthy—what we called "growth" policies in the introduction—and for the poor—what we termed "survival" policies. These comparisons highlight their differential effects. First, because the wealth-building policies of asset-building growth approaches have a multiplier effect, through the generation of additional income and wealth, they have a greater impact than the size of the original investment.[58] Second, the effects of, on the one hand, encouraging wealth building and, on the other, only subsidizing consumption, are not only unequal during individuals' lifetimes. These approaches also have very different consequences for future generations. Most policies that subsidize survival do not allow lower-income families to store money for use even in the proximate future and certainly not to pass down to their children. At the same time, higher earners whose asset growth is facilitated by institutions have vehicles through which they can store wealth, watch it accumulate (often tax-free), and then transmit it to their children.

From this perspective, at least some of the government's investment in asset-based welfare may accumulate over time in families. This is why it may be said that policies like the Homestead Act, which began in 1862, may still confer benefits on many of the 1.5 million families that received 160 acres through its provisions.[103,117] Shanks estimates that in 2000, 46 million US adults were descendants of families who received land as a result of this policy.[117] Because property wealth positions families for financial security and upward mobility across generations, serving as a repository from which parents can invest in their children's chances, the benefits of these government-facilitated holdings echo still today, as do the wealth inequalities amplified when this policy disproportionately favored Whites.[103,117,118] Analysis by the Tax Policy Center suggests that unfair allocation of government wealth-building expenditures continues. African Americans comprise 13.2% of the population but receive only 3.5% of public tax expenditure investments in individual wealth building, resulting in what Shapiro terms an estimated "$35 billion discriminatory race penalty each year."[1,119]

Wealth Inequality Alters Bargaining Power

Assets can alter the interactions those with wealth have with the systems around them. Wealth can even change people's vision of themselves and the world. As a result, wealthy individuals may be blinded to the importance of wealth in catalyzing their success, instead focusing on their individual actions as though determinant of their outcomes. This is evident in people like Mitt Romney and President Donald Trump, both of whom have talked about their careers as though they built their wealth on their own, in accountings that deny the importance of family wealth as an input. From the beginning of the United States, individuals have needed some initial wealth—seed corn, a plot of land, a horse—that can be put to productive use in order to generate more wealth. Today, when the cost of entrance is greater and the stakes higher, the significance of initial resources looms particularly large, even if these effects are not always apparent, including to the individual herself. If someone starts off with $1 million and is today worth well over $250 million, there is much to be attributed to his own effort, and it is easy to assume that the $1 million is immaterial. However, the reality is that to build assets in America, one almost always has to have assets to draw from—their own, their family's, or someone else's.

Importantly, then, wealth inequality is not just about dollars—who has them and who does not. The effects of wealth inequality on individual and household well-being are also manifest through subtler influences on attitudes and behavior, at both ends of the distribution. In an analysis of institutions and rational choice, North talks about embedded thought processes, explaining that "much of what passes for rational choice is not so much individual cognition as the embeddedness of the thought process in the larger social and institutional context."[120] This means that individuals' connections to or separation from key institutions, including the labor market, education system, housing market, and the financial system, help to shape how they think about their world, in ways that eventually become second nature. In the case of wealth building, once higher-income families are connected to financial institutions, these institutions help to provide them with an embedded thought process that facilitates additional asset accumulation and cultivates an ability to think differently about their lives.

While Michael Sherraden does not call them "embedded thought processes," he describes a similar process where what is seen as rational choices are actually thought processes captured in an institutional context, which, in turn, replace the need for conscious thought.[14] As an example, he observes that the middle class "participates in retirement pension systems . . . not [as] a matter of making superior choices. Instead, a priori choices are made by social policy, and individuals walk into the pattern that has been established."[14,p.127] Wealth inequality helps to provide higher-income families with the initial assets they need to connect to wealth-building institutions, and then these institutions provide embedded thought processes that help to catalyze additional asset accumulation. Similarly, those whose social environments prime them to orient to postsecondary education often perceive themselves as on a "college track," where higher education is not as much a conscious choice as a foregone conclusion.[121]

This means that those who are denied access to educational or asset-building institutions miss out on more than just degrees, dividend payments, and interest earnings. They are also separated from the thought processes these institutions engender. Further, as these thought processes are translated into patterns of behavior, they have implications for the types of expectations society forms about individuals, depending on their economic status. As those expectations solidify into institutional arrangements, they determine the amount of bargaining power each wields to maintain or change their position in society. Sociologist Annette Lareau discusses bargaining power using slightly different terms.[122] Lareau discusses how middle-class parents and children display a level of comfort in academic settings that facilitates interaction with adults and authority figures. Parents transmit this competency, primarily via parenting practices, and the resulting cultural capital is then a substantial contributor to the inequitable capacity that students carry with them to school.[122,123]

Specifically, middle-class students, whose parents constantly question and negotiate with them, have a greater level of comfort with teachers and other authority figures than do poorer students. They often participate in extracurricular activities that further improve interactions with adults and groom students for subsequent steps on the path to higher education.[124] As they prod educational institutions to reward their efforts and privilege their experiences, these advantaged students reshape institutions in ways that affect the trajectories of those who do not wield this same capital. This may manifest in different teacher expectations, as teachers respond based on their perceptions of students' likely outcomes, or in expectations of extensive extracurricular involvement as a prerequisite for elite college admission.[125,126] Within schools, privileged students and their parents may angle for additional advantages such as advanced courses and separate academic tracks to ensure that their children stay where they started—ahead.[127–129] While this distribution of resources is sometimes contested, it is also the case that privileged actors often see these accommodations as nothing less than what institutions should do for them.

A simple example Willie often uses to explain the advantages that a sense of bargaining empowerment can confer is the difference between buying a car when he was poor versus buying a car now. As a poor young adult, when Willie went to buy a car, he had no money down, no trade-in, and poor credit. These dynamics fundamentally shaped the process. First, he knew he could not just go and get a car anywhere. He needed special financing and someone willing to potentially call multiple institutions to complete the deal. The car salesperson (in his experience almost always a

White male) also knew this and quite often would state it. As a result, pretty much all of the bargaining power was in the hands of the dealership. Rarely did Willie get even close to a fair deal. In contrast, when he goes to buy a car now, he comes with money down, a vehicle to trade in that is typically already paid off, and a good credit score. In effect, Willie knows that he is in a strong position; he can purchase a car anywhere. Therefore, he feels empowered to negotiate and even to walk out if the dealership is unwilling or unable to give him what he wants.

This power that having assets gives a person to bargain is not to be underestimated. It brings a change in attitude and in how institutions respond. We discussed this idea briefly in chapter 1, related to the power Melinda and her father had to negotiate the best deal when she entered college. Not everyone can negotiate a good deal. Crucially, such ability does not simply depend on personal attributes, such as charisma or knowledge. Financial assets also matter. In our capitalistic society, where the rules have been crafted to benefit those who hold most of the wealth, assets matter a lot. This is something the super-wealthy and many who help to design the institutions that then shape distributional consequences sometimes ignore, even as their lives bear witness to its truth. They have always bargained from a position of power that influences the outcomes their efforts can achieve, whether or not they realize it.

Strategic Actors Seek to Define Life Chances for Others

The power that assets provide allows the wealthy to act strategically to bring about their desired distributional outcomes—what we refer to as defining their life chances. We think about life chances as people's perceptions about their future capabilities, or what they expect to be able to do. Life chances are assessed in light of what individuals possess, what they understand about how well their possessions gird them from what may come, and how well they can use what they possess to realize their American dream.[130] In other words, individuals' assessments of their life chances are based on what they perceive as the restrictions or lack of restrictions on their ability to achieve their desired selves. In today's America, wealth increasingly sets the parameters that define one's life chances. Indeed, wealth may even determine what people consider within the realm of remote possibility, as people may not even be able to dream of what they have never had the resources to really consider. In today's highly unequal America, then, what ends up looking like "choice" is often a reflection of what wealth will allow.[131]

Political scientist Jack Knight discusses how people act strategically to bring about their own desired distributional outcomes.[132] To do this, he introduces the concept of social expectations, which we refer to as "role expectations" in order to more clearly describe the function we see them playing in people's lives. Role expectations are shared expectations about how a person can be expected to act as a member of a group.[132] As such, they can be thought of as specifying a role that a person is to play in society. As Knight suggests, role expectations are formed as part of an epic struggle between strategic actors who are motivated by a desire to maximize their own goals and then attempt to shape expectations so that they produce their preferred ends.

This is not a new phenomenon. What is particular to this moment is the concentration of power—in the form of wealth—which then gives some Americans an outsized ability to shape expectations in order to meet their own preferences.[23] There are many examples of people acting strategically to produce their desired distributional outcomes today. When then-candidate Donald Trump defended paying little in taxes, he is quoted saying that tax avoidance, "Is just smart."[133] His campaign further elaborated on this rationale, "Mr. Trump is a highly skilled businessman who has a fiduciary responsibility to his business, his family, and his employees to pay no more tax than legally required."[133] Wealthy elites' strategic use of the rules to favor themselves is attributed to their superior use of effort and ability ("highly skilled businessman"). According to this interpretation, then, the fact is not that they benefit from having a lot of wealth and paying expensive advisors, nor that they should pay taxes for the public good; instead, it is that they have above-average effort and ability and, therefore, deserve the gains these advantages accrue.

Rather than their behavior being seen as unjustly taking advantage of the rules for their own benefit, the super-wealthy are further defended as having the "responsibility" to act strategically, which seems to confer morality on actions to maximize one's own position. The expectation is thus set. Certainly, President Trump is not alone in working these expectations for his own benefit. Minimizing taxes is a common practice among wealthy individuals, even as less wealthy individuals are forced to pay substantially higher real tax rates.[134] Beyond the tax code, social science research has found that elites prefer distributional consequences that advance their own positions rather than egalitarian aims and, notably, that these preferences persist whether elites identify with the Democrat or the Republican Party.[135] In other words, when it comes to determining how they want institutions to work, many wealthy Americans seem to care more about how they will personally fare than what is *fair*.

Poor Americans do not enjoy such favorable expectations. They are not encouraged to act in ways that optimize their outcomes. Instead, the role assigned to the poor is usually that they are lazy and lack sufficient skill. When they act to bring about the best distributional outcomes for themselves, these actions are perceived as illegitimately hurting society. As a result, they are often sanctioned. Increasingly, this battle over role expectations is decisively won by the wealthy. As a result, ideas once considered viable policies by politicians both conservative and liberal, such as wealth transfers or progressive taxation, are no longer seen as legitimate proposals. Instead, these ideas and the people who would dare to bring them up are branded as un-American, even though it is today's dramatic escalation of wealth inequality that poses the greatest threat to American democratic ideals, social stability, the US constitutional order, and even capitalism itself.[25,111,136,137]

In addition to precluding the development of certain approaches to social policy, role expectations can also be codified into law, thereby solidifying prescribed social roles for entire groups. This was the case when the US Constitution set the expectation that Blacks are three-fifths of a person, when localities and states enacted Jim Crow laws to define African Americans' economic and social roles, and when women were long denied the right to vote. In each case, strategic actors were able to constrain the expectations of and for others for their own self-interest, usually with financial gain at stake. For example, slave owners and their industrial allies shaped laws to protect their property interests while arguing that slavery was a divinely ordained social institution.[138] After emancipation, discriminatory laws and their repressive enforcement ensured that southern economic interests had a large supply of nearly captive workers.[139] Importantly, in each case these expectations ran counter to normative expectations that governed interactions for the rest of society. The intent of the law was therefore to set a different set of expectations for a particular social group. While often less overt, the pernicious effects of inequitable role expectations continue to constrain the life chances of disadvantaged Americans. Examples abound, including when low-income people are disenfranchised because they cannot pay legal fines required to restore their suffrage, as well as policing and sentencing practices that disproportionately deprive people of color of their liberty.[140] In the past and still today, these role expectations are possible because disadvantaged groups lack the bargaining power to negotiate fairly.

While role expectations can be enshrined formally in law books, many more operate informally. These informal role expectations index a set of societal beliefs, broadly but not universally shared. Some examples of informal expectations are the idea that a woman's "place" is in the house or that women are not capable of doing math as well as men or should be paid less than men. These expectations do not carry the weight of law. Nonetheless, they can exert powerful forces on how individuals see themselves and others, ultimately influencing the bargaining power individuals have for negotiating a deal most likely to bring about their desired distributional outcomes. For example, stereotypes about gender differences in math ability influence girls' achievement, and occupational wages decline as fields become more female-dominated. Strict beliefs in traditional gender roles can even increase the risk of domestic violence.[141,142]

The fact that people act strategically to gain their best distributional outcome does not suggest that they are "bad," nor that self-interested maneuvering in and around institutions is inevitably malevolent. Capitalism depends on and encourages competition. However, the reality of self-interested angling by the privileged does raise the importance of having institutions that balance out power so that the game is not unfairly rigged. Otherwise, a perception that the outcome is determined before one even starts can diminish motivation. Why even attempt to compete with others who are so far ahead? When one group fails most of the time despite their best efforts, while another group usually succeeds, can we blame those stuck in cycles of failure if they give up? We think not. In this context, it is no wonder that lower-income groups may despair of watching those with more resources climb so high while they struggle to even remain standing. As a result, inequality denies the larger society the chance to benefit from the contributions of talented people who are staying out of the "race." These patterns of inequality beg questions about whether institutions are doing a good job of leveling the playing field so that effort and ability are actually the deciding factors, rather than one's starting place.

Conclusion

The significance of the inequitable distribution of wealth in the United States is not exclusively, or even primarily, found in the arena of wealth itself. Instead, it is the power that wealth affords and what that power represents that are particularly valuable. Even the far from random distribution of wealth and the persistent wealth gaps by education, age, and, in particular, race, do not tell the most important story about why wealth inequality is a critical threat to American ideals. Instead, in a society where so many "goods"—access to opportunity, health, overall well-being, even basic respect—hinge on some level of asset ownership and accompanying economic empowerment, the distributional consequences of the systems that perpetuate wealth disparity extend far beyond the merely economic.[143]

Central to the policy proposal we lay out in this book is the fact that, in an economy where so many of the trappings of prosperity are secured and preserved through the medium of education, American children who approach that system without a wealth advantage have to push against powerful forces. This experience is like running into a headwind. As a result, they will find it difficult—if not impossible—to leverage even considerable exertion of effort and innate ability for a realistic chance at success. In contrast, children clothed in the advantages that wealth brings have a tailwind at their backs propelling them toward success. Headwinds are often visible only to those straining against the adverse conditions. To those whose races are thrust forward, everything seems to be working as expected. However, as more Americans reckon with what seems like an elusive finish line and the perennial victory of the same groups of runners, these countervailing forces undermine our values and imperil our identity. It is not the length of the climb that Americans find most discouraging, after all, or even alarming; it is the widening space between the rungs and the growing sense that some may be missing entirely.

These headwinds and tailwinds chart children's courses in the education system, helping some coast to nearly sure success while sentencing others to arduous slogs through persistent obstacles. This describes our own stories and largely explains the disparate outcomes realized by privileged and disadvantaged children today. Nor is education the only plane on which these winds buffet Americans' journeys. Following school, young adults carry their accumulated advantages and disadvantages, rooted in disparate family upbringings and magnified in inequitable school systems, to confront the critical task of transitioning to adulthood. Admittedly, to a certain degree, all American young adults today face economic and social challenges.[144] Research indicates that, even when they exceed their parents' earnings, young adults do not experience the asset position or overall financial security of previous cohorts.[145] Tenuous labor market arrangements—frequent job changes, higher-than-historical unemployment, stagnant wages, irregular and part-time employment—make it difficult for young adults to build a sound economic future. However, these economic forces are not "levelers," equitably afflicting an entire generation.

Instead, parents' economic standing may prove even more instrumental in today's economy than for generations past, as new realities further elevate the role of capital income and transfers—from government policy and/or family resources—in the establishment of a firm financial foothold. In this landscape, the ability of some advantaged young people to rely on family wealth into adulthood can prove decisive.[65] When the risk of "falling" is so great, the significance of a cushion becomes even greater. Young people who were able to accumulate human capital without accruing debt can face the task of "launching" into independence bolstered with initial assets, in addition to educational attainment, while those who succeeded in education despite the odds posed by their origins seldom find that they are commensurately rewarded for their accomplishment.

These relative advantages continue to multiply as privileged young adults are able to leverage family asset holdings for capital gains and productive risk-taking, or, at the least, to immediately begin to accumulate their own savings, without having to divert income to debt repayment.[1] Meanwhile, young adults struggling to establish themselves without such assistance confront a context where their efforts are not only more difficult but also often maligned. When their independence is delayed for want of a financial foundation or they cannot find and maintain employment that allows them to reap the rewards of their educational attainment, these challenges are frequently attributed to character failings or, at least, held up for unfavorable comparisons against the triumphs of their peers or their parents.[146] With the significance of wealth inequality for determining the distribution of opportunities and institutional rewards obscured, we seldom notice how much where one starts determines what one gets. Yet again, Americans' eyes are on the individual's pace—rapid or belabored—rather than on the telltale signs of which way the winds are blowing.

Note

a. At the median, the trends remain the same. The gap is $123,200 between Blacks/Whites and $120,500 for Hispanics/Whites, both for 2013.[21]

3 Effort Appears Inadequate in the Modern World
OUR IDENTITIES ARE SHAPED BY OUR REAL-LIFE CHANCES

IN ITS SIMPLEST form, the American dream is the belief that success should be determined by effort, not unfair advantage. This idea is embedded in the psyche of most Americans and shapes the way we collectively view individuals' outcomes. It forms the lens through which we judge social policies that undergird opportunities or compound disadvantage. It is powerful enough to influence the way that people see their own success and failure and that of others. It can blind Americans to the structural forces that chart our fates.[1,2] Indeed, Americans who want so badly to believe that there is a logic to the forces that shape their outcomes and a real path to their promised future may even excuse patently unfair institutions and the injustices they perpetuate. While these system-justifying beliefs can buffer people from the stress of contemplating abject inequity, as evidence mounts that things are not working as they should, defenses slip, doubts rise, and cracks emerge in the American dream.[3]

Today, there is a growing sense that this dream is more nostalgic memory than an accurate representation of the way the world works. A 2014 survey found that 48% of Americans believed that the American dream once was true but is not true anymore.[4] These doubts represent more than just whispered anxieties or casual statements of political frustration. Instead, we contend that belief in the American dream is an expression of deeply rooted faith in our institutions and their ability to deliver on their promises, which in turn becomes a covenant in modern governance. This means that Americans' increasing skepticism about whether institutions will ensure that their efforts pay off threatens the foundation of civil society.[5] In other words, our inclination to rationalize societal arrangements has limits.[6] When we can no longer explain away inequitable outcomes from schools, the labor market, and government policies, the social contract Americans have forged together is broken.

For America to "work," people need to believe that institutions provide them with a chance to thrive and that structures will allow their kids to get ahead. Otherwise, the norms and expectations essential for society to function begin to break down. From the perspective of someone facing a bleak landscape of life chances, why study hard in school if the fruits of those labors are unfairly denied? Why work hard if financial well-being increasingly hinges on where I start, not what I do? We are not the first to make this connection between institutional failures to catalyze fair chances and the democratic processes Americans cherish. Coming out of the Great Depression and the New Deal response, Roosevelt told his fellow Democrats in 1936 that, "Liberty requires opportunity to make a living decent according to the standard of the time, a living that gives man not only enough to live by, but something to live for." Without this opportunity, he continued, "life was no longer free; liberty no longer real; men could no longer follow the pursuit of happiness."[7]

While the precise threats to the American dream are different than in Roosevelt's era, the foundation on which it is supposed to stand is similarly destabilized. Many forces have converged and likely share some of the blame, including mechanization and globalization,[8,9] but our focus in this book is specifically on the role of wealth inequality. This emphasis stems in part from our orientation as asset researchers who study the effects of wealth and its absence on a range of outcomes. It is confirmed by other analyses that also place most of the blame for the erosion of the American dream—in rhetorical power and in reality—at the feet of growing economic inequality.[10–13] And it is informed by our own life experiences, as we reflect on how wealth has influenced how well we have done. However, this analysis reverses the dominant understanding of the causality between wealth and outcomes. Citing wealth disparities for institutions' failure to deliver equitable opportunities to all Americans situates wealth as the *precursor*, rather than the *result*, of the gaps we observe. We concur with others that the wealth gap does not stem from individual choices.[14] Instead, wealth inequality constrains individuals' options by making it harder for those on the losing end of the unequal wealth distribution to realize outcomes commensurate with their efforts, while allowing those who have benefitted from unjust arrangements to write the rules.

Focusing on wealth inequality and the threat it poses to the American dream also clearly situates the dream's declining fortunes as an urgently relevant crisis, notwithstanding progress made in the past. Understanding wealth as the fulcrum of the upward mobility promised by the American dream underscores the requirement of equal chances, not just aggregate progress. Yes, a higher percentage of Americans enroll in college now than in generations past, but they do not realize equal returns on those educations.[15,16] Yes, Blacks face less social exclusion than in the days of Jim Crow, but they still contend with injustices born of systematic rejection from the best American institutions. Yes, the general trend has been toward less overt discrimination; however, some Americans are still disadvantaged by class and race and oppressed by institutional rules that frustrate their efforts to change their outcomes.

Finally, framing wealth inequality as the central menace to the American dream places its restoration and redemption squarely within the purview of US policy. In order to change the opportunity landscape and place the American dream truly within the reach of all—in a way that only our ideals, not our history, have conceived—we need to correctly identify the thumbs pressing unfairly on the scale. Americans must understand the role that institutional resources play in determining whose efforts and ability generate meaningful success. We must force policymakers to grapple with the ways in which institutional arrangements give some groups a head start, while building a steep wall over which others must climb. And we must reckon with how incompatible institutional inequality is with American values and the fuel of American prosperity: our brand of capitalism.

Economist Hernando De Soto has argued that American capitalism is different from other forms because it gives "most people access to property and the tools of production," unlike in non-Western countries where only a few have such access.[17] This idea that American capitalism is characterized by broad constitutional rights to own property is in line with the ideals of the American dream, which hold that all have the basic "stuff" from which to forge their own destinies. In a 2008 poll, 75% of Americans strongly agreed with the notion that "America is unique among all nations, because it is founded on the ideals of freedom, equality, and opportunity."[18] Notably absent in this conceptualization of the US economic model is the centrality of institutions in shaping outcomes. Instead, they are here relegated to the periphery.

De Soto further argues that where capitalism fails, it is because governmental structures do not facilitate access to the tools of production.[17] However, because these are the systems that are supposed to carry us to success, our desire to protect the legitimacy of institutional arrangements is strong.[19] So we buy into the mantra that everyone has requisite access to the institutions that facilitate production—financial services, the education system, property and labor markets—and blame individuals who do not prosper. We might say, for instance, that a disadvantaged person became that way because of insufficient effort or, perhaps somewhat more benevolently, because he is trapped in a "culture of poverty."[20] While the precise words used to center analysis on individual pathology rather than systemic barriers vary, Americans are mostly blind to the far-reaching effects of wealth inequality even as they manifest in our lives. When institutional failings are made visible, we are often reluctant to acknowledge them, because that would mean recognizing how arduous, perilous, and potentially fruitless our own climbs will be. Instead, we celebrate our theoretical right to prosper, buy a home, and go to college. We deny or overlook the obvious: a growing number of people lack the power to use institutions to bring about their desired outcome.

If we accept DeSoto's analysis that America's version of capitalism has succeeded because it gives most people access to the means of production, then his predictions may forewarn difficult times ahead.[17] At some point, wealth inequality is likely to grow too extreme to sustain itself. When this time comes, inequality may topple American capitalism and, quite possibly, take democratic institutions with it.[21,22] Janet Yellen, former Federal Reserve board chair, warned that inequality can "have grave effects on social stability over time."[23] Addressing wealth inequality in America is therefore an imperative, not just in the interest of broadening opportunity and improving people's sense of what is possible in their own lives, but as a rescue mission for the foundations of US economy and governance. It also means that wealth inequality is not just a problem for the poor but a threat to all.

The wealthy have a bigger stake in improving outcomes for the poor than they may realize. The experiences of many nations reveal the difficulties of preserving privilege for wealthy individuals without a robust infrastructure to supply the workers and consumers on whose efforts their fortunes depend. In the context of our consideration of wealth inequality's effects on educational outcomes, while the immediate calculus may consider poor strivers as competition for wealthy elites who are trying to hoard opportunities for their own children, interdependence makes it likely that the wealthy will suffer from inequality in the long run. When education fails to provide equitable incentives and returns, it lacks utility in an economic sense. This makes participation in higher education less attractive and may lead students to turn to alternatives that require fewer investments in order to minimize risk in what appears an uncertain and unequal exchange. The collapse of the "deal" education was supposed to offer, in other words, may lead Americans to pursue other paths, reshaping not only their lives but the economic arrangements on which many depend.

In the remainder of this chapter we provide a rationale for how the American dream works, including within the minds of children, especially those disadvantaged. We examine why, in this time of widespread wealth inequality, there is a need to elevate and recalibrate the public discourse about the role that institutions play in determining winners or losers. Part of this argument is that technology—not just iPhones and PCs but also educational innovations and privatized enrichment—has advanced so much that when people lack access to it, the differences in the outcomes they can achieve are so great that competition can no longer be said to exist. For the American economy through which the American dream runs, this is a problem. Competition is a key tenet of capitalism; without it there is little reason to strive.

Effort and Ability Alone Do Not Determine Winners

When Americans lived their lives comparatively free from institutional influence, they unsurprisingly believed that their success was derived from their own efforts. Even the institutions that were constructed—particularly early public schools— were often seen as protections against undue external influence in individuals' affairs, as in Thomas Jefferson's argument for compulsory public education as a defense against monarchy and tyranny.[24] These beliefs were passed down and are evident in policies such as local control of public schools and in many Americans' skepticism of particular government interventions to level the playing field.[24] As a result, institutions have been sidelined in the conception of the American dream. In this articulation, effort and ability are held out as what matters, rather than the contributions of institutional structures. This framing is particularly advanced by those seeking to undermine any redistributive policy, since little arouses the ire of the American public like thinking that someone is getting something she has not "earned."[25,26] Indeed, explaining outcomes as stemming from one's own hard work, rather than luck or structural forces, can make even disadvantaged Americans dubious about redistributing wealth more equitably, even when they would benefit.[27]

More and more, however, this ethos of self-reliance has come under scrutiny by Americans who work just as hard as—if not harder than—others but continue to fall further behind. A poll conducted in 2014 underscored this shift in American political opinion. In 1995, most Americans said that poverty was caused by "people not doing enough"; 20 years later, nearly half attributed poverty to factors *other than* individual initiative.[28] Another recent poll found that larger percentages of the populace attributed poverty to circumstances beyond one's control than to lack of effort; similarly, they were more likely to attribute wealth to advantages than to working harder.[29] This shift likely results at least in part from the growing concentration of wealth: in 2010, the wealthiest 1% possessed over 35% of the nation's wealth, while the bottom 90% owned only about 23%.[30] Holding such resources endows individuals with power to shape the world to work in their favor. As wealth concentrates in the hands of a very few and increasingly determines life chances, more people are forced to recognize the role that institutions play in determining winners and losers.

This recognition of institutional forces is a turning point, of sorts, in the saga of the American dream. While individualism has inherent appeal as part of this ethos, taking an accounting of the workings of modern society requires acknowledging how institutional inequality determines how people do. This is a reckoning Americans increasingly welcome. Almost two-thirds believe that the economic system in this country favors powerful interests, and majorities see the gap between wealthy Americans and those disadvantaged as a "major problem" that the government should do more to reduce.[31-33] Looking at their own prospects, Americans wonder whether societal structures level the playing field so that individuals can compete fairly or, conversely, amplify the advantages of some so that conclusions are nearly foregone. As they gauge whether these same institutions deserve their trust and allegiance—and whether they can count on any assistance as they work toward the outcomes they seek—this verdict matters.

An American Dream in the 21st-Century Reality

Institutions amplify people's innate abilities. Particularly in today's sophisticated and complicated world, success hinges not on exertion alone but on effort combined with *institutional might*. Here, "institutional might" refers to the way people use tools—social, cultural, and organizational—to compete more effectively. Nowhere is the concept of achieving more through systemic intervention than would be possible through individual effort alone more prominent than in education. This dynamic is the reason that most discussions of the declining fortunes of Americans include an exhortation to use education to improve one's chances.[34-36] The problem with these discussions, however, is that in order to achieve one's full potential today, institutions have to augment one's efforts, through a process that has been called institutional facilitation.[37] And institutions—including the education system—do this insufficiently and inequitably for many, producing outcomes, then, that are patently unfair.

Technological Advancements Have Amplified the Effects of Institutional Inequality

Advances in human knowledge and technology have substantially amplified the importance of institutional resources in determining who succeeds and who fails. Steve Jobs once said, "Humans are tool builders and we build tools that can dramatically amplify our innate human abilities. I believe that the computer will rank near, if not at the top, as history unfolds—it is the most awesome tool that we have ever invented."[38] Even as they fuel productivity and innovation, these developments simultaneously have made inequality an ever-greater threat to the American system of capitalism. It has always been the case that humans build tools that augment their effort and ability, and it has often been true that technological change creates winners and losers.[39] The Industrial Revolution eventually "lifted all boats," but it also widened social divides.[40] This is even more likely today, with tools that dramatically augment what individuals can do. Unequal access to these advanced tools calls into question the "deal" of the American dream—that hard work should be enough. As technologies continue to advance, the difference between having access to them or not multiplies. Even more pertinent to our thinking about the opportunity pipeline and the need for intervention all along it, lacking access to tools with which to wrest desired outcomes from institutions at a particular point may so disadvantage someone that it is difficult to compensate, even with the same tools, at a later stage. This is a prime reason why a policy such as free college is unlikely to equalize outcomes; when it comes to the "tool" of financial resources for postsecondary education, those who wield them at earlier points in the opportunity pipeline may preserve a distinct advantage over those who acquire them late in the game.

The relationship between tools and outcomes played out in our own stories. While technology has advanced considerably since we started college, Melinda remembers the experience of completing multiple scholarship applications on what was then a relatively "high-tech" tool: a word processor. Having a new tool at home that allowed her to quickly substitute out the names of colleges and scholarship providers made it feasible to submit a larger number of applications than would have otherwise been possible. A student who lacked those resources could have outperformed her, maybe even garnering more acceptance letters, but only by expending far greater effort. Today, educators acknowledge that insufficient access to computers compromises the achievement of low-income students, but Americans often overlook the ways in which other institutional arrangements[41,42]—many less tangible than the difference between a spiral notebook and a laptop—similarly send outcomes in divergent directions.

To illustrate this concept of institutional facilitation and how it can work—seemingly invisibly—to determine individuals' chances of success, Willie often tells a story from when his son was too young to ride a bike and Willie had to pull him behind in a cart. This felt like riding a bike with a parachute dragging behind, particularly on windy Kansas afternoons. Willie would ride with his two young daughters and his wife and watch in dismay as they pulled away from him. He started to think that he must be in really bad shape because it was taking so much more effort to ride the same distances. Then his wife bought him a new bike to replace his old one. That same day, he was out in front despite having to pull the cart. It was not that he was suddenly in better shape. What gave him the advantage was the new resource of a much better bike. The bike augmented the effort Willie put into pedaling and resulted in a better outcome. Importantly, his increased success also increased his desire to go on bike rides. When his efforts yielded better returns, his motivation to exert himself increased accordingly. Again, Melinda remembers this effect from her experience applying for college scholarships. It was far easier to motivate herself to apply for relatively small-dollar awards that nonetheless added up, when doing so only meant modifying an application already saved on the word processor. In this way, differential access to tools can create artificial winners and losers.

Institutional facilitation recognizes that in a highly specialized and advanced society like ours, institutions augment effort and ability in unfair ways. When the role of institutions is ignored or when institutional access hinges on an unequally distributed resource such as wealth, these effects are magnified. If one person has access to tools—technology, education, networks—and another does not, or if one person's tools are superior, or if one person has opportunities to apply the tools that are denied to others, those who do not have access will be at a disadvantage. They will be unlikely to overcome this unequal position even with more effort.

An Opportunity Framework for Adapting the American Dream to the Modern World

Although the values on which it stands are much older, the term "American dream" was coined by James Truslow Adams in 1931. In his "Epic of America," Adams defined the American dream as "that dream of a land in which life should be better and richer and fuller for every man, with opportunity for each according to his ability or achievement."[43] Despite Adams' inspirational words, he was writing during the Great Depression and had witnessed firsthand the devastation wrought by the collapse of financial and labor markets—the same institutions touted as agents of upward mobility. As a result, his enthusiasm for the American ideal of equitable rewards for equal effort and ability was tempered with warnings that America must work to maintain its dream, which was already imperiled by collision with the harsh economic context. As Adams noted then, "too many of us . . . have grown weary and mistrustful of [the dream]."[44] The lesson should be clear: the American dream is not invincible. As to Adams, today's warning signs of shakiness should sound alarms, not only to those whose chance of rising to prosperity depends on the dream being more reality than myth, but also to those at the top, whose legitimacy and security in that position similarly depend on its perpetuation.

On the heels of the Great Recession and in the midst of tremendous political mistrust, many Americans find themselves in the same place that Adams was nearly a century ago when he acknowledged uncertainties about the American dream. This is an uncomfortable place. It may become even more so when we examine the past. In Adams' time, policymakers acted decisively to mitigate threats to the American dream. They penned a new social contract between people and their government and forged new institutions whose purpose was to build ladders that would help Americans ascend. These measures enabled policymakers to assure Americans that their efforts could result in real prosperity. Their climbs would be facilitated by social insurance and enhanced regulatory oversight, which lessened the risks individuals bear; infrastructure development, which contributed to stronger economic growth; and expansion of educational opportunities, which allowed thousands to access new roles in the changing landscape. Today, when the American dream is similarly shaky, it is unclear whether—or how—it will be rescued. Few of the approaches pursued during the Great Depression to preserve the American dream are even being considered. Instead, the stakes rise alongside our fears, as we watch the foundations of the American dream crumble around us.

SELF-EFFICACY AND THE POWER OF THE AMERICAN DREAM TO ACT AS A MOTIVATOR

To transition from the American dream as we understand it today—primarily predicated on individual efforts and the returns they promise—to what we see as a more accurate and equitable opportunity framework bracketed by institutional efficacy, we first use the social psychology construct of self-efficacy to explain how the American dream acts as a motivator. This lays the foundation for examining the breakdowns in these processes today and how incorporating an institutional dimension could help. The concept of self-efficacy, which has parallels in the ethos that serves as the foundation of the traditional American dream, has been shown to be an important predictor of people's behavior.[45] Bandura defines self-efficacy as "people's beliefs about their capabilities to produce designated levels of performance that exercise influence over events that affect their lives."[46] Individuals make self-efficacy assessments that incorporate their observations of the requirements to reach particular aims. An individual's self-efficacy assessment might sound like this: "I can put forth the designated level of effort, and I have the ability to perform the task; therefore, I will achieve my desired outcome." Simply put, self-efficacy represents "I can do" beliefs.

We suggest that the foundation the American dream is built on is people's "I can do" beliefs. As such, when people's faith in the American dream is weakened, their perception of what they can do is also weakened. The American dream also mirrors self-efficacy theory in that both concepts are based on the assumption that a "normal contingency" exists[47]—a level playing field on which performance is the primary predictor of outcomes. These beliefs matter for more than just how people *feel* about their chances; they also shape behavior, including in ways associated with educational attainment. Social scientists suggest that self-efficacy is a critical factor in academic engagement and success.[45,47–51] Self-efficacy helps to determine how hard a child will work in school and whether the child will persist when faced with difficulties.[52] Critically, however, as our own life stories and the data traced in chapters 1 and 2 underscore, the American education landscape today does not appear to meet the criteria for "normal contingency." From both Melinda's position of privilege and Willie's uphill climb against disadvantage, the playing field looks anything but level.

Inasmuch as the American dream resembles a self-efficacy belief, then, its survival has more than just rhetorical value as a story we tell ourselves. Much like self-efficacy, the American dream provides people with a vision of their futures and a sense of the ways in which they can move toward them. Importantly, both articulate the expectation that one's desired future can be attained through sustained effort. As a result, when self-efficacy beliefs and their idealized manifestation in the American dream are shared by many, they build cohesion and motivate people to work toward goals that, while individually articulated, can serve as common fuel for shared prosperity. By linking the American dream to self-efficacy beliefs, then, what we are contending is that the American dream has a real role to play in society, not only at the level of the individual but also on a much grander scale.

However, while the American dream works to build up self-efficacy and cultivate the "I can do" spirit that has made America great, it has an inherent flaw: it overemphasizes the role of individual behavior and obscures how institutional inequality determines individual outcomes. Even when institutions are discussed in the context of the American dream, it is often assumed that everyone has equal access to them.[53–55] If that were the case, institutions' influence would be effectively canceled out when it comes to determining individual outcomes. All that would matter is innate ability and exertion of effort. However, this is not the way that people experience their life chances today.

LEGITIMIZING THE ROLE OF INSTITUTIONS IN THE AMERICAN DREAM

While not fully accounting for institutional influences on individual outcomes, self-efficacy theory does provide some hints as to why institutions are important determinants of winners and losers. Bandura distinguishes between two forces that might influence people's behavior in a given situation.[45] One is their judgment about whether they are capable of performing a given act, which Bandura calls a self-efficacy judgment.[45,56] The second is their judgment about the connection between actions and outcomes, which Bandura calls an outcome expectation. According to the latter, people take into consideration institutional factors when they make decisions about whether a particular behavior will lead to a desired outcome. As Gurin and Brim explain, "The environment is critical in one—the outcome expectancy. . . . The self is critical in the other—the efficacy expectation."[57] They elaborate that although "Actual behavior theoretically depends on both expectancies . . . Bandura's work [on self-efficacy] primarily has dealt with the efficacy expectation."[57] In this respect, self-efficacy's emphasis on the self over the environment parallels the American dream, which exalts individualism even when conceding that not all have truly equal chances.

The American dream places the individual in the metaphorical driver's seat when it comes to controlling her life circumstances. Sometimes referred to as "personal causality" within the social-psychology literature, this belief is at the heart of the rugged individualism that often accompanies articulations of the American dream.[54,47] It is firmly entrenched in the thinking of many Americans. Notwithstanding the emerging cracks in people's confidence in their control over their own destinies, as mentioned earlier, more than 70% of Americans still believe that it is "very important" to work hard to get ahead in life; assessing their own track records, they often say that outside forces have little effect on their success in life.[29] Even viewed alongside growing concerns about the viability of the American dream, this may not be as contradictory as it seems. Some research suggests that it is precisely when people feel dependent on a system that is under threat that they are most motivated to justify it.[58] In this case, even as more Americans worry that their path to the American dream may not work out as they had hoped, they may yet be particularly reluctant to abandon its premises.

As a result, while a modern understanding of the American dream would include not only individual effort and ability but also institutions that support and enhance those exertions, this is seldom how Americans see our lives. Instead, Americans buy into self-efficacy, which gives us a sense of security by cultivating the idea that we largely control our own fates. However, many Americans are surrounded daily by evidence that institutions matter a great deal for determining how well we do. For example, the outcomes children achieve in school are not always within their control. Some go to schools that give them ample resources to learn, while others struggle in adverse conditions. Some find that their zip code or the cache of their school set them on a path to near-certain success, while others have to overcome their disadvantaged starting point. As a result, Americans are increasingly concluding that their hard work and talent are not sufficient to secure the returns they desire. Instead, without institutions that complement their efforts, individuals routinely come up short.

It must be acknowledged that there is much to be said about the role of individual effort and ability in personal achievement. At the same time, it can also be true that institutions are responsible for ensuring that there is a level playing field on which these efforts can play out. Some evidence suggests that Americans can simultaneously accommodate both of these beliefs, valuing hard work and also wanting less inequality, perhaps in pursuit of the "normal contingency" they believe their right.[59] In this way, American institutions can be thought of like referees. Their job is to make sure the game is won by the person who exerts the most effort and displays the most ability. Further, because US institutions have set forth rules that favor certain groups over others, providing a "level playing field" may require providing additional resources and opportunities to disadvantaged groups.

INSTITUTIONAL INEQUALITY UNDERSCORES THE ROLE OF INSTITUTIONS

When a normal contingency exists, the individual is unlikely to even notice the role that institutions play in his success or failure. That is, when institutional arrangements function properly in an individual's life, they can be taken for granted. However, in the United States, this is a luxury only granted to some, not a right for all. For those who have such privilege, the path towards the American dream is unobstructed and easy to traverse; institutions have paved their way. These fortunate individuals might travel down this path for their entire lives without ever stopping to think that their journey was facilitated by anything other than their own efforts. Here, we might use breathing as an analogy. We all breathe thousands of times every day, but how often do we stop to think about taking a single breath? You might be thinking about it right now since we brought it up, but our guess is that most people spend very little time thinking about each breath. For those with privilege, institutional facilitation is like breathing. They never have to think about how institutions helped them get where they are unless they find themselves short of breath, which may never happen as they pursue their vision of the American dream.

According to Bandura, when people make a self-efficacy judgment in the absence of a normal contingency, they must judge not only their personal capability to perform a task but also the role that institutions play in their performance:

Self-appraisal of efficacy is, therefore, a judgmental process in which the relative contribution of ability and non-ability factors to performance success and failure must be weighed. The extent that people will alter their self-percepts of efficacy from performance experiences will depend upon such factors as the difficulty of the task, the amount of effort they had to expend . . . *the amount of external aid they receive, the situational circumstance under which they perform, the quality of the apparatus.*[60]

Bandura further distinguishes between the role of personal and institutional factors in forming efficacy beliefs:

There are two aspects to exercise of control. The first concerns the level and strength of personal efficacy to produce changes by perseverant effort and creative use of capabilities and resources. The second aspect concerns the modifiability of the environment. This facet represents the constraints and opportunities provided by the environment to exercise personal efficacy.[61]

Working from these passages, we assert that in order for self-efficacy—or, then, the American dream—to be an accurate predictor of behavior, individuals must have access to sufficient resources that have utility for influencing outcomes that matter. Without such resources, a person's effort and ability has insufficient expected impact. In other words, when a normal contingency does not exist— when the playing field is not level and people know it—the individual is forced to make a judgment about the actual connection between her actions and the outcomes she is able to achieve. Central to our purpose, these assessments are implicated in inequitable educational outcomes. Influencing them is a key part of how children's assets work.

PROVIDING A WAY TO TALK ABOUT INSTITUTIONS AS PART OF THE AMERICAN DREAM

The American lexicon is full of positively charged idioms for speaking about individual initiative: consider "pulling one's self up by the bootstraps," the "self-made man," or "rags-to-riches." Conversely, popular discourse and political dialogue lack phrases that allow us to talk about the idea that institutions also influence people's outcomes. We therefore struggle to even think about institutional facilitation in the context of the American dream. If individuals do not understand how and why institutions matter for their success, they may lose faith in themselves even when their failures have little to do with their own actions. Or they may end up blaming other people when institutional inequality was really at fault.

Here, the concept of institutional efficacy may provide an American lexicon around the affirmative role of institutions in determining winners and losers. Institutional efficacy can simply be defined as a person's judgment about her power to summon and use institutional capabilities to bring about her desired ends.[37] This is not an entirely foreign idea. Americans can draw on their own experiences to understand how, for example, having a computer can make the task of revising applications easier, or going up a steep hill seems less daunting on a good bicycle. Similarly, the concept of institutional efficacy can help people understand how those who can summon institutional resources in order to pursue a desired aim have a decisive advantage over those working without such tools. Unlike self-efficacy, which focuses on the part of a task people perceive as resulting from their own effort and ability, institutional efficacy judgments take place when people become aware that part of performing a task successfully is the power they have to make institutions augment their effort and ability.

In this way, the concept of institutional efficacy brings to the forefront what might otherwise fade to the background. Where self-efficacy assessments center on people's presumed control over their own outcomes, institutional efficacy judgments take into account systemic differences in the ways institutions respond to various groups. This process helps people make sense of what might otherwise be inexplicably frustrating disappointments, as they consistently find their best efforts insufficient, just like Willie laboring up the hill on his old bike. Institutional efficacy can also give privileged Americans a more accurate lens on their own achievements, highlighting the influences that have facilitated them. In other words, institutional efficacy makes one focus on breathing and on the many things that can inhibit it.

The concept of institutional efficacy also explains how the pull of the American dream may ebb in the presence of institutional inequality. If an institution is consistently unresponsive, individuals may develop low institutional efficacy—limited reason to believe that institutions will work with and for them. When the institutions essential for a chance at the American dream are inequitable or even unavailable to a given individual, the dream itself can recede. For example, if schools do not provide a child with the resources he needs to perform a task successfully, such as the quality preparation and adequate financial aid that will help him to transition to and complete college, he may lose faith in education's ability to facilitate his upward mobility.

What this suggests is that the American dream can be a powerful motivator but only when (a) individuals believe that their success and failure depend on their own effort and ability or (b) individuals believe that they can leverage institutions in ways that augment their own effort and ability. The first condition requires either justification of unjust systems, of the type associated with negative self-concept and demoralization among marginalized individuals, or an abandonment of the sophisticated tools and advanced technologies responsible for much of our modern progress.[62] This brings us to the second case, which we see as a 21st-century American dream, centered on institutional efficacy, rather than exclusively individual means. From this perspective, institutions have to be designed to allow individual actions to lead to desired ends, equitably for all tasked with making judgments about whether this is so. Otherwise, people may perceive that an institution does not respond to their efforts in the same way as others'. This conclusion may lead to rejection of the institutions, as when Americans conclude that college is not a good bet, or may even prompt dismissal of the objectives themselves, if people conclude that trying to climb is just not worth the effort.

The Process Through Which Life Chances Are Integrated into Individual Behavior—The Role of Outcome Expectations

In the remainder of this chapter, we discuss how life chances are internalized and integrated into identity in ways that can shape behavior. While admittedly sometimes fairly academic, this discussion is the foundation for the Opportunity Investment Account policy outlined in chapter 6. It is because individuals' views of themselves and their chances affect their interactions with and outcomes from crucial institutions that interventions such as early assets can have substantial effects on multiple spheres. We endeavor to connect these dots for a theoretical foundation for the empirical evidence base on which children's assets policy rests.

Our view of the forces that shape individuals' life chances blends well-held beliefs among institutional theorists that life chances are determined by institutions with other principles that weave in behavioral dimensions for a fuller understanding of how life chances are ultimately formed.[63-65] According to this view, people are not free to form any set of life chances they want. Instead, social and environmental forces, such as family economic status and institutional access, determine their starting point. People like Willie can still play a role in determining their own life chances, despite initial disadvantages. However, the level of success they will be able to achieve will be less than if they had the full support of institutions.

This inequity is seen today when children of color who complete at least some college have less median wealth than White high-school dropouts, and poor children who graduate from college have less wealth than their counterparts who have better starting points.[14,66] The educational efforts and accomplishments of these children improve their individual positions but cannot erase disadvantages. These Americans cannot help but take stock of how the same institutions deliver different returns to differently positioned groups. These experiences become part of how they see themselves, institutions, and the promise of the American dream. Recognizing that life chances become internalized parts of one's identity underscores the imperative of leveling the playing field once and for all. Institutional inequity reshapes what groups of Americans see when they look in the mirror. This is a sobering call to attend to systematic patterns of entrenched but not unchangeable inequality. There is an imperative to select interventions that redress inequities where they begin: at the start.

We introduced an opportunity framework by which to understand the internalization of life chances in chapter 2, with the concept of role expectations. Here we continue that discussion by also introducing normative and cognitive expectations. However, first we draw a distinction between efficacy judgments (as the building blocks of cognitive expectations) and outcome expectancies, so that we begin with a shared foundation for understanding how individuals' beliefs about themselves and their contexts help to determine their futures.

DISTINGUISHING BETWEEN AN EFFICACY JUDGMENT AND
AN OUTCOME EXPECTANCY

Efficacy judgments are a specific form of expectancy, made in the moment when an individual is confronted with a choice of acting or not acting.[47] To make an efficacy judgment, an individual has to stop to think, even if for a very short time. Efficacy judgments are a person's perceptions about whether she can produce the required level of performance for a specific task. They do not, however, encompass a judgment about whether, after acting, ultimate success or failure will be achieved. For example, a student's judgment about whether he can complete a complex math problem is an efficacy judgment that does not require his assessment about whether performing well in math will lead to success as an engineer. From an efficacy perspective, people will continue to perform behaviors even if failure results, so long as they believe they have the effort and ability required to perform them.[45] This is important in understanding the power of the American dream, which motivates people to persist when confronted with difficult tasks, faced with daunting circumstances, or contending with persistent disappointment.

Outcome expectancies come at the point when similar results are achieved repeatedly and it no longer makes sense to expend the energy needed to make efficacy judgments.[45] At this point, the outcome is stored in memory and no longer appears changeable. A person who has formed an outcome expectancy might say something like, "I have performed these math problems successfully and received an A on my math test, so I expect that I will continue to perform well in math and that I 'have what it takes' to succeed in a career that demands math ability." Of course, experiences with institutions do not cultivate outcome expectancies equitably for all.

WEALTH HELPS TO SHAPE THE KINDS OF EFFICACY JUDGMENTS PEOPLE CAN MAKE

As stated, an efficacy judgment (self- or institutional) is basically a person's perception of what she is capable of doing (with or without institutional support). Because capabilities are based on "what a person wants to achieve *and what power she or he has* to convert primary goods to reach her or his desired ends," we view wealth as a critical determinant of success.[67] Wealth increases people's capability for controlling their lives. More specifically, the accumulation of wealth leads to the expansion of individuals' capabilities for participating in, negotiating with, influencing, and holding accountable the institutions that affect them.[68] This becomes even more important to have in mind when we discuss how early assets work to change how children see themselves, their futures, and the institutions that are supposed to help them achieve the American dream.

NORMATIVE EXPECTATIONS

Normative expectations lay out what society says you can expect to happen if you invest your effort and ability into socially prescribed behaviors such as education.[69–72] Based on an ideal, normative expectations do not necessarily come to pass for everyone, even though they are assumed to apply to everyone. The American dream, then, is a type of normative expectation, rooted in self-efficacy beliefs.

Because the United States purports to offer equitable chances, the American dream is supposed to adhere to the promise that all people will have opportunities to reach their full capabilities. Normative expectations follow a formula of, "if I do X, I can expect Y to happen." They are evoked when parents tell their children to study hard so that they can get good jobs, or when college students take out student debt with the assumption that it will be "worth it" one day. In a speech to the Democratic Leadership Council in 1993, President Bill Clinton described the American dream in terms consistent with how we see normative expectations when he said, "The American Dream that we were all raised on is a simple but powerful one: if you work hard and play by the rules you should be given a chance to go as far as your God-given ability will take you."[73] As described earlier, most Americans still ascribe to this accounting. People want to believe that they live in a just society, so they cling to the hope that their children can rise, even if they have personally failed to attain the American dream.[74] The alternative is anarchy, as individuals give up on the institutions that have failed them, or abject despair, as they give up on themselves.

COGNITIVE EXPECTATIONS

Cognitive expectations are the responses an individual expects to receive to her investment of effort and ability in socially-prescribed arenas. Cognitive expectations are formed through personal experiences with the institutions used as resources to achieve outcomes. These institutions become integrated parts of identities only when people are able to form cognitive expectations about their own positions in relation to the institutions around them.[37] Because young children lack the cognitive capacity required to make efficacy judgments and the cognitive expectations that come with them, normative and role expectations are particularly important in early childhood.[45,75] Much of what young children consider to be fact is accepted at face value because they do not have sufficient grounds for doubting and cannot yet comprehend abstract concepts.[76–79] When children gain the ability to form abstract concepts, such as cognitive expectations, they begin to construct a world of their own.

Of course, normative and role expectations are not perfectly predictive of behavior. People are thinking beings, not forced to blindly respond to stimuli. Instead, beginning around age 12, children are able to mediate their actions through forethought and planning.[45,78,80,81] In planning, a person mentally anticipates constraints to performance and opportunities to perform based on his perception of what he is capable of doing.[79,82] This ability to plan allows individuals to alter normative and role expectations based on cognitive expectations established through their previous interactions with institutions. Crucially, then, children whose experiences have not given them any grounds for forming cognitive expectations of institutional facilitation may instead form expectations that their efforts will be insufficient and exertion is, therefore, relatively pointless. Other research has found that it is in early adolescence that holding an unquestioning view of the American "deal" as inherently just becomes detrimental; it is at that point when system-justifying views that ignore the role of institutions may be associated with poorer outcomes, such as decreased academic persistence.[83]

COGNITIVE EXPECTATIONS BECOME AUTOMATIC
RESPONSES TO CUES IN THE ENVIRONMENT

Once people have sufficient evidence of patterns in the outcomes their effort and ability achieve, they stop making efficacy judgments and act based on the outcomes they already expect.[45] That is, their actions become outcome expectancies, which are automatic responses to environmental cues. Here, "automatic responses" differ from reflexes. They are not unthinking but instead represent stored self-knowledge learned through socialization, the process of making efficacy judgments, and observations of the outcomes from acting on those judgments. We internalize cognitive expectations to preserve precious personal resources for the intentional act of making efficacy judgments.[84] However, although expectations are eventually woven into children's ways of seeing themselves and their worlds, they are not always seamlessly integrated into their mental lives. Our own stories highlight this.

Melinda's cognitive expectations aligned well with normative and role expectations. She made plans for college that hinged on her presumed ability to win admission to desired schools, pay for a college degree through scholarships and her family's assets, and leverage this educational attainment for subsequent career opportunities. Her parents, teachers, and other influential adults conveyed consistent expectations that higher education would be part of her future; indeed, these expectations were so much part of the fabric of her life that it is impossible to recall specific instances when they were communicated. When she achieved academically, those accomplishments were implicitly and explicitly framed as confirmatory evidence of the fit between expectations and her outcomes. She cannot remember a moment when anyone expressed surprise when she received a scholarship or earned a high grade. Instead, it was as if everything was working as it "should." However, this is certainly not always true.

As revealed in Willie's story, cognitive expectations may exert powerful influences on the experiences of groups of Americans for whom institutional arrangements have seldom resulted in fair chances to achieve desired outcomes. Willie's parents wanted him do well, but he also received competing messages about the importance of contributing to the family's immediate needs, even when doing so distracted from his schoolwork. Similarly, some of Willie's teachers and school administrators expressed disapproval when he quit playing football, even though it was the religious mission work to which he turned that ultimately facilitated his acceptance into a selective college. The education literature offers other examples of the collision between normative and cognitive expectations and the ways they can compromise educational outcomes. When students receive messages that they do not "belong" in school, it can imperil their academic success, whether these messages come from disparate school discipline policies or the absence of low-income students on an elite college campus.[85-87] Ogbu explicitly examines the psychological processes at work in adverse contexts and suggests that Black children form negative perceptions about the possible return on education due to the ceiling their parents face in the labor market.[88] These negative perceptions may lead Black children to disengage from school and underperform academically.[88] Further, while their observations of their parents' experiences conflict with normative expectations, evidence suggests that these cognitive expectations are based in reality. For example, research has found that college degrees confer less return on the educational efforts of students of color.[89]

More recent research aligns with Ogbu's insights about the conflicting messages some children receive and how these contexts may shape expectations and subsequent outcomes. Low-income African American students are more likely to aspire to college if they have at least one Black teacher between third and fifth grade, an effect researchers ascribe to the presence of role models, which can serve to cue a particular version of a possible future self.[90] White teachers are 30% less likely than Black teachers to think Black students will graduate from college.[91] Crucially, low expectations are not only communicated to students in ways that clash with normative messages about education; they may also influence the support that institutions provide to help particular groups of students achieve.

Seen from the perspective of disadvantaged students' experiences with the actual institutions that normative expectations say are supposed to facilitate their attainment of the American dream—schools, in particular—cognitive expectations that contradict normative ideals appear not irrational or countercultural but as learned adaptations. At issue is not a difference in values but a rational response to accommodate inequitable situations.[92] What disadvantaged groups learn to doubt through personal experience is that the institutions that surround them will sufficiently or equitably augment their own abilities. As such, perhaps it is not surprising that Ogbu and Simons find that Black parents often send a double message to their children.[93] On the one hand, they tell their children to work hard in school to be successful—a normative expectation. On the other hand, Black parents may also send children messages of mistrust about the way schools will treat them and question whether schools will facilitate their success. These beliefs reflect a negative cognitive expectation forged from parents' own experiences, powerfully projected onto a child's sense of self.

COGNITIVE EXPECTATIONS AS BUILDING BLOCKS FOR CONSTRUCTING
POSSIBLE SELVES

Cognitive expectations are a step toward thinking about the self in terms of the future or what Identity-Based Motivation theorists refer to as "possible selves."[94,95] Oyserman, Terry, and Bybee state, "Youth construct possible selves by synthesizing what they know about their traits and abilities and what they know of the skills needed to become various future selves."[95] A student contemplating her future self might think, "I work hard in junior high and am successful; in turn, I can expect to be able to perform the tasks required to go to college in the future." Unlike an outcome expectancy, where the student only has to assess that working hard in junior high will lead to good grades *in junior high*, considering the possible self requires thinking beyond the outcomes present behavior can realize. In other words, projections of a possible self require that an individual make an assessment about what one's future capability will be and what outcomes that future performance will realize. To put this in perspective, think about a junior high student who is just starting to think about how her current abilities and achievements relate to her future as a college student. This student would need to extrapolate from what she knows about her current abilities in order to conceive of what she is capable of in the future as a college student and, in turn, what that future performance will mean.

While useful as an illustration, this example oversimplifies this process. In reality, people hold multiple and sometimes conflicting identities. We do not necessarily act consistently with all of these identities when it comes to thinking about our futures.[96] Instead, we act on identities when they are important, feel congruent with beliefs about our group memberships, and provide a strategy for overcoming difficulties encountered in trying to live consistently with the identity.[96] When a particular possible self is cued, cognitive expectations associated with that identity are emphasized, and people have an automatic psychological and, in turn, physiological response.[97]

Cognitive expectations are therefore highly determinant of which of an individual's multiple identities may shape his projections of a possible self at any given time. For those Americans whom experience has taught to trust institutions to facilitate their desired outcomes, again, alignment of cognitive expectations and desired identities occurs seamlessly. However, when individuals have been disadvantaged by institutional arrangements, their cognitive expectations may run counter to their desired identities—as a college student, for example, or as a professional. For these cognitive expectations to be changed, the automatic response must be interrupted by a change in the environment that alters the cues children receive from their school, their parents, and their community. This interruption allows a child to search for another way of viewing an outcome. For example, exposure to college preparation resources might help children to see college as a viable opportunity. As a result, they may begin to construct versions of their future "possible selves" that include being successful college students. More directly related to our policy proposal, owning assets designated for college may send messages to children and their parents that postsecondary education is within reach and, further, is an outcome toward which their own efforts can propel them, supported by the institution of an endowed account.

This chapter is only the beginning of the discussion about possible selves. Our opportunity framework helps to explain how and why asset accumulation can have significant effects on children's identities and, therefore, on their educational outcomes. In the next chapter, we return to this subject to examine Identity-Based Motivation within the specific context of Children's Savings Accounts. There, evolving theory and mounting empirical evidence suggest that assets can interrupt the formation of negative cognitive expectations that may otherwise prevent realization of a "college-bound" possible self. In the process, development of identities as savers headed for postsecondary education can trigger changes in actions, which may lead to success in higher education and as wealth builders. These changes are crucial to our understanding of how children's asset interventions work and why policies such as Opportunity Investment Accounts could be transformative in children's lives. After all, changing how individuals act today requires changing what they expect for their futures. As Knight puts it, "if we want to use self-enforcing institutions to constrain the actions of others, we must do so by affecting their future expectations."[98]

Conclusion

The policy intervention we outline in chapter 6 is designed to improve children's outcomes all along what we are terming the "opportunity pipeline," from early childhood through adulthood. To a large extent, the early and substantial children's assets that Opportunity Investment Accounts would deliver exert their effects by simultaneously shaping children's expectations—what they expect they will be able to do as their future selves—and the institutional responses they receive, which then serve to bolster those expectations. As we explain in the following chapters, we view understanding how assets work in children's lives as essential to building political will for these investments. In other words, we have to get people to think about breathing—and the context that makes breathing not only possible but seemingly effortless—if we are to convince policymakers and the public they represent to adopt policies to ensure that all children can breathe freely.

Today, in what may be the greatest crack in the American dream façade, there is little evidence that the poorer outcomes realized by disadvantaged children stem from inferior exertion or insufficient innate ability. Instead, superior results are secured by privileged Americans largely through unfair institutional arrangements. As such, success is largely the result of having wealth, growing up in wealthy communities, and attending affluent schools, all levers that serve to amplify the efforts of some, while blocking others. When the curtains of inequality are peeled back, the achievements of the privileged appear illegitimate and the failure of the disadvantaged almost unavoidable. Many Americans end up ahead because they started there.

Nonetheless, even in the face of evidence that directly contradicts our cherished beliefs in equal opportunity, we try to hold on to the American dream because we want to retain faith that this is the way the system works.[6] We perform mental contortions to justify unequal patterns of success and failure. We label scholarships that hinge on high grades and extracurricular accomplishments "merit aid" in order to obscure the mechanisms that determine who wins them. We exalt narratives of people who succeed against all odds while minimizing the importance of institutional factors. We delude ourselves in the service of the "effort plus ability equals success" equation. In the process, we turn this illusion into a weapon that injures disadvantaged children, who are forced to either give up on the system that is supposed to deliver success or to conclude that their own inadequacy is to blame for their failure.[99]

In order for our education system to treat "effort" as we would prefer, we need institutions that augment children's potential and allow them to live into the normative expectations they have been sold. We need systems that extend equitable life chances to all young people so that they cultivate images of their possible selves that align with the hopes they once had. And we need to intervene early enough for these new institutional forces to be incorporated into children's automatic responses. Otherwise, while outcomes such as financial preparation for college, entrance to selective universities, and achievement scores tell us who the winners are, they tell us little about the amount of effort and ability the winners put forth relative to the losers and how, then, our values would actually prefer to reward them.

Our opportunity framework highlights how institutions amplify individuals' abilities. It situates this institutional facilitation as a key dimension of a modern American dream and sets the backdrop for discussion of policy changes that could dramatically alter the distributional consequences of education. This positioning distinguishes Opportunity Investment Accounts from other proposals for education reform. While likely needed and potentially valuable, changing how education is delivered will fail to craft the US education system into a potent force for equity and upward mobility. As our education system evolves and schools get better at what they do, individual students and the country as a whole will surely benefit. However, as has been the case in every institution that has propelled human progress to date, equitable distribution of resources is far from guaranteed. Instead, maximal maintenance of inequality suggests that those already privileged will continue to benefit most from innovations in instructional technology, teacher training, and assessment.[100] What we really need in order to improve our education system and the rewards it distributes is a new approach that directly reduces wealth inequality and equips all students with equitable bargaining power.

Going forward, we must make every effort to create institutions that give everyone a chance to obtain the best life chances that their efforts and abilities allow. It is a moral and strategic imperative. The education system is the central conduit through which Americans climb toward their dream. It is the primary arena in which it is contested. That is *why* education matters and why it is within education that we must reckon with our institutional failings. The American dream cannot survive in the context of current education policies. Just as surely, it is our responsibility to preserve the dream now so that it survives to motivate future generations.

4 Moving from the Status Quo to a 21st-Century Financial Aid System

WITH THE CREATION of the first federal student loans as part of the National Defense Education Act of 1958, the US postsecondary financial aid system was set on a path from which it has not fundamentally deviated in the intervening decades.[1] While college financing has trended almost inexorably toward greater reliance on student borrowing as costs have outpaced families' incomes, the major components of the financing "mix" have remained unchanged. Financial aid policy is sometimes tweaked around the edges to lighten the burden of student debt, give colleges a competitive edge, or address undesirable disincentives. For the most part, however, these reforms bear more resemblance to the classic "shell game" than to authentic innovations. What American students *need* are more powerful tools with which to approach their futures—tools that help them prepare for higher education, persist to completion, and then leverage returns on their degrees. What they *get*, however, are repackaged versions of the same blunt instruments.

While everyone wants improved outcomes from our financial aid investments, the nation's apparent inability or unwillingness to innovate truly novel approaches to paying for higher education stands in the way of progress. The goal of financial aid policy has been narrowly framed as only helping young adults pay for college, a low bar that completely ignores the role financial aid could play in influencing early education, postsecondary completion, and post-college financial health. As a result, instead of receiving support at critical junctures along the opportunity pipeline to a prosperous adulthood, students are largely left to their own devices except at the moment when the tuition bill becomes due. To capitalize on the resulting missed opportunities, the United States needs more than different loan repayment schedules or loosened rules on grant disbursement. What we need is a fundamental shift in how we think about financing higher education and what we believe about why it matters. Even a cursory glance at headlines makes the case for a sea change in financial aid. If college is "a ludicrous waste," our postsecondary education system is "broken," and the American dream is "dead," instead of minor modifications, we need a revolution.[2–4]

The Current Financial Aid System

Mention that you work on higher education financing to anyone—friends, neighbors, people standing in line with you at the grocery store—and you will hear stories about the high cost of college. Keep the conversation going long enough and talk will often turn to how complicated financial aid is, as well as to Americans' sense—no matter where they fall in the income and wealth distributions—that financial aid is comparatively more available and adequate for other people than for them. These three themes—*inadequacy, complexity,* and *inequity*—characterize much of what plagues US financial aid policy today. Together, these limitations help to explain why evidence of the efficacy of financial aid investments is relatively scarce. Indeed, many of our policies do poorly against all three yardsticks. Clearly, something must be wrong. While the availability and expansion of financial aid is largely credited with increasing enrollment in postsecondary education and helping to democratize the idea that college could be for everyone, the divides in educational attainment by race and class traced in chapter 1 persist.[5,6] Although financial aid is certainly not the sole cause of these gaps, its failure to close them should give us pause. And when measured against goals beyond mere access, including catalyzing equitable return on degree and fueling broad prosperity, the American financial aid system clearly leaves much to be desired.

TOO LITTLE, TOO LATE—ADEQUACY

Financial aid is big business in the United States. In the 2015–2016 school year, expenditure on financial aid totaled a seemingly substantial $158.3 billion, reflecting a 57% increase over 10 years.[7] However, because the base objective of financial aid policy is to cover the cost of enrollment in order to facilitate access to higher education, assessing adequacy requires considering these sums against the prices students and families confront. This, of course, is a moving target. As other investors retreat, tuition makes up an ever-larger part of institutional budgets, particularly at public colleges and universities.[8,9] As a result, financial aid has become increasingly crucial to families' accounting. But most students' financial aid packages still leave holes. In 2015–2016, undergraduates in the United States received an average of $14,460 in financial aid per full-time equivalent student.[7] This figure stacks up fairly well for students attending in-state public universities, where average tuition and fees were $9,650 in 2016–2017, but looks far less sufficient for those attending private colleges or out-of-state public institutions, where average prices were $33,480 and $24,930, respectively.[10]

Additionally, few financial aid packages fully account for the nontuition costs of college, including foregone earnings, which are particularly significant for lower-income students.[11,12] Even students at more "affordable" institutions may struggle to afford living expenses. These costs can result in a financial squeeze that propels greater work participation while in school, which can depress achievement and make it harder for graduates to launch into promising careers.[13,14] One analysis estimated that available financial aid only places 1% of postsecondary institutions in the country within financial reach of low- and moderate-income students.[15]

When financial aid does not equal what it costs to go to college, the resulting gap is termed unmet need. Because this figure depends on a complex interplay of individual characteristics, institutional offerings, and public policy, it can vary dramatically, even for two students pursuing the same degree at the same school.[12] Students facing unmet need grapple with an array of less than optimal choices. They may turn to credit cards, private loans, or additional work, or they may be deterred from higher education entirely.[16,17] And the adequacy of financial aid matters beyond enrollment. While there is relatively little evidence of the effects of financial aid on college persistence, research has found that net prices (defined as tuition and fees, minus nonrepayable aid) influence both enrollment and completion.[18-21]

Determining what is "adequate" is not as easy as just comparing the tuition price to the financial aid package. Evidence suggests that different types of financial aid may have different effects, even when awards lump them together.[16,22] In other words, financial aid dollars are not all created equal. Of the $14,460 in financial aid received by the average student, $8,390 comes from grants. In 2015–2016, 34% of grant aid came from the federal government, 43% from postsecondary institutions—much of it awarded based on merit, as discussed in chapter 1—14% from employers and other private sources, and 8% from states.[7] While state grant aid has increased each year since 2011–2012, it remains a rather insignificant part of most students' aid, averaging only $750 per full-time equivalent undergraduate in 2014–2015.[7] The largest single source of grants is the Pell Grant, awarded based on family financial need. Federal funding for Pell Grants peaked in 2010 with an infusion from the recovery stimulus package. In that year, total Pell Grant expenditures were $39.1 billion (in 2015 dollars); this declined to $28.2 billion in 2015–2016.[7] Similarly, the number of Pell Grant recipients today is smaller than at the peak, although more than one-third of undergraduates receive Pell and participation has increased 46% from a decade ago.[7]

For those who receive them, Pell Grants constitute 55% of the funding used to confront the cost of postsecondary education.[7] While an important contribution toward affordability, Pell Grant purchasing power has failed to keep pace with rapid increases in tuition.[23] In 2015–2016, the average Pell Grant recipient received only $3,724.[7] Even the maximum Pell Grant, received by only approximately one-quarter of recipients, covered only 60% of average public and 17% of average private, nonprofit four-year tuition and fees during 2016–2017.[7] This declining potency may help to explain a vexing contradiction in Pell Grant literature. The Pell Grant program is an important investment in higher education affordability and a centerpiece of the federal government's commitment to assisting low- and moderate-income Americans with paying for college. However, most research has found relatively weak effects from Pell Grants on the most important postsecondary education metric: degree completion.[12] Pell Grants appear, then, simultaneously as a valuable aid to many who aspire to climb the economic ladder through higher education and, unfortunately, as not entirely up to that task, perhaps particularly in the post-recession landscape.[24] When it comes to getting students from a childhood in poverty all the way to college graduation, grants that partially subsidize tuition are apparently not enough.

Beyond grants, the rest of a student's financial aid package is composed of sources that bear little resemblance to "aid." This is particularly true of student loans, which of course have to be repaid and can then exert downward pressure on students' returns on their degrees.[25] In 2015–2016, the average financial aid package included $4,720 in student loans. Beyond the inequitable post-degree effects Willie has observed in his own life, there is evidence that student loans may not have grants' positive effects on enrollment because they do not reduce net price in the same way.[6,12]

Also included in the total financial aid budget of a typical student are education tax credits and deductions ($1,290 in 2015–2016).[7] However, because this tax aid is only available *after* postsecondary expenses have been incurred, it is not helpful in actually meeting those obligations on the front end. Additionally, most education tax benefits only cover "qualified higher education expenditures" in excess of student aid. This definition excludes living expenses and makes education tax benefits of almost no use to most lower-income students, whose tuitions (but not other expenses) are often covered by Pell Grants and institutional aid.[26,27] Some analysis has found that as many as 40% of undergraduate students are ineligible for higher education tax benefits altogether.[28] Not surprisingly, then, researchers have found that education tax benefits exert little effect on postsecondary enrollment or completion,[29] exactly the outcome many predicted when these tax-side benefits were rolled out.[30]

In 2016–2017, federal work-study added another $60 to the average student's financial aid receipt.[7] While some research has suggested that this relatively insubstantial program may be particularly useful in increasing persistence to degree, advocates have criticized the insufficient supply and ill distribution of work-study dollars.[18] More specifically, some work-study practices tend to exclude students with the greatest needs, even though lower-income students might benefit most from work-study opportunities.[31,32]

Importantly, students may pay a high price for some of the financial aid they seek in an often desperate attempt to scrounge up enough dollars to enroll. Specifically, some awards may come with strings that distort academic decisions and hinder attainment. For example, financial aid policies may discourage students from taking course loads that would lead to timely degree completion or encourage them to enroll in schools with poorer completion outcomes, both actions that may constrain aggregate attainment.[5,33]

Most crucially, an assessment of whether or not financial aid is adequate requires more than just a financial accounting. Instead, we suggest that adequate financial aid should be defined as that which helps students overcome all of the challenges they face. This means not just being equal to the task of paying for college but also helping to influence student achievement upstream. Here, as Mundel concludes in a review of the literature regarding grants' effects on educational outcomes, policies that merely subsidize the price can only do so much to counter accumulated disadvantages.[34] While increases in Pell Grants did temporarily narrow the enrollment gap between low- and high-income students, there is relatively little evidence that financial aid, overall, is moving the needle on the dimensions necessary to facilitate degree completion.[12,35,36] Indeed, the percentage of low-income students enrolling in college immediately after high school declined steeply even at the same time that public and private financial aid investments increased.[37] Such findings add to doubts about the wisdom of the status quo.

Grant aid does not seem to affect students' educational expectations or high school course-taking or the actions of other important institutions that influence students' success.[38] And other forms of financial aid perform even more poorly on these dimensions of preparation. In fact, the mere prospect of student loans may deter some students from higher education.[39–41] Student loan usage may decrease course credit accumulation[42] and persistence to degree, particularly for low-income students.[43–46] In sum, scholars attempting to assess financial aid policies according to a benchmark of whether they are potent enough to catalyze the educational attainment of those who might not have otherwise made it have largely concluded that, while larger awards seem to have greater effect than smaller amounts and some evidence is mixed, for the most part, current financial aid is not even *designed* to do much more than pay the bills.[18,47]

CONFUSING MAZE LEADS TO . . . FINANCIAL AID?—COMPLEXITY

For financial aid to influence students' outcomes on the way to higher education, students and parents must believe that financial assistance will be available to them and then form expectations that take this aid into account. In other words, they need to be bolstered by institutional efficacy, trusting that the institution of financial aid will complement their own exertions.[48] Here, the complexity of financial aid programs is problematic.[20] This is particularly the case for low-income students and those otherwise disadvantaged, whom research reveals have less understanding of how financial aid works than do privileged students, even though their college plans may hinge on availability of financial assistance.[49,50]

Instead of one single financial aid policy, assistance with college financing is provided through a fragmented patchwork of federal, state, and institutional policies, each with its own rules and entry point.[18] Need-based financial aid—including Pell Grants and federal loans—requires completion of the Free Application for Federal Student Aid (FAFSA). Three questions on the FAFSA require additional worksheets with as many as 40 questions each, resulting in a process longer than most tax returns.[12] The FAFSA has recently been simplified, but the changes only reduced the number of required questions from 127 to 116.[6] Additionally, the formula used to calculate eligibility for Pell Grants is opaque, making it hard to determine in advance how much help one will actually receive.

Complexity in financial aid is about more than just nuisances. For students who cannot draw on family assets, paying for college is a high-stakes exercise that requires wading through eligibility guidelines and meeting different application deadlines, usually to still come up short at the end.[51] The communications that educational institutions, government agencies, and private contributors share to help families navigate options and make decisions often leave serious questions.[52,53] The resulting confusion can affect students' choices about whether and where to continue their schooling. Evidence suggests that complexity may actually stand between some students and the education they seek.[54]

Even for those who successfully run this gauntlet, determinations may come too late to be of maximal utility to students on the financial margins.[12] In recognition of the problems that financial aid complexity creates for students and for the postsecondary education system, recent policy changes have taken some steps in the direction of greater transparency and timely notification. In September 2016, President Obama issued an executive action to allow the use of income data on the FAFSA from two years back, instead of requiring the prior year. This change allows students to apply for financial aid at least somewhat earlier in their postsecondary planning, so that they have more advance notice of how much financial aid they will receive, at least from the federal government.

However, the FAFSA is not the only maze in the financial aid process. Education tax credits are also poorly publicized and complicated, leading to low utilization among some of the households that would be eligible to recoup costs through the tax code.[27,30,55] The complexity of available tax credits and deductions likely also contributes to the skew toward higher-income recipients. As explained in chapter 2, these are the strategic actors best positioned to maximize their tax positions.

COMPOUNDING INEQUITY

Financial aid, then, can be critiqued because it is simply not enough. Remedying this, while politically difficult, is technically straightforward: provide more funding to bring financial aid closer to the true cost of college, and deliver aid when and where it is needed most. Addressing the complexity of the financial aid system seems even more feasible. Some measures recently enacted may help students navigate options, and more efforts are underway.[56] From our perspective, then, the greatest failing of financial aid, and the greatest argument for a revolution, is evidence that financial aid policy may be increasing inequities within the US higher education system. Pell Grants are concentrated on those economically disadvantaged and have helped to make college affordable for low-income students since their introduction in 1972.[5,24] However, a large portion of other financial aid expenditures aims toward students already privileged in the pursuit of postsecondary degrees. In 2014–2015, while three-quarters of dependent students receiving Pell Grants came from families with incomes below $40,000 per year, the distribution of merit aid and tax aid, in particular, looks almost the inverse.[7]

As discussed in chapter 1, an overarching trend in financial aid has been the shift from need-based assistance to that which instead hinges on various definitions of "merit" and ignores financial considerations.[57] This trend has led some to conclude that, in the aggregate, financial aid policy has abandoned its original goals, principally, to facilitate educational attainment by those who might otherwise be priced out of college.[12] While total grant aid increased by 89% between 1995 and 2006 and by another 79% in the last 10 years, much of this spending has been directed at recruiting desirable (often privileged) undergraduate students, rather than ensuring that low-income students can overcome financial obstacles to higher education.[58] When institutions wield financial aid as a tool with which to compete for students, these practices result in a diversion of resources away from those with the greatest need, thereby undermining the progressivity of federal investments.[59,60]

It may be that a more accurate label for "merit aid" is "non-need-based" aid, since these funds may be more accurately characterized by what they do not do—progressively meet the needs of disadvantaged students—than what they do. In 2014–2015, 24% of state grant aid for undergraduates was awarded without regard to students' financial need, a formula that usually results in more resources flowing toward those who already start out with advantages.[7,57] This is a dramatic increase from 13% in 1994–1995. Additionally, and critically, evidence suggests that merit aid is not determined solely or even primarily by actual academic performance. Instead, analysis of some merit aid policies has found disproportionate benefit to higher-income students, even holding demonstrated achievement constant.[61] By further augmenting the chances of those who already begin ahead, some merit programs may even widen attainment gaps by race and class, as was the case when Georgia introduced its HOPE Scholarship.[62]

Other forms of financial aid even more explicitly amplify existing advantages. Particularly notable here are tax credits and deductions for higher education. Fueled by middle-class demands for action on college affordability, these tax expenditures are growing. Apparently undeterred by analysis that has found sparse evidence of any substantial contributions to educational outcomes, federal education tax benefits now reach more students than subsidized and unsubsidized Direct Loans combined and almost twice as many students as Pell Grants.[7,29] Additionally, in 2014, a greater share of the benefit from education tax benefits went to households with adjusted gross income (AGI) between $100,000 and $180,000 than to households with AGI below $25,000.[7] Critically, then, higher education tax benefits can be indicted not only for failing to help poor students but also for further privileging wealthy students. By subsidizing the educational expenses of high-income households after the fact, these tax expenditures effectively underwrite privileged families' escalating investments in their children's achievement, while lower-income households that are taxed at lower rates realize little to no benefit from these policies.

The Future: More of the Same?

While there is much that is uncertain about the policy landscape of tomorrow—in financial aid or otherwise—a scan of what is likely to come reveals continued concerns on each of the fronts where US financial aid policy today comes up short. As states fail to restore public funding for postsecondary education, even well into economic recovery, public institutions continue to shift costs to students and families, and these actions render existing financial aid even less adequate.[63] Pending congressional reauthorization of the Higher Education Act was once thought to offer promise to update financial aid policies. Now, however, fiscally conservative leadership in Congress could use this vehicle to freeze the maximum Pell Grant and eliminate its entitlement nature, "reforms" that could lock some lower-income students out of college altogether.[64]

President Trump's proposed budget cuts have the potential to double-down on already problematic aspects of America's financial aid system, while unraveling its strongest supports for disadvantaged students. President Trump requested $1.3 billion in cuts from the Pell Grant program from the 2017 budget.[65] This would be followed by a raid of almost $4 billion from the Pell Grant surplus reserved to cover potential increases in enrollment or awards.[66] The president's proposed "skinny budget" would also reduce federal work-study and eliminate the Supplemental Educational Opportunity Grant, which awards $732 million per year to mostly low-income students.[66] Juxtaposed with rising college prices, these declines in need-based aid could decimate the already inadequate financial aid system. Compounding this risk, President Trump's proposed cuts to the National Institutes of Health and other federal agencies that award research grants could also squeeze postsecondary institutions and force them to lean even more heavily on tuition dollars.[67]

From the standpoint of complexity, financial aid policy may fare somewhat better in the coming years, particularly given the changes already underway. However, when resources are tight, the trade-off between universal simplicity and strict targeting often shifts in favor of greater hoops that people have to jump through, in an effort to weed out some applicants.[68] And, of course, transparency is not a cure-all; if the factual, digestible information students and parents receive is that there is not much financial assistance available to help them pay for higher education, they may have clarity, but they will not have anything that looks like a promising path to upward mobility.

Most imperiled of all is the quest for equity. Federal education policy at all levels is trending toward privatization. The US Secretary of Education is committed to vouchers that would divert funding from public schools in order to facilitate parental "choice." While the details of such a policy shift would likely determine its precise effects, review of similar policy pivots in other countries suggests potentially dramatic increases in educational stratification.[69-71] US educational institutions are already sharply divided by race and class, with students of color and those from poor families underrepresented on elite campuses and unable to access the same institutional opportunities as their privileged peers.[72,73] Against this baseline, policies that intensify divisions may make it nearly impossible for a talented student to climb all the way to the top.

Initial policy overtures from the Trump administration suggest that fears about the future of financial aid are well-founded. In addition to diversion of Pell Grant funds, the Trump administration's US Department of Education budget would make substantial cuts to TRIO and GEAR UP programs that prepare first-generation college students for success.[66] Withdrawing these supports from disadvantaged students may reduce their college completion rates, widen gaps in educational attainment, and potentially saddle more students with debt they cannot repay. Further compounding the damage, the negative effects of spending reductions on low-income students would be amplified by their counterpoint—increased tax cuts for wealthy Americans and increased government subsidy of families' preferences for private schools.[74-76] As privileged strategic actors take advantage of these institutional supports to advance their own interests and secure optimal life chances for their children, wealth will likely exert a growing influence on children's outcomes.

The Special Case of Student Debt: Wealth Inequality Baked into Higher Education Financing

Even as awareness of the inadequacy, unnecessary complexity, and unfairness of many aspects of education and college financing in the United States has grown, the fundamental inequity of debt-dependent financial aid has only recently come into sharper focus. Conventional wisdom has largely held that, as long as student debt does not become so onerous that borrowers buckle under the pressure of repayment, there is nothing inherently wrong with asking some students to borrow while others finance their degrees from parental asset stores or other transfers. Within this paradigm, when movements of college students and indebted young adults have highlighted the strain that debt can impose, the "solution" has usually been to tweak policy to somewhat blunt the effects. This was the impetus for expansion of Income-Based Repayment (IBR) plans as well as proposals to reduce interest rates and strengthen pre-loan counseling.[77,78] These efforts are assumed to make loans safer for borrowers and to reduce defaults, thereby making them safer for lenders and guarantors as well. Absent an analysis of how a dollar of student debt differs from a dollar in educational assets in economic mobility potential, little policymaking energy is expended to make financial aid fairer. However, as our own journeys underscored, these are the financial aid reforms Americans need in order to create the education system the nation—and our powerful but elusive dream—deserve.

The effects of wealth inequality on students' progress through higher education and prospects for prosperity after graduation were vividly illustrated in our own lives. The student loans that paid for Willie's undergraduate and graduate degrees were simultaneously essential to helping him complete postsecondary education and dramatically less potent an institutional support than Melinda's family's transferred assets. The differences in our financial positions today reflect the accumulated outcomes from our diverging college financing experiences more than any differences in our innate abilities, applied efforts, or personal choices. This is not the equation that is supposed to explain the American dream. And it is not the foundation on which an American opportunity pipeline can rest.

Against the three criteria for financial aid policy laid out here, Melinda's access to family assets stacks up far more favorably than Willie's debt dependence. Melinda's family was able to absorb even unexpected financial demands relatively easily, such as when she chose Washington University's more expensive graduate program and decided to extend her studies by a semester in order to complete advanced fieldwork. She never had to take on extra paid work, defer enrollment because of financial constraints, or expend mental energy worrying about bills. There was always enough. Financing college from an asset base was also more adequate for preparing her for success post-college too. She had experiences navigating financial institutions, garnered through managing transfers from the account she co-controlled with her father. She graduated with about $1,500 left in that account and used it to open her first Individual Retirement Account. The funds reserved for her higher education, in other words, did more than just pay for college. They were the metaphorical tailwind even hard-working young people need to transition to adulthood. She was able to leverage those resources to extend her family's asset advantages to her husband as well. With her grandparents' blessing, their money paid off her husband's student loan and supported him through his own graduate studies. In contrast to financial aid that can only pay for tuition, this is a tangible example of the multiplier effect of assets, particularly as her husband's advanced degree secured a stronger financial future for Melinda's children than she could have delivered herself.

Additionally, where Willie had to maneuver through different eligibility requirements, strategically pay bills to adjust for financial aid disbursement dates, and deal with uncertainty as he waited for each award, Melinda's reliance on her family's education savings was straightforward. She knew from an early age that there would be money for college. She could check the balances and knew the purposes for which she would be allowed to spend the savings. It was an institutional support on which she could depend. To the extent that it was somewhat complex, what she learned about investment returns and inflation risks was knowledge that served her upward mobility interests, rather than complexity used as a gatekeeper.

Finally, our passages through the US opportunity pipeline have convinced us that there is undeniable and irreconcilable inequity in a system that delivers disparate returns to two groups of students who are both chasing the American dream but separated by a wealth gap. To us, this is what matters most. It is the failing of the status quo that is most resistant to reform. It is both a symptom and contributor to widening wealth inequality in the United States. It is, therefore, the most urgent reason why we need a revolution in financial aid.

Correctly assessing the contributions of debt-centric financial aid to wealth inequality in the United States begins with acknowledging that student borrowing is neither universal nor randomly distributed. Although headlines portray student loans as ubiquitous features of the American postsecondary education experience, many students from higher-income families are able to navigate to degree completion—at least at the undergraduate level—without resorting to borrowing. Huelsman finds that only 46% of bachelor's degree recipients at public colleges whose incomes are too high to qualify for Pell Grants take out student loans, while 84% of students who are eligible for Pell Grants take out loans.[79] Similarly, Elliott, Lewis, and Johnson find that only 53% of high-income individuals with bachelor's degrees have outstanding student loans, compared to 76% of low-income college graduates.[80] As our own stories show, individuals who confront the task of paying for college with more money in their pockets have greater ability to avoid student loans, which are often considered a last resort.

Considering racial disparities adds another layer to the difficulties lower-income students encounter in financing postsecondary degrees. Elliott, Lewis, and Johnson find that, among those with bachelor's degrees at all income levels, 82% of Blacks, 77% of Latinos, and 64% of Whites have student loans.[80] Illustrating overlapping dimensions of disadvantage, Grinstein-Weiss and colleagues find that the odds of a Black low- or moderate-income (LMI) student having outstanding student debt were twice as high as a White LMI student. Moreover, Black LMI students carried more student debt than White LMI students[81]—about $7,721 more over the course of their studies.[81] This finding is particularly notable because students of color are under-represented at more expensive institutions.[82] Finally, there is evidence that a racial debt divide persists even after students complete their degrees.[79] Scott-Clayton and Li found that four years after earning a bachelor's degree in 2008, Black graduates held $24,720 more in student debt than their White counterparts ($52,726 versus $28,006).[83] Addo, Houle, and Simon found that Black young adults have substantially more student debt than their White peers and, further, that differences in young adults' net worth explain a portion of the overall racial wealth divide.[84]

Importantly, Addo and colleagues found the disparity between the debt of White and Black young adults to be greatest at the highest levels of parental net worth.[84] This difference suggests that privileged White young adults enjoy greater advantage from their parents' economic standing than do similarly situated students of color. As a result, White students are better able to avoid student borrowing. These authors conclude that "student loan debt may be a new mechanism by which racial economic disparities are inherited across generations."[84] McKernan and colleagues report that 42% of African Americans ages 25 to 55 had student debt in 2013, compared with 28% of Whites.[85] Again, these figures are particularly stark given Whites' higher rate of degree completion.[86] The fact that Willie's journey to and through the George Warren Brown School of Social Work depended on student debt while Melinda's did not is not, then, surprising or rare or somehow particular to our own experiences. Students of color and those from low-income families, like Willie, have few avenues for avoiding student borrowing, while maneuvering through higher education without debt is fairly routine for White students from financially-secure families, like Melinda.

Student debt is certainly not the only factor contributing to the wealth gap in the United States. However, it is just as certainly playing a critical and often unnoticed role. We note it in our own lives and in a growing body of research. Collectively, these data point to the need for a new direction in how we finance postsecondary education. Ideally, financial aid would be not only how students pay their tuition bills but also a valuable tool that augments students' efforts within institutions that facilitate their pursuit of the American dream. By this standard, it is clear that a dollar of assets is a world away from a dollar of debt.

Analysis of the effects of student debt on wealth inequality must account for the influence of timing. There is evidence that students who finance their educations with student loans are, like Willie, forced to delay wealth-building activities such as homeownership during the early part of their working lives.[87–91] Contrary to the characterizations of some student debt apologists, these are not inconsequential inconveniences.[92] Instead, delays that suspend wealth accumulation have lasting implications for individuals' financial well-being. Beyond the tangible and compounding financial effects is the psychological damage done to those who experience prolonged dampening of the return on their degrees while they watch their peers without debt prosper. These wounds ripple. They imperil our collective confidence in the American dream and prompt rising doubts about whether higher education continues to pay off or, at least, whether college is "worth it" when financed with debt.[93–96]

Trends suggest that worries about the wisdom of financing college with loans are not misplaced panic. Some indicators of return on degree are indeed moving in the wrong direction. The average length of time to repay student loans grew from about seven years in 1992 to a little more than 13 years in 2010.[97] This extension reflects not only the larger debt loads that force many borrowers to consider mechanisms such as deferment, but also the rising uptake of IBR plans. IBR, also known as Income-Driven Repayment, puts borrowers on a repayment schedule of up to 25 years rather than a 10-year one and forgives unpaid balances after 25 years. This accounting softens the monthly blow to borrowers, particularly if IBR adjusts obligations in order to keep them below a set percentage of the borrower's income. Critically, however, IBR is an expensive commitment for borrowers and for US taxpayers.[98]

The imposition of interest on student loans means that extending the period of repayment makes total debt service more expensive, just as a television purchased on a credit card may be paid for many times over before the debt is discharged. According to the Government Accountability Office, assuming a standard 10-year payback at 7% annual interest, the average student borrower paid a $6,000 premium for his degrees.[99] As a result of schemes like IBR as well as deferment and forbearance options (used by about 21% of borrowers), nine years after leaving school, the 2005 cohort had paid down only 38% of its original student debt.[100,101] Under a standard 10-year amortization schedule, it would have been approximately 90% discharged.[101] Slow repayment is not the worst possible outcome, however; 22% of high-balance borrowers actually had *higher* student loan balances in 2014 than in 2009, even without having fallen into severe delinquency or default.[101]

Students of color appear more vulnerable to negative amortization. Forty-eight percent of Black graduates owe more on their federal undergraduate loans than they did at graduation, compared to just 17% of White graduates.[83] These rising debts hinder forward progress. Further, because IBR benefits flow disproportionately to borrowers with the high balances that often reflect attendance at elite institutions and/or pursuit of advanced degrees, providing student loan "relief" through IBR schemes is regressive as well.[102]

Financial aid policy responds to political imperatives as much as to economic needs. Therefore, despite their limitations, eligibility for, marketing of, and enrollment in IBR plans have grown alongside widespread public discontent with student debt. In June 2013, 10% of federal Direct Loan borrowers were repaying their loans on IBR schedules; by June 2016, this figure had grown to 24%.[98] As more students find their way to IBR, further increases in average periods of indebtedness are likely. In other words, treating only the symptoms of student debt may worsen the underlying problem. While IBR relieves repayment pressures and may reduce default, extending the time that some Americans' incomes are diverted from wealth creation to debt management will likely exacerbate the contribution of student debt to wealth inequality.

It is an axiom that those with postsecondary degrees are supposed to be doing better financially than those without such credentials, even if some analysis suggests that this may no longer be true, at least in the case of net worth.[103] What should be the benchmark for the financial aid system is not whether this basic hurdle is still met but rather whether the way we pay for college is compromising equity in return on degree among those who achieve similar academic feats. Here, scholarship suggests that student debt can greatly limit a graduate's ability to ascend the economic ladder. In a recent study that directly analyzes student debt's effects on the ability to capitalize on a degree, Elliott and Rauscher considered the likelihood and rate of achieving median household net worth among those at least age 22 who have at least a four-year college degree.[25] After controlling for key differences such as race and parental education, they found that acquiring the relatively small amount of $10,000 in student loans is associated with a 16% decrease in the rate of achieving median net worth. Crucially, student borrowers' ascent is slowed even when the amount of student debt is excluded from net worth calculations. In other words, it appears to be the mere *presence* of student debt, rather than its *amount*, that keeps college graduates from "making it."

Again, we see this truth in our own stories. Melinda's ability to avoid debt—thanks to her families' resources and how they helped her to position herself—allowed early investments that jumpstarted asset accumulation. On the flipside, Willie's accounting of the toll student loans have taken on his financial well-being is not limited to just what he owes but also to what he has lost—in terms of delayed homeownership and reduced retirement saving—under the shadow of student debt. Willie is the first to concede that he is better positioned, financially and otherwise, than if he had not continued his education. Indeed, it is hard to imagine his life without the doors his degrees have opened. That does not negate, however, the simultaneous acknowledgement that he is not where he would be, at least financially, if he had not had to borrow for college.

This erosion of equitable return on degree is in part the result of compounding, multifaceted, and intergenerational effects of student debt on wealth inequality and of wealth inequality on educational attainment. How much college "pays" depends on who one is and where one starts. Differences in return on degree can be quantified. Researchers at the Federal Reserve Bank of St. Louis found that Hispanic ($68,379 income/$49,606 net worth) and Black students ($52,147 income/ $32,780 net worth) receive less benefit from having obtained a college degree than their White ($94,351 income/$359,780 net worth) and Asian ($92,931 income/

$250,637 net worth) counterparts.[104] Wealth gaps remain even at the postgraduate level.[105] These gaps are large and likely stem to a significant extent from the direct effects of the student borrowing that is unavoidable for many students of color and those from low-income families.[79]

Black and Hispanic college-goers seem to be particularly vulnerable to the forces constraining return on degree. As a result, race appears to be a determining factor in how far college graduates can climb and how much their degrees protect them from falls. Emmons and Noeth, for instance, found that during the Great Recession, Black and Hispanic college-graduate families experienced greater wealth declines than White families without a college degree.[104] This outcome is contrary to what Americans believe about postsecondary education and its economic rewards. Lower-income Blacks and Hispanics are not the only groups who experience these inequities. Hershbein found that young adults from *any* race/ethnicity who grow up poor receive less return on their degrees than young adults who do not grow up poor.[106] They struggle more than their privileged classmates in times of economic hardship, and, even when they prosper, they are often haunted—like Willie is—by the specter of student debt long after graduation.

Observations of these inequitable returns appear to have profound impacts on public perceptions about the viability of the higher education path to the American Dream. For example, in a survey of 900 adult college graduates, more than half said that those leaving college with a degree today will see lower returns than those 10 to 15 years ago.[94] This prediction strikes at the foundation of the deal Americans think they have. Financial aid today makes a mockery of the ideal that education is supposed to be an equalizer. Student debt undermines the wealth accumulation of those who have to borrow, undercuts the value proposition of American postsecondary education, and leaves millions of children without an institution capable of supporting their upward climb. In turn, the chorus demanding a new approach to education financing grows—in numbers and in volume.

Free College Does Not Represent a Fundamental Shift in How We Finance College

If financial aid policy can be characterized as a series of experiments to increase access and affordability of higher education, recent moves toward "free college" may be more incremental innovation than revolutionary departure, despite their framing as the preeminent "left flank" of college financing. Between 2014 and 2017, 29 states considered 77 bills related to free college.[12,107] The idea of free—or, at least, tuition-free—college gained national prominence during the 2016 presidential election, when Senator Bernie Sanders proposed eliminating tuition at four-year public colleges and universities. Some in the postsecondary community were effusive in their praise. Alexandra Flores-Quilty, vice president of the United States Students Association, said, "Senator Sanders' proposal is exactly what the broken US higher education system needs. A free education means a free society."[108] In the months since, states as demographically and politically diverse as New York, Tennessee, and Oregon, as well as some cities and specific institutions, have made at least some types of higher education "free."[109,110] However, when evaluated through a lens of wealth inequality, the evidence suggests that nationwide free college would be simultaneously more—at an estimated price tag of $70 billion—and less than what American students really need.

Free college proposals do not address most of the ways in which wealth inequality distorts the educational experiences of both disadvantaged and privileged students. Indeed, given the disproportionate rate at which high-income students participate in higher education and the absence of any upper income thresholds in some free college plans, these policies could end up transferring resources from low-income families to those already advantaged.[111] Analysis of free college policies that provide only "last-dollar" financial aid to those with unmet need finds that they mostly help students from households earning relatively high incomes. In many cases, they do not change the affordability calculation for LMI students at all.[112] At the same time, subsidizing the higher education costs of households like the one in which Melinda grew up would have exacerbated her advantage post-degree, making all of the money that her parents had saved for her education available for later wealth building and likely allowing her husband to graduate debt-free as well.

Even more problematic are free college proposals that provide tuition-free access only to public two-year community colleges or divert funds from need-based aid in order to pay for across-the-board tuition reductions. In these cases, while the concept of "free college" may sound like a dramatic change from the status quo, the net impact on the accounting and educational outcomes of disadvantaged students may be relatively modest or even negative.[113] Such policies would likely increase institutional stratification and further compromise the return on degree of students funneled into lower-status schools.

Particularly troubling are analyses that suggest that free college proposals may do little to reduce student debt among the neediest students. For example, in Sweden, where tuition is currently free, about 85% of students leave with debt that averages around $19,000.[114] This is because there, as in the United States, tuition is not the only cost students face. They also must pay for things like rent, transportation, fees, and food, and "free college" does not reduce costs for any of those essentials. At each of the universities Willie attended, living expenses were onerous and often prompted him to make decisions that compromised his education, including commuting a long distance while in law school.

Critically, then, free college proposals fail to address the inequality in return on degree that stems from one's starting point, unfairness that can only be remedied by directly tackling its root—wealth inequality itself. Hamilton and colleagues find that Black families who have a head of household who graduated from college have about 33% less wealth than White families who have a head of household who dropped out of high school.[115] This is effort resulting in educational attainment but not what that attainment was supposed to secure—financial status commensurate with achievement. Traub, Sullivan, Meschede, and Shapiro determine that even if Blacks graduated college at the same rate as Whites, this feat would only slightly reduce the racial wealth gap.[116] In addition to unequal dependence on student debt, other differences in college financing contribute to inequitable return on degree. For example, research by Rauscher finds that predicted household income and net worth are higher for adults who received parental financial support for education than for those receiving no such support.[117] Crucially, parental assets likely do more than just help students avoid debt. It is also the case that, as described earlier, students who approach institutions armed with assets engage differently with those institutions, compel different responses, and reap different rewards. While government investments to mimic these transfers could reduce wealth inequality, it is not at all clear that simply taking tuition off the table will do the same.[118]

Viewed from a perspective centered on wealth inequality and the obstacles it poses to upward mobility through education, proposals to make college free miss the mark. They fail to tackle the overlapping and accumulating effects of wealth inequality and instead treat inequality in higher education as only a problem of access. Defining the solution as "free college" presumes that what ails the withering American dream is just lack of money to pay for tuition, when in reality the problem goes much deeper, starts much earlier, and lasts much longer. Conversely, we propose that what the United States needs for the 21st century is a truly novel approach to financial aid that directly addresses wealth inequality all along the opportunity pipeline. That is what a financial aid revolution should aim for. It is what financial aid policy should deliver.

Children's Savings Accounts, New Tools for Educational Equity

The United States invests in education—particularly higher education—as the principal path to affluence and the purveyor of opportunity. These aims cannot be realized without a financial aid system that enhances, rather than compromises, education's potency as an equalizer. In the remainder of this book we outline how an American financial aid revolution could aim to better fulfill education's equalizing role. We contend that Children's Savings Accounts (CSAs) combined with a significant, progressive initial deposit—a combination we later call Opportunity Investment Accounts (OIAs)—could spark such a revolution. As manifestations of asset-based approaches to financial aid, these policies are potentially powerful tools for improving children's outcomes in the domains of early childhood development, college preparation, postsecondary access and completion, and postcollege financial health.

We contend that CSAs have the potential to perform better than current US financial aid policies with respect to adequacy, simplicity, and equity. CSAs serve as an institution that complements and enhances education's capacity as an economic mobility agent. As described in greater detail in the next chapter, evidence suggests that CSAs are associated with children's educational attainment, which itself is a conduit of economic mobility.[119,120] CSAs stand alone among financial aid policies in their ability to equip children with assets capable of altering their interactions with the institutions that help determine how well Americans do. In addition to fueling ascent through education, CSAs can be gateways to mainstream financial markets, including by providing assets that facilitate capital accumulation and fuel upward mobility.[121,122] This is true financial *aid*, capable of unlocking the door to the 21st-century American dream.

DEFINITION OF A CSA

CSAs are interventions that aim to equip children with assets and cultivate the development of identities consistent with educational attainment.[123,124] In recognition of the steep obstacles facing disadvantaged children and the need to influence not only college affordability but also preparation, CSAs start early.[125] Ideally, children receive CSAs at birth, although some CSA programs begin in kindergarten or early in primary school.[126] By essentially beginning the financial aid process in early childhood, this timeline takes advantage of the longer period of asset accumulation to build balances and influence children's development. CSAs provide families with a financial instrument into which they can funnel any saving for their children's futures.[123] This is an important feature for catalyzing equity, since many high-income families in the United States already use such vehicles to save for education.[127] However, asset accumulation in CSAs does not hinge entirely or even primarily on families' own savings. Instead, CSAs are capitalized with an initial deposit and augmented by transfers in the form of benchmark incentives and savings matches.[123, 128–129]

CSAs are gaining traction around the country as more policymakers, philanthropists, and educators concerned about rising student debt and the declining fortunes of America's youth are exposed to research regarding assets' potential to improve educational outcomes.[130–135] At the end of 2016, there were nearly 313,000 children with a CSA in 42 programs operating in 29 states, a 39% increase in enrollment from the previous year.[a,136]

These CSA programs all have roughly the same purpose: improving how well children do—particularly those disadvantaged. However, CSAs vary in operational and funding structures. CSA programs may operate through school districts, as in San Francisco's Kindergarten-to-College (K2C); through state 529 college savings plans, as in Nevada's College KickStart and Promise Indiana; or under the auspices of local organizations, as in Albuquerque, New Mexico's Prosperity Kids and at the Tacoma, Washington Housing Authority. CSAs also differ in how they are funded. They may be financed by private philanthropy, as in Maine's Harold Alfond College Challenge; by individual donors; or by corporate partners, as in the case of Rhode Island's CollegeBound*Baby*.[137–139]

Some CSA programs have leveraged existing financial aid dollars.[140] In Oakland, California, and the Kansas City region, CSAs are integrated with "promise" programs that make an early commitment to pay for most of a child's college education. Potentially particularly instructive for future policy development, some CSA programs are funded with dedicated public revenues, as in St. Louis' College Kids and Connecticut's CHET Baby Scholars. States and municipalities have turned to various sources of public funding for CSAs, including not only general appropriations but also fees paid by out-of-state investors in the 529 state college savings plan, as in Nevada, or other restricted funds. For example, Kansas' Child Support Savings Initiative is financed by reducing unpaid child support arrears.[141,142]

Illustrative of the origins and development of the CSA field are two of the oldest and most prominent CSAs in the country: Maine's Harold Alfond College Challenge (HACC) and San Francisco's K2C. When it started, HACC required parents to open an account in Maine's NextGen 529 college savings plan in order to receive the $500 seed deposit.[143] In 2014, HACC became the first in the nation statewide CSA that automatically awards initial deposits to all babies born Maine residents, a decision driven by a desire to increase operational efficiency and ensure that the most disadvantaged children were included.[139,144] Demonstrating that children's assets can be delivered automatically and universally, at scale, the HACC is expected to enroll more than 62,000 more Mainers over the next five years.[138] In addition to initial deposits and savings matches, families in the HACC also receive quarterly statements and information about child development milestones as children grow.[145]

The first universal CSA in the United States was San Francisco's K2C, which has provided savings accounts automatically to all incoming kindergartners in the San Francisco Unified School District since full implementation in 2012.[146] Framed from inception as an initial step toward college, K2C helped to position CSAs as tools for educational attainment.[147] Over the years, K2C has offered assistance to communities inspired by the promise of children's asset building and innovated features such as the use of a deposit institution—rather than a state 529 college savings plan—to administer a high volume of accounts, as well as financial incentives that reward savings behaviors rather than the amount deposited. CSAs in other jurisdictions have adopted many aspects of K2C's approach.

MORE THAN AN ACCOUNT: CSAS AS A CONDUIT FOR WEALTH TRANSFER

CSAs provide a financial product or facilitate access to one. Children with CSAs have an account—either a deposit account at a bank or credit union or an investment account in a state 529 college savings plan—that holds assets reserved for their futures. This design bridges access to the financial institutions that cultivate wealth in America. Equipped with a CSA in their own name, children have experiences saving and navigating financial systems far earlier than they likely would otherwise. However, CSAs are about more than just increasing children's comfort with financial institutions. They also aim to change the distribution of power. By directly countering wealth inequality, CSAs give disadvantaged children a better chance to make institutions complement their own efforts. CSAs, in other words, are more than just tools for families to exercise their own, often limited, capacities. They also position more families to interact strategically with institutions in ways that *increase* their capacities.

Much of the attention to and ascent of CSAs is owed to their effects on how parents and children see themselves and their futures, described later. Essential to their potential as a centerpiece of a 21st-century financial aid system, however, CSAs also have a lot to offer when it comes to transferring wealth and the power it confers to those who need it most. Today's CSAs field reveals some of this wealth accumulation potential. For example, with its initial seed and available matches, a family saving $50 per month in Maine's HACC could have more than $30,000 in educational assets by age 18.[148] Even CSA models with smaller transfers can facilitate significant balances. Back-of-the-envelope calculations suggest that a family saving $50 per month in Promise Indiana's CSA, starting at kindergarten, could expect to have more than $10,000 at age 18. Substantial tax credits for deposits into Indiana's 529 college savings plan could help families deposit even more. A family saving $25 per month in New Mexico's Prosperity Kids CSA could have approximately $5,650 by the time their child finishes elementary school, even with the lower returns realized in credit union accounts.

However, existing programs have only begun to tap into CSAs' full asset-building potential. While CSAs provide the opportunity to garner third-party contributions from extended family members, employers, philanthropists, and community organizations, recent examination of saving in CSAs underscores the imperative to adequately and progressively reward the relatively modest contributions families can make toward their children's futures.[149] As outlined in the discussion of OIAs, such investment is essential, if new children's asset-building structures are to serve disadvantaged families more fairly than existing wealth structures do.

CSAs' greatest potential to counter the corrosive effects of wealth inequality is found at the nexus of their financial account structure and their demonstrated ability to galvanize significant changes in how children and parents see themselves and their futures. CSAs can become a conduit for wealth transfers robust enough to serve as a meaningful institution capable of equitably facilitating success, but this outcome is likely only politically possible due to CSAs' effects on families' expectations and the actions they take in accordance with these future selves. Sparked in individuals and multiplied across entire communities, these changes can create a political context in which more substantial public transfers are viewed as investments in educational equity and restoration of the American dream. In turn, this could result in federal policy to construct what we are calling OIAs, an intervention capable of making real inroads in the maldistribution of wealth in the United States today. In other words, CSAs' ultimate contribution to reducing wealth inequality and mitigating its threat will be measured not only in the assets already transferred and the models already built but also in how changing the understanding of what asset-based financial aid can accomplish may change what the nation is politically willing to do.

UNDERSTANDING THE POTENTIAL OF CSAS TO CHANGE HOW PARENTS AND
CHILDREN THINK ABOUT THEIR FUTURES

From the beginning of the movement toward asset-based welfare policy, the power of wealth to change people's psychology, as well as their balance sheets, has been central to the appeal of asset interventions.[123,150,151] As explained in greater detail in the next chapter, CSAs can change how children and their parents think about their futures. These effects have been demonstrated in rigorous research and revealed in analysis of every CSA program investigated to date.[152,153] The question is: How? How does having money set aside for college make a difference in a student's academic achievement? How do children come to see themselves as likely to go to college? How does this expectation influence how they see the educational institutions with which they engage, and then, how do those interactions help to determine how well they do in school?

To better understand how CSAs help children live into a desired future possible self as college-bound, we have turned to Identity-Based Motivation theory, which has been widely researched and well-documented by Daphna Oyserman and her colleagues.[154,155] Particularly for disadvantaged children who have identified postsecondary education as an important goal but are uncertain as to how to move forward to act on that vision, motivating oneself to live into an identity as a future college student means more than wearing a particular college's apparel or even announcing plans to go to college. What these students need in order to persevere on the path to higher education is an institution that aligns their aspirations for college with their sense of what they are capable of accomplishing. They have to not just *feel* that they are going to college but actually trust that institutional supports will help them get there. This is where CSAs come in, specifically in terms of the college-saver identities that they can cultivate.

As discussed in chapter 3, research shows that people have more than one identity and that not all identities are acted on.[156,157] In this case, children may want to continue their educations beyond high school and may even be academically prepared for that step but still unable to imagine how to overcome the barriers they will face. All of these factors may lead to "wilt," which occurs when children with the ability and desire to attend college fail to transition after high school.[134] However, a college-saver identity can counteract wilt. Toward this end, CSAs can make a real difference. In contrast to other forms of financial aid, CSAs can help children to create and sustain college-saver identities. More specifically, CSAs equip children and parents with not only the *idea* of college as part of their futures but also *tangible strategies* for pursuing that aim.[124] A college-saver identity helps students interpret difficulties that they encounter when pursuing higher education as normal, rather than reasons to abandon their goals.[154] Given the high financial and academic odds many students face, this may be a crucial protection against a "difficulty as impossible" interpretation that might otherwise derail education.[158] A student with a college-saver identity expects to go to college *and* has a valuable tool to help her get there. Especially if she participates in a CSA program that publicly invests in her plans to go to college, she comes to see higher education as something that *people like her* do, aligned with the role expectations that shape her identity.

It is through the complementary effects of asset accumulation and assets' effects on identity that CSAs can best mitigate wealth inequality's corrosion of higher education as an equalizer in society. CSAs are institutions that can equip students with both the competencies and the balance sheets needed to succeed in college and beyond. As we describe in chapter 6, correctly designed and progressively funded, they can do so equitably in every household in the nation.

Conclusion

Americans are wise to be initially skeptical of claims that sound too good to be true. At first glance, the research that has found positive effects on children's educational outcomes as a result of CSAs with relatively small balances would seem to fall into that category.[132] After all, how could problems as grave as gaping achievement gaps, which then drive persistent inequities in educational attainment and keep economic mobility stubbornly out of reach, really be addressed by opening educational savings accounts for children and putting a few hundred dollars in them? Over the past several years, initially dubious responses have transformed into growing enthusiasm, as CSA research has fleshed out a more complete picture of how early educational assets cultivate the types of sustained orientations to college that drive better outcomes. As CSA evangelists have increasingly taken up the mantle of "small-dollar" CSAs as a near-panacea, however, a new threat has emerged, in the form of those convinced that merely opening accounts or, at most, very modestly jumpstarting them, is enough. Our analysis of the importance of wealth inequality in explaining the dire straits of the American dream clearly suggests that this is not the case. American children disadvantaged by race, class, ethnicity, geography—or some confluence of all these dimensions—need more than just college-saver identities. They need more than their thinking about their future to change. They also need bargaining power, so that others' thinking *about them* changes as well. In other words, they need wealth transfers that give them real reason to believe that their CSA is up to the challenges they will face as they pursue higher education. They need more than their own effort and ability, even bolstered by self-efficacy. They need a powerful institution on their side.

The truly revolutionary potential of children's assets, then, is not *either* meaningful asset accumulation, catalyzed by wealth transfers, *or* the college-saver identity effects realized through account ownership. It is the melding of both. It is precisely because the problems are so deep and so wide that the nation must bring its very best tools to confront this task. Here, that means that children need more than just money. They have to also live into expectations that align with their hugest hopes for their future selves. But they do need money, because as college tuitions rise and privileged parents leverage their resources to buy their own children a leg up, expectations alone will not get the job done.

Our contention in this book is that early children's assets are not only uniquely capable of improving children's chances but also rare in their political viability and operational feasibility. Without CSAs' effects on children's college-saver identities and related behaviors, they would likely be considered just another "handout" to poor families. However, when stakeholders from any political persuasion witness the transformation that early asset ownership catalyzes in children's lives, their perceptions of and expectations for these children change. We have seen it happen in communities from rural Indiana to urban San Francisco. Children become future college students. They and their families talk about and start to plan for their college futures. They approach institutions differently, expecting to have their efforts and abilities augmented by educational and financial systems. They wring better outcomes from these institutions in the process.

As a result, in the eyes of those who control the resources that so desperately need to be more equitably distributed, these children start to look like very good investments. CSAs' effects on identities are valuable, then, not only because they can change how children see themselves and how parents think about their children's futures. The cultivation of college-saver identities also changes how previously disadvantaged children interact with institutions that determine success. And, then, just like when Willie goes to buy a car today and secures better terms than he ever imagined, entirely new arrangements become possible. In other words, CSAs make "college savers" out of children and families who otherwise would not have been. When it comes to determining who gets what—in education reform, financial aid, college admissions, and incentives for asset building—this may make all the difference.

However, while it may not take much money to set a child on a college-saver path, as a child advances through school and contends with high college costs and insufficient, complex, and inequitable financial aid, small dollars can only go so far toward true institutional efficacy. Children also need a fairer distribution of American wealth. To get there, policy must put powerful American institutions to work in the service of children's interests. This is an end only accomplished by coalescing policymakers and other stakeholders around an asset-building vision robust enough to propel children all the way to their desired future selves. Therefore, we argue that building the political will necessary to capitalize CSAs substantially enough to meaningfully reduce wealth inequality begins with understanding the dimensions of a college-saver identity, how CSAs help to foster it, and how such an identity may help to chart a child's course. If American policymakers have shown little appetite in recent years for progressive wealth transfers *for their own sake*, wealth transfers explicitly designed to address our greatest collective imperative—to create the conditions where children can realistically expect their hard work in school to pay off in equitable life chances—may be a different proposition.

Note

a. An exhaustive inventory of CSA programs is beyond the scope of this book and would be difficult given continuous changes in this landscape. The appendix provides an overview of some of the most prominent CSA initiatives in operation around the United States as of June 2017.

5 Children's Savings Accounts' Influence on the Opportunity Pipeline

THE RAPID PROLIFERATION of Children's Savings Accounts (CSAs) around the United States has somewhat outpaced research into how early children's assets influence multiple aspects of children's lives. As they contend with operational details and the challenges inherent in trying to make disconnected systems cooperate in the interests of children and their families, practitioners in the field often lack nuanced understanding of how a particular incentive might work or what to expect as a benchmark outcome at a specific stage of child development. Their efforts rest, however, on a burgeoning body of research that provides a sense of how CSAs may differ from other forms of financial aid and how these differences could make them powerful tools for facilitating children's success. According to this research, CSAs are understood to begin working early in a child's life, thereby affecting not only college affordability but also early preparation and achievement. Also distinct from other financial aid approaches are CSAs' effects on students' asset holdings and overall economic positions. When taken together, CSAs demonstrate unique potential to alter both educational and financial outcomes. More specifically, as articulated here, CSAs are understood to affect children at four stages of what we are calling the *opportunity pipeline*: (a) early childhood, (b) school years, (c) college years, and (d) post-college years. Success in all four stages is crucial to the realization of strong returns on postsecondary educational attainment and the construction of a solid ladder of equitable upward mobility.

By introducing the phrase "opportunity pipeline," we intend to expand the notion of what financial aid really is or, at least, should be. CSAs are an investment in the ideal that every child in America should have an equal opportunity to achieve the American dream. Given education's role in facilitating equitable chances at economic well-being, we see this as the standard to which financial aid policies should be held. Unfortunately, this view contrasts with perceptions of financial aid only as a way to help solve the problem of not having enough money to pay for tuition. Asset interventions such as CSAs can and do help pay for college. However, they are also capable of more. Specifically, they attempt to address inequity in opportunity, taking aim at the root causes and pernicious consequences of wealth inequality, which were discussed in earlier chapters of this book (e.g., unequal power over setting expectations, unequal preparation for college, unequal access to selective schools, unequal return on a degree). We speak of financial aid as facilitating students' travel through the opportunity pipeline to convey the need for tools that better align with education's function as an equalizer.

The four stages along the opportunity pipeline are critical times for developing one's actual life chances. While most people know someone, maybe like Willie, who manages to compensate for disadvantages and "leap over" crucial developmental moments, for the most part those who struggle at some point along the opportunity pipeline will pay for those deficits at other points. The cumulative nature of both achievements and failures cannot fully be understood unless researchers systematically examine the influence of interventions such as CSAs on all four stages. Otherwise, efforts to intervene at one point will be unlikely to produce true equity, as inequality continues to plague other parts of the pipeline. For example, if everyone is given free access to college but wealth inequality still constrains early childhood development, it will be hard for students to equitably take advantage of the opportunities presented by free tuition. Similarly, if school reform efforts improve the provision of college-preparatory curriculum but wealth inequality inhibits some families' development of strong expectations of college attendance, these gains will be inequitably distributed. Finally, if universities change their practices to increase completion but wealth inequality fuels unequal returns on degrees, life chances will remain inequitable. The unavoidable conclusion is that policies that only address one stage of the opportunity pipeline—free college or school reform or college completion—will not solve America's equity problem. Education's role in facilitating realization of the American dream can only be redeemed through change in all of the domains where inequity reigns today. In the next section, we review research across the four opportunity stages to examine the case that children's assets are uniquely capable of supporting equitable progress along the way.

Methodological Considerations in CSA Research

In this chapter, we trace the evidence on which CSAs stand, pulling from studies conducted by different scholars at different institutions and using different data sources and measures. This diversity and the breadth of scholarship it reflects are strengths. While no one study can answer every question and every study has some limitations, the expanding constellation of CSA findings can be knit together into a robust case for creating a national policy for children's asset building. This evidence appears particularly strong against the paucity of evidence supporting many of our current financial aid investments. Especially when contrasted with the debt-dependent status quo,[1] even a cautious reading of CSA research underscores the crucial truth: at every point along the opportunity pipeline, children do better with assets.

Despite the fact that CSAs are a relatively new intervention, there is a growing body of research that informs consideration of their potential to help construct a more equitable opportunity pipeline. In order to accurately assess the strength of these findings, it is important to understand how CSA research has unfolded within the inherent methodological constraints associated with assessing any policy. As with other forms of financial aid, much of the research on CSAs has been limited to secondary data analysis. Research using secondary data typically tests whether there is an association between an intervention, such as receipt of grants or holding of educational assets, and a particular outcome, such as college enrollment or completion. As a result of limitations in this methodology, such research must be interpreted with some caution. Specifically, findings from studies using secondary data are typically viewed as not capable of fully ruling out the possibility that an observed association represents a spurious relationship. For example, it may not be that having a CSA causes someone to enter college but, instead, that this outcome is caused by a third, unobserved factor, not controlled for in the study.

Only experimental research can completely control for potential outside influences. However, it is difficult to design such studies to examine existing policies, particularly since factors other than research interests (e.g., funding limitations, political priorities, and jurisdictional boundaries) often determine who participates in a policy and when data can be collected. This often means that policy development rests on an evidence base constituted primarily by secondary research. These limitations are not unique to CSA research but also compromise much of the research on other financial aid polices, such as the student loan program. Nonetheless, policies have moved forward, even in the absence of definitive evidence that they solve the problems to which they are supposed to respond.

THE COMMON SENSE TEST

As with any research, consideration of the validity and implications of findings related to CSAs includes what might be thought of as the "common sense test." This can be thought of as an effort to examine research claims in light of real-world knowledge. It also looks at research through eyes similar to those with which the public will view findings. Using this test, a researcher might ask two questions about CSA research findings: (a) Do children who grow up in wealthier families have better opportunities for achieving the American dream than children who grow up in poorer families? and (b) Do children who have access to greater resources have better prospects for getting to and through higher education than those who do not? Common sense tells us that the answers to these questions would be yes. Moreover, as described in Chapter One, evidence also supports this conclusion.

In seeking to understand how equipping children with assets for education could improve their chances of succeeding along the opportunity pipeline and specifically in postsecondary education, the common sense relationship between resources for college and children's postsecondary outcomes offers some confirmatory utility. At the same time, opportunity costs are real. Public money and policymaker energy expended in the direction of CSAs are not available for other investments in children's life chances. The existence of these trade-offs means that we should not adopt a new policy direction solely because it seems like it should make sense. That conviction is why CSA research and its careful interpretation are so essential.

RIGOROUS EVIDENCE OF CSA EFFECTS

In the earliest days of the CSA field, secondary data analysis was used to make the case for the relationship between children's assets and educational outcomes. Increasingly, however, stronger experimental evidence is available from the SEED for Oklahoma Kids (SEED OK) randomized control trial, conducted by the Center for Social Development at Washington University. The SEED OK experimental sample was drawn randomly from birth records provided by the Oklahoma State Department of Health for all infants born during certain periods in 2007.[2] As the first randomized control trial testing the principles of universal CSA access and automatic account opening in the United States, SEED OK is of particular importance in establishing the effects of CSAs. As the children in SEED OK pass through stages along the opportunity pipeline, we gain new insights and inform new lines of inquiry, including other relationships to explore with secondary data analysis and other questions to ask of CSAs that use different models with different populations.

The Case for CSAs across the Opportunity Pipeline

GETTING A GOOD START: CSAS IN EARLY CHILDHOOD

Social and Emotional Development

Research has demonstrated that social and emotional competency is the foundation of intellectual development, essential for progress in school. Children who are socially and emotionally developed are better able to "manage their emotions, calm themselves when angry, establish positive relationships, make responsible and safe decisions, and handle challenging situations constructively and ethically."[3] They are better able to avoid negative consequences in school and to exhibit the self-regulatory behaviors that predict academic and career performance.[4] Crucially, then, social and emotional development is not just about ensuring that children are "well-behaved" or have "social skills." It is essential for the mastery of cognitive tasks.[5,6] Learning, especially early on, requires social interaction. Children who begin school with abilities to express themselves, manage their feelings, and have healthy exchanges with adults and peers will be able to take better advantage of educational opportunities presented to them.[7–11]

Early measures of social and emotional development are predictive of academic achievement in the primary grades,[12,13] an outcome that then determines later success. Rigorous experimental studies conducted by education researchers have clarified the direction of this relationship.[14] Durlak and colleagues conducted a meta-analysis of 213 school-based, universal social and emotional learning (SEL) programs involving 270,034 students.[14] They used an experimental randomized design to compare SEL participants to students who did not receive these interventions on a number of measures of social and emotional competency. The results revealed that SEL participants demonstrated significantly improved social and emotional skills, attitudes, and behavior when compared to the control students. Moreover, the SEL participants showed an 11 percentile point gain in academic achievement, which was positively correlated with their future college enrollment. Although schools increasingly recognize the centrality of social-emotional development to children's chances,[15] much of children's social and emotional well-being is determined by family and environmental influences.[16–18] This is where CSAs may come in. The relationship between social-emotional health and academic achievement may be key to understanding how and why CSAs can make a difference in educational outcomes.

Social and emotional measures were an early focus of SEED OK research. SEED OK tested the effects of CSAs on children's social and emotional skills directly and found that infants who were randomly assigned to receive the SEED OK account at birth demonstrated significantly higher social-emotional skills at age four than their counterparts who did not receive the CSA.[19] These findings align with other literature that shows that effects of parental investment on children's well-being are detectable around age five.[20] The SEED OK effects were strongest among families with household incomes less than 200% of the federal poverty line and, importantly, not confined only to those children whose parents were saving their own money for their children's education.[19] This research underscores the value of CSAs as an equalizing force on children's early development.

SEED OK's findings regarding CSAs' effects on children's early social and emotional competency propelled examination of dynamics that may explain them. Within the randomized control trial, researchers examined CSAs' effects on predictors of children's well-being and found relationships that are likely multidirectional and overlapping and, crucially, often pass through parents. For example, one predictor of children's social and emotional health is maternal depression.[21] Often exacerbated by the material deprivation of poverty, maternal depression can interfere with relationships between caregivers and children in ways that threaten children's immediate well-being and long-term development.[22-24] Findings from SEED OK have indicated that mothers whose children have a CSA report lower levels of depressive symptoms than mothers whose children do not have a CSA.[25] This may be one way that CSAs improve the conditions that influence children's outcomes. In addition to directly affecting maternal/child interactions, reducing maternal depression may have indirect effects on child well-being, even facilitating actions that change parental occupation or reduce family stress.[26-29]

SEED OK findings have also revealed that ownership of a CSA mitigates about 50% of the negative association between material hardship and children's social and emotional development.[30] This is particularly notable since the funds in the SEED OK account are not accessible to the family while the child is young. Researchers believe that these developmental benefits are transmitted through influences on parenting practices and parental expectations. This again suggests that the transformations CSAs catalyze in families may affect children in complex and far-reaching ways.[30]

Notably, a recent study found that the SEED OK CSA reduced the disparity in social and emotional development between children of unmarried mothers and their peers with married mothers by almost 90%.[31] While it may seem surprising that owning a relatively small amount of children's assets could make such a substantial difference in child well-being, these SEED OK findings align with other research that has underscored the value of intervening with parents to improve children's outcomes. Conger and colleagues explain how parental psychological well-being and parenting practices mediate the association between family structure and child development.[32] Other research has found that the effects of single motherhood on children's social and emotional development may matter more than its impacts on children's economic outcomes.[33] Taken together, SEED OK's rigorous examination of the effects of early educational assets on children's development paints a compelling picture. Even though CSAs cannot change the underlying conditions that challenge children and families, including poverty and family instability, they may interrupt the processes by which these factors affect how well-positioned children are to move successfully through the opportunity pipeline, particularly as they reach school age.

How CSAs Improve Early Environments: Parental Expectations

Survey research suggests that nearly all parents aspire to see their children attain college degrees.[34] However, these hopes may not be sufficient to influence outcomes. We hope a lot of things: that we will achieve financial security, get along with our relatives, or even lose 10 pounds, although we may have little reason to believe that these things will occur. For these wishes to translate into action that makes their realization more likely, they have to become expectations—not just what we hope but what we really plan for. We suspect that this process underlies much of CSAs' potency in the lives of children and families. While *wanting* the best for our children is a universal experience, having assets helps parents to truly *expect* the best. And, particularly when children are young and largely dependent on their parents' construction of reality, this evolution from what others have termed "vague hopes" to "active aspirations" may make all the difference.[35]

Asset researchers have consistently found that having assets can enhance what parents and their children expect for their futures. Zhan and Sherraden used the National Longitudinal Survey of Youth to establish a temporal order between assets, educational expectations, and children's later college graduation.[36] This early study helped to affirm the theoretical foundation of asset-based social welfare, specifically that assets work differently than income to influence perceptions, motivation, and behavior.[37] Using experimental data from SEED OK, Kim, Sherraden, Huang, and Clancy directly examined the impact of CSAs on the durability of parents' educational expectations from birth to age four.[38] They found that parents whose children received the CSA have higher expectations for their children's future educations and that their expectations are more likely to remain constant or increase, compared to parents whose children did not receive the CSA. In a follow-up study, Kim, Huang, Sherraden, and Clancy examined one of the possible pathways through which SEED OK affects parental expectations.[38] Specifically, they investigated whether opening a parent-owned OK 529 college savings plan account in order to "save alongside" the SEED OK account mediates the relationship between the SEED OK treatment and parental expectations. Findings from this study indicate that (a) the SEED OK treatment has a positive and significant causal effect on parental expectations and (b) parents who open their own 529 college savings plan account have higher expectations than those who do not. Further, the SEED OK treatment increases caregivers' likelihood of opening an account to save for their child's education. In tracing CSAs' effects on parental expectations to their encouragement of early educational account ownership, this research provides further evidence for the importance of institutions in shaping how families see their futures. Additionally, evidence of positive effects early in a child's life may be particularly significant, since the educational expectations of many disadvantaged parents tend to erode as they confront obstacles to their children's success.[39] Intervening before these corrosive forces can undermine a family's intentions for their children's expectation may, then, be particularly valuable.

Educational expectations may be an especially important target for equalizing children's outcomes. Specifically, while research suggests that most parents expect their child to complete a four-year degree, when the data are disaggregated, just 63% of parents with income less than $35,000 said their children were very likely to attend college, compared with 81% for parents with at least $100,000 in income.[40] Independent of household income, parental education level is a significant predictor of expectations for children's education.[41] Significantly, low expectations can be transmitted from parent to child.[42,43] Representing more than just a diffuse hope for the future, then, what parents expect for their children may influence interactions that later affect achievement. Hess, Holloway, Dickson, and Price found that a mother's expectations of her preschool child are positively linked to the child's proficiency in sixth-grade math and vocabulary.[44] Research has linked parents' educational expectations with children's academic achievement and later college enrollment.[45–49] This also means that lower expectations may translate into a reduced chance of low-income children completing college.[50] As is the case with many dynamics influencing children's outcomes, these effects are likely realized through multiple channels, including parental engagement and investment in children's schooling.[43,51]

Apart from social and emotional development and parental expectations, other research suggests that factors such as parental education and occupation, neighborhood poverty, high-quality early education, and quality of home environment are predictors of children's social and emotional well-being.[52,53] By influencing parental expectations, having a CSA may mitigate the effect of these household and neighborhood variables as well. For example, greater expectations of college enrollment may spur parents to act strategically in charting their children's educational path, perhaps taking actions that actually increase children's chance of academic success, such as seeking out better-quality early education or even finding a way to move to a neighborhood with better-performing schools.[54-58]

ACADEMIC ACHIEVEMENT DURING THE SCHOOL YEARS

It can be hard to maintain political momentum for CSA programs—and hard to sustain needed financial support—since it takes so long to ultimately demonstrate CSAs' effectiveness. Most CSAs start by the time children are in kindergarten. The years between that point and the time that children begin to enroll in and complete college (what asset champions promise) can seem like, well, a lifetime, particularly for the policymakers, philanthropists, and school officials who have staked resources and reputations on CSA outcomes. Therefore, identifying interim metrics that can be used as a starting point for assessing CSAs' delivery on their long-term promises is important for the field and for the children whose futures are still unfolding. In the following section we discuss some potential interim CSA metrics for which there is growing evidence.[59]

Effects on Children's Educational Expectations

Parents' expectations are powerful forces on children's achievement, but they are not the only expectations that matter. Additionally, education research consistently shows that children's own college expectations lead to increased academic efforts and achievement.[60-65] Research on children's identity development and academic achievement has used children's educational expectations as proxies for possible selves, the development of which influences current behavior.[65] In other words, what children expect for their futures may influence what they do, even when those futures still seem far away.

While SEED OK has directly examined CSAs' effects on parental expectations and confirmed earlier asset research, to date, only research using secondary data has tried to determine how assets might affect children's own expectations.[36] This makes it difficult to disentangle what is undeniably a complex relationship. Absent data from a randomized control trial, how can we know whether children have savings accounts for college because they expect to go, expect to go because that savings account serves as an important cue about their future college attendance, or some measure of both? To explore how assets might affect children's educational expectations, Elliott, Choi, Destin, and Kim conducted a simultaneous test of whether children's savings predict college expectations or vice versa.[66] They found that children's educational savings have a slightly stronger relationship with children's expectations than children's expectations have with savings. This could reflect parents' greater willingness to invest in the college savings of children whose own high expectations signal likely continued educational attainment.[67-69] According to Elliott and Friedline, "positive student expectations may provide parents with much needed confidence that the student will graduate."[67]

Qualitative research in CSA programs provides some evidence that receiving an account dedicated for college contributes to children's expectations. Even when CSAs do not "plant" the idea of expecting to go to college, cultivation of the college-saver identities discussed in chapter 4 may make that expectation seem more attainable and, thus, more actionable. Second-grade Joey[a] has a CSA through Promise Indiana but might not otherwise be expected to have strong college expectations. He lives in a single-parent household earning less than $30,000 per year, and his mom did not go to college. Joey, however, has picked out which college he plans to attend and expresses confidence that he will get there, "because I'm working hard in saving up a lot of money" and his mom is contributing too. He emphasizes, "We're saving up money for my college funds." In New Mexico, Amalia's kindergartner has a Prosperity Kids account. She claims that she had not talked with her son about college before opening the CSA but that, now, she "always" does, explaining to him, "Son, we are saving because it's for your school, your studies later on. Now you may be little but years go by really fast."

Reading and Math Achievement

It is important to point out that we believe the strongest evidence to date of CSAs' potential to improve children's college outcomes is in their ability to positively affect children's social and emotional development and parents' and children's educational expectations. Affecting how children and parents see their futures can change interactions within families and between families and educational institutions, in ways that may transform children's progress through the opportunity pipeline. As a potential example of these tangible effects, there is some evidence to suggest that CSAs may be able to improve children's math and reading scores during the school years, effects that would also position children for improved higher education outcomes. In many school systems today, students' satisfactory progress along the opportunity pipeline toward high school graduation and college readiness is operationalized by their scores in reading and math.

The relationship between reading proficiency and overall academic achievement is documented in education research and ensconced in state and federal policy.[70,71] Children who cannot read well cannot use reading as a tool to engage with school, do their homework, or study for exams.[72] These deficiencies can compromise later educational attainment. In a longitudinal study of nearly 4,000 students, Hernandez found that students who do not read proficiently by third grade are four times more likely than proficient readers to leave high school without graduating.[73] The odds are even worse for the least proficient readers. Children who have not mastered even the basic skills by third grade are nearly six times less likely to graduate high school than proficient readers.[73] The effects of reading on educational attainment are particularly strong for low-income and minority students. Looking further down the opportunity pipeline, research indicates that third-grade reading is a positive predictor of college attendance.[70] While the research supporting standardized math scores as predictors of college completion is not as extensive as for reading, triangulating across national data sets, Lee demonstrates the effects of early math performance on eighth-grade math achievement and on the likelihood of entering and completing two- and four-year colleges.[74] As school systems increasingly emphasize science and technology within their curricula, the importance of early math scores for later success may grow.

In recent years, school districts have put increasing weight on standardized achievement measures, and these trends inflate the influence of these measures on children's lives. Schools that use such assessments to make decisions about academic tracking, in particular, may send children powerful messages about their academic potential. In the educational landscape, where so much is sequential and getting behind early can derail later achievement, students steered away from college-bound curriculum may struggle to catch up later.[75–79] In this way, children's math and reading scores may not only reflect authentic likelihood of future academic success[80] but also signal to teachers a given child's academic potential. These dynamics may affect interactions between teachers and students in ways that independently affect achievement.[81–84] Parents, too, use their children's academic achievement to figure out potential career paths and begin to make college plans.[85]

Until recently, the only evidence linking assets with math and reading achievement came from secondary data analysis. Relatively few children with CSAs have had the accounts long enough to expect that they would produce any effects on academic achievement. Indeed, few of these children have even reached a grade level where these assessments are administered. Scholars have sought to compensate for this limitation in two principal ways. On the one hand, CSA research, particularly in SEED OK, has connected children's assets to predictors of achievement documented in education research. On the other hand, analysis of secondary datasets has linked assets to math and reading scores, although, as described earlier, these findings cannot control for potentially confounding factors, nor evaluate CSA interventions, specifically.

On the first front, school readiness indicators, including cognitive capabilities and self-regulation, are strongly associated with academic achievement.[86] Some research suggests that children's orientation to learning may help to explain achievement as they progress through school.[87] CSAs can affect children's social and emotional development by influencing parenting practices.[88–90] The effects of stronger social and emotional competency can continue to shape children's trajectories once they start school. Thinking again in terms of common sense, students who today display the social and emotional competencies that education research has linked to later academic achievement can be expected to demonstrate commensurate outcomes when they take assessments in the future. CSAs' effects on children's achievement may be further reinforced by the use of benchmark incentives to explicitly encourage behaviors associated with reading and math performance. For example, some CSA programs make additional deposits into children's accounts to encourage such actions as regular school attendance and participation in summer learning loss prevention programs.

Analysis of secondary data provides some evidence of asset effects on children's math and reading scores. By framing children's asset building as essential to schools' missions and illuminating CSAs' potential to close achievement gaps, these findings have played a role in catalyzing educators' interest in CSAs. In one study, Elliott examined the association between children's savings and the math scores of children ages 12 to 18.[91] Here, children with savings designated for school had significantly higher math scores than their peers who lacked savings dedicated for postsecondary education. The analysis further suggested that this relationship can be partly explained by the effects of children's savings on children's college expectations, which encourage behavior that may be associated with greater achievement. This study helped establish that savings designated for school may be associated with improved math scores even when comparing children with similar incomes. Huang, Guo, Kim, and Sherraden later found that early liquid assets increase college going by improving children's achievement in school.[92]

Several other studies seem to confirm the positive association between children's assets and academic achievement. Elliott, Jung, and Friedline examined how children's ownership of any type of savings correlates with higher math scores.[93] Findings revealed that savings set aside for a child are positively related to higher achievement for all children but a stronger predictor of better math scores for children in wealthier families than for those less advantaged. To further examine how different types of assets affect achievement, the same authors also examined the effect of children's savings designated specifically for college on math scores.[93] Here, they found that college savings are associated with higher math scores and, further, that this effect does not vary according to overall family wealth, as does the relationship between general savings and children's math scores. These findings suggest that assets designated for college have a stronger and more equalizing effect on achievement than undesignated assets.

Research has also examined how the effects of children's assets may vary by race. Elliott, Kim, Jung, and Zhan examined separately the relationship of savings with Black and White children's math and readings scores.[94] Children's savings designated for school were significantly related to White children's math scores but not their reading scores. Conversely, savings were directly related to Black children's reading scores but not their math scores. Clearly, more research is needed, as CSA evidence cannot yet definitively answer important questions, including how long children have to have a CSA before one sees effects, whether these effects occur at different developmental stages, how other factors may alter assets' effects on achievement, or which CSA features make a difference in terms of effects on academic achievement.

Further, while research on potential interim metrics underlines CSAs' equalizing potential, findings that academic outcomes associated with children's savings may vary by race highlight racial inequities in the education system and the ways that this inequality affects children at different points. In turn, this analysis underscores an important reality: while explicitly countering wealth inequality is key to constructing an equitable opportunity pipeline, no single intervention can completely close the gaps plaguing disadvantaged students today.

Support for the CSA Intervention, from the CSA Field

Early research from Promise Indiana, a CSA intervention begun in Wabash County, Indiana, reveals some promising results when it comes to the effects of CSAs on children's math and reading scores. In this study, Elliott and colleagues used regression analysis to separately analyze achievement for the full sample of children and those eligible for free or reduced-price lunch.[95] While the full sample displayed some differences between students without a CSA/not contributing to the account and those saving in Promise Indiana, effects were stronger for the subsample of students eligible for free or reduced-price lunch. For this group, having a CSA had a positive, statistically significant relationship with both reading and math scores, accounting for nearly 29% of the variance in reading and 23% of the variance in math scores. Considering only those students who have a CSA allowed researchers to further examine the effect of the amount saved on achievement, in order to examine how differences in the extent or ways families engage with the CSA may affect the strength of the assets' effects. Here, regression analysis revealed that, for every additional $100 contributed, reading scores increased by 2.08 units and math scores by 2.02 units.[95]

Elliott and colleagues' findings align with research using secondary data to consider assets' effects on achievement: (a) assets dedicated to education may exert effects on children's achievement, (b) educational assets may have a stronger association with the achievement of disadvantaged students than of students as a whole, and (c) there may be some value in account ownership even apart from asset accumulation.[95] Findings from Promise Indiana are preliminary, however, and should be interpreted with some caution. Forthcoming analysis with new waves of data will allow for more rigorous tests of the relationship between Promise Indiana CSAs and children's achievement at different points during their school years.

Besides Promise Indiana, research is also underway in other CSA programs around the country, including New Mexico (Prosperity Kids), San Francisco (Kindergarten-to-College), and Maine (Harold Alfond College Challenge). These studies will help fill a gap in existing scholarship by specifically analyzing CSAs' effects on math and reading achievement with rigorous designs and considering not only the effect of having the CSA, but also any differential effect from different CSA models and different levels of engagement with the account. While earlier studies of assets' effects on math and reading employed secondary datasets and a proxy (i.e., children who have savings reserved for education) for CSA ownership, the newest research will directly test expected relationships between ownership of a CSA, asset accumulation, and academic achievement using more advanced methods such as propensity score matching or regression-discontinuity designs. Additionally, these investigations of operational CSAs will benefit from data collected in the current, somewhat constrained, opportunity context, in contrast to earlier studies that relied on data collected prior to the Great Recession, a period which marked a turning point in US attention to wealth inequality, stagnant economic mobility, college unaffordability, and student debt.[96] This context matters. American children need asset-based financial aid powerful enough to support their successful passage through the opportunity pipeline they will actually confront.

THE COLLEGE YEARS: COMBATING WILT AND ENCOURAGING PERSISTENCE

CSAs are understood primarily as interventions to increase postsecondary educational attainment, particularly among students underrepresented in higher education today. To test this aim, correlational research has considered whether assets improve college outcomes, for whom, and how. To date, evidence suggests that assets do facilitate postsecondary enrollment and completion. Some of these effects are catalyzed early, as assets encourage students and families to prepare early for educational success, engage in school in ways associated with increased achievement, and sustain expectations of college. However, there is evidence from secondary data that assets may also help to determine outcomes at the point of enrollment. This is an important part of educational asset research, particularly since this is the most crowded point in the opportunity pipeline, where most financial aid interventions kick in.

Students who expect to attend college are more likely to actually make it to postsecondary education when they have savings designated for their studies.[97] One way that children's assets appear to increase educational attainment is by bridging the distance between high school and postsecondary education for those students who have the desire and ability to continue but often fail to make the transition.[98] This derailing of college hopes—which Willie has termed "wilt"[98] and others call "melt"[99]—is particularly common among students of color and those with low incomes. Reducing these "no-shows" is a frustratingly elusive aim for many postsecondary institutions.[100] CSAs counter wilt through the cultivation of college-saver identities, which help students to overcome inevitable difficulties in their path.[101] College-saver identities transform vague hopes for postsecondary education into concrete plans. In this way, some research even suggests that assets may matter more than income for encouraging college completion.[36]

Small amounts of educational assets can have large impacts on postsecondary enrollment and graduation rates, especially among students from low- and moderate-income (LMI) households. In one study, Elliott used propensity score weighting to examine the relationship between educational assets and subsequent outcomes observed in the Panel Study of Income Dynamics.[102] He found that a child with less than $500 in assets designated for school is three times more likely to enroll in college and two and a half times more likely to complete postsecondary education than a child without such savings.[102] These effects are even somewhat larger for LMI students, again illustrating the equalizing power of children's assets. Elliott, Song, and Nam found that LMI students with education savings were three times more likely to graduate from college than LMI students without education savings.[97] Similarly, Elliott, Constance-Huggins, and Song found that LMI students with school-designated savings were two times more likely to be "on track"[103]—having either already graduated or still attending college—than those without such savings. Notably, these asset effects were not statistically significant for high-income students. This research emphasizes CSAs as a valuable intervention for sustaining disadvantaged students' effort toward postsecondary completion. This outcome, in turn, may be crucial to closing the attainment gap, which today stems even more from differences in completion than enrollment.[104,105]

Increasing disadvantaged students' college completion is the driving motivation of many CSA champions today. Because CSAs begin at birth or early in a child's school years, it will be a long time before research can directly examine their effects on underrepresented students' college graduation rates. While we wait for these investments to reach the point where effects on completion can be analyzed, however, analysis of the literature examining college persistence may provide early indication of mechanisms through which assets may help students sustain their effort toward graduation.

Assets can help students graduate both directly—by providing resources and reducing the strain of unmet financial need[106]—and also indirectly, by strengthening students' positioning for successful college completion. Children's assets can help to foster many of the attributes and accomplishments associated with degree persistence. These include high school preparation and achievement,[107-110] completion of college-preparatory curriculum,[111-113] early college planning,[114] strong college expectations,[115] and immersion in a context that provides encouragement of college going.[116]

For many students, getting through college is even more daunting than getting to college.[117] And while we fully acknowledge that studies using secondary data have limitations, the good news is that, in line with our common sense beliefs about what it takes for prospective students to become degree-holders, there is empirical evidence to suggest that assets equip students with more than just money. All along the opportunity pipeline, they also confer educational advantage.

POST-COLLEGE: COLLEGE IS JUST THE BEGINNING—FINANCIAL HEALTH AND CSAS

CSAs diverge from other forms of financial aid in many ways. Where student loans and even most grants and scholarships aim at the narrow window surrounding enrollment, CSAs begin working early—often from birth—to improve outcomes. Where loans and grants are designed to be used to the point of exhaustion, CSAs are long-term assets that provide a platform for future economic mobility. And where most other financial aid is seen as a tuition consumption subsidy, CSAs are financial instruments that connect young people to institutions that can facilitate lifelong prosperity. These differences make CSAs unique not only because they improve a child's preparation for postsecondary education while helping to finance it. They are also particularly capable of strengthening return on degree, catalyzing healthy balance sheets, and facilitating ownership of a diversified asset base.

In a nation of insufficient savers where financial well-being increasingly hinges on ownership, CSAs may be instrumental in creating positive savings behaviors among American youths.[118] Studies have found that saving as a child or adolescent can predict saving as an adult.[119,120] In recognition of the importance of cultivating saving and initiating wealth building early in a child's life, schools, community-based organizations, and even state treasurers have sought to increase the financial knowledge and improve the financial habits of young people by incorporating financial instruction into math and life-skills courses, offering standalone financial counseling, and creating online financial education portals. Unfortunately, outcomes from this instruction have been mixed at best.[121,122]

However, equipping children with an actual account and tangible assets may increase their motivation to learn financial concepts and overcome the psychological and cultural distance that otherwise separate disadvantaged youth from financial systems.[123] Additionally, there is evidence of a direct, positive relationship between the future orientation CSAs can help to cultivate and young adult savings.[124,125] When young people are primed to look to their futures, they may be more likely to prepare for them financially. While all young people could arguably benefit from stronger preparation for financially healthy adulthood, some research suggests that the effect of youth savings on subsequent saving as an adult may be greatest for low-income youth and even greater for those involved in CSA structures rather than saving in unrestricted accounts.[120]

CSAs are also noteworthy because they can serve as gateways to diversified asset portfolios. The research of Terri Friedline and her colleagues has found that youth who have education savings are more likely to hold assets in other vehicles such as stocks, retirement accounts, and real estate as adults.[126,127] Compared to traditional savings accounts, these investments carry some risk but also the opportunity for greater returns. In an economy like ours, where institutions influence outcomes, addressing wealth inequality requires more than just shaping individual behavior. It hinges on equitable participation in capital-generating systems. This is another way that CSAs help to equalize children's life chances, by connecting them early to the same institutions that strategic actors use to accumulate wealth and wield power. CSA research suggests that helping families understand, navigate, and be rewarded for owning stakes in their children's futures makes a difference for those who would otherwise be excluded.

Conclusion

Yes, there are still some questions about CSA design and operation, including the best account vehicle through which to deliver CSAs, the precise calibration of seed deposits and other incentives, and the ideal complements in financial education and college-saver identity support. There will be important opportunities to ask and hopefully answer many of these questions in the coming years as children with CSAs move through the opportunity pipeline. Scholars can then examine how these children fare compared to those without such an institution on which to rely. Even today, however, CSAs stand on a comparatively strong base of evidence that aligns with our common sense assessment that assets matter for determining how well children do. They have demonstrated potential to improve outcomes in all the domains of the opportunity pipeline where, today, many children find their dreams diverted or their progress stunted.

Having assets from birth can cultivate a sense of institutional efficacy that complements individual efforts. With an image of their possible future college-graduate selves firmly in mind, students may engage differently with educational institutions, setting up a virtuous cycle where outcome expectancies align with a norm of college-going. When they reach postsecondary education and confront high costs and insufficient, complex, and inequitable financial aid, students with assets can approach institutions from a stance of empowerment and secure better outcomes on their way to a diploma. And CSAs can help students complete higher education equipped to benefit equitably from the wealth-building engines of the American economy. These effects compound as children progress through the opportunity pipeline. They culminate in what looks like the best chance for American children to have equitable life chances. Social science has tested—on many fronts, in many studies, by many scholars—whether early assets designated for education truly hold great promise to help children do well, fairly. As we review the mounting evidence, we conclude: the answer is yes. There is no substitute, after all, for money in the "bank" (or other wealth-building instrument)—and asset approaches are the only financial aid vehicles capable of delivering that.

Note

a. All names are pseudonyms assigned in the data coding process.

6 Toward an Equitable Opportunity Pipeline
THE CREATION OF A UNIQUELY AMERICAN PROPOSAL FOR THE 21ST CENTURY

THE PROMISING EFFECTS of relatively small-dollar Children's Savings Accounts (CSAs) have catalyzed tremendous energy for universal provision of early asset accounts.[1] Within the CSA field and among many close observers, there is consensus that CSA policy should start with an account for every child in the United States. As described in chapter 4, however, the promise of small-dollar CSAs is a bit of a double-edged sword. For some, the policy objective has become the account itself. Some proponents of this view believe that Children's Savings Accounts are like infrastructure, a sort of social utility that has to be put in place—like plumbing—so that the benefits that these structures confer can then "flow." Others may be eager for what seems like an easier win and consoled by the prospect of getting "something"—like the college-saver identities that early assets can cultivate—for nearly "nothing."

However, because this policy conceptualization fails to fully account for the problem of wealth inequality and its devastating effects on equitable educational attainment and upward mobility, such CSAs will likely fall short of the potentially transformative impact of children's asset ownership. In this chapter, we discuss our understanding of CSA policy evolution in order to present a case for how CSAs can go beyond mere "plumbing" to truly revolutionize higher education finance. In accordance with Kingdon's theory of how agendas advance,[2] we then outline a policy suited to the problem to which our political system must respond: fractures in the opportunity pipeline that derail children's futures and threaten the American dream. Instead of starting with what might be the easiest immediate win, we frame a vision of the powerful institutional tool children need: Opportunity Investment Accounts (OIAs), an essential investment in an American opportunity pipeline.

Our emphasis on OIAs as conduits for meaningful wealth transfer rather than empty pipes does not mean that there are no benefits to small-dollar children's savings. As described in chapter 5, a growing body of evidence attests to the intrinsic value of dedicated educational assets, early in a child's life, even when small in amount. Nor does our insistence that "plumbing" cannot be the end to which children's asset-building policy aims mean that there is not a need for pipes to be laid. Without an account infrastructure capable of delivering meaningful assets to every child, an asset-based intervention becomes difficult to design and even harder to implement. However, crucially, if the goal is to eliminate or even substantially reduce wealth inequality in America, accounts alone will not be sufficient. Further, we contend that Americans' hunger for solutions to wealth inequality's effects on mobility and opportunity means that proposing CSA policy insufficient to tackle wealth inequality will be unlikely to inspire much passion. Devoid of an inequality-fighting context, CSAs may be seen as a nice program but far from a policy imperative. Even more unconscionably, given imbalances in participation and wealth accumulation within current asset-building structures, providing another vehicle through which those best-positioned to build wealth can do so, without attending to inclusion and equity, may further entrench wealth inequality.

The Current State of US CSA Policy

As described in chapter 5, what CSAs have to offer to American children—particularly those disadvantaged by race and/or class—is the uniquely potent combination of wealth transfers and college-saver identity effects. Enacting policy to deliver this powerful institutional support will require careful strategizing and skillful communication, but it starts with articulating a bold call. For advocates and the policymaker champions they hope to rally, that begins with summoning courage. Our own thinking about where CSA policy sits today includes reckoning with the extent to which fear paralyzes the pursuit of dramatic changes. While fear of losing hard-fought gains is pervasive in the current political climate, for advocates of children's asset building, fear is rooted in more than aversion to potential loss. It also stems from memories of disappointing setbacks when legislative success seemed tantalizingly within reach. In 2007, in talking to the Congressional

Black Caucus, then-Senator and Democratic presidential candidate Hillary Clinton said, "I like the idea of giving every baby born in America a $5,000 account that will grow over time."[3] Clinton's statement was almost immediately attacked by the Republican National Committee, who called it a "budget busting baby fund," and by conservative groups who piled on criticism. Shortly after, Senator Clinton backed away from the idea of even small-dollar accounts for all children.[3-5]

This rebuke became a defining moment for the CSA field. Undoubtedly engrained into the minds of many leaders, it is often cited in private conversations to argue that proposing anything grander than small-dollar accounts would be irrational and maybe even irresponsible. This fear has only deepened as CSAs have multiplied around the country but children's savings proposals have found little traction in gridlocked Congress.

FEDERAL CSA PROPOSALS

A review of children's savings legislation in the recent Congress underscores the paucity and inadequacy of current proposals. CSAs have not received the congressional attention that might be expected given the proliferation of initiatives around the country. Additionally, the few proposals that have garnered some momentum often bear little resemblance to CSAs as we understand them. Instead, much of what passes for "children's savings policy" would do little to level the financial or educational playing fields. Some proposals would likely even increase inequality by further facilitating the educational investments of already-privileged families while providing few resources to help disadvantaged households keep up. Table 6.1 provides an overview of congressional policy proposals related to children's savings.[a]

As Table 6.1 illustrates, few congressional proposals would even deliver small-dollar accounts to every child in the nation. Few reflect bipartisan commitment to equitable asset ownership opportunities. And very few provide the progressive benefits needed to overcome wealthy households' built-in advantages in current wealth-building systems.

Current Legislation Ignores the Basic Tenets of CSA Theory

Current congressional children's savings legislation does not adhere to the vision of CSAs as universal, automatic, progressive, long-term asset-building instruments.[6] Far from leveraging the regulatory and fiscal power of the federal government to expand upon the promise of children's assets, most proposals fall short of the best models currently operating at the state and local levels, which generally include at

TABLE 6.1

Children's Savings Legislation in the 114th Congress

Bill #	Title	Bipartisan	Universal	Automatic	Progressive	Long-Term	Seeded	Matched	Pro-Savings[a]	Status
S101	A bill to amend the Internal Revenue Code of 1986 to expand the Coverdell education savings accounts to allow home school education expenses, and for other purposes	NO	NO	NO	NO	NO	NO	NO	NO	Introduced
S195	401(Kids) Education Savings Account Act of 2015	NO	NO	NO	NO	NO	NO	NO	NO	Introduced
S243	ACE Act	NO	NO	NO	NO	NO	NO	NO	NO	Introduced
S306	Enhancing Educational Opportunities for all Students Act	NO	NO	NO	NO	NO	NO	NO	NO	Introduced

Bill	Description								Status
S1973	A bill to amend the Internal Revenue Code of 1986 to expand the deduction for interest on education loans, to extend and expand the deduction for qualified tuition and related expenses, and eliminate the limitation on contributions to Coverdell education savings accounts	NO	NO	NO	NO	NO	NO	NO	Introduced
S2471	401(Kids) Education Savings Account Modernization Act of 2016	NO	NO	NO	NO	NO	NO	NO	Introduced
S335	A bill to amend the Internal Revenue Code of 1986 to improve 529 plans	YES	NO	NO	NO	NO	NO	NO	Became law
S473	SONG Act	NO	NO	NO	NO	NO	NO	YES	Introduced
S687	American Dream Accounts Act	YES	NO	YES	YES	YES	NO	YES	Introduced
S2455	Educational Freedom Accounts Act	NO	NO	NO	NO	NO	NO	NO	Introduced

(continued)

TABLE 6.1 Continued

Bill #	Title	Bipartisan	Universal	Automatic	Progressive	Long-Term	Seeded	Matched	Pro-Savings[a]	Status
S2703	ABLE Financial Planning Act	YES	NO	NO	NO	NO	NO	NO	NO	Introduced
S2711	Native American Education Opportunity Act	NO	NO	NO	NO	NO	NO	NO	NO	Passed committee
S2869	Boost Saving for College Act	YES	NO	NO	NO	NO	NO	NO	NO	Introduced
S3083	Housing Opportunity Through Modernization Act of 2016	YES	NO	NO	NO	NO	NO	NO	YES	Became law
S3091	EMPOWER Act of 2016	YES	NO	NO	NO	NO	NO	NO	YES	Introduced
HR553	To amend the Internal Revenue Code of 1986 to encourage the use of 529 plans and Coverdell education savings accounts, and for other purposes	NO	NO	NO	NO	NO	NO	NO	NO	Introduced
HR554	Enhancing Educational Opportunities for all Students Act	NO	NO	NO	NO	NO	NO	NO	NO	Introduced

Bill	Name								Status
HR701	Helping Families Save for Education Act	YES	NO	NO	NO	NO	NO	NO	Introduced
HR1928	Empowering Parents to Invest in Choice Act of 2015	NO	NO	NO	NO	NO	NO	NO	Introduced
HR529	To amend the Internal Revenue Code of 1986 to improve 529 plans	YES	NO	NO	NO	NO	NO	NO	Passed House
HR1125	Start Saving Sooner Act of 2015	YES	NO	NO	NO	YES	NO	YES	Introduced
HR1359	American Dream Accounts Act	NO	NO	YES	YES	YES	NO	YES	Introduced
HR1377	RAYS Act	YES	NO	NO	NO	YES	NO	YES	Introduced
HR2029	Consolidated Appropriations Act, 2016	NO	NO	NO	NO	NO	NO	NO	Became law
HR2681	Training Highly Skilled Americans Act of 2015	YES	NO	YES	YES	YES	YES	NO	Introduced
HR3170	Student Debt Repayment Fairness Act	NO	NO	NO	NO	NO	NO	NO	Introduced
HR3700	Housing Opportunity Through Modernization Act of 2016	YES	NO	NO	NO	NO	NO	YES	Became law

(continued)

TABLE 6.1 Continued

Bill #	Title	Bipartisan	Universal	Automatic	Progressive	Long-Term	Seeded	Matched	Pro-Savings[a]	Status
HR4045	USAccounts: Investing in America's Future Act of 2015	NO	YES	YES	YES	YES	YES	YES	YES	Introduced
HR4222	Higher Education Savings Accounts Act of 2015	NO	NO	YES	YES	YES	YES	NO	NO	Introduced
HR4236	Financial Security Credit Act of 2015	NO	NO	NO	YES	YES	NO	YES	NO	Introduced
HR4426	Educational Freedom Accounts Act	NO	NO	NO	NO	NO	NO	NO	NO	Introduced
HR4794	ABLE Financial Planning Act	YES	NO	NO	NO	NO	NO	NO	NO	Introduced
HR4872	Save for Success Act	NO	NO	NO	YES	YES	NO	YES	NO	Introduced
HR5186	Help All Americans Save for College Act of 2016	NO	NO	NO	NO	NO	NO	NO	NO	Introduced
HR5191	Help for Students and Parents Act	YES	NO	NO	NO	NO	NO	NO	NO	Introduced
HR5193	529 and ABLE Account Improvement Act of 2016	NO	NO	NO	NO	NO	NO	NO	NO	Introduced
HR5214	CSA Opportunity Act	YES	NO	NO	NO	NO	NO	NO	YES	Introduced
HR5517	Local Education Freedom Act of 2016	NO	NO	NO	NO	NO	NO	NO	NO	Introduced

[a] Here "pro-savings" refers to provisions that encourage saving and asset accumulation by low-income families, particularly exemption of children's savings from asset limits in means-tested public assistance programs.

least some key CSA features: universal enrollment, seed deposits, progressive savings matches, benchmark incentives, and inclusive outreach approaches.[7]

Instead of incorporating features that could provide meaningful opportunities for equitable life chances for American children, the bulk of current legislation embraces limited or even punitive measures that are not in the best interests of low-income Americans. For instance, 28 of the 38 children's savings bills introduced in Congress maintain asset limits that penalize low-income Americans for saving.[8] In other words, although ensuring that poor families are protected from explicit punishment for trying to build wealth should be considered the "floor" of acceptable children's savings initiatives, less than a third of recent congressional efforts pass this test. While there is little to applaud within these bills, seven do include progressive benefits and one would provide universal accounts.[8] Of particular concern, however, these are not the proposals with bipartisan support or legislative momentum.

Current Legislation Helps the Privileged

Current congressional proposals mostly make it easier and more lucrative for already-privileged Americans to accumulate assets in incentivized accounts, particularly state 529 college savings plans, which are owned in far greater concentration by high-income households.[9] Five bills would ease rollovers in 529s to allow accountholders to shelter savings from taxation and shift them to retirement or other accounts. Ten bills would raise contribution caps for tax-advantaged Coverdell accounts.[8] As described in chapter 2, these policies facilitate tax-advantaged wealth accumulation and are of far greater value to those with higher incomes and tax liabilities. Clearly, while often cloaked in the language of CSAs and, in some cases, even touting research about the benefits of saving for higher education, most of these policies would not only fail to tackle wealth inequality but, perversely, could make it worse.

The Meaning of Compromise in an Environment of Political Warfare

From the CSA field, we see reluctance to push for substantial wealth transfers within children's asset policy as reflective of a long-standing liberal strategy to not ask for too much for fear of being left empty-handed. For liberals, compromise has too often come to mean pursuing incremental policies they think will garner the votes needed for passage rather than looking at policy from the perspective of what people need to be successful. By this accounting, victories are measured in bills passed or elected seats retained, not policy impact. In contrast, for conservatives, compromise has come to be seen as a sign of weakness and an unacceptable concession. For example, John Boehner, who was soon to become the Speaker of the House, said of President Obama's agenda, "We're going to do everything—and I mean everything we can do—to kill it, stop it, slow it down, whatever we can."[10] When one side in a war—political or otherwise—is perennially more willing to compromise than the other, the outcomes will be predictably lopsided. And when "compromise" means adopting policies unlikely to bring about the best results in order to put another check in the "win" column, the American people lose.

The national tendency to talk about our politics in terms of winners and losers hardens the positions of the respective actors, obscures the real issues to which policies should respond, and reduces the likelihood of policymaking in the national interest. Media often further entrench the notion that policy creation is a battle to be won instead of a mechanism through which to pursue a better society and, in this case, to restore the American dream. CSA champions are not immune to the lure of hollow victories. While we understand this impulse, if a desire to win obscures the focus on improving lives through transformative children's assets, the battle for CSAs is lost before it even begins.

We Must Free Our Minds and Hope Once Again

Today, as the United States contends with wealth inequality and its crushing effects on equitable chances of upward mobility, we need policy revolutions that transcend mere reforms.[11] While that prospect may seem daunting, particularly within our context of polarized national politics and entrenched opposing interests, it is certainly not the first such moment in our history. During the space race in the early 1960s, President John F. Kennedy articulated the nation's desire to be the first to walk on the moon, saying, "I believe we possess all the resources and all the talents necessary. But the facts of the matter are that we have never made the national decisions or marshalled the national resources required for such leadership."[12] These same words could be spoken today in reference to our uninspiring reliance on debt-dependent financing of higher education, our failure to build an asset-building system for the economically disadvantaged, or our apparent unwillingness to commit to closing the opportunity gap by creating institutions that equitably facilitate the success of all children.

To advance a vision of children's savings policy up to the challenge of countering wealth inequality and rescuing the American dream, we once again need to imagine the possibilities. Only then will we be able—as a CSA field, yes, but more importantly as a country—to dare to reach for what might seem to be the stars. If we are free to imagine what CSAs can be instead of limited by our preconceptions, $5,000 accounts for each child may seem quite modest in the face of vast wealth inequality and poor children's inability to routinely overcome their from-behind starts. If we consider what is possible instead of what seems immediately attainable, we might discover untapped sources of asset-building potential by unwinding regressive wealth-building subsidies or abandoning financial aid policies with dubious returns. Our history reminds us that ours is a wealthy nation capable of mustering tremendous resources for the objectives we deem priorities. In our past, the United States has invested in wealth-building programs as grand as the Homestead Act or the GI Bill. We have marshalled policymaking apparatuses to redress injustices and open doors of opportunity. We can do so again.

The path to the CSA policies that disadvantaged children so direly need will be difficult, but the American dream is worth the fight. And the United States is at its best when Americans stretch toward what we want, rather than try to convince ourselves that we are content with what we have. As President Kennedy said of the space race, "We choose to go to the moon in this decade and do the other things, not because they are easy, but because they are hard, because that goal will serve to organize and measure the best of our energies and skills, because that challenge is one that we are willing to accept, one we are unwilling to postpone, and one which we intend to win."[12] This exhortation holds lessons for our present challenge. It reminds us that, while securing the national children's asset-building policy we really need will not be easy, articulating a bold policy vision makes it more likely that we reach our distant goal. Reworking the mechanisms in state-supported 529 plans so that they work progressively and powerfully for all children will not happen overnight. Obtaining funding so that wealth flows all along the opportunity pipeline will be harder than just laying the pipes. None of this, however, looks as daunting as flying to the moon must have seemed in 1961.

So while we recognize that there are details to determine and allies to enlist, we suggest that revolutionizing financial aid in pursuit of an equitable opportunity pipeline begins with removing the constraints that limit our vision. We need to reimagine the possibilities when it comes to what Congress can accomplish with CSAs. We need to go beyond small-dollar accounts to make financial aid a true investment in upward mobility. We need to be unafraid to insist on the robust transfers on which poor children's futures depend. We need to dare to ask the right questions about return on degree and whether education as currently financed and delivered is really serving as an equalizer. We need to reevaluate the benefits and trade-offs in different policy options to consider, for example, that CSAs might be better paths to equitable life chances than "free college." We must free our minds so that we can dare to make a better future for our children and so that we can construct systems that will help them to expect this better future for themselves. If we "win," we will have saved the American dream from becoming just a story we tell ourselves about the way things used to be. And even if we do not—at least not now—we will have made valuable strides toward exposing how wealth inequality robs Americans of fair life chances. We will have begun to mobilize an increasingly demoralized populace around early children's assets as a rescue for our imperiled dream. Among the many lessons of our history, surely, is this: there is value in shooting for the moon.

Moving Beyond Children's Savings Accounts toward OIAs

Perhaps unsurprisingly for a field that has grown and diversified as much and as rapidly as that of CSAs, CSAs have a bit of identity confusion. Some literature refers to these interventions as Child Development Accounts, consistent with Michael Sherraden's original terminology.[13] Even among those who consistently use "CSA," variations in program design and operation can lead to very different views of what a CSA even is. Given that most existing CSAs are of the relatively small-dollar variety, we think that our policy proposal, which couples a universal CSA with a substantial wealth transfer, needs a new name. We are referring to this policy as an "Opportunity Investment Account" (OIA) to draw a distinction between local/state CSA programs and federal policy, the latter of which would aim more explicitly to reduce wealth inequality.

The development of small-dollar CSAs at the local and state levels has been critical for developing the CSA evidence base, building momentum around children's asset policies, and learning best practices. These efforts have galvanized stakeholders to collaborate and invest in new ways to pursue better outcomes for children, particularly those currently disadvantaged. Elements of state and local CSA models offer important lessons to inform federal CSA policy. On many fronts, this policy innovation has proven the concepts that undergird children's asset building. The CSA field—and the thousands of children and families whose lives have been changed by this work—owe sincere thanks to these program administrators and policy entrepreneurs. Nonetheless, CSA programs at the state and local levels cannot perform at the same scale as federal policy. Specifically, local and state CSA programs often lack the financial resources to make CSAs more than small-dollar accounts. While their efforts could certainly be layered onto a federal investment, we see key points of distinction between the children's savings policy America needs and the CSA policy that has paved the way for it.

By designating assets for children at birth and linking them to opportunities for higher education, OIAs would mirror CSAs' effects on children's college-saver identities. However, unlike current CSA initiatives, OIAs would harness the fiscal capacity of the federal government to equip all American children with assets from which to finance postsecondary education and launch into adulthood. In this way, OIAs could set a generation on a path to broadly shared prosperity, narrow the wealth gap, and disrupt cycles of disadvantage—feats that small-dollar CSAs cannot accomplish on their own.

An aim as urgent as salvaging the resonance of the American dream makes constructing OIA policy worthwhile even if doing so required a huge increase in public investment or a major break with popular opinion. Not to discount the spectacle of the race to the moon, there is arguably no more noble purpose to which to direct American policy ingenuity than to uphold the American value that how well one does should depend on how hard one works, not where one starts. However, crucially, the groundwork is already in place to implement national OIA policy. The United States already spends billions on financial aid that fails to facilitate equitable educational outcomes or create wealth. Repurposing those dollars frees resources for OIAs. The evidence base that would inform OIA policy, while certainly with limitations, is stronger than that which undergirds many existing investments. Scaling OIAs is technically feasible, as well, in large part thanks to the work of CSA programs whose innovations have demonstrated viable approaches and identified needed infrastructure. And there are political reasons to pursue children's asset building in this moment, as Americans demand a pivot from the failed legacy of debt dependence to a system that catalyzes broadly shared wealth.[14,15] OIAs are ideologically compatible with historic American ideals of equality of opportunity and with contemporary values of rewarding effort and leveraging ability. In an era when nearly everything seems to be a political battleground, OIAs speak to an urgent need that cuts across traditional dividing lines. On the left and right, in red states and blue states, Americans want to believe that education offers their children a fair chance at upward mobility.

By leveraging the distributive power of financial markets[16] and building on families' own contributions, OIAs avoid the dependency label that has sunk other redistributive policies. They are also consistent with important policy precedents. While we have obviously never erased legacies of racism and class discrimination, some of our greatest successes have come from using federal power to facilitate access to education and give people robust ladders on which to climb to greater prosperity. For example, the GI Bill was an extensive investment that made higher education possible for millions of veterans.[17] It redefined higher education from a largely private good to an investment in collective growth. And it worked.

According to a congressional cost-benefit analysis, the GI Bill had returned every dollar invested nearly seven-fold in economic output and federal tax revenue within eight years of enactment.[18] A similarly bold investment in widespread human capital development can realize comparable returns again.

OPPORTUNITY INVESTMENT ACCOUNT PROPOSAL

To confront the high cost of college and get to a uniquely American version of "free college" that delivers equal life chances, we propose that every child receive an OIA with an initial deposit. All children need an institution capable of facilitating their pursuit of the American dream. While the accounts must be universal, we join others who have proposed children's assets as weapons against inequality in designing a progressive initial deposit.[19] Because OIAs must equip children with enough assets to make higher education seem valuable, not impossible, if they are to support identities consistent with educational exertion and attainment,[20] low-wealth children would have their accounts seeded with $10,500 at birth. Consistent with others' analyses,[21] we use wealth instead of income as the criterion for determining the amount of the seed deposit because, as detailed in chapter 2, it is wealth inequality we believe is ultimately most determinant of outcomes. These initial deposits would be invested in stock/bond portfolios of the type that privileged households use to amplify their returns. To cultivate savings behaviors associated with financial well-being and ensure that families are actively preparing for their children's postsecondary educations, these deposits would be augmented by $5 in monthly family contributions.

As family wealth increases, the amount of the initial public seed would be reduced and family deposits increased, according to a formula that will allow every American child to turn 18 with approximately $40,000 in dedicated educational assets. This amount is enough to finance a debt-free public higher education or place a degree from a private institution within realistic reach. While this may be a moving target, as tuition prices and financial aid policy change, calibrating OIA accumulation to approximate the cost of postsecondary education is essential, both functionally and symbolically. As a practical matter, if OIAs leave substantial gaps between available resources and necessary expenses, they will fail disadvantaged children as predictably as the status quo. Politically, framing OIAs as fuel for the education "engine" of upward mobility requires that the policy be well-suited to facilitating children's progress in that particular arena. While the details may be somewhat complex, our federal policymaking apparatus is surely up to the challenge.

We recognize that, for families at or below the poverty line, even $60 in annual deposits may prove onerous, particularly if they have multiple children. Indeed, our research examining savings patterns in CSA programs have found that, on average, 40% to 50% of participants are making contributions, at least on any regular basis.[22-24] To accommodate the obstacles that many low- and even moderate-income households face to long-term saving,[25-27] national OIA policy could allow monthly contributions to be deposited by philanthropic sources, local governments, or other third-party sponsors. OIA policy could take advantage of emerging innovations to encourage family asset-building, such as the rewards cards offered by the Community Link Foundation, with which families can add up to $900 per year to a college savings account just through realizing rewards from their existing spending.[27] Even better, as discussed in more detail in the final chapter, the United States could adopt policies similar to those in Canada[28] and Israel,[29] which leverage family allowances as complements to children's savings policy. Considerable savings challenges notwithstanding, evidence from CSA programs suggests that families will use innovative strategies and make substantial sacrifices to contribute as much as they possibly can to secure their children's futures.[30,31] Aligning income supports with asset-building policy would amplify these efforts and give parents the tools they need to successfully leverage this powerful new institution.

We Can Afford It

Universal OIAs would cost the federal government significantly less than current financial aid programs. Given the number of American children born each year, financing the federal government's seeding of universal OIAs would cost an estimated annual $42 billion. Particularly considering the potential for substantial positive returns, this figure pales in comparison to expenditures such as regressive loan repayment in Income-Driven Repayment plans ($74 billion in FY2017).[32] It is far less than the total expenditures in other forms of financial aid, some of which could be repurposed to pay for OIA investments. For example, tax credits and deductions for higher education cost the federal government $30 billion in 2015.[33] While there would likely be some political cost of withdrawing these tax-side subsidies,[34] there would not be much lost in postsecondary outcomes. Analysis has found no evidence of anything more than "negligible" effects from education tax incentives on a variety of outcomes, including college enrollment and attendance.[35-37] Beyond the efficacy argument for reinvesting these funds are questions of equity. Today, those earning more than $75,000 per year are more than twice as likely to receive tuition tax benefits as those earning less than $25,000 per year.[38] Giving privileged families a break on their taxes for actions they are motivated to take anyway is consistent with incentives for wealthy homeowners and retirement savers[39] and makes sense for a system that allows privileged actors to shape their own life chances and to define the life chances of others. However, it is not the way to finance an education system that would give all children a chance to pass successfully through the opportunity pipeline. It is not the way that most Americans truly want to see billions of postsecondary education dollars disbursed.[40]

Higher education tax credits and deductions are not the only part of US tax policy that offers potential revenue with which to finance OIAs. Rough analysis by the Tax Foundation estimates that the United States could free up most of the resources needed to finance universal children's accounts by reducing the threshold of estates excluded from inheritance taxes to $3.5 million, which would bring in $30 billion in annual revenue.[41] While recent tax policy changes largely moved in the opposite direction, polling suggests likely support for such progressive policies. Specifically, while 61% of Americans viewed their own federal income tax obligation as fair in 2017, approximately 60% were disturbed that "some corporations" and wealthy people do not pay their fair shares.[42] If the United States paid for an opportunity pipeline in a way that also restores equity to US tax policy, the combination could be a particularly potent investment in reducing wealth inequality.

Beyond the core commitment of the federal government and families' own saving, private institutions and state and local governments could also augment funding for universal OIAs. Existing CSA programs could be layered onto the OIA infrastructure to meet particular, local objectives and/or amplify support for specific communities. Foundations and other entities could also restructure when and how they invest in children's futures. These organizations spend billions in the final months before high school graduation, when students' paths are largely already set. These funds could be used, instead, by local scholarship providers and even postsecondary institutions to amplify government investments in ways that would build students' institutional efficacy early enough to actually alter their outcomes.

OIA POLICY MUST BE UNIVERSAL AND AUTOMATIC

A national OIA policy must be universal. OIAs should automatically open accounts for every child in order to ensure that the children who most need these assets accrue them seamlessly, at the beginning of their journeys through the opportunity pipeline. The CSA field has already experimented with models that require families to sign up for accounts and has learned that only universal and automatic models work equitably for disadvantaged children.[43] For example, while Promise Indiana incorporates extensive engagement and embeds the CSA within the existing institution of the school, even there, enrollment peaked at 63% of eligible kindergartners,[30] a rate that proved unsustainable with expansion to new geographies. Even CSAs that only require parents to check a box on the birth certificate form in order to open the account fall short of universal delivery, with some evidence that relatively advantaged families are more likely to take that step.[44] Importantly, ensuring that valuable interventions actually reach their intended targets is not a challenge unique to CSAs. Incomplete take-up is not a particular failing of families with children. Other policies have had to similarly contend with the importance of institutions in shaping behavior.[45] Retirement savings structures have demonstrated that even active outreach and recruitment cannot overcome the distance that separates disadvantaged households from essential financial services.[46] Given this reality, without making universal participation the default, high OIA take-up among already advantaged families could lead to intensification of the disadvantages buffeting poor children's fates.

Instead, to equalize children's life chances, OIAs should take the initial onus off parents and vest it with institutions. There are already models that use "opt-out" enrollment to provide CSAs to every child in the target population who does not explicitly decline to participate. Using this approach, SEED for Oklahoma Kids' universal design has eliminated inequity in account holding and asset ownership.[47] Every child in the San Francisco Unified School District receives a savings account automatically at kindergarten. Maine's Harold Alfond College Challenge uses birth records to automatically transfer assets to every child born a Maine resident. St. Louis' College Kids automatically opens accounts, as does Nevada's College Kickstart. The evidence of assets' effects on children's outcomes all along the opportunity pipeline makes inclusion imperative. If dedicated children's accounts are as valuable as research suggests, every child deserves one.

OIA POLICY CHALLENGES

While universality is the goal and, we contend, well within reach, policy changes are needed to construct federal systems capable of delivering truly universal and automatic asset-building opportunities. Today, CSA programs seeking to automatically include everyone often struggle with regulatory barriers that necessitate workarounds such as the utilization of "omnibus" 529 accounts that hold incentive deposits in a master fund, to be disbursed once parents open their own, parallel account or, conversely, laborious construction of custodial deposit account systems.[48] To move beyond such maneuvering, OIAs will require automatic account opening without an owner's signature or disclosure of a beneficiary's Social Security number.

Other regulatory reforms would make existing financial structures, such as state 529 college savings plans, friendlier to financially-marginalized consumers, in order to facilitate completely universal engagement. This means that accounts opened automatically should provide easy customer interface options such as cash and mobile deposits. Account information should be provided in accessible language, and financial institutions should be required to manage servicing and customer support, in exchange for the opportunity to hold sizable new balances. Achieving the goal of delivering equitable opportunities for financial inclusion and asset accumulation to all Americans requires (a) bridging divides that separate disadvantaged families from sophisticated instruments and (b) altering these institutions' distributional consequences. No child's educational future should hinge on her parent's ability to navigate the disclosures that accompany 529 college savings plan accounts. Crucially, we believe that winning reforms will be far more feasible once low-income households bargain with financial institutions from a position of greater power, a natural result of their collective ownership of billions of dollars in educational assets.

Making the case for reforms to financial systems in order to deliver universal OIAs also requires framing the principles of automatic account opening and universal eligibility as not only equitable but also efficient and effective. The CSA field has discovered that universal designs allow budgets to be focused on incentives and transfers, rather than expended for recruitment.[49] Importantly, this efficiency does not compromise outcomes. Friedline found that savings accounts in children's names may produce effects independent from accounts in which parents save on children's behalf.[50] This means that even passive ownership of educational assets, without any family deposits, can profoundly affect a child's trajectory. In SEED OK, accounts' effects on children's social and emotional competency and mothers' educational expectations do not require parents to have taken any action.[51] Institutions matter. For children's futures, there seems to be something powerful about *owning assets*, regardless of their origin.

SAVING AND THE POOR: EVEN MORE VALUABLE POLITICALLY
THAN FINANCIALLY

American families—even those living in and near poverty—can and will save.[52] They will prioritize saving for their children's higher educations if they are supported in doing so with access to accounts and financial incentives that make their saving worthwhile.[53] However, as should be apparent, our understanding of American wealth inequality suggests that low-income families cannot save their way to equitable life chances. Closing the opportunity gap requires changing the institutions that create and perpetuate their disadvantages. Nonetheless, the insufficiency of poor families' saving does not mean that it is unimportant. Even if it does not yield sizable balances, this saving often represents a disproportionate sacrifice, compared to the efforts of higher-income families.[54,55] CSAs' cultivation of savings behavior is a valuable component of their effects on children's life chances.

While the evidence base is still unfolding, it may even be the case that CSAs' effects are stronger when families actively engage with the accounts, including by saving.[56] Perhaps even more significant for our consideration of the path to federal OIA policy, the demonstrated savings performance of poor families may provide potent political ammunition in the battle to level the playing field.

Families Save in CSAs

Over the history of CSA interventions in the United States, savings participation can be characterized as modest in amount but earnest in effort. Almost 60% of participants in the national Savings for Education, Entrepreneurship, and Downpayment (SEED) CSA demonstration, which ran from 2003 to 2013, saved their own funds for their children's higher education.[57] Our recent research examining saving in some of the nation's most prominent CSA programs has found somewhat lower savings rates for CSAs where families opt in, perhaps due to the constrained financial context, post-recession: 46% in Promise Indiana, 44% in New Mexico's Prosperity Kids, and 40% in the opt-in iteration of Maine's Harold Alfond College Challenge.[22-24] Approximately 18% of accountholders have saved in their San Francisco Kindergarten-to-College (K2C) CSAs, a figure that should be considered in light of K2C's completely automatic account opening, which means that the program is attempting to engage the entire population, rather than those who have already signaled some interest in and capacity for saving for their children's educations.[58]

While there are noteworthy parallels in savings rates among these CSAs, savings totals vary more substantially, likely reflective both of differences in CSA design and the financial positions of target populations. Net quarterly contributions in the national SEED demonstration averaged $30 per participant.[57] In Promise Indiana, savers' median contributions after an average 24 months of account ownership were $50.[59] Quarterly deposits by the mostly low-income Latino families saving in Prosperity Kids average $20 to $70.[23] During the period of opt-in enrollment (2009–2013) in Maine's HACC, the median amount saved by contributing families was $1,400.[22] Among savers in San Francisco's K2C, deposits have averaged $907 over four years.[58]

Parents Sacrifice to Save for Their Children's Futures

As in so many domains, wealth shapes outcomes in the children's savings arena. Dramatic differences in the wealth positioning and relative power of most CSA participants and more privileged college savers make savings totals an incomplete and even misleading assessment. Indeed, saving by low- and moderate-income families can resemble the proverbial iceberg, with much happening below the surface in order for relatively modest outcomes to emerge. Complementing the quantification of saving is qualitative CSA research, which is replete with examples of families' commitment to saving for their children's futures. These actions range from modest behavioral modifications to dramatic sacrifices. Collectively, they demonstrate to policymakers that CSA policy expects parents to do their part to build wealth for their children. They also provide evidence that saving even small amounts can be a step toward a child's brighter future. Parents with CSAs go without so that their children's savings stay on track. From Indiana, mom Lindsay described, "I make us do it [save] no matter if it's a tight month or not because it's auto, but you know, things pop up, cars need new tires, Christmas. So you just have to find different ways to scrimp on other things so that the money still goes into the account and you're still okay." Mom Margaret earns less than $15,000 a year in San Francisco. Asked to describe the strategies she uses to come up with money to deposit into her child's K2C account, she responded immediately, "To stay broke. Not buy anything. Just save." Families leverage CSAs' institutional supports to build their financial capability and incorporate new practices that stretch their limited incomes. After a year in Prosperity Kids, mom Angelina had $570 in her child's college savings account. She described how she has come up with this money on her annual income of less than $45,000. "I told [my son], this week you are not eating out. We will find the way. We will make lunch home and you will take it with you. But you will not spend money. You have to spend as little as possible. . . . He also learned that if he found a penny, a dime, he should pick it up. They have piggy banks and there they deposit that change."

In contrast to both traditional financial aid policies and welfare programs that subsidize survival, then, CSA participation shapes families' interactions with money. In this way, children's asset-building initiatives build the next generation's financial capability. As mom Susana described from New Mexico, "If [her children] see me buying things we don't need, they will say, 'Mommy, you don't need it'." Bolstered by these experiences and socialized to see themselves as financially capable, it is not difficult to imagine that children who grow up managing their own investment accounts will live into possible selves that deal differently than they might have otherwise with the wealth-building institutions that are the source of much of their prospective prosperity.

The Institution of a CSA Facilitates Savings Patterns That Build Wealth

CSA evidence illustrates the role of institutions in facilitating wealth building. For many families, including those only tenuously connected to financial institutions, the CSA transforms household finances. Mom Sydney said what she values most about San Francisco's K2C CSA is, "Just the existence; I mean it's just that it's structured for you, so it enables, again to having another structure and having it be part of an intentional community that saves for their kids is important." Parents in CSA programs use financial tools to discipline their behaviors, as described by Laura, whose son has a Promise Indiana account. "I really like direct deposit. I think there is . . . when you aren't making the move to put it in, it is easier to not miss it." Even when their finances are distressed, families appreciate CSA restrictions that protect their children's assets. Elizabeth's grandson has a Promise Indiana account. "It is something that I can't just go to the bank when I am short of money and say, 'Hey, I need fifty bucks.' It is in a place where I can't get to it. It is a lot easier to just ignore it. It is not there." Emilia, who saves in her child's Prosperity Kids account despite earning less than $15,000 per year, echoes this. "We always tried to save, and sometimes we'd look at the savings account and we'd say, oh wow! Yes! We're doing good. But suddenly it was again in zeros . . . And the money would be gone, where? Who knows? It was gone. And that account has helped us a lot, because the money is there, it doesn't go anywhere, and we can't touch it, and we can't take it out."

As has been demonstrated among higher-income households, policy features shape individual behavior. US policy uses incentives to encourage Americans to save for retirement, own homes, and, indeed, save for their children's postsecondary educations. Because these incentives are delivered through the tax code, however, they have little to no value for lower-income families—and, therefore, no effect on—their behaviors and balance sheets. Within CSA programs, savings incentives, including matches and other rewards, can spark families' motivation to save.[60] These features change the distributional consequences of savings vehicles and transform them into institutions that equitably facilitate wealth building. Families with CSAs testify to these effects and how they have transformed their financial lives. For example, mom Elizabet, whose child has a New Mexico Prosperity Kids account, said, "They [matches] motivate us because I say; I am not going to lose two hundred dollars that they will give me for my son's savings." Our research has allowed us to observe how CSA programs are operating and, most poignantly, how families are responding to the opportunities CSAs extend. We are convinced that there is tremendous promise for children's assets to transform individual lives. Even more importantly, we see in CSAs the foundation of an institution on which entire generations can stand to stretch toward their American dreams.

OIAS: A BRIDGE TO TRUE COMPROMISE

The selfless saving we have observed of parents whose children have CSAs stands in stark contrast to perceptions about how low-income people use their money.

By defying expectations and incorporating a dimension of individual sacrifice and responsibility, OIAs may be more politically viable than other investments aimed at facilitating upward mobility. In this way, children's asset policy may help to clear a path to substantial policy change. OIAs avoid the dichotomy of work versus dependency that has doomed many redistributive attempts.[16] Instead, by encouraging the kind of behavior people want to see from those who are poor,[61] OIAs may be the best available bridge to broader prosperity and real compromise. This may be particularly essential in today's political climate, although skepticism about the thrift of the poor is, perhaps, as old as poverty itself. President Donald Trump has been especially vocal that people in poverty should shoulder responsibility for pulling themselves out of it. He has said that, "Benefits should have strings attached to them"[62] and that, "If [people] can stay poor for so many generations . . . how smart can they be? They're morons."[63] The president is hardly alone in these sentiments. Congressional candidates have derided the "slothfulness and laziness" of people in poverty.[64] Pertinent given the racial dimension of American wealth inequality,[65] poverty has often been framed in Black and White terms. While campaigning for the presidency, former Senator Rick Santorum criticized welfare by stating, "I don't want to make black people's lives better by giving them somebody else's money."[66] These attitudes have also permeated some Americans' opinions. Recent polls suggest that a majority of White Republicans agree that African Americans are worse off economically than Whites "because most just don't have the motivation or will power to pull themselves up out of poverty."[67]

In general, however, the American people are more inclined than many politicians to locate the causes of poverty in fundamental economic inequities rather than individual moral failings. A recent *Huffington Post* poll found that 44% of Americans think poor people's straits are mostly due to a lack of opportunities, while only 30% blame individual actions.[68] Despite political platitudes that work is the key to prosperity,[69] 47% of Americans believe that poverty has more to do with the fact that good jobs are not available, while only 28% perceive that poor people have a poor work ethic.[68] Importantly, polls suggest that Americans can—and do—simultaneously place their faith in hard work and express concern that inequality is undermining the likelihood that their work will pay off.[40] Policy to close the American opportunity gap must resonate with American values that demand equitable life chances. Otherwise, while Americans have always been more concerned with inequitable opportunity rather than unequal outcomes, the reality of extremely unequal outcomes will threaten the opportunity structure that determines the next generation's success. The case for OIAs can be further bolstered by evidence that people in poverty will put their own stake in their children's futures.

Crucially, then, public opinion suggests an opening for policies like OIAs, which create opportunities while incorporating individual effort.

Even some politicians otherwise scornful of anti-poverty programs may be persuaded to invest in policies such as OIAs. In his Tea Party response to the 2014 State of the Union address, Senator Rand Paul, usually identified as a Libertarian, said, "We must choose a new way, a way that empowers the individual through education and responsibility to earn a place alongside their fellow Americans."[70] The following year, his response included this statement: "I think peace will come when those of us who have enjoyed the American Dream become aware of those who are missing out on the American Dream. The future of our country will be secure when we break down the wall that separates us from 'the other America'."[71] Ben Carson, current Secretary of the US Department of Housing and Urban Development, has written, "If we really want to eradicate poverty, we should allocate significant resources and personnel toward providing education and opportunity for the poor."[72] These statements reflect preference for the type of policy that OIAs represent and suggest that, if the policy is well-constructed and framed as responding to the pressing problem of the eroding American dream, the streams of policy change may indeed converge to make OIA passage possible.[2]

Substantial partisan divides notwithstanding, Americans of all political persuasions generally want action to address wealth inequality and create opportunity. Media analysis and public opinion suggest that our collective appetite for action to counter inequality has increased since the Great Recession and its recovery, as fortunes diverged and the American dream appears increasingly threatened.[40] While a Pew Research Center poll found some divided opinions among Republicans and Democrats about whether the federal government should act to counter widening wealth inequality; nonetheless, 69% of those polled wanted some government action to shrink wealth divides.[73] There seems to be support for the more specific policy proposal of OIAs too, at least historically. A 2007 poll found support for CSA policy among those of differing political affiliations and ideologies (74% of liberals, for example, and 62% of conservatives) and in all regions of the country.[74] Crucially, this same poll found the strongest support—by a wide margin—for a CSA-type policy specifically designed to help families pay for college and to level the playing field.[75]

In the aggregate, public opinion appears to underscore the importance of crafting OIA policy robust enough to accomplish the ambitious goal of restoring higher education's equalizing role. Speaking to the particular features that OIA policy would include, the earlier poll found that more than two-thirds of voters and 78% of parents favored a CSA policy that included automatic accounts, initial seed deposits, and savings incentives.[74] As concerns about student debt, stagnant mobility, and economic polarization have grown and more Americans have been exposed to CSAs, openness to progressive children's savings policy has likely increased. OIAs have never been more urgently relevant.

A NATIONAL POLICY MUST CONTAIN A SIZABLE OPPORTUNITY INVESTMENT

Gaining support for a level of investment that will give American children a meaningful institution, not a mere instrument, will require more than just alignment with the noble rhetoric of the American dream. Marshalling this political will hinges on helping policymakers understand how assets affect educational outcomes and what low-income families have demonstrated they can do, through CSAs, on their own behalf. Still, even with progressive matches, seamless account interface, and other supportive structures, saving alone will not close the wealth gap. Furthermore, if saving is rewarded equally for those who face huge hurdles and those with baked-in advantage, already-privileged families will always stay ahead. Instead, if OIAs are to catalyze upward mobility, they will have to be sufficiently progressive. Family saving, in other words, is a fundamental component of the OIA intervention. It is just as surely only a part.

Distinct from savings matches, CSAs' initial seed deposits are more analogous to the wealth transfer we envision in OIAs. These deposits build in wealth creation from the moment of account opening. Seeding accounts sends children an important message that institutions stand poised to facilitate their success. Robust seeds spur accumulation substantial enough to help children interpret paying for college in terms of difficulty-as-importance, not difficulty-as-impossible.[20] This is the down payment on equitable life chances that OIAs can represent. The initial seeds invested in current CSA programs vary. As a sampling, accounts are seeded with $25 in Promise Indiana, $50 in St. Louis and San Francisco's K2C, $100 in Rhode Island's CollegeBound*Baby*, $500 in Maine's Harold Alfond College Challenge, and $1,000 in the SEED for Oklahoma Kids experiment. In all of these iterations, seed deposits jumpstart asset accumulation[76,77] and make CSAs instruments of more equitable wealth distribution.

Seed deposits illustrate what is undeniably true in other wealth-building systems as well: asset accumulation in CSAs does not hinge entirely—or, usually, even primarily—on families' own saving. Across the SEED sites, third-party contributions accounted for approximately 50% of median asset accumulation.[77] Perhaps the most compelling example of the importance of initial seeds in catalyzing accumulation is SEED OK, where the average value of educational assets held by children in the treatment group is $1,851, $1,426 of which comes from the automatic initial seed and its earnings within the Oklahoma 529 college savings plan.[78] These returns illustrate a particular advantage of OIA-type interventions: harnessing market outcomes to alter the distribution of the fruits of economic growth.[16]

As we consider how to craft OIAs into the most potent institution possible, we must grapple with what recent CSA research has revealed about how inequities can unfold even within relatively progressive systems. For example, in San Francisco's K2C, asset accumulation outcomes are nearly equalized in the first two years of account ownership for families eligible for free or reduced-price lunch and those who are not, but after that point, higher-income families begin to pull away from economically disadvantaged ones.[58] This finding simultaneously underscores the equalizing potential of CSAs, even in one of the most difficult economic contexts low-income families face, and suggests the need for additional institutional supports.[79] On the other side of the country, Maine's Harold Alfond College Challenge delivers the CSA through the state 529 plan instead of a deposit account, as in K2C. There, too, analysis found that higher-income households not only save more than low-income Mainers; they also receive larger return on their contributions, likely a function both of investment choices and the greater earning potential of their larger asset stores.[22]

Assets Beget Assets, But Only Through Institutions

CSA policy and program implementation experiences provide evidence, then, that sizable initial deposits are important seed capital. In OIA policy, initial opportunity investments would fuel asset accumulation and serve as the linchpin to OIAs' effects on reducing wealth inequality. However, as the discussion in chapter 3 highlighted, institutions are increasingly determinant of individuals' outcomes, including their wealth building. As we construct OIA policy that optimizes children's chances along the opportunity pipeline, we must consider the role for institutions in delivering, leveraging, and growing children's assets. Here, CSA experiences suggest that state-supported 529 college savings plans may be the best available institutional vehicle.

While some elements of the 529 college savings plan system are less than ideally suited to the delivery of a progressive wealth transfer,[48] CSAs show stronger asset accumulation when administered on the 529 platform.[80] This is an important metric. If OIAs are to counter today's wealth divide, the assets of low-income people must earn returns commensurate with those of the financially advantaged. While the potential for asset loss is not insubstantial in the portfolios purchased by state 529 plans,[81] this risk may be better addressed with policies that cushion economically vulnerable families from catastrophic loss rather than those that restrict them to products that offer comparatively little yield. Particularly since wealthy Americans will continue to save in higher-growth investments, OIA policy must not relegate those already disadvantaged to institutions that deliver lower returns. OIA policy should change the distributional consequences of investment systems, rather than cede these institutions to the strategic actors who use them to their advantage.

Conclusion: OIAs as the Foundation for a Reimagined Economic Mobility System

As a lifelong investment in children's outcomes, OIAs stand in sharp contrast to the just-in-time nature of today's financial aid instruments. OIAs are asset building, while current financial aid is designed to be consumed to the point of exhaustion. Another potential distinction between asset-based financial aid and most financial aid policy is the purpose toward which it can be put. Today, most financial aid is conceived narrowly, as a way to meet higher education expenses—often, just those payable directly to the educational institution. Conversely, although accounts held in most current CSAs are restricted for postsecondary education, a national OIA policy could and should move beyond these constraints. OIAs could provide the foundation for a reimagined economic mobility system, with broader allowable asset uses that can facilitate successful transition to secure adulthood.

Some CSAs, such as New Mexico's Prosperity Kids, already permit balances to be applied to finance homeownership, entrepreneurship, or retirement saving.[82] These programs operate on the premise that children's assets should finance more than just a diploma. Although we believe that such efforts are on the right track, they cannot solve the national crisis that separates poor children from the American dream. To tackle that problem, "we need also to alter the power dynamics of the current economy so that the fruits of economic growth are more fairly divided."[16] As inequities in US labor,[83] housing,[84] and financial markets[85] make abundantly clear, these fruits are not harvested exclusively in the realm of postsecondary education.

Existing CSA programs provide a framework for more expansive national policies. Even more fundamentally, the ascendance of CSAs as a state and local policy innovation has broadened the understanding of what financial aid can do and the domains in which it can affect children's outcomes. Granted, there are technical complications to be hurdled in order to ensure that OIA policy serves to facilitate children's progress in arenas other than education. Specifically, today, assets in state 529 plans are subject to penalties on noneducational disbursements.[86] These rules would unjustly penalize children whose path to the American dream passes through institutions other than postsecondary education. Prohibitions on early

CSA disbursements also complicate efforts to construct "sidecar" accounts that families could use on the way to higher education, such as for enrichment or technology, as children's asset policy has done in some global contexts.[87] However, regulatory reform could protect families from these consequences and thereby fit the 529 structure to OIAs' larger aims. There are also ways to ensure—if we have the political will to do so—that these assets are used to reduce disparities in educational investments during primary and secondary school, rather than exacerbating inequities through the subsidizing of private school for privileged children, even if the converse seems more likely in the current context.[88] As is often the case, the technical fix is the easier one.

More crucial will be ensuring that public support for children's asset building is not eroded by the removal of restrictions that ensure funds are expended only for postsecondary education. This is particularly important given what many have pointed to as the most urgent task facing advocates for children's asset building: clearly defining the problem to which CSAs respond, so that children's assets avoid the "Swiss Army knife" characterization as a useful but not necessarily essential tool.[5,75] To preserve the public's appetite for investments in children's wealth building, even outside the confines of college financing, OIAs' universality is especially essential. In marked contrast to perceptions of means-tested welfare benefits, Americans demonstrate strong support for universal social investments.[89] As evidence of this double standard in policymaking and public opinion, older adults' spending of Social Security benefits is not subjected to the same scrutiny as welfare beneficiaries' spending. By extension, Americans may be far more willing to extend some flexibility regarding the use of OIAs if they have reason to trust that they or their children will receive the same resources and the same consideration. Structuring OIAs as a front-end investment in children's well-being across the board will create the space and, ultimately, foster the political will, to entrench OIAs as institutions. Then, designed correctly, they would represent a completely reimagined financial aid, not just a new way to finance college. This is financial aid as an institution broadly conceived as facilitating transition to successful American adulthood.[90] Yes, OIAs would place higher educational attainment within reach of American young people whose futures hinge on college completion. OIAs would also facilitate the advancement of those who choose another path of ascent.

OIAs and the infusions of assets they would transmit could make a dramatic dent in the wealth divide. The wealth held in OIAs would, itself, provide a platform of upward mobility for those who start with little.[91] It is hard to get ahead in the American economy without a wealth foundation.[92] This is particularly true today, given the increasingly volatile nature of US labor markets, the chasm between productivity and income, the growing association between wealth and educational attainment, and widespread financial instability.[93–95] This context makes particularly significant analyses that universal children's asset accounts could reduce the racial wealth gap by about 20% to 80%, depending on funding and participation, while simultaneously raising the wealth of the entire population.[96] If we had implemented a universal and progressive children's asset policy a generation ago, we would have wiped out the wealth gap for today's 18 to 34 year-olds.[96] In turn, this could have transformative effects for American democracy, which is imperiled today by the profound depth and breadth of the wealth divide.[97–99]

OIAs are powerful in their own rights because they give poor children an ownership stake in American prosperity that mirrors the strong starts that wealthier parents transmit to their children.[100] Not merely financial, these effects also provide psychological benefits. Coming to college with money in their figurative pockets and literal accounts would vest low-income children with real bargaining power. This could change their orientation to the institutions that broker opportunity. Just as a car buyer with money in hand may approach the decision differently than one requesting financing, students who see college through an asset-empowered lens may interact differently with the systems that constitute the opportunity pipeline.

Where, today, they struggle toward their futures, poor children with OIAs would have real reason to believe that powerful tools are at their disposal and potent winds at their backs. In this way, national OIAs have the potential to transform higher education. Asset-empowered students may demand, for example, prudent administration of postsecondary institutions and accountability for measures that drive return on degree. Certainly, the education system will have to bend to accommodate a growing number of college-bound students, from all corners of the country and all demographics, armed with a plan for how they will realize their educational expectations. This, after all, is how strategic actors engage with institutions that determine their outcomes. In turn, these students may reshape those systems so that they work for everyone, not just those who start with privilege.

We do not pretend to be able to predict the future of policymaking. We do not deny that the current political landscape presents few opportunities for substantial policy change,[101] particularly that which aims for dramatic reversal of gaping wealth divides and low mobility. We recognize that there is crucial work to do in order to create the conditions in which starting all American children with assets is seen as a prudent response to our 21st-century economic arrangements and, therefore, a political imperative. However, we believe that the streams that must come together in order for policy to change—problem, policy, and politics[2]—are, indeed, converging. OIAs are a persuasive answer to one of the most fundamental questions of our age: How can we make the American dream into a promise instead of a fable? They present an opportunity all too rare in US policymaking, when the best available science aligns with smart politics and deeply held values.

When correctly framed as an intervention that aligns with the American ideal of equitable opportunity for upward mobility, OIAs have the potential to serve political and functional aims. Educators are eager for ways to really mean it when they tell students that they can achieve their dreams. Millions of parents are desperate for some way to put their children on equal footing with their peers,[102] even if they were born a rung below. OIAs can fill those bills. They represent a policy around which an influential constituency can be built. Bolstered by a growing evidence base illustrating real educational and economic returns, the discussion about OIAs becomes not *if* they could strengthen the ladder of American ascent but instead precisely *how* we should structure, finance, and scale them. These are questions we can and must answer. The future of what the nation cares about most—if not the disadvantaged children whose life chances depend on policy change, then the core principle that America should be a land where effort and ability are what carries people up the ladder—depends on it.

Note

a. Our sincere appreciation to Justin King of New America for allowing us to use the analysis he compiled of this federal legislation, prepared for AEDI's CSA Symposium in November 2016.

7 Conclusion
THE AMERICAN DREAM NEEDS A WEALTH AGENDA

THE AMERICAN DREAM is imperiled. Nearly half of Americans who report having once believed that Americans who work hard will get ahead are no longer convinced that is the case. Many doubt that their children's generation will be better off financially than theirs.[1] Even more alarming, new research suggests that such fears are well-founded.[2] As Americans take stock of their chances to "make it" and find that their realities lag behind their aspirations, the dream withers. Some scholars have even linked recent declines in life expectancy of middle-aged Whites to the hollowing of the American dream, attributing rising mortality rates to "deaths of despair."[3] Dimming prospects for climbing the economic ladder may threaten the survival of the American experiment.

If the verdict was already rendered and the American dream beyond any possible repair, this would be a very different book. Certainly, there are no guarantees that narratives, even broadly shared, endure forever. However, we believe that the American dream is not only salvageable but eminently worth saving. It still holds considerable sway over personal ambitions and collective aspirations in the United States and around the world. In 1931, Adams credited the dream with having "lured tens of millions of all nations to our shores";[4] today, immigrants and their descendants are the most optimistic about the central premise of the dream: that all who work hard have a fair chance to succeed.[5,6] Admittedly, the idea that working hard should help people get ahead is not peculiarly "American." What makes the American Dream uniquely ours is (a) the contention that institutions should aim to create conditions that roughly equalize opportunity and (b) the confidence born of generations' experiences seeing the dream materialize, albeit unequally.

We see the American dream as worth a fight because it defines not only how Americans see themselves and their possible tomorrows but also how they see their nation and the opportunities they believe that nation should extend. Without a belief that the United States is a place where people can rise from any depths to any heights, it is hard to imagine why Americans would work so hard,[7] even as the fruits of their labors diminish.[8] A nation that did not believe that everyone should have a chance to climb would be less likely to invest in public education as the central mechanism of American opportunity. As we see it, then, the American dream is not merely part of our national identity and an inspirational comfort to those dissatisfied with their current station. It is also the force that legitimizes the institutions that construct pathways out of poverty. For those who want to see prosperity more fairly distributed, it is our best rhetorical and political bet. Indeed, it may be our only hope.

A Wealth Agenda to Revive the American Dream

As we have emphasized throughout this book, we see wealth inequality as the primary threat to the American dream and the principal target of our children's savings policy. Americans have not rejected the American dream's fundamental premise. The vitality of the dream has not been beset by some mysterious force. Instead, the widening wealth gap and associated concentration of economic, political, and social power are distorting the institutions that are supposed to provide the ladders of American upward mobility.[9] When it would take the average Black family 228 years to accrue the same wealth that the average White family has today, structures cannot be said to extend anything resembling equitable life chances.[10] Further, as outlined in chapter 2, wealth inequality manifests in fissures other than the racial divide. The top 0.1% of Americans hold almost as much wealth as the bottom 90%, a figure that suggests that many White households are locked out of asset accumulation by forces similar to those that beset many communities of color.[11] While Blacks' wealth disadvantage is deep and "toxic,"[12] completely racializing wealth inequality makes it harder to build a movement for its reduction. What the United States needs is a wealth agenda that will close the opportunity gap for those disadvantaged, a group that includes most households of color, certainly, and many Whites as well.

On nearly every measure—health, educational attainment, career satisfaction, even overall well-being [13-17]—there are profound disparities between wealthy "haves" and disadvantaged "have-nots." Because wealth inequality is the common thread running through every assault on the American dream, we contend that all US policy should be assessed through a lens of equitable opportunities for wealth accumulation. However, while policymakers occasionally champion a particular program or policy that could catalyze greater wealth creation, we see no clear American wealth agenda advocated from either end of the ideological spectrum. It is our hope that Opportunity Investment Accounts (OIAs) can inform such an agenda. Aimed explicitly at reducing wealth inequality and creating viable paths to equitable opportunities, OIAs are more than another anti-poverty policy. They provide an example of the policymaking possible with a new paradigm through which to assess where, how, and for whom institutions facilitate wealth. The United States needs a wealth-building agenda not simply because we think people on the bottom should have more. The point is not to string together a series of policy innovations that seem like they would be useful to the downtrodden. What we have in mind is the beginning, at least, of a plan to counter the core threat to the American dream. Ultimately, that is a mission as integral to the fortunes and futures of those with considerable privilege as to those who are disadvantaged. Other unequal societies' experiences offer abundant cautions about the ways in which extreme economic disparities hinder economic growth[18] and democratic governance.[19] Perhaps promisingly, as Thomas Shapiro has stressed, "toxic inequality" is constructed, not inevitable.[19] This means that it can also be *unmade* by intentional intervention.

Toward this end, we identify failings in key institutions implicated in inequitable opportunities for wealth building. We have compiled this admittedly incomplete list of policies according to what we see as their alignment with our primary proposed wealth-building structure: OIAs. Our objective here is to place OIAs within the context of a broader wealth agenda. We intend to outline how policy changes in other domains would complement OIAs and increase the efficacy of this new institution. The point here is not to specify precise policy solutions nor, certainly, to exhaustively document all of the reforms that could benefit disadvantaged Americans. Instead, we hope to (a) acknowledge that OIAs are not a silver bullet but can be an important part of a larger wealth agenda, (b) articulate the lessons we have learned from CSA research about the institutional supports families need in order to build assets, and (c) extend our examination of key American institutions through a lens of wealth inequality, in order to identify some of the policies that may improve Americans' chances.

The lessons of our CSA research have convinced us of an axiom of children's asset building: progressive features and laudable enthusiasm notwithstanding, families with stronger financial positions are better-positioned to leverage the opportunities that CSAs extend. When family budgets are shocked by sudden job loss or unexpected health expenses, all the commitment in the world cannot materialize the dollars to put into a child's account. Policy should not expect families to forego their essential survival needs in order to extend their children a chance to get ahead. And while research suggests that accounts are valuable even when families are not saving and that children's assets may be valuable[20]—perhaps especially so—even when families are still struggling with disadvantages, OIAs cannot deliver maximal equalizing force if many families lack the capacity to participate equitably in all these accounts have to offer.[21] Indeed, this is the lesson of existing wealth-building structures in the United States.

CSA research has explored obstacles that prevent families from engaging as they would like with their children's accounts, including debt obligations and high housing costs that siphon away their already low wages.[22] In our own qualitative examinations of CSA programs, families have told us about these struggles, often in very personal terms. In many cases, financial circumstances defy even their best efforts. Elizabet is 51, earns less than $25,000 per year, and is saving in her child's Prosperity Kids (New Mexico) CSA. Reciting her financial challenges, she concludes, perhaps a bit exasperated with the interviewer and her family's situation, "The obstacle I find is that there is not enough money to cover all the necessities." In some cases, incomes are not only insufficient but also irregular. Gabriela attends Prosperity Kids events and encourages her daughter in school but has not yet been able to contribute to the CSA. She cites her husband's sporadic work as the cause. "When there is work . . . Right now it is slow. When there is work . . ." These problems are not limited to particular demographics or geographic areas. In San Francisco's K2C, 30-year-old Margaret explains that "All the money that you have goes towards bills." Caleb, 41, has a son with a K2C account. He concurs with Margaret, explaining that "Well, most of the bills that you have got to pay and, uh, you know, you have got to buy food and everything, you know. You really ain't left with much." Thirty-six-year-old Alice recently lost her job. She became emotional speaking about the constraints on her saving in her son's K2C account. "The rent has gone crazy here [in San Francisco]; I'm slowly being priced out, and in June I'll be evicted because my landlord wants to triple my rent, so that's a lot of stress for me, I'm sorry . . . It's just really hard; we're really struggling." Even families with higher incomes experience savings challenges. Surveying those around her in San Francisco, mom Raquel summarized, "It's very hard to save because it's so expensive here. I mean . . . even teachers. Teachers are leaving the city because they can't afford it. It's hard. It's hard to save here." Almost without exception, these families still value their CSAs. They would undoubtedly be grateful for the larger investment and more powerful institution of OIA. They just as surely deserve a policy infrastructure that provides them truly equitable chances to successfully leverage these policies to support their children toward prosperous futures.

EDUCATION: WHERE INEQUALITY BEGINS, AND COULD END

Our accounting of the American dream centers on educational attainment and the equalizing role education is supposed to play. It is to education, then, that we turn first to consider where the American dream is failing its adherents. As we detail in chapter 1, too many American children's hopes of prosperity through academic achievement are dashed against inequitable realities that, in the aggregate, ensure that wealth *predicts* educational outcomes more than *results* from them.[14] Even when children play by the rules of the American dream, they often find that the rewards they can reap hinge largely on where they started.[23] For us, this erosion of the American dream is profoundly personal. Our scholarly examination of the role of wealth in shaping children's prospects parallels our own diverging experiences. We see our respective stories in data that underscore how difficult it is for disadvantaged students to use education to climb and how easily privileged families can manipulate systems to ensure that their children rarely fall.[24]

Of course, the effects of wealth inequality on educational outcomes are not confined to attainment itself. Because education also unlocks opportunity in other domains, countering wealth's influence on postsecondary education and its returns is not merely the primary goal of our work. It is also the starting point for nearly everything we believe matters. On average, Americans with college educations fare better in the labor market than those without degrees.[25] They secure jobs that facilitate access to wealth-building retirement accounts and to protective institutions such as health insurance.[26] Well-educated Americans are generally healthier than those with less education, a relationship that becomes a virtuous cycle.[27] Particularly when financed from assets rather than student debt, postsecondary education is also associated with engagement in wealth-creating financial and housing markets. Those with college educations are more likely to own homes.[28]

In sum, higher education confers privilege, albeit to differing extents, depending largely on initial conditions.[29,30] Those who succeed in education are positioned to engage strategically with influential institutions and to bend those institutions to meet their needs. They are even expected to do so, presumed to possess the intelligence, drive, and moral acuity to merit such authority. Education matters, in other words, not only in its own right, as the primary way that a child born into poverty in America can leave it.[31] It also matters because one's educational attainment, the roots of which begin in infancy, determines how one fares the rest of the way through the opportunity pipeline.

There are valuable ideas for education reform, many of which are supported by at least some evidence that attests to their potential to improve outcomes and close gaps. However, there is little chance that the US education system will be the leveler that disadvantaged children need unless and until low-income households wield enough power to mold it to serve their interests. That is where the principal policy proposal of this book—OIAs—comes in. As outlined in chapter 6, OIAs would provide all American children with a dedicated account and enough initial wealth to fuel substantial accumulation, finance a debt-free college education, and cultivate the early expectations associated with greater educational achievement. Universal OIAs would be an institution aligned with children's hopes for their possible selves, potent enough to make the American dream attainable for millions of talented young people who are limited today only because, as fast as they run, it is hard to catch up when one starts from behind and runs into the wind.

The evidence detailed in chapter 5 suggests that OIAs have the potential to improve outcomes in early childhood, K-12 schooling, college enrollment and completion, and post-college financial health. However, OIAs' true impact cannot be captured in the measure of their direct effects. Because OIAs would also increase the bargaining power of children and families, they would make other valuable interventions more politically possible. Progressive reforms to public school funding formulas and universal quality early childhood education could make education more equalizing.[32-35] When those whose fortunes depend on such investments wield more power at the tables where these decisions are made, we predict that the prospects for such changes will markedly improve. Additionally, effects of children's assets on early social and emotional competency[21,36] and educational expectations[37,38] may increase families' capacity to take advantage of other investments, as when parents seek out the best early childhood program or push their children to take college-preparatory classes. Children's assets can have ripple effects, multiplying the value of other investments. With national OIA policy, these ripples could reach across the nation.

OTHER EDUCATION POLICIES MUST SUPPLEMENT OIAS

OIAs are admittedly long-term approaches. Even if established today, they would do little to help current college students and recent graduates who struggle to convert their credentials into financial security. As we acknowledged in our earlier book about student debt, for these Americans, the American dream of upward mobility through higher education has not paid off, at least not as they were told to expect.[39] While the promise of a brighter future for their children would bring some consolation, their own balance sheets need immediate intervention. Here, targeted and progressive student debt forgiveness is a necessary concession. Importantly, as with "free college," student debt relief is an area where rising tides do not lift all boats. Across-the-board student debt reduction would increase the racial wealth gap and offer comparatively less value to disadvantaged Americans. However, eliminating student debt for those making $50,000 per year or less would reduce racial wealth disparity by nearly 37% at the median among low-wealth households, while eliminating debt among those making $25,000 or less would reduce this gap by more than 50%.[40]

Even if not repurposed to finance OIAs, as we have recommended, there is perhaps no postsecondary education policy more in need of reform than higher education tax benefits. As described in chapter 4, providing financial aid through the tax code performs poorly against any benchmark. Higher education tax benefits are insufficient to meet the financial needs of low-income students, too complex to figure into families' college financing, and skewed heavily toward those who least need assistance.[41,42] Replacing tax benefits with direct support[43] for those with greatest need would redirect essential resources and make education a more potent institution for equalizing wealth building.

HEALTH CARE: ABOUT WEALTH, NOT JUST HEALTH

In the United States, poor Americans are also sicker Americans. While lack of wealth compromises health in many ways, our emphasis here is on the inverse of this relationship: the financial consequences suffered by individuals not fated with good health and the ways in which these effects thwart asset building.[44] While expansions in health insurance have reduced the risk of catastrophic medical debt, 24% of all nonelderly Americans and 31% of nonelderly Blacks have past-due medical debts.[45,46] These liabilities cause families to compromise their asset accumulation in multiple ways, including draining savings, running up credit card bills, and/or taking out predatory loans.[47] All but the most privileged Americans are one serious injury or illness away from a major blow to their wealth. As Willie's family has witnessed, poor health can lead to reliance on public assistance, with its attendant prohibitions on saving and asset building. Without universal provision of health care coverage, poor health may continue to doom many to asset poverty.

As in the institution of education, there is a need for interim policy measures during the transition to broader and more equitable health coverage. Those whose ability to save and invest is compromised by the burden of medical debt need progressively-targeted debt forgiveness. And to ensure that no Americans have to choose between meeting basic needs today and building wealth for their tomorrows, policy should eliminate asset limits in means-tested safety-net programs, including those that provide health benefits.[48] Otherwise, those who rely on these supports will remain locked out of asset-building institutions and punished for trying to build wealth, while tax policy encourages the wealthy to save. Asset limits in means-tested benefit programs are damning examples of how institutional arrangements contribute to wealth inequality.[48] They are unfair, unproductive, and—in the context of the American dream and its promise to reward effort—un-American.

In addition to the obvious uncertainties health concerns—crisis or chronic—can introduce into a family's finances, we see another point of intersection between children's wealth building and health care policy, with important technical and political implications for policy reform. As health insurance providers seek to maximize profit, they by necessity seek to find ways to avoid paying for care. We have seen a similar dynamic in the CSA field. Banks and 529 college savings plan providers are profit-driven organizations that have little motivation to serve low-income families who are small-dollar savers. This can lead to tensions that may constrain efforts to scale equitable asset building. As CSAs proliferate, there are signs that financial institutions remain somewhat resistant to robustly servicing low-income constituencies. This suggests that intrusion of profit motives will likely be at least as problematic in children's savings as in health care. Even though financial institutions appreciate CSAs because they bring in more middle- and higher-income savers, they often fail to offer the products or make the modifications that would be necessary to serve poor families well. Additionally, evidence from CSAs such as Maine's Harold Alfond College Challenge reveal that financial systems often produce superior earnings for higher-income households, even with the progressive features of initial deposits and universal enrollment.[49] OIAs may change these dynamics, as more substantial initial deposits make profit motive and compound interest begin to work in favor of low-income families. However, this is not an outcome children's savings advocates can take for granted. Instead, health care policy offers some important lessons about the regulatory environment and incentives required when for-profit entities have a role to play in delivering crucial public investments.

LABOR: AMERICANS WANT TO WORK THEIR WAY UP

Americans are, for the most part, hard-working people.[7] A strong work ethic is a part of the culture of all demographic groups and bolstered by the American dream's promise to reward those who put in the requisite effort. Today, however, Americans find it increasingly hard to work their way to financial security, to say nothing of upward mobility.[50] This is particularly true for those with lower levels of education or who live in regions where jobs have nearly disappeared.[51,52] Even

Americans with college educations find their livelihoods increasingly threatened by automation,[53] global competition, and the persistent gap between productivity and compensation.[54] Households with the capacity to invest have responded by relying more heavily on asset earnings to support their standard of living.[55] Those without this wealth advantage, however, have no cushion in the event of individual or societal emergencies, limited capacity to save—even when policies such as CSAs give them access to instruments—and little ability to vault to a higher financial standing.

The increasingly prevalent sense that labor alone is insufficient as a foundation of survival or engine of ascent has contributed to a resurgence of a long-standing policy idea: a universal basic income or universal child/family allowance. Guaranteeing some basic floor of household income would not undermine the incentive to work. Getting *ahead* would still require exerting oneself. It would, however, ensure that no one could fall into abject poverty.[56] It would protect those who lose their jobs to robots or leave the labor market to care for relatives.[57] Additionally and, for our purposes, essentially, an allowance specifically aimed at families with children could serve as a complement to asset-building policies such as OIAs. This is the case in Canada, where 97% of low-income families who have accounts in that nation's Registered Education Savings Plans (RESPs) are saving, even though that is not a condition of receipt of the government's initial seed deposits.[58] Even more instructive are contributions levels by these low-income households: more than $1,000 per year on average.[58] While there has not yet been extensive analysis of the savings strategies employed by low-income Canadian families, our study of the Canadian children's savings system attributed their comparatively high contributions to participation in "group scholarship" savings plans that compel specific savings levels and to the availability of family allowances, worth as much as $6,400 per year, tax-free, to households with young children.[59] A similar connection to universal income supports is also used to finance children's education savings in Israel.[60]

In the United States, proposals for guaranteed universal minimum income or regular child allowances have appeal on the political right and left.[61–63] Explicitly linking such a policy to children's savings structures may further increase its political feasibility. Evidence from CSAs in the United States attests to the potential of a guaranteed allowance to mitigate families' savings obstacles.[22,64,65] Already, families with CSAs often save at levels greater than their limited incomes would suggest possible, once they have access to an institution that facilitates and rewards their efforts. There is reason, then, to believe that many will prioritize asset building for their children's futures once they have a basic income floor on which to stand.

There are other policy reforms that could similarly complement OIAs by augmenting household incomes. Chief among these is an expanded Earned Income Tax Credit (EITC).[43] The EITC lifts millions of Americans out of poverty.[66] With a more generous formula, expanded eligibility, and linkage to financial institutions that offer strong returns, these effects could multiply. If these investments are financed in ways that directly reduce wealth inequality, such as with a progressive tax on extreme wealth or an increase in the inheritance tax, they could address wealth inequality from both the upper and lower ends.[12] If families had incentives and vehicles for transferring tax refunds directly to long-term, asset-building accounts such as OIAs, they might substantially increase their savings propensity, building significant balances and valuable financial competency in the process.[67]

Guaranteeing more adequate income is not, however, sufficient for eradicating wealth inequality and its corrosion of the American dream. If income was sufficient to fuel wealth accumulation, then the wealth gap would merely mirror the income divide. Instead, wealth is even more concentrated than income.[11] While, as described earlier, labor income is of declining importance to the wealthiest Americans, most in the country still depend on their own labors. This means that, in addition to a basic income floor, the US labor market will need to provide equitable wealth-building opportunities. For millions of American children, wealth building could begin with OIAs. Policy to allow families to transfer unspent OIA balances to universal retirement accounts, as is allowed in Canada's RESPs, would extend asset accumulation into adulthood and give newly financially capable savers a lifelong institution to facilitate their wealth building.[59] Here, too, tax policy could be reworked to provide more equitable incentives, such as refundable credits that reward retirement saving.[43] Otherwise, retirement savings opportunities will remain inequitably provided and unfairly subsidized, and these disparities will continue to contribute to wealth inequality.[68–70] Finally, labor policies that complement OIAs, as part of a larger wealth-building agenda, must contend with tomorrow's labor market, particularly the growing number of jobs threatened by automation. Children's assets, after all, are predicated on the American dream calculus that hard work is what delivers success. If people are replaced with machines on a wide scale it is difficult to imagine what could take the place of work in our daily lives or our understanding of the "deal" America offers. As a result, while human welfare—and, certainly, profit maximization—may be advanced by innovations in automation, policy may need to ensure that people have outlets for their efforts and abilities. The "opportunity" in OIAs is a chance to build a good life, through individual exertion on a relatively level playing field. If that exertion is pointless because technology has supplanted humans in all but a few niches, toward what will children strive?

Looking at policy through a lens of wealth inequality reveals how automation figures into wealth inequality in ways other than job loss. Specifically, determining who owns technologies and who profits from their production will provide important parameters for individuals' life chances. Because moving up the ladder is inextricably tied to asset ownership, policies that govern ownership of the machines of automation may determine who can become wealthy. At this moment, on the cusp of change as dramatic as the Industrial Revolution, it is imperative that we institute policies to democratize asset ownership. If US policy can anticipate the shock waves that new technologies will produce, we can prevent further intensification of wealth inequality. If we look at current and future policy through a lens of wealth inequality, we can innovate new approaches that keep the American dream alive in what may otherwise be its final days. Here, Americans' commitment to creating the conditions where individual merit and exertion determine victors compels a revolution in how we think about our wealth-building systems and how they shape outcomes.

FINANCIAL AND HOUSING MARKETS: OPENING DOORS TO WEALTH BUILDING

Iterations of the American dream often include homeownership not because we are inherently a nation of do-it-yourselfers, but because we value the independence—rooted in wealth—that homeownership tangibly represents. However, households' disparate capacities to access, navigate, and profit from institutions where wealth is built perpetuate wealth gaps. Indeed, even when disadvantaged Americans participate in the systems that help others accumulate wealth, they seldom benefit equally. As we have described, this is true in education.[23] Additionally, the extent to which homeownership can contribute positively to a family's balance sheet depends in large part on income,[71] race, and geography.[12,72] When institutions amplify the efforts and capacities of some Americans more than others, we have textbook conditions for inequality. We get widening cracks in the American dream. Critically, from our perspective as wealth researchers proposing asset-based policy that runs through the US education system, indictment of the housing market's inequitable wealth outcomes is of more than corollary interest. Homeownership is one of the primary ways that privileged Americans act strategically with institutions such as school districts, and educational inequities suppress wealth building by disadvantaged communities. Historically and still today, government policy has been complicit in these inequities.[73] Importantly, however, equitable homeownership could be a complement to children's asset policies. Housing wealth can be leveraged to cushion shocks, facilitate productive risks, and transfer assets to future generations.[74]

Where, today, homeownership both results from and contributes to wealth gaps, this could look different within a fair system of asset opportunities. Housing wealth could be a source of family OIA deposits and a tangible representation of the promise that awaits children coming of age as asset owners.

CSAs provide some families' first access to a financial instrument. This financial inclusion matters. Accounts provide the institutional access theorized to make a difference in financial decision-making.[75] Indeed, the entire concept of children's savings is grounded in theory that holds that people require institutions in order to accumulate wealth.[76,77] Because wealth is built within financial institutions, all Americans should have access to savings and investment vehicles. Research has found that low-income households' probability of owning wealth-building investment accounts increases with greater density of mainstream financial institutions.[78] However, financial institutions are not equitably available in communities around the country.[79] Ownership of low-cost, nonpredatory accounts protects people from wealth-stripping financial services such as check cashers and payday lenders.[80] Financial inclusion would allow families to translate competencies gained from interacting with their OIAs to daily financial practices, including the accumulation of emergency savings.

BECAUSE WEALTH IS POWER, THE WEALTH AGENDA MUST BRIDGE THE GAP

Examining US policy institutions through a wealth-building lens is a little like driving on the highway while shopping for a new car; when you are looking for ways wealth influences Americans' outcomes, you start to see them everywhere. The policies highlighted here—in education reform, health care, income support, and housing and financial markets—are only some of the many cases where institutions exacerbate rather than counter wealth inequality. As others have articulated, there are needs for reforms in other domains as well (criminal justice, immigration policy, women's rights, and even climate policy).[81-84] As new dynamics unfold, other issues must be considered as part of a wealth-building agenda. What Americans need, in short, is for every policy to be considered a potential leverage point in the effort to ensure that wealth inequality does not pull any more rungs out of the ladder of opportunity.

It is important to emphasize that a wealth-building agenda is not merely an anti-poverty agenda. It is not designed only to ensure that no Americans suffer the worst that our economy can deliver. Instead, this agenda articulates how existing institutions will have to change in order to facilitate wealth accumulation for those currently disadvantaged. The aim is to underscore the institutional arrangements that predetermine inequitable outcomes, as a pivot away from blaming those on the losing end of the wealth distribution for their predicaments. We expose some of the ways wealth matters for how well Americans do so that we can provide a playing field on which hard-working, talented Americans profit fairly from their efforts. Less wealth inequality is the goal, not merely for its own financial sake but because wealth is really about power. And if we want to redistribute power, we need to do more than just inch those on the bottom up a few rungs. We need to make sure that the most privileged have some upper bounds on their climb.[85]

This is a crucial distinction. To close the opportunity gap, we have to address wealth inequality from both ends. Assertively progressive taxation is the best-known mechanism for constructing these upper parameters. This includes taxing assets[86] (e.g. capital gains) and intergenerational transfers[87] at higher rates. It has been our contention throughout this book that wealth's value is not just measured in dollars but also in the power wealth confers to shape institutions in ways that put the metaphorical wind at one's backs. To achieve different outcomes on the scale required to save the American dream, we need policy that not only gives every American child a "faster bicycle." We must also ensure that her peers are not being driven to the front of the line.

Where We Begin: OIAs, the Opportunity Pipeline, and the Distribution of Power in America

From the pantheon of essential policy changes for making American institutions better conduits of equitable wealth building, we begin with assets for children at birth, in the form of OIAs, not because we think they are the only answer but because they are a way to distribute wealth and its power at crucial moments along the opportunity pipeline that is supposed to see children to prosperity. To salvage the American dream, we need to expand it to accommodate an understanding of the role institutions play in augmenting individuals' efforts and, ideally, creating the conditions in which exertion can pay off. OIAs can be such an institution. They can also position children to improve the outcomes they wrest from other institutions, thereby bringing the American dream within reach. OIAs are politically feasible, even in today's polarized environment. Their incorporation of family contributions aligns with American value preferences for how policy should complement individual capacity. Early assets' effects on children's college-saver identities and possible future selves provide interim indicators that long-term investment is paying dividends and reassurance to those who want to see changes in individuals' orientations, not just their balance sheets.

Understood as a 21st-century financial aid policy that works all along the opportunity pipeline rather than just at the point of enrollment, OIAs are relatively fiscally manageable as well. Certainly, the United States spends heavily on financial aid policies that are doing little to convince the nation that children will be able to secure the "good life" they envision. Where our financial aid footprint today is inadequate, complex, and inequitable, asset-based approaches have demonstrated potential to catalyze superior outcomes in early childhood, throughout school, during college, and following college completion. Where, today, wealth inequality creates perpetuating cycles of privilege and disadvantage that make it hard for talented but poor children to fairly compete, OIAs are capable of constructing new, positive, reinforcing patterns. Creating universal OIAs and seeding them with a public transfer capable of closing the opportunity gap is a big lift, to be sure. A nation defined by grand aspirations of equitable chances and perpetual progress is just as surely up to the challenge. Our shared dream is on the line. Saving it is our central purpose and, we believe, the definitive task of our age.

Descriptions of Some Children's Savings Account Programs in the Field

Harold Alfond College Challenge (HACC) (ME); https://www.500forbaby.org/; http://myalfondgrant.org

Inception	Started in 2008 as a pilot with two hospitals; went statewide in 2009
Administrator	The HACC grant is provided by the Harold Alfond Foundation (HAF) to the nonprofit Alfond Scholarship Foundation (ASF). Automatic enrollment in the Harold Alfond College Challenge is administered by the Finance Authority of Maine (FAME). Harold Alfond College Challenge grants are deposited in NextGen 529 accounts, administered by Bank of America's Merrill Lynch.
Target Population	All children born Maine residents (HACC awarded at birth)
Enrollment Procedure	The HACC was opt-in from 2008 to 2012 and switched to opt-out (automatic enrollment, facilitated by birth records) for all babies born in 2013 and later. If families want to contribute to the 529 plan, they must open their own NextGen account.
Accountholders as of 1/2017	Total HACC grantees as of 1/31/2017: 70,771 Of these, 32,095 have NextGen 529 college savings accounts where they can save for their children's educations.
Account Type	Maine's 529 college savings plan (NextGen)

Initial Seed & Incentives	Universal $500 initial seed
	NextStep match: 2015–present, 50% match on 529 contributions with a cap of $300 total match per calendar year (no lifetime limit)
	Accounts with direct deposit are eligible for an additional one-time $100 match.
Funding	Private philanthropy funding (HAF) of the initial seed
	NextStep matching grants funded by FAME
	Outreach and educational materials funded by HAF and delivered through ASF partnership with FAME. Additional, charitable incentives available to accountholders in some geographies.
Programmatic Elements	• Universal seed
	• Savings matches
	• Quarterly statements and parent materials re: college, child development, financial management (by mail and online)
	• Funds can be used for any qualified higher education expenses by the child's 28th birthday (must be paid in one disbursement)
	• Payroll deductions, available through a growing number of employers
	• Partnerships with Head Start programs in four counties to expand reach, build trust, and encourage raised aspirations
Research & Evaluation	HACC Evaluation (by Center on Assets, Education, and Inclusion [AEDI]) to quantitatively examine savings patterns, college-saver identity, and outcomes for children enrolled in the opt-in and opt-out phases; qualitative analysis of elements of Identity-Based Motivation

CollegeBound*Baby* (RI) https://www.collegeboundsaver.com/cbb.html

Inception	2010
Administrator	529 account overseen by Rhode Island State Treasurer; sponsored by Rhode Island Higher Education Assistance Authority; accounts are managed by Ascensus College Savings
	Delivery of the $100 seed coordinated by CollegeBound*Baby* and Rhode Island Office of Vital Records
Target Population	Children born in Rhode Island
Enrollment Procedure	Streamlined opt-in enrollment facilitates account opening with a checkbox to opt in for the $100 grant (added to hospital discharge paperwork for state-issued birth certificate).
	*Parents must open a separate CollegeBoundSaver account to contribute their own savings.
Accountholders as of 1/2017	12,702 accounts as of the end of 2016, 12,016 of which were opened after the shift to "checkbox" facilitated enrollment
Account Type	State 529 college savings plan (CollegeBoundSaver)

Initial Seed & Incentives	$100 initial seed deposit if the 529 account is opened by child's first birthday
Funding	Ascensus College Savings (529 provider), as part of their contract with RI
Programmatic Elements	• CollegeBound*Baby* funds are not transferable to other children and can only be used for approved higher education expenses by the child's 25th birthday. • Those receiving the CollegeBound*Baby* seed are exempt from the 529 plan's opening deposit requirement. • Families receive welcome packets with information about paying for college.
Research & Evaluation	RI tracks uptake of CollegeBound*Baby*.

CHET Baby Scholars (CT) https://www.aboutchet.com/buzz/baby.shtml

Inception	Soft launch 2014; marketing rollout 2015
Administrator	CHET Baby Scholars administered by the state treasurer; accounts held in state 529 college savings plan, managed by TIAA-CREF
Target Population	All Connecticut resident babies up to age 1 (for adopted Connecticut resident children, up to first anniversary of adoption)
Enrollment Procedure	Opt-in, parent-initiated enrollment
Accountholders as of 1/2017	4,735 (by the end of 2016), although this is likely to increase more rapidly now that there is an option to ask for information on CHET Baby Scholars on the state's birth certificate application form given to all new mothers. Approximately 45% of new parents have selected the CHET Baby Scholars option on the birth certificate form since that process changed in early 2016, but there is a delay between these births and initiation of the CHET Baby Scholars account.
Account Type	State 529 college savings plan
Initial Seed & Incentives	$100 initial seed and match for the first $150 saved
Funding	Connecticut Student Loan Foundation (residual funds to be used until gone) Provision to allow Connecticut taxpayers to direct a portion of their refunds to the CHET Baby Scholars fund; pursuit of additional corporate and/or philanthropic investment
Programmatic Elements	• $100 initial seed • $25 minimum initial deposit required, which can come from the $100 initial seed • Match the first $150 saved by the child's fourth birthday • Assets excluded from financial aid determinations at state colleges and universities and within means-tested state programs

Research & Evaluation	CHET Baby Scholars was created to help CT families start early to save for future college costs and to increase the affordability of higher education. To date, families who have taken advantage of the CHET Baby Scholars grant by opening their CHET account within the first year of the child's life have generally continued to contribute to those accounts. This savings engagement can be monitored over time.

Inversant (Formerly FUEL Education) (MA) http://www.inversant.org/

Inception	2009
Administrator	Community-based nonprofit organization
Target Population	Low-income families from Chelsea, Lynn, Salem, and Boston neighborhoods
Enrollment Procedure	Opt-in parent or child-initiated enrollment
Accountholders as of 1/2017	Total accountholders since 2009: 1,707 Currently enrolled account holders: 660
Account Type	Credit union savings accounts owned by participants
Initial Seed & Incentives	Match upon high school graduation—varies by school but usually a 1:1 match up to an average of around $1,000 Entered into $100 sweepstakes for responding to e-newsletter survey Other incentives vary by site. For example, some offer a one-time incentive for regular saving or a direct deposit incentive.
Funding	Private philanthropic contributions from funders such as Boston Foundation and Smith Foundation, as well as some individual donors
Programmatic Elements	• Monthly multilingual learning circles for adolescents and/or parents, with meals provided; topics include financial aid and college preparation • Savings matches • Outreach and support in English and Spanish
Research & Evaluation	Three-year study conducted by researchers at the Harvard Graduate School of Education regarding effects of parental engagement and savings on students' academic achievement[1]

$eedMA (MA) https://www.seedma.org/

Inception	Three-year pilot program launched fall 2016
Administrator	Office of the Treasurer and Receiver General of Massachusetts and Massachusetts Educational Financing Authority
Target Population	Kindergarten students in Worcester and Monson Public School Systems
Enrollment Procedure	Opt-in parent-initiated enrollment; parents can enroll online or at community enrollment session

Accountholders as of 1/2017	Not available
Account Type	State 529 college savings plan
Initial Seed & Incentives	$50 initial seed deposit
Funding	Economic Empowerment Trust Fund (501(c)3 organization overseen by MA Treasurer) and support from private partnerships
Programmatic Elements	• $50 initial seed • Information on college planning and financial education • Savings can be used for any postsecondary education expenses
Research & Evaluation	Massachusetts State Treasurer's Office of Economic Empowerment conducting a process evaluation and exploring research partnership for formative and summative evaluations

Boston Saves (MA) BostonSavesCSA.org

Inception	2016 (three-year pilot, five schools for first round 2016-2017)
Administrator	Administered by the Mayor's Office of Financial Empowerment in partnership with Boston Public Schools
Target Population	Boston public (district and charter) school kindergartners in selected schools, with plans to expand, eventually, to all public (district and charter) schools in the city
Enrollment Procedure	Automatic enrollment through the school (opt-out)
Accountholders as of 1/2017	246
Account Type	Seed and incentive held in Boston Education Development Foundation account; the linked account (where parents contribute) can be regular savings, checking, or 529 account or a custodial account
Initial Seed & Incentives	$50 initial seed for all children Sign-up bonus: Linking an account gets an automatic $25 incentive; if account is linked within 60 days, an additional $25 incentive is added. $5 incentive per quarter for each $25 net increase in linked account
Funding	Eos Foundation
Programmatic Elements	• Initial $50 seed and sign-up bonus • Quarterly savings incentives • Financial education and savings tools and events • Classroom activities • Savings can be used for any postsecondary education
Research & Evaluation	During initial rollout, priority metrics include account linkage and dimensions of the savings process.

NYC Kids Rise CSA[2]

Inception	2017 (three-year pilot)
Administrator	Created by New York City (NYC) mayor; overseen by NYC Kids RISE (nonprofit)
Target Population	Kindergartners in one NYC school district (first year is 30 schools in Queens)
Enrollment Procedure	Universal, automatic enrollment for kindergarten students at participating schools
Accountholders as of 1/2017	3,500 projected to be enrolled September 2017
Account Type	NY 529 college savings plan
Initial Seed & Incentives	$100 initial seed Up to $200 in matching if benchmarks (not yet set) are met during first three years
Funding	The Gray Foundation contributed up to $10 million for first three years.
Programmatic Elements	• Initial seed • Matching incentive for meeting benchmarks
Research & Evaluation	Baseline, MDRC conducted focus groups with low- and moderate-income income families regarding their views on college and college savings.

Promise Indiana www.promiseindiana.org

Inception	September 2013
Administrator	Spearheaded by the Wabash County YMCA; implemented in local communities by pilot collaboratives (schools, local government, nonprofit organizations)
Target Population	Students beginning in kindergarten in participating schools (now in 18 Indiana communities)
Enrollment Procedure	Opt-in enrollment, facilitated by staff and volunteers at school registration and outreach events
Accountholders as of 1/2017	10,796 accounts as of March 2017
Account Type	529 college savings account in the state's direct-sold 529 plan, Indiana CollegeChoice, overseen by the Indiana Education Savings Authority and administered by Ascensus College Savings
Initial Seed & Incentives	$25 initial seed deposit in all Promise IN communities, savings matches (ranges from $50 to $100/year)
Funding	Local philanthropic organizations, private donors such as local champions and state government

Programmatic Elements	• College and career discovery activities integrated into elementary classrooms • "Walk into my future" visits to college campuses • Champion support
Research & Evaluation	AEDI studying savings engagement, effects on academic achievement, and evidence of emerging college-saver identities

St. Louis College Kids www.stlofe.org/collegekids

Inception	Fall 2015
Administrator	Office of Financial Empowerment, Treasurer, City of St. Louis
Target Population	Kindergarteners in public or charter schools, citywide
Enrollment Procedure	Automatic (opt-out) enrollment
Accountholders as of 1/2017	6,264 at 65 participating schools
Account Type	Deposit savings account at First Financial Federal Credit Union
Initial Seed & Incentives	$50 initial deposit Dollar-for-dollar matching of family contributions up to $100 per academic year K-12th grades Financial education incentive for parent/guardian
Funding	Treasurer of the City of St. Louis (funded through capture of parking revenues) Private donation marketing by 1:1Fund
Programmatic Elements	• In-person, online, or smartphone app financial education courses • Family Savings Nights • Benchmark incentives for children's school attendance, completion of financial education • Savings match up to $100
Research & Evaluation	The Center for Social Development is studying non-financial outcomes. St. Louis College Kids is working with the Common Cents Lab at Duke University to explore how integration of behavioral economics principles may improve savings outcomes.

SEED for Oklahoma Kids https://www.ok.gov/treasurer/SEED_OK/

Inception	2007
Administrator	Oklahoma State Treasurer, in partnership with Center for Social Development at Washington University
Target Population	Accountholders randomly selected from the full population of Oklahoma children born in certain periods in 2007
Enrollment Procedure	Automatic enrollment in state-owned 529 college savings plan account/opt-in participant-owned 529 college savings plan account

Accountholders as of 1/2017	Randomized control trial 1,358 treatment children/1,346 control children
Account Type	Oklahoma 529 college savings plan
Initial Seed & Incentives	Initial state-owned deposits of $1,000 $100 account opening incentive in participant-owned 529 account $1 or $.50 match for every $1 (depending on income level) up to $250 per year
Funding	Philanthropic support from private donors such as Ford Foundation and Charles Stewart Mott Foundation
Programmatic Elements	• Quarterly account statement (limited engagement, via mail, to avoid contamination of control group)
Research & Evaluation	Rigorous, randomized control trial research by the Center for Social Development, examining saving, effects on parental and child well-being, and assessment of the program model[3]

Prosperity Kids

Inception	Summer 2014
Administrator	Prosperity Works, a private nonprofit organization in Albuquerque, NM
Target Population	Albuquerque public school children and children in the two poorest zip codes, ages birth to 11 years old
Enrollment Procedure	Opt-in enrollment facilitated by nonprofit Prosperity Works after completion of 10 weeks of child development and community leadership training for parents
Accountholders as of 1/2017	524 Children's Savings Accounts and 86 parent Emergency Savings Accounts (ESAs)
Account Type	Deposit savings account at Rio Grande Credit Union
Initial Seed & Incentives	$100 seed deposit Savings matches up to $200 per year for 10 years Benchmark incentive deposits in ESA for parental accomplishment of financial education and parent engagement goals up to $100/year for five years
Funding	Many philanthropic and for-profit donors[4] headed by the Kellogg Foundation; $25,000 from City of Albuquerque
Programmatic Elements	• 10 weeks of culturally-competent, peer-supported child development and community leadership training • Two weeks of financial capability training • Two-generation program with ESAs for parents with an associated secured credit card
Research & Evaluation	AEDI research on college-saver identity development, savings patterns, and effects on academic achievement[5]

San Francisco K2C http://sfgov.org/ofe/k2c

Inception	Spring 2011
Administrator	The City of San Francisco Office of Financial Empowerment, in partnership with San Francisco Unified School District
Target Population	All San Francisco public school kindergarteners, as well as any student entering a San Francisco public school in grades K-4 at some schools and K-5 at other schools
Enrollment Procedure	Automatic enrollment
Accountholders as of 1/2017	21,617 accounts opened (as of July 2016)
Account Type	Deposit savings account at Citibank
Initial Seed & Incentives	$50 initial deposit $10 Save Monthly Bonus (up to $60 for any six months of saving) $10 Save Now Bonus (for new K2C savers) $20 K2C Account Registration Bonus (when families sign up to view the K2C account activity through the online portal)
Funding	Public funding from the City and County of San Francisco for the initial seed Philanthropic support for outreach and incentives
Programmatic Elements	• Age-appropriate financial education in the classroom • Social marketing to encourage college savings • Incentives for certain schools to experiment with approaches to encourage engagement • Citibank field trips for students and parents to encourage saving
Research & Evaluation	EARN conducted analysis on K2C design features and savings barriers[6] AEDI (with American Institute for Research) studied saving in K2C, evidence of college-saver identities, and effects on academic outcomes

Oakland Promise (Two CSA programs: Brilliant Babies and K2C)
http://www.oaklandpromise.org/brilliant-baby.html

Inception	Fall 2016
Administrator	The City of Oakland Mayor's Office
Target Population	Brilliant Baby: Low-income infants (births financed by Medicaid) K2C: Kindergartners in all Oakland Public Schools (Oakland Unified School District or charter-managed)
Enrollment Procedure	Brilliant Baby: Opt in K2C: All kindergartners automatically receive a $100 early scholarship and encouragement/incentives to open a 529 account for college saving

Accountholders as of 1/2017	1,500 babies to be enrolled in Brilliant Baby demonstration in first three years 17 K2C elementary schools as of 2016–2017 academic year
Account Type	California 529 accounts
Initial Seed & Incentives	Brilliant Baby CSAs are seeded with $500 K2C provides up to $100 in account-opening incentive
Funding	The City of Oakland, East Bay College Fund, the Oakland Public Education Fund, and other philanthropic organizations
Programmatic Elements	• Brilliant Baby includes financial coaching and incentives associated with meeting coaching milestones • In addition to the early scholarship and CSA, K2C includes financial education and activities to cultivate college-going cultures, within the classroom experience
Research & Evaluation	Brilliant Baby includes a randomized control trial run through hospital partners. Participants will be randomized into three groups: (1) standard of care, (2) Brilliant Baby with coaching, and (3) Brilliant Baby 529 without coaching. Impact evaluation will begin in the winter of 2017–2018; baseline data will be collected at enrollment. Additionally, AEDI is conducting an investigation into development of CSA components within the larger Oakland Promise initiative and families' experiences with the CSAs.

Nevada College KickStart http://collegekickstart.nv.gov/

Inception	Fall 2013
Administrator	Nevada State Treasurer's Office
Target Population	Kindergartners in Nevada public schools
Enrollment Procedure	Opt-out automatic enrollment, based on information supplied by the schools to the Treasurer's Office, including the child's name and school district ID number
Accountholders as of 1/2017	Approximately 135,000
Account Type	SSGA Upromise 529 plan, owned by the State Treasurer's Office Families are encouraged to open a separate 529 account that will grow their child's savings over time and be owned by the parents. The two accounts can be linked together.
Initial Seed & Incentives	Initial deposit of $50 for each public school kindergarten student If parents open their own account and link it to the automatic account, they may be eligible for additional incentives. For example, for students entering kindergarten in 2016, families who linked the College KickStart account to a parent-owned 529 account were eligible to receive a $200 incentive, on a first-come-first-served basis. On personal accounts in the SSGA Upromise Plan, eligible participants receive 1:1 match for their contributions, up to $300/year, for a maximum of $1,500 over five years.

Funding	The Board of Trustees of the College Savings Plans of Nevada provided funding from inception through 2015–2016 school year. Subsequently, the program uses a portion of the fees paid to the Treasurer's Office by the private companies that serve as program managers for the College Savings Plans of Nevada. In addition, some funding is donated by community partners and donors.
Programmatic Elements	• Treasurer's Office supplies elementary schools with support materials, including fliers, brochures, and posters. • Parents receive regular statements about their children's accounts. • Some schools sponsor events designed to cultivate a college-saving culture.
Research & Evaluation	*Not available*

Tacoma Housing Authority https://www.tacomahousing.net/content/
children%E2%80%99s-savings-account-program

Inception	Fall 2015
Administrator	Tacoma Housing Authority (THA), in partnership with Tacoma Public Schools
Target Population	Families residing in the New Salishan housing community. Initial enrollment occurs when a child enters kindergarten. In fall 2016, children who enroll at Lister Elementary but do not reside at Salishan can also participate in the elementary portion but must live in Salishan to continue in middle/high school.
Enrollment Procedure	Opt-in enrollment via online application, until the program is full. The program can enroll 80 new kindergarteners and 60 new sixth graders per year.
Accountholders as of 1/2017	The program is in its second year; thus far, 43 kindergarten children and 35 sixth-grade children have been enrolled.
Account Type	Savings account at Heritage Bank opened in the child's name, but THA is account custodian and controls withdrawals.
Initial Seed & Incentives	Account is seeded with $50 at opening. THA will match 1:1 any family deposits made, up to $400 per year, between kindergarten and fifth grade. Beginning in sixth grade, individualized plans are made that include goals for the child through high school. For each academic milestone met, an incentive of up to $700/year will be placed into the child's account. Students who fully participate between kindergarten and high school will accumulate $9,700 in their account, available when they enroll in postsecondary education.
Funding	Initially funded by Bill & Melinda Gates Foundation, Bamford Foundation, Heritage Bank, and other smaller partners. Fundraising is ongoing.

Programmatic Elements	• Children receive financial literacy education at their elementary school. • Parents receive financial training and assistance accessing mainstream banking through the THA.
Research & Evaluation	The Urban Institute will complete a three-year evaluation that will examine early progress toward academic and nonacademic medium- and long-range outcomes. Academic outcomes include school attendance, discipline, standardized reading and math scores, high school graduation rates, and enrollment and completion in postsecondary education. Nonacademic outcomes include extent of participation in the CSA, mainstream banking activity, financial literacy for students and parents, attitudes toward saving, and future orientation.

Lansing SAVE (Student Accounts Valuing Education)

http://www.lansingmi.gov/674/Lansing-SAVE

Inception	January 2015
Administrator	Lansing SAVE is a program of the City of Lansing, Office of Financial Empowerment, which has partnered with the HOPE Scholarship, Promise Scholarship, Capital Area College Access Network, and the Financial Empowerment Center to design a continuum for students and their families from kindergarten through adulthood. Other partners include the Lansing School District and Michigan State University (MSU) Federal Credit Union.
Target Population	Kindergarten students in the Lansing School District. Program started at five elementary schools in the 2014–2015 school year, and four more schools were added in the 2015–2016 and 2016–2017 school years. Beginning in 2017, students at all district elementary schools are eligible.
Enrollment Procedure	Opt-out, automatic enrollment for kindergarten students at eligible schools
Accountholders as of 1/2017	The program currently has 1,798 students enrolled, with new cohorts added every school year.
Account Type	Account at MSU Federal Credit Union, with City of Lansing as custodian. At one year, a certificate of deposit (CD) is added for private and philanthropic contributions, to yield a higher interest rate.
Initial Seed & Incentives	Accounts seeded with $5 starting deposit. Family contributions can also be made to accounts. The program currently offers a $10 incentive for attending an annual Lansing SAVE night (added to the CD). Lansing SAVE is in the process of conducting focus groups with parents to design additional incentives/matches.
Funding	The seed is provided by the MSU Federal Credit Union, with matching and incentive funds raised by the program manager.

Programmatic Elements	Financial education is provided to students in their elementary school classrooms.
Research & Evaluation	Lansing SAVE has focused on the savings rate. Additionally, Lansing SAVE and CEDAM have been working with the local college access network and the Lansing Promise (local place-based scholarship) to craft a "financial readiness for success beyond high school" continuum, which includes benchmarks in three categories: financial capability, identifying and securing resources, and creating an individualized financial plan. Lansing SAVE will then look for a research partner to operationalize these benchmarks into metrics.

KS Child Support Savings Initiative
http://www.dcf.ks.gov/services/CSS/Pages/529.aspx

Inception	2013
Administrator	Kansas Department for Children and Families (Kansas Child Support Services), with Kansas State Treasurer
Target Population	Children of noncustodial parents who owe child support arrears or judgments to the State of Kansas or a custodial parent. The CSSI program is available to any eligible noncustodial parent with no enrollment limits.
Enrollment Procedure	Opt-in
Accountholders as of 1/2017	427 total (212 on the state arrears side of the program and 215 on the custodial parent arrears side)
Account Type	Learning Quest 529 Education Savings Account. The Kansas Department for Children and Families is the owner of the account, and the child is named as the beneficiary.
Initial Seed & Incentives	If back child support is owed to the state, for every dollar invested in the child's CSSI account, $2 of child support arrears owed to the state will be forgiven. The minimum $25 deposit required to open the account is paid by the noncustodial parent. If back child support is owed to the custodial parent, a $1:1 match for deposits is available, up to $2,000. Kellogg Foundation funds are used to seed the $25 to open the account. Paying the back child support to the custodial parent qualifies the child's CSSI account for deposits from the Kellogg funds. To receive credit toward arrears, the noncustodial parent must make the current child support payment in full plus pay at least $1 toward the arrears.
Funding	W.G. Kellogg Foundation (for the custodial parent arrears program) In-kind investment by the state of Kansas, in the form of forgiveness of liability of state-owed child support arrears
Programmatic Elements	The Kansas Department of Children and Families sends account statements to custodial parents and children so that they can track asset accumulation in the Learning Quest account.

Research & Evaluation	MRDC used random assignment to one of four behavioral intervention approaches to test the effects of different tactics for increasing noncustodial parents' uptake of the CSSI incentive.

Durham Kids Save[7]

Inception	Spring 2016
Administrator	East Durham Children's Initiative, in partnerships with Self-Help Credit Union, City of Durham, Durham Public Schools, and Prosperity Now (formerly CFED)
Target Population	Six successive cohorts of kindergarteners at YE Smith Elementary School in Durham, NC
Enrollment Procedure	Opt-out automatic, enrollment
Accountholders as of 1/2017	166 savers
Account Type	Savings account at Self-Help Credit Union
Initial Seed & Incentives	Seeded with $100, and then family deposits between kindergarten and fifth grade are matched 1:1, up to $100/year. Durham Kids Save also offers prize-linked savings incentives.
Funding	Private donations by individuals funded initial deposits and matches for six years; regional bank funding for evaluation.
Programmatic Elements	• Children receive basic financial education in the classroom. • Periodic financial education is provided to parents by Latino Community Credit Union. • Regular deposit days are scheduled at the school where cash deposits can be made. • Periodic savings weeks when kids receive piggy banks. • There are incentives available for parents who use the local Volunteer Income Tax Assistance site.
Research & Evaluation	No formal research planned at this point. The Center for Advanced Hindsight at Duke University has completed research to inform program design and suggest behavioral approaches to increase parent engagement.

Notes

1. https://dash.harvard.edu/bitstream/handle/1/14121779/HASHMI-DISSERTATION-2015.pdf?sequence=1; http://www.inversant.org/docs/research/BLong%20-%20FUEL%20Final%20Report%202016-2-8.pdf

2. http://www1.nyc.gov/office-of-the-mayor/news/900-16/mayor-de-blasio-commissioner-menin-newly-created-nonprofit-nyc-kids-rise-child

3. SEED OK research library: https://csd.wustl.edu/OurWork/FinIncl/InclAssetBuild/SEEDOK/Pages/SEEDOKPubs.aspx

4. http://prosperityworks.net/about/our-funders/

5. See http://aedi.ssw.umich.edu/publications/1712-latino-immigrant-families-saving-in-childrens-savings-account-program-against-great-odds-prosperity-kids;http://aedi.ssw.umich.edu/publications/1719-building-college-saver-identities-among-latino-immigrants-a-two-generation-prosperity-kids-account-pilot-program

6. https://www.earn.org/wp-content/uploads/2015/03/130619-K2C-Practitioners-Report-Final.pdf

7. See http://edci.org/en/services/elementary-school/parent-education-and-support/tigers-save

References

PREFACE

1. McCall, L. (2013). *The undeserving rich: American beliefs about inequality, opportunity, and redistribution*. New York, NY: Cambridge University Press.
2. O'Connor, A. (2007). *Social science for what: Philanthropy and the social question in a world turned rightside up*. New York, NY: Russell Sage Foundation, p. 144.
3. Biswas, A. K., & Kirchherr, J. (2015, April 11). Prof, no one is reading you [Opinion]. *The Straits Times*. Retrieved from http://www.straitstimes.com/opinion/ prof-no-one-is-reading-you.
4. Oliver, M. & Shapiro, T. (2006). *Black wealth, White wealth*. New York, NY: Taylor & Francis.
5. Shapiro, T. (2004). *The hidden cost of being African American: How wealth perpetuates inequality*. New York, NY: Oxford University Press.
6. Shapiro, T. (2017). *Toxic inequality: How America's wealth gap destroys mobility, deepens the racial divide, and threatens our future*. New York, NY: Basic Books.
7. Rothstein, R. (2017). *The color of law: A forgotten history of how our government segregated America*. New York, NY: Liveright.
8. Sullivan, L, Meschede, T., Shapiro, T., Asante-Muhammed, D., & Nieves, E. (2016). *Equitable investments in the next generation: Designing policies to close the racial wealth gap*. Waltham, MA: Institute on Assets and Social Policy and CFED. Retrieved from https:// iasp.brandeis.edu/pdfs/2016/EquitableInvestments.pdf.
9. Powell, J. A. (2008). Post-racialism or targeted universalism. *Denver Law Review, 86*, 785. Retrieved from http://scholarship.law.berkeley.edu/facpubs/1633.

10. Shapiro, T., Meschede, T., & Osoro, S. (2013). *The roots of the widening racial wealth gap: Explaining the Black-White economic divide* (pp. 1–7). Waltham, MA: Brandeis University, Institute on Assets and Social Policy.

INTRODUCTION

1. American Enterprise Institute. (2014, December). *What does the American dream mean?* Washington, DC: Author. Retrieved from https://www.aei.org/wp-content/uploads/2014/12/Political-Report-December-20141.pdf.

2. Bowman, K., Marsico, J. K., & Sims, H. (2014). *Public opinion and the American dream.* Washington, DC: American Enterprise Institute. Retrieved from https://www.aei.org/publication/public-opinion-american-dream/.

3. Rothwell, J. (2015). The stubborn race and class gaps in college quality. Retrieved from http://www.brookings.edu/blogs/social-mobility-memos/posts/2015/12/18-stubborn-race-class-gaps-college-rothwell.

4. McCall, L. (2013). *The undeserving rich: American beliefs about inequality, opportunity, and redistribution.* New York, NY: Cambridge University Press.

5. Shapiro, T. (2017). *Toxic inequality: How America's wealth gap destroys mobility, deepens the racial divide, and threatens our future.* New York, NY: Basic Books.

6. Pew Charitable Trusts. (2012). *Pursuing the American dream: Economic mobility across generations.* Washington, DC: Author. Retrieved from http://www.pewtrusts.org/~/media/legacy/uploadedfiles/pcs_assets/2012/pursuingamericandreampdf.pdf.

7. Chetty, R., Hendron, N., Kline, P., & Saez, E. (2014). *Where is the land of opportunity? The geography of intergenerational mobility in the United States.* Stanford, CA: Stanford Center of Poverty & Inequality, Stanford University. Retrieved from http://www.equality-of-opportunity.org/assets/documents/mobility_geo.pdf.

8. Reeves, R., & Venator, J. (2014, June 5). Mobility: What are you talking about? *Social Mobility Memos.* Washington, DC: Brookings Institution. Retrieved from https://www.brookings.edu/blog/social-mobility-memos/2014/06/05/mobility-what-are-you-talking-about/.

9. Bernstein, J., Spielberg, B., & Winship, S. (2015). *Policy options for improving economic opportunity and mobility.* Washington, DC: Peter G. Peterson Foundation. Retrieved from http://www.pgpf.org/what-we-are-doing/grants/grantee-list/policy-options-for-improving-economic-opportunity-and-mobility.

10. Reich, R. (2016). *Saving capitalism: For the many, not the few.* New York, NY: Vintage.

11. Goldfarb, Z. (2012, December 25). Democrats now pushing for tax cuts they once opposed. *The Washington Post.* Retrieved from https://www.washingtonpost.com/business/fiscal-cliff/democrats-now-pushing-for-tax-cuts-they-once-opposed/2012/12/25/bc318a84-4df4-11e2-950a-7863a013264b_story.html?utm_term=.68f63626516f.

12. Hacker, J., & Pierson, P. (2011). *Winner-take-all politics: How Washington made the rich richer—and turned its back on the middle class.* New York, NY: Simon & Schuster.

13. Howard, C. (1999). *The hidden welfare state.* Princeton, NJ: Princeton University Press.

14. Mettler, S. (2011). *The submerged state.* Chicago, IL: University of Chicago Press.

15. Emmons, W. R., & Ricketts, L. R. (2017). College is not enough: Higher education does not eliminate racial and ethnic wealth gaps. *Federal Reserve Bank of St. Louis Review,* 99(1), 7–40. https://dx.doi.org/10.20955/r.2017.7-39

16. Hershbein, B. (2016, February 19). A college degree is worth less if you are raised poor. *Brookings Social Mobility Memos.* Retrieved from http://

www.brookings.edu/blogs/social-mobility-memos/posts/2016/02/
19-college-degree-worth-less-raised-poor-hershbein.

17. McNamee, S. J., & Miller, R. K. (2013). *The meritocracy myth.* Lanham, MD: Rowman & Littlefield.

18. Sullivan, L., Meschede, T., Dietrich, L., Shapiro, T., Traub, A., Ruetschlin, C. & Draut, T. (2015). *The racial wealth gap: Why policy matters.* Waltham, MA: IASP/Demos. Retrieved from http://www.demos.org/sites/default/files/publications/RacialWealthGap_2.pdf.

19. Elliott, W., Lewis, M., Nam, I., & Grinstein-Weiss, M. (2014). Student loan debt: Can parent's college savings help? *Federal Reserve Bank of St. Louis Review, 96*(4), 331–357.

20. Meschede, T., Taylor, J., Mann, A., & Shapiro, T. (2017, First Quarter). "Family achievements?" How a college degree accumulates wealth for Whites and not for Blacks. *Federal Reserve Bank of St. Louis Review, 99*(1), 121–137.

21. Greenstone, M., Looney, A., Patashnik, J., & Yu, M. (2013). *Thirteen economic facts about social mobility and the role of education.* Washington, DC: The Hamilton Project. Retrieved from https://www.brookings.edu/wp-content/uploads/2016/06/THP_13EconFacts_FINAL.pdf.

22. Boshara, R., Emmons, W., & Noeth, B. (2015). *The demographics of wealth: How age, education, and race separate thrivers from strugglers in today's economy* (Essay No. 3). St. Louis, MO: Federal Reserve Bank of St. Louis. Retrieved from https://www.stlouisfed.org/~/media/Files/PDFs/HFS/essays/HFS-Essay-3-2015-Age-Birth-year-Wealth.pdf.

23. Walpole, M. (2003). Socioeconomic status and college: How SES affects college experiences and outcomes. *The Review of Higher Education, 27,* 45–73. http://dx.doi.org/10.1353/rhe.2003.0044

24. Eccles, J., Wigfield, A., Harold, R. S., & Blumenfeld, P. (1993). Age and gender differences in children's self- and task perceptions during elementary school. *Child Development, 64*(3), 830–847.

25. Rauscher, E. (2015). *By my parents' bootstraps: Parent-adult child transfers and the intergenerational transmission of financial standing.* Lawrence, KS: Center on Assets, Education, and Inclusion.

26. Schoeni R. F., & Ross K. E. (2005). Material assistance from families during the transition to adulthood. In R. A. Settersten, F. F. Furstenberg, & R. G. Rumbaut (Eds.), *On the frontier of adulthood: Theory, research, and public policy* (pp. 396–417). Chicago, IL: University of Chicago Press.

27. Rauscher, E. (2016). Passing it on: Parent-to-adult child financial transfers for school and socioeconomic attainment. *The Russell Sage Foundation Journal of the Social Sciences, 2*(6), 172–196.

28. Dynarski, S. (2015, June 2). For the poor, the graduation gap is even wider than the enrollment gap. *New York Times.* Retrieved from https://www.nytimes.com/2015/06/02/upshot/for-the-poor-the-graduation-gap-is-even-wider-than-the-enrollment-gap.html.

29. Huang, J., Sherraden, M., Kim, Y., & Clancy, M. (2014). Effects of Child Development Accounts on early social-emotional development: An experimental test. *Journal of American Medical Association Pediatrics, 168*(3), 265–271.

30. Huang, J., Sherraden, M., & Purnell, J. Q. (2014). Impacts of Child Development Accounts on maternal depressive symptoms: Evidence from a randomized statewide policy experiment. *Social Science & Medicine, 112,* 30–38. doi:10.1016/j.socscimed.2014.04.023

31. Huang, J., Kim, Y., & Sherraden, M. (2016). Material hardship and children's social-emotional development: Testing mitigating effects of Child Development Accounts in

a randomized experiment. *Child: Care, Health and Development, 43,* 89–96. doi:10.1111/cch.12385

32. Elliott, W., Kite, B., O'Brien, M., Lewis, M., & Palmer, A. (2016). *Initial elementary education finding from Promise Indiana's Children's Savings Account program* (AEDI Working Paper 04-16). Lawrence: Center on Assets, Education, and Inclusion.

33. Elliott, W. (2013). Small-dollar children's savings accounts and children's college outcomes. *Children and Youth Services Review, 35*(3), 572–585. doi:10.1016/j.childyouth.2012.12.015

34. Elliott, W., Webley, P., & Friedline, T. (2011). *Two accounts for why adolescent savings is predictive of young adult savings: An economic socialization perspective and an institutional perspective* (CSD Working Papers No. 11-34). St. Louis, MO: Center for Social Development. Retrieved from https://csd.wustl.edu/Publications/Documents/WP11-34.pdf.

35. Friedline, T., Johnson, P., & Hughes, R. (2014). Toward healthy balance sheets: Are savings accounts a gateway to young adults' asset diversification and accumulation? *Federal Reserve Bank of St. Louis Review, 96*(4), 359–89. Retrieved from https://files.stlouisfed.org/files/htdocs/publications/review/2014/q4/friedline.pdf.

CHAPTER 1

1. Pew Research Center. (2012). *The American-western European values gap.* Washington, DC: Author. Retrieved from http://www.pewglobal.org/2011/11/17/the-american-western-european-values-gap/.

2. Mann, H. (1848). *Twelfth annual report of the Board of Education.* Boston, MA: Dutton and Wentworth.

3. Rhode, D., Cooke, K., & Ojha, H. (2012, December 19). The decline of the "great equalizer"? *The Atlantic.* Retrieved from https://www.theatlantic.com/business/archive/2012/12/the-decline-of-the-great-equalizer/266455/.

4. Van Roekel, D. (2010, March 26). Education is the great equalizer. Washington, DC: National Education Association. Retrieved from http://www.nea.org/home/38697.htm.

5. Sorkin, A. R., & Thee-Brenan, M. (2014). Many Americans feel the American dream is out of reach, poll shows. *The New York Times.* Retrieved from https://dealbook.nytimes.com/2014/12/10/many-feel-the-american-dream-is-out-of-reach-poll-shows/.

6. Harvard Institute of Politics. (2015). Harvard IOP fall 2015 poll. Retrieved from http://iop.harvard.edu/survey/details/harvard-iop-fall-2015-poll.

7. Sanders, K. (2013). Is it easier to obtain the American dream in Europe? Politifact. Retrieved from http://www.politifact.com/punditfact/statements/2013/dec/19/steven-rattner/it-easier-obtain-american-dream-europe/.

8. Pew Research Center. (2011). Is college worth it? Washington, DC: Author. Retrieved from http://www.pewsocialtrends.org/2011/05/15/is-college-worth-it/.

9. Strauss, V. (2014). Poll: Most Americans no longer think a college education is "very important." *The Washington Post.* Retrieved from https://www.washingtonpost.com/news/answer-sheet/wp/2014/09/16/poll-most-americans-no-longer-think-a-college-education-is-very-important/?utm_term=.f2e1a34eec43.

10. Fishman, R., Ekowo, M., & Ezeugo, E. (2017). *Varying degrees: New America's annual survey on higher education.* Washington, DC: New America. Retrieved from https://na-production.s3.amazonaws.com/documents/Varying-Degrees.pdf.

11. Winship, S. (2017). *Economic mobility: A state of the art primer.* Washington, DC: Archbridge Institute. Retrieved from https://www.archbridgeinstitute.org/wp-content/uploads/2017/04/Contemporary-levels-of-mobility-digital-version_Winship.pdf.

12. Corak, M. (2006). *Do poor children become poor adults? Lessons from a cross country comparison of generational earnings mobility* (IZA Discussion Paper No. 1993). Bonn, Germany: Institute for the Study of Labor. Retrieved from http://ftp.iza.org/dp1993.pdf.

13. Pew Charitable Trusts. (2014). *A new financial reality: The balance sheets and economic mobility of Generation X.* Washington, DC: Author. Retrieved from http://www.pewtrusts.org/~/media/assets/2014/09/pew_generation_x_report.pdf.

14. Greenstone, M., Looney, A., Patashnik, J., & Yu, M. (2013). *Thirteen economic facts about social mobility and the role of education.* Washington, DC: The Hamilton Project. Retrieved from https://www.brookings.edu/wp-content/uploads/2016/06/THP_13EconFacts_FINAL.pdf.

15. Chetty, R., Grusky, D., Hell, M., Hendren, N., Manduca, R., & Narang, J. (2016). *The fading American dream: Trends in absolute income mobility since 1940* (NBER Working Paper No. 22910). Cambridge, MA: National Bureau of Economic Research. Retrieved from http://www.nber.org/papers/w22910.pdf.

16. Ehrenfreund, M. (2017, April 20). The average millennial worker makes less than the average baby boomer did in 1975. *The Washington Post.* Retrieved from https://www.washingtonpost.com/news/wonk/wp/2017/04/20/census-young-men-are-making-much-less-than-they-did-in-1975/?utm_term=.a8e5cde527c7.

17. Pew Charitable Trusts. (2014). *A new financial reality: The balance sheets and economic mobility of Generation X.* Washington, DC: Author. Retrieved from http://www.pewtrusts.org/~/media/assets/2014/09/pew_generation_x_report.pdf.

18. Carneiro, P., Hansen, K., & Heckman, J. (2003). *Estimating distributions of treatment effects with an application to the returns to school and measurement of the effects of uncertainty on college choice* (NBER Working Paper No. 9546). Cambridge, MA: National Bureau of Economic Research.

19. Haskins, R., Holzer, H., & Lerman, R. (2009). *Promoting economic mobility by increasing postsecondary education.* Washington, DC: Economic Mobility Project, an Initiative of the Pew Charitable Trusts. Retrieved from http://www.pewtrusts.org/~/media/legacy/uploadedfiles/pcs_assets/2009/pew_emp_promoting_upward_mobility.pdf.

20. Heckman, J. J., Lochner, L. J., & Todd, P. E. (2008). Earnings functions and rates of return. *Journal of Human Capital, 2*(1), 1–31.

21. Pfeffer, F. (2016). *Growing wealth gaps in education.* Ann Arbor, MI: National Poverty Center. Retrieved from http://npc.umich.edu/publications/u/2016-06-npc-working-paper.pdf.

22. Baker, C. N., Tichovolsky, M. H., Kupersmidt, J. B., Voegler-Lee, M. E., & Arnold, D. H. (2015). Teacher (mis)perceptions of reschoolers' academic skills: Predictors and associations with longitudinal outcomes. *Journal of Educational Psychology, 107*(3), 805–820.

23. Turner, C., Khrais, R., Lloyd, T., Olgin, A., Isensee, L., Vevea, B., & Carsen, D. (April 18, 2016). Why America's schools have a money problem. National Public Radio. Retrieved from http://www.npr.org/2016/04/18/474256366/why-americas-schools-have-a-money-problem.

24. Giancola, J., & Kahlenberg, R. (2016). *True merit: Ensuring our brightest students have access to our best colleges and universities.* Lansdowne, VA: Jack Kent Cooke Foundation. Retrieved from http://www.jkcf.org/assets/1/7/JKCF_True_Merit_Report.pdf.

25. Burd, S. (2013). *Undermining Pell: How colleges compete for wealthy students and leave the low-income behind.* Washington, DC: New America Foundation, Education Policy

Program. Retrieved from https://s3.amazonaws.com/new-america-composer/attachments_archive/Merit_Aid%20Final.pdf.

26. Reynolds, J. R., & Pemberton, J. (2001). Rising college expectations among youth in the United States: A comparison of the 1979 and 1997 NLSY. *Journal of Human Resources, 36*(4), 703–726.

27. Bjorklund-Young, A. (2016). *Family income and the college completion gap*. Baltimore, MD: Institute for Education Policy, Johns Hopkins School of Education. Retrieved from http://edpolicy.education.jhu.edu/family-income-and-the-college-completion-gap/.

28. Hershbein, B. (2016, February 19). A college degree is worth less if you are raised poor. *Brookings Social Mobility Memos*. Retrieved from http://www.brookings.edu/blogs/social-mobility-memos/posts/2016/02/19-college-degree-worth-less-raised-poor-hershbein.

29. Hochschild, J. L., & Scovronick, N. (2003). *The American dream and the public schools*. New York, NY: Oxford University Press.

30. Bourdieu, P. (1977). Cultural reproduction and social reproduction. In J. Karabel & A. H. Halsey (Eds.), *Power and ideology in education* (pp. 487–511). New York, NY: Oxford University Press.

31. Reeves, R., & Howard, K. (2013). *The glass floor: Education, downward mobility, and opportunity hoarding*. Washington, DC: Brookings Institution.

32. Mollenkopf, J., Zeltzer-Zubida, A., Holdaway, J., Kasinitz, P., & Waters, M. (2002). *Chutes and ladders: Educational attainment among young second generation and native New Yorkers*. New York: Center for Urban Research, City University of New York.

33. Maxwell, L. (2016). School building condition, social climate, student attendance and academic achievement: A mediation model. *Journal of Environmental Psychology, 46*, 206–216.

34. Strauss, V. (2014). Poll: Most Americans no longer think a college education is "very important." *The Washington Post*. Retrieved from https://www.washingtonpost.com/news/answer-sheet/wp/2014/09/16/poll-most-americans-no-longer-think-a-college-education-is-very-important/?utm_term=.f2e1a34eec43.

35. Reynolds, L. (2004). Skybox schools: Public education as private luxury. *Washington University Law Review, 82*(3).

36. Reeves, R. (2017). *Dream hoarders: How the American upper middle class is leaving everyone else in the dust, why that is a problem, and what to do about it*. Washington, DC: Brookings Institution Press.

37. Lareau, A. (2003). *Unequal childhoods: Race, class, and family life*. Oakland: University of California Press.

38. Baker, B., & Corcoran, S. (2012). *The stealth inequities of school funding*. Washington, DC: Center for American Progress.

39. Godoy, M. (2007, June 28). Parsing the high court's ruling on race and schools. National Public Radio. Retrieved from http://www.npr.org/templates/story/story.php?storyId=11507539.

40. Hannah-Jones, N. (2014, December 19). School segregation, the continuing tragedy of Ferguson. ProPublica. Retrieved from https://www.propublica.org/article/ferguson-school-segregation.

41. Thomas, H., Boguslaw, J., Mann, A., & Shapiro, T. (2013). *Leveraging mobility: Building wealth, security and opportunity for family well-being*. Waltham, MA: Institute on Assets and Social Policy. Retrieved from https://iasp.brandeis.edu/pdfs/2013/LM1-building-wealth.pdf.

42. Buchmann, C., Condron, D., & Roscigno, V. (2010). Shadow education, American style: Test preparation, the SAT and college enrollment. *Social Forces, 89*(2), 435–461.

43. Duncan, G. J., & Murnane, R. J. (Eds.). (2011). *Whither opportunity? Rising inequality, schools, and children's life chances.* New York, NY: Russell Sage Foundation.

44. Golden, D. (2006). *The price of admission: How America's ruling class buys its way into elite colleges—and who gets left outside the gates.* New York, NY: Broadway Books.

45. Rauscher, E. (2015). *By my parents' bootstraps: Parent-adult child transfers and the intergenerational transmission of financial standing.* Lawrence, KS: Center on Assets, Education, and Inclusion.

46. Collins, C. (2013, May 29). Wealthy parents, inherited advantage, and declining mobility. Retrieved from http://inequality.org/wealthy-parents-inherited-advantage-declining-mobility/.

47. Mortenson, T. (2004). Bachelor's degree attainment by age 24 by income quartile, 1970–2002. *Postsecondary Education Opportunity, 143*(1).

48. Fernald, A., Marchman, V. A., & Weisleder, A. (2013). SES differences in language processing skill and vocabulary are evident at 18 months. *Developmental Science, 16*(2), 234–248. doi:10.1111/desc.12019

49. Barnett, W. S., & Yarosz, D. J. (2007). *Who goes to preschool and why does it matter?* (Issue 15). New Brunswick, NJ: National Institute for Early Education Research. Retrieved from http://nieer.org/policy-issue/policy-brief-who-goes-to-preschool-and-why-does-it-matter-updated.

50. Kozol, J. (2005). *Shame of the nation.* New York, NY: Random House.

51. National Public Radio. (2017). How the systemic segregation of schools is maintained by "individual choices." *Fresh Air.* Retrieved from http://www.npr.org/sections/ed/2017/01/16/509325266/how-the-systemic-segregation-of-schools-is-maintained-by-individual-choices.

52. Reynolds, A. J., Chen, C. C., & Herbers, J. E. (2009, June). School mobility and educational success: A research synthesis and evidence on prevention. Paper presented at the Workshop on the Impact of Mobility and Change on the Lives of Young Children, Schools, and Neighborhoods, Board on Children, Youth, and Families, National Research Council, Washington, DC.

53. Zaff, J. F., Moore, K. A., Papillo, A., & Williams, S. (2003). Implications of extracurricular activity participation on positive outcomes. *Journal of Adolescent Research, 18*(6), 599–630.

54. Castleman, B. L., & Page, L. C. (2014). *Summer melt: Supporting low-income students through the transition to college.* Cambridge, MA: Harvard University Press.

55. Sacks, P. (2007). *Tearing down the gates: Confronting the class divide in American education.* Berkeley: University of California Press.

56. Snellman, K., Silva, J. M., Frederick, C. B., & Putnam, R. D. (2014). The engagement gap. *The ANNALS of the American Academy of Political and Social Science, 657*(1), 194–207.

57. Wolniak, G., Wells, R., Engberg, M., & Manly, C. (2015). College enhancement strategies and socioeconomic inequality. *Research in Higher Education,* 1–25.

58. Kornich, S., & Furstenberg, F. (2013). Investing in children: Changes in parental spending on children, 1972–2007. *Demography, 50*(1), 1–23.

59. Venator, J., & Reeves, R. (2015). Unpaid internships: Support beams for the glass floor. *Social Mobility Memos.* Washington, DC: Brookings Institution. Retrieved from https://www.brookings.edu/blog/social-mobility-memos/2015/07/07/unpaid-internships-support-beams-for-the-glass-floor/.

60. Valverde, R. (2017). Students of color in Lawrence school district face uneven odss. Retrieved from http://www2.ljworld.com/news/2017/jan/29/students-color-lawrence-school-district-face-uneve/.

61. Brantlinger, E. A. (2003). *Dividing classes: How the middle class negotiates and rationalizes school advantage*. New York, NY: Routledge-Falmer.

62. Rothwell, J. (2012). *Housing costs, zoning, and access to high-scoring schools*. Washington, DC: Brookings Institution.

63. Ehrenberg, R. G. (2002). *Tuition rising: Why colleges cost so much*. Cambridge, MA: Harvard University Press.

64. Thompson, D. (2017). Rich people are great at spending money to make their kids rich, too. *The Atlantic*. Retrieved from https://www.theatlantic.com/business/archive/2015/04/being-rich-means-having-money-to-spend-on-being-richer/389871/.

65. Everson, H. T., & Millsap, R. E. (2005). *Everyone gains: Extracurricular activities in high school and higher SAT scores* (College Board Research Report 2005-2). New York, NY: College Entrance Examination Board. Retrieved from http://research.collegeboard.org/sites/default/files/publications/2012/7/researchreport-2005-2-extracurricular-activities-high-school-higher-sat-scores.pdf.

66. Reeves, R. (2013). The other American dream: Social mobility, race and opportunity. *Social Mobility Memos*. Washington, DC: Brookings Institution. Retrieved from https://www.brookings.edu/blog/social-mobility-memos/2013/08/28/the-other-american-dream-social-mobility-race-and-opportunity/b.

67. Reeves, R. (2017). *Dream hoarders: How the American upper middle class is leaving everyone else in the dust, why that is a problem, and what to do about it*. Washington, DC: Brookings Institution Press.

68. Pell Institute for the Study of Opportunity in Higher Education. (2015). *Indicators of higher education equity in the United States*. Washington, DC: Author. Retrieved from http://www.pellinstitute.org/downloads/publications-Indicators_of_Higher_Education_Equity_in_the_US_45_Year_Trend_Report.pdf.

69. Bahr, A. (2014, July 29). When the college admissions battle starts at age 3. *The New York Times*. Retrieved from https://www.nytimes.com/2014/07/30/upshot/when-the-college-admissions-battle-starts-at-age-3.html.

70. Dynarski, S. (2015, June 2). For the poor, the graduation gap is even wider than the enrollment gap. *The New York Times*. Retrieved from https://www.nytimes.com/2015/06/02/upshot/for-the-poor-the-graduation-gap-is-even-wider-than-the-enrollment-gap.html.

71. Mettler, S. (2014). *Degrees of inequality: How the politics of higher education sabotaged the American dream*. New York, NY: Basic Books.

72. Rauscher, E. (2016). Passing it on: Parent-to-adult child financial transfers for school and socioeconomic attainment. *The Russell Sage Foundation Journal of the Social Sciences, 2*(6), 172–196.

73. Bailey, M. J., & Dynarski, S. M. (2011). Inequality in postsecondary education. In G. J. Duncan & R. J. Murnane (Eds.), *Whither opportunity: Rising inequality, schools, and children's life chances* (pp. 117–132). New York, NY: Russell Sage Foundation.

74. Hartle, T., & Nellum, C. (2015, November 25). *Where have all the low-income students gone?* Washington, DC: American Council on Education. Retrieved from http://higheredtoday.org/2015/11/25/where-have-all-the-low-income-students-gone/.

75. Reardon, S. F. (2013). The widening income achievement gap. *Educational Leadership, 70*(8), 10–16.

76. DeSilver, D. (2014, January 15). *College enrollment among low-income students still trails richer groups.* Washington, DC: Pew Research Center. Retrieved from http://www.pewresearch.org/fact-tank/2014/01/15/college-enrollment-among-low-income-students-still-trails-richer-groups/.

77. Shapiro, T. (2017). *Toxic inequality: How America's wealth gap destroys mobility, deepens the racial divide, and threatens our future.* New York, NY: Basic Books.

78. Yeung, W. J., & Conley, D. (2008). Black-White achievement gap and family wealth. *Child Development, 79,* 303–324.

79. Belley, P., & Lochner, L. (2007). The changing role of family income and ability in determining educational achievement. *Journal of Human Capital, 1*(1), 37–89.

80. Conley, D. (1999). *Being Black, living in the red: Race, wealth and social policy in America.* Berkeley: University of California Press.

81. Conley, D. (2001). Capital for college: Parental assets and postsecondary schooling. *Sociology of Education, 74*(1), 59–72. http://dx.doi.org/10.2307/2673145

82. Haveman, R., & Wilson, K. (2007). Economic Inequality in college access, matriculation, and graduation. In S. Dickert-Conlin, & R. Rubenstein (Eds.), *Economic inequality and higher education: Access, persistence, and success* (pp. 17–43). New York, NY: Russell Sage Foundation.

83. Morgan, S. L., & Kim, Y. M. (2006). Inequality of conditions and intergenerational mobility. Changing patterns of educational attainment in the United States. In S. L. Morgan, D. B. Grusky, & G. S. Fields (Eds.), *Mobility and inequality: Frontiers of research in sociology and economics* (pp. 165–194). Stanford, CA: Stanford University Press.

84. National Center for Education Statistics. (2001). *Students whose parents did not go to college.* Condition of Education. Washington, DC: Author. Retrieved from https://nces.ed.gov/pubs2001/2001126.pdf.

85. DeAngelo, L., Franke, R., Hurtado, S., Pryor, J. H., & Tran, S. (2011). *Completing college: Assessing graduation rates at four-year institutions.* Los Angeles, CA: Higher Education Research Institute, University of California. Retrieved from https://heri.ucla.edu/DARCU/CompletingCollege2011.pdf.

86. Bowen, W. G., Chingos, M. M., & McPherson, M. S. (2009). *Crossing the finish line: Completing college at America's public universities.* Princeton, NJ: Princeton University Press.

87. Nichols, A. H., Eberle-Sudre, K., & Welch, M. (2014). *Rising tide II: Do Black students benefit as grad rates increase?* Washington, DC: Education Trust. Retrieved from https://edtrust.org/wp-content/uploads/2014/09/RisingTide_II_EdTrust.pdf.

88. Astin, A. W., & Oseguera, L. (2004). The declining "equity" of American higher education. *The Review of Higher Education, 27*(3), 321–341.

89. Chetty, R., Friedman, J. N., Saez, E., Turner, N., & Yagan, D. (2017). *Mobility report cards: The role of colleges in intergenerational mobility.* Stanford, CA: Stanford Center of Poverty & Inequality, Stanford University. Retrieved from http://www.equality-of-opportunity.org/papers/coll_mrc_paper.pdf.

90. Mitchell, M., Leachman, M., & Masterson, K. (2016). *Funding down, tuition up: State cuts to higher education threaten quality and affordability at public colleges.* Washington, DC: Center on Budget and Policy Priorities. Retrieved from http://www.cbpp.org/research/state-budget-and-tax/funding-down-tuition-up.

91. Hiltonsmith, R., & Draut, T. (2015). *The great cost shift continues: State higher education funding after the recession.* Retrieved from http://www.demos.org/publication/great-cost-shift-continues-state-higher-education-funding-after-recession.

92. Webber, D. A. State divestment and tuition at public institutions. *Economics of Education, 60*, 1–4. http://dx.doi.org/10.1016/j.econedurev.2017.07.007

93. Quinterno, J., & Orozco, V. (2012). the great cost shift: How higher education cuts undermine the future middle class. Retrieved from http://www.demos.org/publication/great-cost-shift-how-higher-education-cuts-undermine-future-middle-class.

94. Brand, J. E., & Xie, Y. (2010). Who benefits most from college? Evidence for negative selection in heterogeneous economic returns to higher education. *American Sociological Review, 75*(2), 273–302. http://doi.org/10.1177/0003122410363567.

95. Cullen, J. (2003). *The American dream: A short history of an idea that shaped a nation.* New York, NY: Oxford University Press.

96. Noble, K. G., Houston, S. M., Brito, N. H., Bartsch, H., Kan, E., Kuperman, J. M., & Sowell, E. R. (2015). Family income, parental education and brain structure in children and adolescents. *Nature Neuroscience, 18*(5), 773–778. doi:10.1038/nn.3983

97. Halle, T., Forry, N., Hair, E., Perper, K., Wandner, L., Wessel, J. & Vick, J. (2009). *Disparities in early learning and development: Lessons from the early childhood longitudinal study—Birth cohort (ECLS-B).* Washington, DC: Child Trends. Retrieved from http://www.elcmdm.org/Knowledge%20Center/reports/Child_Trends-2009_07_10_FR_DisparitiesEL.pdf.

98. Attewell, P., & Lavin, D. (2007). *Passing the torch: Does higher education for the disadvantaged pay off across the generations?* New York, NY: Russell Sage Foundation.

99. Pfeffer, F. (2015). How has educational expansion shaped social mobility trends in the United States? *Social Forces, 94*(1), 143–180.

100. Kim, Y., & Sherraden, M. (2011). Do parental assets matter for children's educational attainment? Evidence from mediation tests. *Children and Youth Services Review, 33*(6), 969–979.

101. Dubow, E. F., Boxer, P., & Huesmann, L. R. (2009). Long-term effects of parents' education on children's educational and occupational success: Mediation by family interactions, child aggression, and teenage aspirations. *Merrill-Palmer Quarterly, 55*(3), 224–249.

102. Sharkey, P. (2013). *Stuck in place: Urban neighborhoods and the end of progress toward racial equality.* Chicago, IL: University of Chicago Press.

103. Pennsylvania Department of Education. (2017). Pennsylvania school performance profile. Retrieved from http://www.paschoolperformance.org/Profile/41.

104. Kansas Department of Education. (2017). Kansas building report cards. Retrieved from http://ksreportcard.ksde.org/.

105. U.S. Department of Education. (2012). *National assessment of educational progress.* Washington, DC: National Center for Education Statistics.

106. Orfield, G., Frankenberg, E., Ee, J., & Kuscera, J. (2014). *Brown at 60: Great progress, a long retreat, and an uncertain future.* Los Angeles: Civil Rights Project.

107. Spatig-Amerikaner, A. (2012). *Unequal education.* Washington, DC: Center for American Progress. Retrieved from https://www.americanprogress.org/issues/education/reports/2012/08/22/29002/unequal-education/.

108. Farkas, G. (2003). Racial disparities and discrimination in education: What do we know, how do we know it, and what do we need to know? *Teachers College Record, 105*(6), 1119–1146.

109. Reardon, S. F., Robinson, J. P., & Weathers, E. S. (2014). Patterns and trends in racial/ethnic and socioeconomic academic achievement gaps. In H. F. Ladd & M. E. Goertz

(Eds.), *Handbook of research in education finance and policy* (pp. 491–509). New York, NY: Taylor & Francis.

110. Barton, P. E., & Conley, R. J. (2010). *The Black-White achievement gap: When progress stopped*. Princeton, NJ: Educational Testing Service. Retrieved from https://www.ets.org/Media/Research/pdf/PICBWGAP.pdf.

111. McKown, C., & Weinstein, R. S. (2002). Modeling the role of child ethnicity and gender in children's differential response to teacher expectations. *Journal of Applied Social Psychology, 32*(1), 159–184. doi:10.1111/j.1559-1816.2002.tb01425.x

112. Meeks, M. A. (2010). Racial microaggressions by secondary school teachers against students of color (Doctoral dissertation). Georgia Southern University. Retrieved from http://digitalcommons.georgiasouthern.edu/cgi/viewcontent.cgi?article=1355&context=etd

113. Papageorge, N. W., Gershenson, S., & Kang, K. (2016). *Teacher expectations matter*. Bonn, Germany: Institute for the Study of Labor. Retrieved from http://ftp.iza.org/dp10165.pdf.

114. Rist, R. C. (1970). Student social class and teachers' expectations: The self-fulfilling prophecy in ghetto education. *Harvard Educational Review, 40*, 411–450.

115. Rosenthal, R., & Jacobson, L. (1968). *Pygmalion in the classroom*. New York, NY: Holt, Rinehart & Winston.

116. Rydell, R. J., & Boucher, K.L. (2017). Stereotype threat and learning. *Advances in Experimental Social Psychology, 56*, 81–129. http://dx.doi.org/10.1016/bs.aesp.2017.02.002

117. Lewis, A. E., & Diamond, J. E. (2015). *Despite the best intentions: How racial inequality thrives in good schools*. Oxford: Oxford University Press.

118. Useem, E. L. (1992). Middle schools and math groups: Parents' involvement in children's math placement. *Sociology of Education, 65*, 263–279.

119. Godsey, M. (2015, June 15). Inequality in public schools. *The Atlantic*. Retrieved from https://www.theatlantic.com/education/archive/2015/06/inequality-public-schools/395876/.

120. Theokas, C., & Saaris, R. (2013). *Finding America's missing AP and IB students*. Retrieved from https://edtrust.org/wp-content/uploads/2013/10/Missing_Students.pdf.

121. McNamee, S. J., & Miller, R. K. (2013). *The meritocracy myth*. Lanham, MD: Rowman & Littlefield.

122. Clinedinst, M. E., & Hawkins, D. A. (2009). *State of college admission*. Washington, DC: National Association for College Admission Counseling.

123. McDonough, P. M. *Counseling and college counseling in America's high schools*. Retrieved from http://www.nacacnet.org/research/research-data/Documents/WhitePaper_McDonough.pdf.

124. Weissman, J. (2013). The miserable odds of a poor student graduating from college (in 2 graphs). Retrieved from http://www.theatlantic.com/business/archive/2013/03/the-miserable-odds-of-a-poor-student-graduating-from-college-in-2-graphs/274250/.

125. Heckman, J., & Masterov, D. V. (2007). *The productivity argument for investing in young children* (NBER Working Paper No. w13016). Cambridge, MA: National Bureau of Economic Research. Retrieved from http://www.nber.org/papers/w13016.pdf

126. Rothstein, R. (2014). The racial achievement gap, segregated schools, and segregated neighborhoods—a constitutional insult. *Race and Social Problems, 6*(4).

127. Schneider, B., Martinez, S., & Owen, A. (2006). Barriers to educational opportunities for Hispanics in the United States. In M. Tienda & F. Mitchell (Eds.), *Hispanics and the future of America* (pp. 179–227). Washington, DC: National Academies Press.

128. Pew Research Center. (2014). *The rising cost of not going to college.* Washington, DC: Author. Retrieved from http://www.pewsocialtrends.org/files/2014/02/SDT-higher-ed-FINAL-02-11-2014.pdf.

129. Burning Glass Technologies. (2014). *Moving the goalposts: How demand for a bachelor's degree is reshaping the workforce.* Boston, MA: Author. Retrieved from http://burning-glass.com/wp-content/uploads/Moving_the_Goalposts.pdf.

130. Karabel, J. (2005). *The chosen: The hidden history of admission and exclusion at Harvard, Yale, and Princeton.* New York, NY: Mariner Books.

131. Vara, V. (2015). Is college the new high school? *The New Yorker.* Retrieved from http://www.newyorker.com/business/currency/college-new-high-school.

132. Truman, H. (1947). Statement by the president making public a report of the Commission on Higher Education. Santa Barbara, CA: American Presidency Project. Retrieved from http://www.presidency.ucsb.edu/ws/index.php?pid=12802.

133. Horn, L. J., Chen, X., & Chapman, C. (2003). *Getting ready to pay for college: What students and their parents know about the cost of college tuition and what they are doing to find out* (NCES 2003-030). Washington, DC: National Center for Education Statistics. Retrieved from https://nces.ed.gov/pubs2003/2003030.pdf.

134. Pew Charitable Trusts. (2012). *Most parents expect their children to go to college.* Washington, DC: Author.

135. Camera, L. (2015, November 6). A right, not a luxury. *U.S. News & World Report.* Retrieved from http://www.usnews.com/news/the-report/articles/2015/11/06/college-affordability-is-still-an-issue-today.

136. Gerber, T. P., & Cheung, S. Y. (2008). Horizontal stratification in postsecondary education: Forms, explanations, and implications. *Annual Review of Sociology, 34,* 299–318. doi:10.1146/annurev.soc.34.040507.134604

137. Lucas, S. R. (2001). Effectively maintained inequality, education transitions, track mobility, and social background effects. *American Journal of Sociology, 106,* 1642–1690.

138. Hacker, H. K., & Marcus, J. (2015, December 17). The rich-poor divide on America's college campuses is getting wider, fast. Hechinger Report. Retrieved from http://hechingerreport.org/the-socioeconomic-divide-on-americas-college-campuses-is-getting-wider-fast/.

139. Rothwell, J. (2015). *Using earnings data to rank colleges: A value-added approach with college scorecard data.* Washington, DC: The Brookings Institution. Retrieved from https://www.brookings.edu/research/using-earnings-data-to-rank-colleges-a-value-added-approach-updated-with-college-scorecard-data/.

140. National Postsecondary Education Cooperative. (2007). *Deciding on postsecondary education: Final report* (NPEC 2008–850). Prepared by K. MacAllum, D. M. Glover, B. Queen, & A. Riggs. Washington, DC: Author.

141. Shapiro, D., Dundar, A., Wakhungu, P. K., Yuan, X., Nathan, A., & Hwang, Y. (2015). *Completing college: A national view of student attainment rates—fall 2009 cohort* (Signature Report No. 10). Herndon, VA: National Student Clearinghouse Research Center. Retrieved from https://nscresearchcenter.org/wp-content/uploads/SignatureReport10.pdf.

142. U.S. Department of Education. (2015). *The condition of education 2015 (NCES 2015-144), institutional retention and graduation rates for undergraduate students.* Washington, DC: National Center for Education Statistics.

143. Hoekstra, M. (2009). The effect of attending the flagship state university on earnings: A discontinuity-based approach. *The Review of Economics and Statistics, 91*(4), 717–724.

144. Hoxby, C. M. (2015). *Computing the value-added of American postsecondary institutions.* Washington, DC: Internal Revenue Service. Retrieved from https://www.irs.gov/pub/irs-soi/15rpcompvalueaddpostsecondary.pdf.

145. Zimmerman, S. (2014). The returns to college admission for academically marginal students. *Journal of Labor Economics, 32*(4), 711–754.

146. Dancy, K., & Barrett, B. (2017). Is higher education the gateway to the middle class? Washington, DC: New America. Retrieved from https://www.newamerica.org/education-policy/edcentral/higher-education-gateway-middle-class/.

147. Sallie Mae. (2015). *How America pays for college.* Washington, DC: Author. Retrieved from http://news.salliemae.com/files/doc_library/file/HowAmericaPaysforCollege2015FNL.pdf.

148. Goldrick-Rab, S., & Kendall, N. (2016). *The real price of college* (College Completion Series: Part Two). Washington, DC: Century Foundation. Retrieved from https://tcf.org/content/report/the-real-price-of-college/.

149. Higher Education Research Institute. (2011). *Completing college: Assessing graduation rates at four-year institutions* (IHEP Research Brief). Retrieved from https://heri.ucla.edu/DARCU/CCResearchBrief.pdf.

150. Sallie Mae. (2016). *How America pays for college.* Washington, DC: Author. Retrieved from http://news.salliemae.com/files/doc_library/file/HowAmericaPaysforCollege2016FNL.pdf.

151. College Board. (2015). *Trends in college pricing, 2015.* Retrieved from http://trends.collegeboard.org/sites/default/files/2015-trends-college-pricing-final-508.pdf.

152. Zinshteyn, M. (2017). Who benefits from New York's free college plan? *Hechinger News.* Retrieved from http://hechingerreport.org/benefits-new-yorks-free-college-plan/.

153. Poutre, A., Rorrison, J., & Voight, M. (2017). *Limited means, limited options.* Washington, DC: Institute for Higher Education Policy.

154. Kane, T. (1995). *Rising public college tuition and college entry: How well do public subsidies promote access to college?* Cambridge, MA: National Bureau of Economic Research. Retrieved from http://www.nber.org/papers/w5164.pdf?new_window=1.

155. Kelly, A.P. (2011). *Nothing but net: Helping families learn the real price of college.* Washington, DC: American Enterprise Institute. Retrieved from http://www.aei.org/publication/nothing-but-net-helping-families-learn-the-real-price-of-college/.

156. Marcus, J. (2016). Whom do college-affordability efforts help the most? *The Atlantic.* Retrieved from http://www.theatlantic.com/education/archive/2016/05/who-do-college-affordability-efforts-really-help/484019/.

157. Levitz, J., & Thurm, S. (2012). Shift to merit scholarships stirs debate. *Wall Street Journal.* Retrieved from http://www.wsj.com/articles/SB10001424127887324481204578175631182640920.

158. National Center for Education Statistics. (2015). *Trends in undergraduate nonfederal grant and scholarship aid by demographic and enrollment characteristics, selected years: 1999–2000 to 2011–12.* Washington, DC: U.S. Department of Education. Retrieved from https://nces.ed.gov/pubs2015/2015604.pdf.

159. Woo, J., & Choy, S. (2011). *Merit aid for undergraduates: Trends from 1995–96 to 2007–8.* Washington, DC: National Center for Education Statistics.

160. Dynarski, S. (2004). The new merit aid. In C. M. Hoxby (Ed.), *College choices: The economics of where to go, when to go, and how to pay for it* (pp. 67–93). Chicago, IL: University of Chicago Press.

161. Suggs, C. (2016). *Troubling gaps in HOPE point to need-based aid solutions.* Atlanta: Georgia Budget and Policy Institute. Retrieved from https://gbpi.org/2016/gaps-in-hope-point-to-need-based-aid/.

162. Butrymowicz, S., & Kolodner, M. (2017, August 4). $500M in HOPE reserves idle while students drop out, drown in loans. *Atlanta Journal-Constitution.* Retrieved from http://www.myajc.com/news/500m-hope-reserves-idle-while-students-drop-out-drown-loans/yyRVOvXi5xsYBuFBpxTkoI/.

163. Angrist, J., Autor, D., Hudson, S., & Pallais, A. (2016). *Evaluating postsecondary aid: Enrollment, persistence, and projected completion effects* (NBER Working Paper No. 23015). Cambridge, MA: National Bureau of Economic Research. Retrieved from http://www.nber.org/papers/w23015.pdf.

164. Fishkin, J. (2014). *Bottlenecks: A new theory of equal opportunity.* New York, NY: Oxford University Press.

165. Breland, H., Maxey, J., Gernand, R., Cumming, T., & Trapan, C. (2002). *Trends in college admission 2000: A report of a national survey of undergraduate admission policies, practices, and procedures.* New York: College Board.

166. Gerald, D., & Haycock, K. (2006). *Engines of inequality: Diminishing equity in the nation's premier public universities.* Washington, DC: Education Trust. Retrieved from http://1k9gl1yevnfp2lpq1dhrqe17-wpengine.netdna-ssl.com/wp-content/uploads/2013/10/EnginesofInequality.pdf.

167. Kelchen, R., & Stedrack, L. J. (2016). Fewer poor students are being enrolled in state universities. Here's why. *The Conversation.* Retrieved from http://theconversation.com/fewer-poor-students-are-being-enrolled-in-state-universities-heres-why-56898.

168. McPherson, M., & Schapiro, M. (1998). *The student aid game: Meeting need and rewarding talent in American higher education.* Princeton, NJ: Princeton University Press.

169. Marcus, J., & Hacker, H. K. (2014). Poorer families are bearing the brunt of college price hikes, data show. *Hechinger Report.* Retrieved from http://hechingerreport.org/data-show-poorer-families-bearing-brunt-college-price-hikes/.

170. Olbrecht, A. M., Romano, C., & Teigen, J. (2016). How money helps keep students in college: The relationship between family finances, merit-based aid, and retention in higher education. *Journal of Student Financial Aid, 46*(1).

171. McGrath, M. (2013). Does applying for financial aid hurt your college admissions chances? *Forbes.* Retrieved from http://www.forbes.com/sites/maggiemcgrath/2013/10/29/does-applying-for-financial-aid-hurt-your-college-admissions-chances/#20309ad2674c.

172. Rivard, R. (2013). Using FAFSA against students. *Inside Higher Ed.* Retrieved from https://www.insidehighered.com/news/2013/10/28/colleges-use-fafsa-information-reject-students-and-potentially-lower-financial-aid.

173. Hoxby, C. M., & Avery, C. (2012). *The missing "one-offs": The hidden supply of high-achieving, low income students* (NBER Working Paper No. 18586). Washington, DC: National Bureau of Economic Research. Retrieved from http://www.nber.org/papers/w18586.

174. Elliott, W. (2013b). *Evaluation of the 2011 GEAR UP priority: Lessons learned about integrating CSAs within GEAR UP.* Lawrence, KS: Center on Assets, Education, and Inclusion.

175. White House Council of Economic Advisors. (2016). *Investing in higher education: Benefits, challenges, and the state of student debt*. Retrieved from https://www. whitehouse.gov/sites/default/files/page/files/20160718_cea_student_debt.pdf.

176. Woodhouse, K. (2015). Public colleges' revenue shift. *Inside Higher Ed*. Retrieved from https://www.insidehighered.com/news/2015/04/13/ report-shows-public-higher-educations-reliance-tuition.

177. Snider, S. (2015). Colleges that report meeting full financial need. *U.S. News and World Reports*. Retrieved from http://www.usnews.com/education/best-colleges/paying-for-college/articles/2015/09/14/colleges-that-report-meeting-full-financial-need

178. Butler, S. (2015, January 20). Obama's SOTU free college plan is bad for poor Americans [Op-Ed]. Washington, DC: Brookings Institution. Retrieved from http://www.brookings. edu/research/opinions/2015/01/20-obama-free-community-college-bad-idea-sotu-butler.

179. Chingos, M. M., & Blagg, K. (2017). *Do poor kids get their fair share of school funding?* Washington, DC: Urban Institute. Retrieved from http://www.urban.org/sites/default/ files/publication/90586/school_funding_brief.pdf.

180. Saunders, K. (2015). *Barriers to success: Unmet financial need for low-income students of color in community colleges*. Washington, DC: Center for Postsecondary and Educational Success. Retrieved from http://www.clasp.org/resources-and-publications/publication-1/Barriers-to-Success-Unmet-Financial-Need-for-Low-Income-Students-of-Color.pdf.

181. Juszkiewicz, J. (2015). *Trends in community college enrollment and completion data, 2015*. Washington, DC: American Association of Community Colleges.

182. Wyner, J., Bridgeland, J. M., & DiIulio, J. J. (2008). *Achievement trap: How America is failing millions of high-achieving students from lower-income families*. Landsdowne, VA: Jack Kent Cooke Foundation. Retrieved from http://www.jkcf.org/assets/1/7/Achievement_Trap.pdf.

183. Hersch, J. (2014). *Catching up is hard to do: Undergraduate prestige, elite graduate programs, and the earnings premium* (Vanderbilt Law and Economics Research Paper No. 14-23; Vanderbilt Public Law Research Paper No. 16-17). http://dx.doi.org/10.2139/ssrn.2473238

184. De Alva, J. K., & Schneider, M. (2015). *Rich schools, poor students: Tapping large university endowments to improve student outcomes*. San Francisco, CA: Nexus Research and Policy Center. Retrieved from http://nexusresearch.org/wp-content/uploads/2015/06/Rich_ Schools_Poor_Students.pdf.

185. Card, D. (1995). Using geographic variation in college proximity to estimate the return to schooling. In L. Christofides, E. K. Grant, & R. Swidinsky (Eds.), *Aspects of labor market behaviour: Essays in honour of John Vanderkamp* (pp. 201–222). Toronto: University of Toronto Press.

186. Dale, S. B., & Krueger, A. B. (2002). Estimating the payoff to atending a more selective college: An application of selection on observables and unobservables. *The Quarterly Journal of Economics, 177*(4), 1491–1527.

187. Matsudaira, J. (2016). *Defining and measuring institutional quality in higher education*. Ithaca, NY: Cornell University. Retrieved from http://sites.nationalacademies.org/cs/ groups/pgasite/documents/webpage/pga_170937.pdf.

188. Ost, B., Pan, W., & Webber, D. (2016). *The returns to college persistence for marginal students: Regression discontinuity evidence from university dismissal policies* (IZA Discussion Paper9799). Bonn, Germany: Institute of Labor Economics.

189. Stohl, J., & Carnevale, A. (2013). White flight goes to college. *Poverty and Race*. Washington, DC: Poverty and Race Research Action Council. Retrieved from http:// www.prrac.org/pdf/SeptOct2013Carnevale_Strohl.pdf.

190. Hillman, N. (2012). *Economic diversity among selective colleges: Measuring the enrollment impact of "no-loan" programs* (IHEP Issue Brief). Washington, DC: Institute for Higher Education Policy. Retrieved from http://www.ihep.org/sites/default/files/uploads/docs/pubs/brief_economic_diversity_among_selective_colleges_august_2012.pdf.

191. Bromberg, M., & Theokas, C. (2014). *Falling out of the lead: Following high achievers through high school and beyond*. Washington, DC: Education Trust. Retrieved from http://edtrust.org/wp-content/uploads/2013/10/FallingOutoftheLead.pdf.

192. Santelices, M. V., & Wilson, M. (2010). Unfair treatment? The case of Freedle, the SAT, and the standardization approach to differential item functioning. *Harvard Educational Review, 80*(1).

193. Carnevale, A., & Strohl, J. (2013). *Separate and unequal: How higher education reinforces the intergenerational reproduction of white racial privilege*. Washington, DC: Georgetown University, Center on Education and the Workforce. Retrieved from https://cew.georgetown.edu/report/separate-unequal/

194. Letukas, L. (2015). *Nine facts about the SAT that might surprise you*. Washington, DC: College Board. Retrieved from http://research.collegeboard.org/sites/default/files/publications/2015/1/sat-rumors-stat-report.pdf.

195. Nguyen, T. (2016). How to predict financial attrition. Washington, DC: EAB. Retrieved from https://www.eab.com/research-and-insights/enrollment-management-forum/expert-insights/2016/unmet-need-cliff.

196. Goldrick-Rab, S. (2016). *Paying the price*. Chicago, IL: University of Chicago Press.

197. Hamilton, L. (2013). More is more or more is less? Parental financial investments during college. *American Sociological Review, 78*(1), 70–95. Retrieved from http://dx.doi.org/10.1177/0003122412472680.

198. Krupnick, M. (2015). Low-income students struggle to pay for college, even in rare states that offer help. *Hechinger News*. Retrieved from http://hechingerreport.org/low-income-students-struggle-to-pay-for-college-even-in-rare-states-that-offer-help/.

199. U.S. Department of Housing and Urban Development. (2015). *Barriers to success: Housing insecurity for U.S. college students*. Washington, DC: Author. Retrieved from https://www.huduser.gov/portal/periodicals/insight/insight_2.pdf.

200. Walpole, M. (2003). Socioeconomic status and college: How SES affects college experiences and outcomes. *The Review of Higher Education, 27*, 45–73. http://dx.doi.org/10.1353/rhe.2003.0044

201. Reich, D., & Debot, B. (2015). House Budget Committee plan cuts Pell Grants deeply, reducing access to higher education. Washington, DC: Center on Budget & Policy Priorities. Retrieved from http://www.cbpp.org/research/house-budget-committee-plan-cuts-pell-grants-deeply-reducing-access-to-higher-education.

202. Cunningham, A. F., & Santiago, D. A. (2008). *Student aversion to borrowing: Who borrows and who doesn't*. Washington DC: Institute for Higher Education Policy; Washington, DC: Excelencia in Education. Retrieved from http://www.ihep.org/sites/default/files/uploads/docs/pubs/studentaversiontoborrowing.pdf.

203. Perna, L. (2008). Understanding high school students' willingness to borrow to pay college prices. *Research in Higher Education, 49*(7), 589–606. Retrieved from http://www.jstor.org/stable/25704587.

204. Heller, D. E. (2008). The impact of student loans on college access. In S. Baum, M. McPherson, & P. Steele (Eds.), *The effectiveness of student aid policies: What the research tells us* (pp. 39–67). New York, NY: College Board.

205. St. John, E. P., Andrieu, S., Oescher, J., & Starkey, J. B. (1994). The influence of student aid on within-year persistence by traditional college-age students in four-year colleges. *Research in Higher Education, 35,* 455–480.

206. Fox, M. (1992). Student debt and enrollment in graduate and professional school. *Journal of Applied Economics, 24*(7), 669–677.

207. Millett, C. M. (2003). How undergraduate loan debt affects application and enrollment in graduate or first professional school. *The Journal of Higher Education, 74*(4).

208. Tsapogas, J., & Cahalan, M. (1996, May). Incidence of and factors related to progression to graduate school among recent science and engineering bachelor's degree recipients: Results from a national study. Paper presented at the annual meeting of the Association of Institutional Research, Albuquerque, NM.

209. Zhan, M. (2013). *Youth debt and college graduation: Differences by race/ethnicity.* St. Louis, MO: Washington University, Center for Social Development.

210. Kahlenberg, R. (2004). *America's untapped resource.* Washington, DC: Century Foundation.

211. Phillips, J. P., Petterson, S. M., Bazemore, A. W., & Phillips, R. L. (2014). A retrospective analysis of the relationship between medical student debt and primary care practice in the United States. *Annals of Family Medicine, 12*(6), 542–549. doi:10.1370/afm.1697

212. Rothstein, J., & Rouse, C. E. (2011). Constrained after college: Student loans and early-career occupational choices, *Journal of Public Economics, 95*(1), 149–163.

213. Leonhardt, D. (2014, September 8). Top colleges that enroll rich, middle class, poor. *The New York Times.* Retrieved from http://www.nytimes.com/2014/09/09/upshot/top-colleges-that-enroll-rich-middle-class-and-poor.html?_r=0andabt=0002andabg=1.

214. Dew, J. (2008). Debt change and marital satisfaction change in recently married couples. *Family Relations, 57*(1), 60–71.

215. Dugan, A., & Kafka, S. (2014, August 7). Student debt linked to worse health and less wealth. Retrieved from http://www.gallup.com/poll/174317/student-debt-linked-worse-health-less-wealth.aspx.

216. Walsemann, K. M., Gee, G. C., & Gentile, D. (2014). Sick of our loans: Student borrowing and the mental health of young adults in the United States. *Social Science & Medicine, 124,* 85–93.

217. Fry, R. (2014). *The changing profile of student borrowers.* Washington, DC: Pew Research Center. Retrieved from http://www.pewsocialtrends.org/2014/10/07/the-growth-in-student-debt/.

218. Traub, A., Sullivan, L., Meschede, T., & Shapiro, T. (2017). *The asset value of whiteness: Understanding the racial wealth gap.* Washington, DC: Demos and IASP. Retrieved from http://www.demos.org/publication/asset-value-whiteness-understanding-racial-wealth-gap.

219. Bulman, G. B., & Hoxby, C. M. (2015). The returns to the federal tax credits for higher education. *Tax Policy and the Economy, 29*(1), 13–88. doi:10.1086/683364.

220. McKernan, S. M., Ratcliffe, C., Simms, M., & Zhang, S. (2011). *Private transfers, race, and wealth.* Washington, DC: Urban Institute. Retrieved from http://www.urban.org/sites/default/files/alfresco/publication-pdfs/412371-Private-Transfers-Race-and-Wealth.PDF.

221. Lederman, D., & Fain, P. (2017, January 19). The higher education president. *Inside Higher Ed.* Retrieved from https://www.insidehighered.com/news/2017/01/19/assessing-president-obamas-far-reaching-impact-higher-education.

222. Thompson, D. (2016). Things are about to get much worse for poor Americans. *The Atlantic*. Retrieved from http://www.theatlantic.com/business/archive/2016/11/things-are-about-to-get-much-worse-for-poor-americans/507143/.

223. Neate, R. (2016). Trump's tax plan: Massive cuts for the 1% will usher "era of dynastic wealth." *The Guardian*. Retrieved from https://www.theguardian.com/us-news/2016/nov/23/trump-tax-plan-cuts-wealthy-low-income-inequality.

224. Emma, C., Wermund, B., & Hefling, K. (2016, December 9). DeVos' Michigan experiment gets poor grades. *Politico*. Retrieved from http://www.politico.com/story/2016/12/betsy-devos-michigan-school-experiment-232399.HERE

225. Kainz, K., & Dynarski, M. (2015). *Why federal spending on disadvantaged students (Title I) doesn't work* (Vol. 1). Washington, DC: Brookings Institution.

226. Reardon, S. F. (2011). The widening academic achievement gap between the rich and the poor. In G. J. Duncan & R. J. Murnane (Eds.), *Whither opportunity? Rising inequality, schools, and children's life chances* (pp. 91–115). New York, NY: Russell Sage Foundation.

227. Mazumder, B. (2011). *Black-White differences in intergenerational economic mobility in the U.S.* (Working Paper No. 2011-10). Chicago, IL: Federal Reserve Bank of Chicago. Retrieved from https://www.chicagofed.org/publications/working-papers/2011/wp-10.

228. Carnevale, A., & Strohl, J. (2010). How increasing college access is increasing inequality, and what to do about it. In R. D. Kahlenberg (Ed.), *Rewarding strivers: Helping low-income students succeed in college*. Washington, DC: Century Foundation Press. Retrieved from http://tcf.org/assets/downloads/tcf-CarnevaleStrivers.pdf

229. Johnson, H. B. (2006). *The American dream and the power of wealth: Choosing schools and inheriting inequality in the land of opportunity*. New York, NY: Taylor & Francis.

CHAPTER 2

1. Shapiro, T. (2017). *Toxic inequality: How America's wealth gap destroys mobility, deepens the racial divide, and threatens our future*. New York, NY: Basic Books.

2. Thomas, H., Meschede, T., Mann, A., Boguslaw, J., & Shapiro, T. (2014). *The web of wealth: Resiliency and opportunity or driver of inequality?* Waltham, MA: Institute on Assets and Social Policy. Retrieved from https://iasp.brandeis.edu/pdfs/2014/Web.pdf.

3. Weissman, J. (2013). The miserable odds of a poor student graduating from college (in 2 graphs). *The Atlantic*. Retrieved from http://www.theatlantic.com/business/archive/2013/03/the-miserable-odds-of-a-poor-student-graduating-from-college-in-2-graphs/274250/.

4. Bjorklund-Young, A. (2016). *Family income and the college completion gap*. Baltimore, MD: Institute for Education Policy, Johns Hopkins School of Education. Retrieved from http://edpolicy.education.jhu.edu/family-income-and-the-college-completion-gap/.

5. Reynolds, L. (2004). Skybox schools: Public education as private luxury. *Washington University Law Review, 82*(3).

6. Chingos, M. M., & Blagg, K. (2017). *Do poor kids get their fair share of school funding?* Washington, DC: Urban Institute. Retrieved from http://www.urban.org/sites/default/files/publication/90586/school_funding_brief.pdf.

7. Rothwell, J. (2015b). Using Earnings Data to Rank Colleges: A Value-Added Approach with College Scorecard Data. Washington, DC: The Brookings Institution. Retrieved from https://www.brookings.edu/research/using-earnings-data-to-rank-colleges-a-value-added-approach-updated-with-college-scorecard-data/.

8. Haskins, R., Holzer, H., & Lerman, R. (2009). *Promoting economic mobility by increasing postsecondary education*. Washington, DC: Economic Mobility Project, an Initiative of the Pew Charitable Trusts. Retrieved from http://www.pewtrusts.org/~/media/legacy/uploadedfiles/pcs_assets/2009/pew_emp_promoting_upward_mobility.pdf.

9. Chetty, R., Friedman, J. N., Saez, E., Turner, N., & Yagan, D. (2017). *Mobility report cards: The role of colleges in intergenerational mobility*. Stanford, CA: Stanford Center of Poverty & Inequality, Stanford University. Retrieved from http://www.equality-of-opportunity.org/papers/coll_mrc_paper.pdf.

10. Zaback, K., Carlson, A., & Crellin, M. (2012). *The economic benefits of postsecondary degrees*. Washington, DC: State Higher Education Executive Officers. Retrieved from http://www.sheeo.org/sites/default/files/publications/Econ%20Benefit%20of%20Degrees%20Report%20with%20Appendices.pdf.

11. Schwartz, C.R., & Mare, R.D. (2005). *Trends in educational assortative marriage from 1940 to 2003*. Los Angeles: UCLA California Center for Population Research. Retrieved from http://escholarship.org/uc/item/1t89v0vz.

12. Eika, L., Mogstad, M., & Zafar, B. (2017). Educational assortative mating and household income inequality. *Federal Reserve Bank of New York Staff Reports, 682*. Retrieved from https://www.newyorkfed.org/medialibrary/media/research/staff_reports/sr682.pdf.

13. U.S. Census Bureau. (2015). Educational attainment in the United States. Retrieved from https://www.census.gov/hhes/socdemo/education/data/cps/2015/tables.html.

14. Sherraden, M. (1991). *Assets and the poor: A new American welfare policy*. Armonk, NY: M. E. Sharpe.

15. Chambers, M., Garriga, C., & Schlagenhauf, D. E. (2016). *The postwar conquest of the home ownership dream*. St. Louis, MO: Federal Reserve Bank of St. Louis. Retrieved from http://research.stlouisfed.org/wp/2016/2016-007.pdf.

16. Fetters, D. K. (2010). *Housing finance and the mid-century transformation in U.S. home ownership: The VA home loan program* [Job Market Paper]. Retrieved from https://www.researchgate.net/publication/228672634_Housing_finance_and_the_mid-century_transformation_in_US_home_ownership_the_VA_home_loan_program.

17. Rosen, H., & Rosen, K. T. (1980). Federal taxes and home ownership: Evidence from time series. *Journal of Political Economy, 88*(1), 59–75.

18. Shiller, R. J. (2007). Understanding recent trends in house prices and homeownership. Proceedings, Economic Policy Symposium, Jackson Hole, Federal Reserve Bank of Kansas City, pp. 89–123.

19. College Savings Plan Network. (2016). 529 report: An exclusive end-of-year review of 529 plan activity. Retrieved from http://www.collegesavings.org/wp-content/uploads/2015/09/FINAL-CSPN-Report-March-15-2016.pdf.

20. Piketty, T., Saez, E., & Zucman, G. (2016). Distributional national accounts: methods and estimates for the United States. Cambridge, MA: National Bureau of Economic Research. Retrieved from http://www.nber.org/papers/w22945.

21. McKernan, S. M., Ratcliffe, C., Steuerle, C. E., Kalish, E., & Quakenbush, C. (2015). *Nine charts about wealth inequality in America*. Washington, DC: Urban Institute. Retrieved from http://apps.urban.org/features/wealth-inequality-charts/.

22. Rosenberg, J. (2013). *Measuring income for distributional analysis* (pp. 1–14). Washington, DC: Tax Policy Center, Urban Institute, and Brookings Institution.

23. Freeland, C. (2012). *Plutocrats: The rise of the new global super-rich and the fall of everyone else*. London: Penguin Press.

24. Gilens, M., & Page, B. I. (2014). Testing theories of American politics: Elites, interest groups, and average citizens. *Perspectives on Politics, 12*(3), 564–581. doi:10.1017/S1537592714001595

25. Sitaraman, G. (2017). *The crisis of the middle-class constitution: Why economic inequality threatens our republic.* New York, NY: Knopf.

26. Cohen, P. (2015, April 10). Middle class, but feeling economically insecure. *The New York Times.* Retrieved from https://www.nytimes.com/2015/04/11/business/economy/middle-class-but-feeling-economically-insecure.html?_r=0.

27. Vallas, R., & Valenti, J. (2014). *Asset limits are a barrier to economic security and mobility.* Washington, DC: Center for American Progress. Retrieved from https://www.americanprogress.org/issues/poverty/reports/2014/09/10/96754/asset-limits-are-a-barrier-to-economic-security-and-mobility/

28. Greer, J., & Levin, E. (2014). *Upside down: Tax incentives to save and build wealth* (CFED Federal Policy Brief). Retrieved from http://preview.cfed.org/assets/pdfs/Policy_Brief_-_Tax_Incentives.pdf.

29. Bernstein, J., & Spielberg, B. (2016, November 24). Thankful for the fight for $15. *The Washington Post.* Retrieved from https://www.washingtonpost.com/posteverything/wp/2016/11/24/thankful-for-the-fight-for-15/?utm_term=.b4d22214e4fd.

30. Associated Press. (2010, January 12). Hundreds protest social services cuts. *Bangor Daily News.* Retrieved from https://bangordailynews.com/2010/01/12/politics/hundreds-protest-social-service-cuts/.

31. Pew Charitable Trusts. (2015). *Americans' financial security: Perception and reality.* Washington, DC: Author. Retrieved from http://www.pewtrusts.org/~/media/assets/2015/02/fsm-poll-results-issue-brief_artfinal_v3.pdf.

32. Bankrate. (2016). Financial Security Index. Retrieved from http://www.bankrate.com/finance/consumer-index/financial-security-charts-0621.aspx.

33. Federal Deposit Insurance Corporation. (2015). *National survey of unbanked and underbanked households* [Executive Summary]. Washington, DC: Author. Retrieved from https://www.fdic.gov/householdsurvey/2015/2015execsumm.pdf.

34. Mullainathan, S., & Shafir, E. (2013). *Scarcity: Why having too little means so much.* New York, NY: Time Books.

35. Iyengar, S., Jiang, W., & Huberman, G. (2003). *How much choice is too much? Contributions to 401(k) retirement plans* (PRC Working Paper 2003-10). Philadelphia, PA: Pension Research Council. Retrieved from https://pensionresearchcouncil.wharton.upenn.edu/publications/papers/how-much-choice-is-too-much-contributions-to-401k-retirement-plans/.

36. Cole, A. J., Gee, G., & Turner, N. (2011). The distributional and revenue consequences of reforming the mortgage interest deduction. *National Tax Journal, 64*(4), 977–1000.

37. Office of the Press Secretary. (2013). Remarks by the president on economic mobility. Washington, DC: White House. Retrieved from https://www.whitehouse.gov/the-press-office/2013/12/04/remarks-president-economic-mobility.

38. Krugman, P. (2014, September 21). Those lazy jobless. *The New York Times.* Retrieved from https://www.nytimes.com/2014/09/22/opinion/paul-krugman-those-lazy-jobless.html?_r=0.

39. Everett, B., & Bresnahan, J. (2015, September 14). McConnell's fall mandate: Keep calm, avert catastrophe. *Politico.* Retrieved from http://www.politico.com/story/2015/09/mitch-mcconnell-agenda-2015-shutdown-213582#ixzz3libLARAk.

40. Grim, P. (2012, October 2). Paul Ryan: 30% "want welfare State," 70% "want the American dream." *Huffington Post.* Retrieved from http://www.huffingtonpost.com/2012/10/02/paul-ryan-30-percent-welfare-state_n_1933730.html.

41. Montopoli, B. (2010, January 25). S.C. Lt. Gov. Andre Bauer compares helping poor to feeding stray animals. *CBS News*. Retrieved from http://www.cbsnews.com/news/sc-lt-gov-andre-bauer-compares-helping-poor-to-feeding-stray-animals/.

42. American Presidency Project. (2004). Fact sheet: America's ownership society: expanding opportunities. Retrieved from http://www.presidency.ucsb.edu/ws/?pid=81211.

43. Yadama, G. N., & Sherraden. M. (1996). Effects of assets on attitudes and behaviors: Advance test of a social policy proposal. *Social Work Research, 20*(1), 3–11. https://doi.org/10.1093/swr/20.1.3

44. Rubio, M. (2014). Take next step in War on Poverty: Provide opportunity. *Face the Nation*. Retrieved from http://www.ontheissues.org/Economic/Marco_Rubio_Welfare_+_Poverty.htm.

45. Moran, J. (2012). Sens. Moran, Wyden form first-ever senate economic mobility caucus. Washington, DC: Author. Retrieved from https://www.moran.senate.gov/public/index.cfm/news-releases?ID=a2208204-0e09-4b70-b708-9d44593a6aa9.

46. Jenson, J. (2003). Redesigning the welfare mix for families: Policy challenges (CPRN Family Network Discussion Paper) Ottawa: Canadian Policy Research Networks.

47. Peck, J., & Tickell, A. (2007). Conceptualizing neoliberalism, thinking Thatcherism. In H. Leitner, J. Peck, & E. S. Sheppard (Eds.), *Contesting neoliberalism: Urban frontiers* (pp. 26-50). New York, NY: Guilford Press.

48. Lister, R. (2003) Investing in the citizen-workers of the future: Transformations in citizenship and the state under New Labour. *Social Policy and Administration, 37*(5), 427–443.

49. Luccisano, L. (2006) The Mexican Oportunidades Individual Development Account Program: Questioning the linking of security to conditional social investments for mothers and children. *Canadian Journal of Latin American & Caribbean Studies, 31*(62), 53–85.

50. Moyers, B., & Winship, M. (2016, June 9). Debbie can't save herself: The Democratic National Committee Chair has to go for the good of the party. *Salon*. Retrieved from http://www.salon.com/2016/06/09/debbie_cant_save_herself_the_democratic_national_committee_chair_has_to_go_for_the_good_of_the_party_partner/.

51. Badger, E., & Ingraham, C. (2015, April 9). The rich get government handouts just like the poor. Here are 10 of them. *The Washington Post*. Retrieved from https://www.washingtonpost.com/news/wonk/wp/2015/04/09/the-rich-get-government-handouts-just-like-the-poor-here-are-10-of-them/?utm_term=.ce46780df8cc.

52. Elliott, W., & Lewis, M. (2014). *Harnessing assets to build an economic mobility system: Reimagining the American welfare system*. Lawrence, KS: Center on Assets, Education, and Inclusion.

53. Shapiro, T., Meschede, T., & Osoro, S. (2013). *The roots of the widening racial wealth gap: Explaining the black-white economic divide*. Waltham, MA: Brandeis University, Institute on Assets and Social Policy.

54. Piketty, T. (2014). *Capital in the twenty-first century*. Translated by Arthur Goldhammer. Boston, MA. Belknap Press.

55. Saez, E., & Zucman, G. (2014). *Wealth inequality in the United States since 1913: Evidence from capitalized income tax data* (Working Paper 20625). Cambridge, MA: National Bureau of Economic Research.

56. Wolff, E.N. (1995). *Top heavy. A study of the increasing inequality of wealth in America*. New York, NY: Twentieth Century Fund Press.

57. Lindert, P. H., & Williamson, J. G. (2012). American Incomes, 1774–1860. Cambridge, MA: National Bureau of Economic Research. Retrieved from http://www.nber.org/papers/w18396

58. Shapiro, T., Meschede, T., & Osoro, S. (2013). *The roots of the widening racial wealth gap: Explaining the Black-White economic divide.* Waltham, MA: Brandeis University, Institute on Assets and Social Policy.

59. U.S. Census Bureau. (2016). *Quarterly residential vacancies and homeownership.* Retrieved from http://www.census.gov/housing/hvs/files/currenthvspress.pdf.

60. Newman, S. J., & Holupka, C. S. (2016). Is timing everything? Race, homeownership and net worth in the tumultuous 2000s. *Real Estate Economics, 44,* 307–354. doi:10.1111/1540-6229.12118

61. Rothstein, R. (2017). *The color of law: A forgotten history of how our government segregated America.* New York, NY: Liveright.

62. Gudell, S. (2017, January 11). Homes in Black neighborhoods twice as likely to be underwater as homes in White neighborhoods. Seattle, WA. https://www.zillow.com/research/negative-equity-race-q3-2016-14063/

63. Meschede, T., Taylor, J., Mann, A., & Shapiro, T. (2017, First Quarter). Family achievements? How a college degree accumulates wealth for Whites and not for Blacks. *Federal Reserve Bank of St. Louis Review, 99*(1), 121–137.

64. McKernan, S. M., Ratcliffe, C., Simms, M., & Zhang, S. (2011). *Private transfers, race, and wealth.* Washington, DC: Urban Institute. Retrieved from http://www.urban.org/sites/default/files/alfresco/publication-pdfs/412371-Private-Transfers-Race-and-Wealth.PDF.

65. Rauscher, E. (2015). *By my parents' bootstraps: Parent-adult child transfers and the intergenerational transmission of financial standing.* Lawrence, KS: Center on Assets, Education, and Inclusion.

66. Chang, M. L. (2015). *Women and wealth: Insights for grantmakers.* New York, NY: Asset Funders Network. Retrieved from http://www.marikochang.com/AFN_Women_and_Wealth_Brief_2015.pdf.

67. Ruel, E., & Hauser, R. M. (2013). Explaining the gender wealth gap. *Demography, 50*(4), 1155–1176. http://doi.org/10.1007/s13524-012-0182-0

68. McCullough, H. (2017). *Closing the women's wealth gap.* Asset Building Strategies. Retrieved from http://assetbuildingstrategies.com/wp-content/uploads/2017/01/Closing-the-Womens-Wealth-Gap-Jan2017.pdf.

69. TIAA. (2016). *Income insights: Gender retirement gap.* Retrieved from https://www.tiaa.org/public/pdf/income_gender.pdf.

70. Jacobsen, L. A., Lee, M., & Pollard, K. (2013). *Household wealth and financial security in Appalachia.* Washington, DC: Appalachian Regional Commission. Retrieved from www.arc.gov/assets.

71. Zaw, K., Bhattacharya, J., Price, A., Hamilton, D., & Darity, W. Jr. (2017). *Women, race & wealth.* Oakland, CA: Samuel DuBois Cook Center on Social Equity. Retrieved from http://www.insightcced.org/wp-content/uploads/2017/01/January2017_ResearchBriefSeries_WomenRaceWealth-Volume1-Pages-1.pdf.

72. Emmons, W. R., & Noeth, B. J. (2015). *Why didn't higher education protect Hispanic and Black wealth?* (In the Balance, Issue 12). St. Louis, MO: Federal Reserve Bank of St. Louis. Retrieved from https://www.stlouisfed.org/publications/in-the-balance/issue12-2015/why-didnt-higher-education-protect-hispanic-and-black-wealth.

73. Autor, D. (2014). Skills, education, and the rise of earnings among the "other 99 percent." *Science, 23,* 843–851.

74. Boshara, R., Emmons, W., & Noeth, B. (2015). *The demographics of wealth: How age, education, and race separate thrivers from strugglers in today's economy* (Essay No. 3). St.

Louis, MO: Federal Reserve Bank of St. Louis. Retrieved from https://www.stlouisfed. org/~/media/Files/PDFs/HFS/essays/HFS-Essay-3-2015-Age-Birth-year-Wealth.pdf.

75. Pew Research Center. (2010). *How the Great Recession has changed life in America.* Washington, DC: Author. Retrieved from http://www.pewsocialtrends.org/2010/06/30/ how-the-great-recession-has-changed-life-in-america/.

76. Thompson, D. (2012). Adulthood, delayed: What has the recession done to millennials? *The Atlantic.* Retrieved from https://www.theatlantic.com/business/archive/2012/02/ adulthood-delayed-what-has-the-recession-done-to-millennials/252913/.

77. Pew Research Center. (2015). *The American middle class is losing ground.* Washington, DC: Author. Retrieved from http://assets.pewresearch.org/wp-content/uploads/sites/3/ 2015/12/2015-12-09_middle-class_FINAL-report.pdf.

78. Pfeffer, F. T., Danziger, S., & Schoeni, R. F. (2013). Wealth disparities before and after the Great Recession. *The Annals of the American Academy of Political and Social Science, 650*(1), 98–123. http://doi.org/10.1177/0002716213497452.

79. Smeeding, T. (2012). *Income, wealth, and debt and the Great Recession.* Palo Alto, CA: Russell Sage Foundation and the Stanford Center on Poverty and Inequality. Retrieved from https://web.stanford.edu/group/recessiontrends/cgi-bin/web/sites/all/ themes/barron/pdf/IncomeWealthDebt_fact_sheet.pdf.

80. Kochhar, R. & Fry, R. (2014). *Wealth inequality has widened along racial, ethnic lines since end of Great Recession.* Washington, DC: Pew Research Center. Retrieved from http:// www.pewresearch.org/fact-tank/2014/12/12/racial-wealth-gaps-great-recession/.

81. Zakaria, F. (2015, December 31). America's self-destructive Whites. *The Washington Post.* Retrieved from https://www.washingtonpost.com/opinions/americas-self-destructive-whites/2015/12/31/5017f958-afdc-11e5-9ab0-884d1cc4b33e_story.html?utm_term=. b4d4f32d4bde.

82. Casselman, B. (2017, January 9). Stop saying Trump's win had nothing to do with economics. *FiveThirtyEight.* Retrieved from https://fivethirtyeight.com/features/stop-saying-trumps-win-had-nothing-to-do-with-economics/.

83. Cox, D., Lienesch, R., & Jones, R. P. (2017). *Beyond economics: Fears of cultural displacement pushed the white working class to Trump.* Washington, DC: Public Religion Research Institute. Retrieved from https://www.prri.org/research/white-working-class-attitudes-economy-trade-immigration-election-donald-trump/.

84. Congressional Budget Office. (2016). *Trends in family wealth, 1989–2013.* Washington, DC: Author. Retrieved from https://www.cbo.gov/publication/51846.

85. Burd-Sharps, S. & Rasch, R. (2015). *The impact of the U.S. housing crisis on the racial wealth gap.* Brooklyn, NY: Social Science Research Council. Retrieved from https://www.aclu. org/files/field_document/discrimlend_final.pdf.

86. Tankersley, J. (2016, August 18). The wealthy have nearly healed from recession. The poor haven't even started. *The Washington Post.* Retrieved from https://www. washingtonpost.com/news/wonk/wp/2016/08/18/the-wealthy-have-nearly-healed-from-recession-the-poor-havent-even-started/?utm_term=.f1dfdfc2b401.

87. Washington Post-Miller Center. (2013). *Post-Miller Center Poll: American dream and economic struggles.* Retrieved from http://www.washingtonpost.com/page/2010-2019/ WashingtonPost/2013/09/28/National-Politics/Polling/release_266.xml?uuid=uD8cGiiSE eOKs7WqzJ4RZQ.

88. McCall, L. (2013). *The undeserving rich: American beliefs about inequality, opportunity, and redistribution.* New York, NY: Cambridge University Press.

89. Chetty, R., Grusky, D., Hell, M., Hendren, N., Manduca, R., & Narang, J. (2016). *The fading American dream: Trends in absolute income mobility since 1940* (NBER Working Paper No. 22910). Cambridge, MA: National Bureau of Economic Research. Retrieved from http://www.nber.org/papers/w22910.pdf.

90. Boshara, R., Clancy, M., Newville, D., & Sherraden, M. (2009). *The basics of progressive 529s*. St. Louis, MO: Washington University, Center for Social Development; Washington, DC: New America Foundation.

91. Clancy, M., Lasser, T., & Taake, K. (2010). *Saving for college: A policy primer*. St. Louis, MO: Washington University, Center for Social Development. Retrieved from http://csd.wustl.edu/Publications/Documents/PB10-27.pdf.

92. Adelman, C. (2011). *Why 529 college savings plans favor the fortunate*. Washington, DC: Education Sector.

93. U.S. Department of Treasury. (2009). *An analysis of Section 529 college savings and prepaid tuition plans: A report prepared by the Department of Treasury for the White House Task Force on Middle Class Working Families*. Washington, DC: U.S. Department of Treasury. Retrieved from http://www.treasury.gov/press-center/press-releases/Documents/529.pdf.

94. Phillips, L. (2014, March 27). *Presentation at the children's savings account roundtable*. New York, NY: Ford Foundation.

95. College Board. (2015). *Trends in college pricing, 2015*. Retrieved from http://trends.collegeboard.org/sites/default/files/2015-trends-college-pricing-final-508.pdf.

96. Government Accountability Office. (2012). *A small percentage of families save in 529 Plans* (GAO-13-64). Washington, DC: Author. Retrieved from http://www.gao.gov/assets/660/650759.pdf.

97. Hannon, S., Moore, K., Schmeiser, M., & Stefanescu, I. (2016, February 3). Saving for college and section 529 plans. FEDS Notes. Washington, DC: Federal Reserve Bank. Retrieved from https://www.federalreserve.gov/econresdata/notes/feds-notes/2016/saving-for-college-and-section-529-plans-20160203.html.

98. Sallie Mae. (2016). *How America saves for college*. Washington, DC: Author. Retrieved from https://www.salliemae.com/plan-for-college/how-america-saves-for-college/.

99. Reeves, R. (2017). *Dream hoarders: How the American upper middle class is leaving everyone else in the dust, why that is a problem, and what to do about it*. Washington, DC: Brookings Institution Press.

100. Weisman, J. (2015). Obama relents on proposal to end "529" college savings plans. *The New York Times*. Retrieved from https://www.nytimes.com/2015/01/28/us/politics/obama-will-drop-proposal-to-end-529-college-savings-plans.html?_r=0.

101. Emmons, W. R., & Ricketts, L. R. (2017). *College unintentionally increases racial and ethnic disparity in income and wealth* (In the Balance, Issue 16). St. Louis, MO: Federal Reserve Bank of St. Louis. Retrieved from https://www.stlouisfed.org/~/media/Publications/In-the-Balance/Images/Issue_16/ITB16_february_2017.pdf.

102. Traub, A., Sullivan, L, Meschede, T., & Shapiro, T. (2017). *The asset value of whiteness: Understanding the racial wealth gap*. Washington, DC: Demos and IASP. Retrieved from http://www.demos.org/publication/asset-value-whiteness-understanding-racial-wealth-gap.

103. Shapiro, T. (2004). *The hidden cost of being African American: How wealth perpetuates inequality*. New York, NY: Oxford University Press.

104. Callahan, D. (2013, November 11). How the GI Bill left out African Americans. Washington, DC: Demos. Retrieved from http://www.demos.org/blog/11/11/13/how-gi-bill-left-out-african-americans.

105. Turner, S., & Bound, J. (2003). Closing the gap or widening the divide: The effects of the G.I. Bill and World War II on the educational outcomes of Black Americans. *Journal of Economic History, 63*(1), 145–177.

106. Biggs, A. (2016, December 23). Middle class retirement accounts at record levels; Low-income households still saving little [Opinion]. *Forbes.* Retrieved from http://www.forbes.com/sites/andrewbiggs/2016/12/23/middle-class-retirement-accounts-at-record-levels-low-income-households-still-saving-little/#2c32294d113f.

107. Butrica, B. A., & Johnson, R. W. (2010). *Racial, ethnic, and gender differentials in employer-sponsored pensions.* Washington, DC: Urban Institute. Retrieved from http://www.urban.org/sites/default/files/alfresco/publication-pdfs/901357-Racial-Ethnic-and-Gender-Differentials-in-Employer-Sponsored-Pensions.PDF.

108. Kim, C., & Tamborini, C. (2016, August). Disadvantages of the less educated: Education and contributory pensions at work. Paper presented at the American Sociological Association's 111th annual meeting.

109. Morrissey, M. (2016). *The state of American retirement: How 401(k)s have failed most American workers.* Washington, DC: Economic Policy Institute. Retrieved from http://www.epi.org/publication/retirement-in-america/.

110. Oliver, M., & Shapiro, T. (2006). *Black wealth, White wealth.* New York, NY: Taylor & Francis.

111. Reich, R. (2016). *Saving capitalism: For the many, not the few.* New York, NY: Vintage.

112. Black, R. (2014). *Rebalancing the scales: The 2015 assets budget.* Washington, DC: New America. Retrieved from https://www.newamerica.org/asset-building/policy-papers/rebalancing-the-scales/.

113. Spar, K., & Falk, G. (2016). *Federal benefits and services for people with low income: Overview of spending trends, FY2008–FY2015.* Washington, DC: Congressional Research Service. Retrieved from https://fas.org/sgp/crs/misc/R44574.pdf.

114. Faricy, C. (2017, March 15). Donald Trump's tax plan would mean huge breaks for millionaires like Trump. *The Washington Post.* Retrieved from https://www.washingtonpost.com/posteverything/wp/2017/03/15/donald-trumps-tax-plan-would-mean-huge-breaks-for-millionaires-like-trump/?utm_term=.7796db6fd1fc.

115. Mufson, S., & Jan, T. (2017, March 16). If you're a poor person in America, Trump's budget is not for you. *The Washington Post.* Retrieved from https://www.washingtonpost.com/news/wonk/wp/2017/03/16/if-youre-a-poor-person-in-america-trumps-budget-is-not-for-you/?utm_term=.0750bb07afc3.

116. Johnson, S., Campbell, N., Spicklemire, K., & Partelow, L. (2017, March 17). The Trump-DeVos budget would dismantle public education, hurting vulnerable kids, working families, and teachers. Washington, DC: Center for American Progress. Retrieved from https://www.americanprogress.org/issues/education/news/2017/03/17/428598/trump-devos-budget-dismantle-public-education-hurting-vulnerable-kids-working-families-teachers/.

117. Shanks, T. R. W. (2005). The Homestead Act: A major asset-building policy in American history. In M. Sherraden (Ed.), *Inclusion in the American dream: Assets, poverty, and public policy* (pp. 20–41). New York, NY: Oxford University Press.

118. Haskins, R. (2016). *Wealth and economic mobility.* Washington, DC: Brookings Institution. Retrieved from https://www.brookings.edu/wp-content/uploads/2016/07/02_economic_mobility_sawhill_ch4.pdf.

119. Harris, B., Steuerle, C. E., McKernan, S. M., Quakenbush, C., & Ratcliffe, C. (2014). *Tax subsidies for asset development: An overview and distribution analysis.* Washington,

DC: Urban Institute. Retrieved from http://www.urban.org/research/publication/tax-subsidies-asset-development-overview-and-distributional-analysis.

120. North, D.C. (2005). *Understanding the process of economic change*. Princeton, NJ: Princeton University Press.

121. Brownstein, R. (2014, April 11). Are college degrees inherited? *The Atlantic*. Retrieved from https://www.theatlantic.com/education/archive/2014/04/are-college-degrees-inherited/360532/.

122. Lareau, A. (2002). Invisible inequality: Social class and childrearing in Black families and White families. *American Sociological Review, 67*(5), 747–776.

123. Lareau, A. (2003). *Unequal childhoods: Race, class, and family life*. Oakland: University of California Press.

124. Lareau, A. (2011). *Unequal childhoods: Race, class, and family life, 2nd edition, with an update a decade later*. Oakland: University of California Press.

125. Boser, U., Wilhelm, M., & Hanna, R. (2014). *The power of the Pygmalian Effect*. Washington, DC: Center for American Progress. Retrieved from https://www.americanprogress.org/issues/education/reports/2014/10/06/96806/the-power-of-the-pygmalion-effect/.

126. Papageorge, N. W., Gershenson, S., & Kang, K. (2016). *Teacher expectations matter*. Bonn, Germany: Institute for the Study of Labor. Retrieved from http://ftp.iza.org/dp10165.pdf.

127. Godsey, M. (2015, June 15). Inequality in public schools. *The Atlantic*. Retrieved from https://www.theatlantic.com/education/archive/2015/06/inequality-public-schools/395876/.

128. McNamee, S. J., & Miller, R. K. (2013). *The meritocracy myth*. Lanham, MD: Rowman & Littlefield.

129. Useem, E. L. (1992). Middle schools and math groups: Parents' involvement in children's math placement. *Sociology of Education, 65*, 263–279.

130. Sen A. (1999). *Development as freedom*. New York, NY: Oxford University Press.

131. Jez, S. J. (2017). Not all college is equal when it comes to wealth and race. *Federal Reserve Bank of St. Louis Review, 99*(1), 45–51. https://dx.doi.org/10.20955/r.2017.45-51

132. Knight, J. (1992). *Institutions and social conflict*. Cambridge, MA: Cambridge University Press.

133. Blake, A. (2016, October 2). Donald Trump's defenses of not paying taxes pretty much say it all. *The Washington Post*. Retrieved from https://www.washingtonpost.com/news/the-fix/wp/2016/09/28/donald-trumps-defense-of-not-paying-taxes-is-remarkable/?utm_term=.7df000afac6d.

134. Winters, J. (2011). *Oligarchy*. New York, NY. Cambridge University Press.

135. Fisman, R., Jakiela, P., Kariv, S., & Markovits, D. (2015). The distributional preferences of an elite. *Science, 349*(6254), doi:10.1126/science.aab0096.

136. Jacobs, L. R., & Skocpol, T. (Eds.). (2007). *Inequality and American democracy: What we know and what we need to learn*. New York, NY: Russell Sage Foundation.

137. Jones, R., Cox, D., & Navarro-Rivera, J. (2014). *Economic insecurity, rising inequality, and doubts about the future: Findings from the 2014 American Values Survey*. Washington, DC: Public Religion Research Institute. Retrieved from http://www.prri.org/wp-content/uploads/2014/09/AVS-web.pdf.

138. Dew, T. (1832). *The pro-slavery argument*. Retrieved from http://www.encyclopedia.com/history/dictionaries-thesauruses-pictures-and-press-releases/text-pro-slavery-argument-1832-thomas-dew.

139. Blackmon, D. (2009). *Slavery by another name: The re-enslavement of black Americans from the Civil War to World War II*. New York, NY: Anchor Books.

140. Alexander, M. (2012). *The new Jim Crow*. New York, NY: New Press.

141. Spencer, S. J., Steele, C. M., & Quinn, D. M. (1999). Stereotype threat and women's math performance. *Journal of Experimental Social Psychology, 35*, 4–28.

142. Reidy, D. E., Berke, D. S., Gentile, B., & Zeichner, A. (2015). Masculine discrepancy stress, substance use, assault and injury in a survey of US men. *Injury Prevention, 22*(5), 370–374. doi:10.1136/injuryprev-2015-042599

143. Kochhar, R., & Fry, R. (2014). *Wealth inequality has widened along racial, ethnic lines since end of Great Recession*. Washington, DC: Pew Research Center. Retrieved from http://www.pewresearch.org/fact-tank/2014/12/12/racial-wealth-gaps-great-recession/.

144. Kamenetz, A. (2006). *Generation debt*. New York, NY: Riverhead Hardcover.

145. Pew Charitable Trusts. (2014). *A new financial reality: The balance sheets and economic mobility of Generation X*. Washington, DC: Author. Retrieved from http://www.pewtrusts.org/~/media/assets/2014/09/pew_generation_x_report.pdf.

146. Dowdy, L. (2015, April 21). Why do millennials get such a bad rap at work? *CNBC*. Retrieved from http://www.cnbc.com/2015/04/20/are-millennials-lazy-entitled-narcissists.html.

CHAPTER 3

1. MacLeod, J. (2009). *Ain't no makin' it: Aspirations and attainment in a low-income neighborhood* (rev. ed.). Boulder, CO: Westview Press.

2. Jones, A. (2016, October 3). The myth of meritocracy: Reframing the American dream. Retrieved from https://rowlandfoundation.wordpress.com/2016/10/03/the-myth-of-meritocracy-reframing-the-american-dream/.

3. Jost, J. T., & Hunyady, O. (2002). The psychology of system justification and the palliative function of ideology. *European Review of Social Psychology, 13*, 111–153. https://doi.org/10.1080/10463280240000046.

4. Jones, R., Cox, D., & Navarro-Rivera, J. (2014). *Economic insecurity, rising inequality, and doubts about the future: Findings from the 2014 American Values Survey*. Washington, DC: Public Religion Research Institute. Retrieved from http://www.prri.org/wp-content/uploads/2014/09/AVS-web.pdf.

5. Packer, G. (2014). *The great unwinding: An inner history of the new America*. New York, NY: Farrar, Straus and Giroux.

6. Jost, J. T., & Banaji, M. R. (1994). The role of stereotyping in system justification and the production of false consciousness. *British Journal of Social Psychology, 33*, 1–27. http://dx.doi.org/10.1111/j.2044-8309.1994.tb01008.

7. Roosevelt, F. D. (1936, June 27). Acceptance speech. Democratic National Convention, Philadelphia, PA. Retrieved from www.2austin.cc.tx.us/1patrick/his2341/fdr36acceptancespeech.htm.

8. Rotman, J. (2013, June 12). How technology is destroying jobs. *MIT Technology Review*. Retrieved from https://www.technologyreview.com/s/515926/how-technology-is-destroying-jobs/.

9. Ebenstein, A., Harrison, A., & McMillan, M. (2015). *Why are American workers getting poorer? China, trade, and offshoring* (NBER Working Paper No. 21027). Cambridge, MA: National Bureau of Economic Research. Retrieved from http://www.nber.org/papers/w21027.

10. Chetty, R., Grusky, D., Hell, M., Hendren, N., Manduca, R., & Narang, J. (2016). *The fading American dream: Trends in absolute income mobility since 1940* (NBER Working Paper No. 22910). Cambridge, MA: National Bureau of Economic Research. Retrieved from http://www.nber.org/papers/w22910.pdf.

11. Jackson, D. (2013, December 4). Obama: Income inequality threatens the American dream. *USA Today*. Retrieved from http://www.usatoday.com/story/news/politics/2013/12/04/obama-income-inequality-speech-center-for-american-progress/3867747/.

12. *The Economist*. (2006, June 15). Inequality and the American dream. Retrieved from http://www.economist.com/node/7059155.

13. Zuckerman, M. (2015, March 27). Making a mockery of the American dream. *US News and World Reports*. Retrieved from http://www.usnews.com/opinion/articles/2015/03/27/income-inequality-makes-a-mockery-of-the-american-dream.

14. Traub, A., Sullivan, L., Meschede, T., & Shapiro, T. (2017). *The asset value of Whiteness: Understanding the racial wealth gap*. Washington, DC: Demos and IASP. Retrieved from http://www.demos.org/publication/asset-value-whiteness-understanding-racial-wealth-gap.

15. Rampell, C. (2013, June 12). Data reveal a rise in college degrees among Americans. *The New York Times*. Retrieved from http://www.nytimes.com/2013/06/13/education/a-sharp-rise-in-americans-with-college-degrees.html.

16. Hershbein, B. (2016, February 19). A college degree is worth less if you are raised poor. *Brookings Social Mobility Memos*. Retrieved from http://www.brookings.edu/blogs/social-mobility-memos/posts/2016/02/19-college-degree-worth-less-raised-poor-hershbein.

17. DeSoto, H. (2000). *The mystery of capital: Why capitalism triumphs in the West and fails everywhere else*. New York, NY: Basic Books.

18. White, J. K., & Hanson, S. L. (Eds.). (2011). *The American dream in the 21st century*. Philadelphia, PA: Temple University Press.

19. Godfrey, E. B., & Wolf, S. (2016). Developing critical consciousness or justifying the system? A qualitative analysis of attributions for poverty and wealth among low-income racial/ethnic minority and immigrant women. *Cultural Diversity and Ethnic Minority Psychology, 22*(1), 93–103.

20. Wilson, W. J. (2009). *More than just race: Being Black and poor in the inner city*. New York, NY: Norton.

21. World Economic Forum. (2017). Global risks report 2017. Davos, Switzerland: Author. Retrieved from http://reports.weforum.org/global-risks-2017/.

22. Goering, L. (2016, April 15). Growing wealth inequality "dangerous" threat to democracy: Experts. Reuters. Retrieved from http://www.reuters.com/article/us-democracy-wealth-inequality-idUSKCN0XC1Q2.

23. Jones, S. (2014, May 8). Fed chair unsure if capitalism or oligarchy describes the U.S. *CBS News*. Retrieved from http://cbsnews.com/news/article/susan-jones/fed-chair-unsure-if-capitalism-or-oligarchy-describes-us.

24. Walker, B. (1984). The local property tax for public schools: Some historical perspectives. *Journal of Education Finance, 9*(3), 265–288. Retrieved from http://www.jstor.org/stable/40703424.

25. Tanner, M. D., & Hughes, C. (2013). *The work v. welfare trade-off: 2013*. Washington, DC: Cato Institute. Retrieved from https://www.cato.org/publications/white-paper/work-versus-welfare-trade.

26. Hochschild, A. R. (2016). *Strangers in their own land: Anger and mourning on the American Right*. New York, NY: New Press.

27. Ashok, V., Kuziemko, I., & Washington, E. (2016). Support for redistribution in an age of rising inequality: New stylized facts and some tentative explanations. *Brookings Papers on Economic Activity, 2015*(1), 367–433.

28. Wessler, S. F. (2014). Poll: Fewer Americans blame poverty on the poor. *NBC News.* Retrieved from http://www.nbcnews.com/feature/in-plain-sight/poll-fewer-americans-blame-poverty-poor-n136051.

29. Pew Research Center. (2014). *Most See inequality growing, but partisans differ over solutions.* Washington, DC: Author. Retrieved from http://www.people-press.org/2014/01/23/most-see-inequality-growing-but-partisans-differ-over-solutions/.

30. Mishel, L., Bivens, J., Gould, E., & Shierholz, H. (2012). *The state of working America* (12th ed.). Ithaca, NY: Cornell University Press.

31. Fingerhut, H. (2016, February 10). Most Americans say U.S. economic system is unfair, but high-income Republicans disagree. Washington, DC: Pew Research Center FACTTANK. Retrieved from http://www.pewresearch.org/fact-tank/2016/02/10/most-americans-say-u-s-economic-system-is-unfair-but-high-income-republicans-disagree/.

32. *The Washington Post.* (2015). Washington Post-ABC news poll. Retrieved from https://www.washingtonpost.com/politics/polling/americans-thinking-wealthy-problem/2015/01/22/5838c72e-a0fc-11e4-91fc-7dff95a14458_page.html.

33. Schieber, N., & Sussman, D. (2015). Inequality troubles Americans across party lines, times/CBS poll finds. *New York Times.* Retrieved from https://www.nytimes.com/2015/06/04/business/inequality-a-major-issue-for-americans-times-cbs-poll-finds.html?_r=0.

34. Berger, N., & Fisher, P. (2013). *A well-educated workforce is key to state prosperity.* Washington, DC: Economic Policy Institute. Retrieved from http://www.epi.org/publication/states-education-productivity-growth-foundations/.

35. *Portland Press-Herald.* (2015, January 25). Our view: Public education must lead the fight against poverty. Retrieved from http://www.pressherald.com/2015/01/25/our-view-public-education-must-lead-fight-against-poverty/.

36. Rhee, M. (2010, March 1). Education is key to our nation's prosperity. *The Hill.* Retrieved from http://thehill.com/special-reports/science-a-math-march-2010/84345-education-is-the-key-to-our-nations-prosperity.

37. Elliott, W., & Sherraden, M. S. (2013). Institutional facilitation and CSA effects. In W. Elliott (Ed.), *Building expectations, delivering results: Asset-based financial aid and the future of higher education, Biannual report on the assets and education field* (pp. 30–49). Lawrence, KS: Center on Assets, Education, and Inclusion.

38. Steve Jobs quotes. (2012, November 16). Retrieved from http://stevejobsquote.tumblr.com/post/35839003377/humantoolbuilders.

39. Goldin, C., & Katz, L. (2010). *The race between education and technology.* Cambridge, MA: Belknap Press.

40. Freeland, C. (2012). *Plutocrats: The rise of the new global super-rich and the fall of everyone else.* London: Penguin Press.

41. Pachon, H. P., Macias, E. E., & Bagasao, P. Y. (2000). Minority access to information technology: Lessons learned (ERIC Document Reproduction Service No. ED455990).

42. Purcell, K., Heaps, A., Buchanan, J., & Friedrich, L. (2013). *How teachers are using technology at home and in their classrooms.* Washington, DC: Pew Research Center's Internet & American Life Project. Retrieved from http://www.mydesert.com/assets/pdf/J12142481024.PDF.

43. Wener-Fligner, Z. (2014). People in this country believe in individualism even more than Americans. *Quartz*. Retrieved from https://qz.com/279343/people-in-this-country-believe-in-individualism-even-more-than-americans/.

44. Bayles, M. (2015, October 10). How the world perceives the new American Dream. *The Atlantic*. Retrieved from https://www.theatlantic.com/international/archive/2015/10/american-dream-world-diplomacy/410080/.

45. Bandura, A. (1997). *Self-efficacy: The exercise of control*. New York, NY: W. H. Freeman.

46. Bandura, A. (1994). Self-efficacy. In V. S. Ramachaudran (Ed.), *Encyclopedia of human behavior* (pp. 71–81). San Diego, CA: Academic Press.

47. Scheier, M. F., & Carver, C. S. (1987). Dispositional optimism and physical well-being: The influence of generalized outcome expectancies on health. *Journal of Personality, 55*, 169–210.

48. Eccles, J., Wigfield, A., Harold, R. S., & Blumenfeld, P. (1993). Age and gender differences in children's self- and task perceptions during elementary school. *Child Development, 64*(3), 830–847.

49. Jonson-Reid, M., Davis, L., Saunders, J., Williams, T., & Williams, J. H. (2005). Academic self-efficacy among African American youths: Implications for school social work practice. *Children & Schools, 27*(1), 5–14.

50. Schunk, D. H. (1995). *Self-efficacy and education and instruction*. New York, NY: Plenum Press.

51. Zimmerman, B. J. (1995). Self-efficacy and educational development. In A. Bandura (Ed.), *Self-efficacy in changing societies* (pp. 203–231). New York, NY: Cambridge University Press.

52. Pajares, F. (2002). Gender and perceived self-efficacy in self-regulated learning. *Theory into Practice, 41*(2), 116–126.

53. Alkire, S. (2005). Subjective quantitative studies of human agency. *Social Indicators Research, 74*(1), 217–260.

54. Franzblau, S. H., & Moore, M. (2001). Socializing efficacy: A reconstruction of self-efficacy theory within the context of inequality. *Journal of Community & Applied Social Psychology, 11*(2), 83–96.

55. Rosenbaum, J., Reynolds, L., & DeLuca, S. (2002). How do places matter? The geography of opportunity, self-efficacy and a look inside the black box of residential mobility. *Housing Studies, 17*(1), 71–82.

56. Bandura, A. (1986). *Social foundations of thought and action: A social cognitive theory*. Englewood Cliffs, NJ: Prentice-Hall.

57. Gurin, P., & Brim, O. G. Jr. (1984). Change in self in adulthood: The example of sense of control. In P. B. Baltes & O. G. Brim (Eds.), *Life-span development and behavior* (Vol 6, pp. 281–334). New York, NY: Academic Press.

58. Kay, A. C., & Friesen, J. (2011). On social stability and social change: Understanding when system justification does and does not occur. *Current Directions in Psychological Science, 20*, 360–364. http://dx.doi.org/10.1177/0963721411422059

59. McCall, L. (2013). *The undeserving rich: American beliefs about inequality, opportunity, and redistribution*. New York, NY: Cambridge University Press.

60. Bandura, A. (1984). Recycling misconceptions of perceived self-efficacy. *Cognitive Therapy and Research, 8*(3), 231–255. doi:10.1007/BF01172995

61. Bandura, A. (1993). Perceived self-efficacy in cognitive development and functioning. *Educational Psychologist, 28*(2), 117–148.

62. Jost, J. T., & Thompson, E. P. (2000). Group-based dominance and opposition to equality as independent predictors of self-esteem, ethnocentrism, and social policy attitudes among African Americans and European Americans. *Journal of Experimental Social Psychology, 36*, 209–232.

63. North, D.C. (1990). *Institutions, institutional change, and economic performance.* Cambridge, UK: Cambridge University Press.

64. Sen A. (1999). *Development as freedom.* New York, NY: Oxford University Press.

65. Sherraden, M. (1991). *Assets and the poor: A new American welfare policy.* Armonk, NY: M. E. Sharpe.

66. Campbell, A. (2017). Why does wealth vary among college graduates? *Federal Reserve Bank of St. Louis Review, 99*(1), 41–43. https://dx.doi.org/10.20955/r.2017.41-43

67. Morris, P. M. (2002). The capabilities perspective: A framework for social justice. *Families in Society: The Journal of Contemporary Human Services, 83*(4), 365–373.

68. World Bank. (2002). *Empowerment and poverty reduction: A sourcebook.* Washington, DC: Author.

69. Cook, T. D., Church, M. B., Ajanaku, S., Shadish, W. R., Kim, J. R., & Cohen, R. (1996). The development of occupational aspirations and expectations among inner-city boys. *Child Development, 67*(6), 3368–3385.

70. Gould, M. (1999). Race and theory: Culture, poverty, and adaptation discrimination in Wilson and Ogbu. *Sociological Theory, 17*(2), 171–200.

71. Luhmann, N. & Albrow, M. (1985). *A sociological theory of law.* Boston, MA: Routledge & Kegan Paul.

72. Mickelson, R. A. (1990). The attitude-achievement paradox among black adolescents. *Sociology of Education, 63*, 44–61.

73. Clinton, W. J. (1993, December 3). Remarks to the Democratic Leadership Council [Transcript]. Online by Gerhard Peters and John T. Woolley. The American Presidency Project. Retrieved from http://www.presidency.ucsb.edu/ws/?pid=46193.

74. Lerner, M. J., & Miller, D. T. (1978). Just world research and the attribution process: Looking back and ahead. *Psychological Bulletin, 85*, 1030–1051.

75. Schunk, D. H., & Pajares, F. (2002). The development of academic self-efficacy. In A. Wigfield & J. Eccles (Eds.), *Development of achievement motivation* (pp. 16–31). San Diego, CA: Academic Press.

76. Wittgenstein, L. (1969). *On certainty.* Translated by D. Paul and G. E. M. Anscombe. New York, NY: Harper Torchbooks.

77. Harter S. (1990). Developmental differences in the nature of self-representations: Implications for the understanding, assessment and treatment of maladaptive behavior. *Cognitive Therapy and Research, 14*(2), 113–142.

78. Piaget, J. (1955). *The construction of reality in the child.* Translated by Margaret Cook. New York, NY: Routledge and Kegan Paul.

79. Vygotsky, L.S. (1986). *Thought and language.* Cambridge, MA: MIT Press.

80. Gudiano, V. F. (1987). *Complexity of the self: A developmental approach to psychopathology and therapy.* New York, NY: Guilford Press.

81. Vygotsky, L. S. (1978). *Mind in society: The development of higher psychological processes.* Cambridge, MA: Harvard University Press.

82. Rogoff, B., Baker-Sennett, J., & Matusov, E. (1994). Considering the concept of planning. In M. Haith, J. Benson, R. Roberts, & B. Pennington (Eds.), *The development of future-oriented processes* (pp. 353–374). Chicago, IL: University of Chicago Press.

83. Smalls, C., White, R., Chavous, T., & Sellers, R. (2007). Racial ideological beliefs and racial discrimination experiences as predictors of academic engagement among African American adolescents. *Journal of Black Psychology, 33,* 299–330. https://doi.org/10.1177/0095798407302541

84. Bargh, J. A., & Chartrand, T. L. (1999). The unbearable automaticity of being. *American Psychologist, 54*(7), 462–479.

85. Walton, G. M., & Cohen, G. L. (2007). A question of belonging: Race, social fit, and achievement. *Journal of Personality and Social Psychology, 92,* 82. https://doi.org/10.1037/0022-3514.92.1.82

86. Wallace, J. M., Goodkind, S., Wallace, C. M., & Bachman, J. G. (2008). Racial, ethnic, and gender differences in school discipline among U.S. high school students: 1991–2005. *The Negro Educational Review, 59*(1–2), 47–62.

87. Foster, B. L. (2015, April 9). What's it like to be poor at an Ivy League School? *Boston Globe.* Retrieved from https://www.bostonglobe.com/magazine/2015/04/09/what-like-poor-ivy-league-school/xPtql5uzDb6r9AUFER8R0O/story.html.

88. Ogbu, J. (1983). Minority status and schooling in plural societies. *Comparative Education Review, 27*(2), 168–190.

89. Emmons, W. R. ,& Noeth, B. J. (2015). *Why didn't higher education protect Hispanic and Black wealth?* (In the Balance, Issue 12). St. Louis, MO: Federal Reserve Bank of St. Louis. Retrieved from https://www.stlouisfed.org/publications/in-the-balance/issue12-2015/why-didnt-higher-education-protect-hispanic-and-black-wealth.

90. Gershenson, S., Hart, C. M. D, Lindsay, C. A., & Papageorge, N. W. (2017). *The long-run impacts of same-race teachers* (IZA Discussion Paper No. 10630). Bonn, Germany: Institute of Labor Economics.

91. Papageorge, N. W., Gershenson, S., & Kang, K. (2016). *Teacher expectations matter.* Bonn, Germany: Institute for the Study of Labor. Retrieved from http://ftp.iza.org/dp10165.pdf.

92. Della Fave, L.R. (1974). On the structure of egalitarianism. *Social Problems, 22*(2), 199–212.

93. Ogbu, J. U., & Simons, H. D. (1998). Voluntary and involuntary minorities: A cultural-ecological theory of school performance with some implications for education, *Anthropology and Education Quarterly, 29*(2), 155–188.

94. Markus, H., & Nurius, P. (1986). Possible selves. *American Psychologist, 41*(9), 954–969.

95. Oyserman, D., Terry, K., & Bybee, D. (2002). A possible selves intervention to enhance school involvement. *Journal of Adolescence, 25,* 313–326.

96. Oyserman, D., & Destin, M. (2010). Identity-based motivation: Implications for intervention. *The Counseling Psychologist, 38*(7), 1001–1043. doi:10.1177/0011000010374775

97. Murru, E. C., & Ginish, K .A. M. (2010). Imagining the possibilities: The effects of a possible selves intervention on self-regulatory efficacy and exercise behavior. *Journal of Sport & Exercise Psychology, 32,* 537–554.

98. Knight, J. (1992). *Institutions and social conflict.* Cambridge, UK: Cambridge University Press.

99. Godfrey, E. B., Santos, C. E., & Burson, E. (2017). For better or worse? System-justifying beliefs in sixth-grade predict trajectories of self-esteem and behavior across early adolescence. *Child Development,* 1–16.

100. Raftery, A. E., & Hout, M. (1993). Maximally maintained inequality: Expansion, reform, and opportunity in Irish education, 1921–75. *Sociology of Education, 66,* 41–62.

CHAPTER 4

1. National Defense Education Act (P.L. 85-864; Stat. 1580).
2. Reich, R. (2014). Robert Reich: College is a ludicrous waste of money. *Salon.* Retrieved from http://www.salon.com/2014/09/03/robert_reich_college_is_a_ludicrous_waste_of_money_partner/.
3. Nisen, M. (2013). America's increasingly broken college system, in three charts. *Business Insider.* Retrieved from http://www.businessinsider.com/americas-broken-college-system-2013-5.
4. Peters, A. (2015). The American dream is dead: Here's where it went. *Fast Company.* Retrieved from https://www.fastcompany.com/3049643/the-american-dream-is-dead-heres-where-it-went.
5. Baum, S. (2015). The Federal Pell Grant program and reauthorization of the Higher Education Act. *Journal of Student Financial Aid, 45*(3), 23–34. Retrieved from http://publications.nasfaa.org/jsfa/vol45/iss3/4.
6. Scott-Clayton, J. (2015). The role of financial aid in promoting college access and success: Research evidence and proposals for reform. *Journal of Student Financial Aid, 45*(3), Article 3. Retrieved from http://publications.nasfaa.org/jsfa/vol45/iss3/3.
7. College Board. (2016). *Trends in student aid, 2016.* Retrieved from https://trends.collegeboard.org/sites/default/files/2016-trends-student-aid.pdf.
8. Mitchell, M., Leachman, M., & Masterson, K. (2016). *Funding down, tuition up: state cuts to higher education threaten quality and affordability at public colleges.* Washington, DC: Center on Budget and Policy Priorities. Retrieved from http://www.cbpp.org/research/state-budget-and-tax/funding-down-tuition-up.
9. Quinterno, J., & Orozco, V. (2012). The great cost shift: How higher education cuts undermine the future middle class. Washington, DC: Demos. Retrieved from http://www.demos.org/publication/great-cost-shift-how-higher-education-cuts-undermine-future-middle-class.
10. College Board. (2016). Trends in college pricing. Retrieved from https://trends.collegeboard.org/college-pricing/figures-tables/average-published-undergraduate-charges-sector-2016-17.
11. Goldrick-Rab, S., & Kendall, N. (2016). *The real price of college* (College Completion Series: Part Two). Washington, DC: Century Foundation. Retrieved from https://tcf.org/content/report/the-real-price-of-college/.
12. Long, B. T. (2008). *What is known about the impact of financial aid? Implications for policy* (NCPR Working Paper). New York, NY: National Center for Postsecondary Research.
13. Carnevale, A. P., Smith, N., Melton, M., & Price, E. W. (2015). *Learning while earning: The new normal.* Washington, DC: Georgetown University, Center on Education and the Workforce. Retrieved from https://cew.georgetown.edu/wp-content/uploads/Working-Learners-Report.pdf.
14. Perna., L. (Ed.). (2010). *Understanding the working college student: New research and its implications for policy and practice.* New York, NY: Stylus Publishing.
15. Poutre, A., Rorrison, J., & Voight, M. (2017). *Limited means, limited options.* Washington, DC: Institute for Higher Education Policy.
16. Long, B. T., & Riley, E. (2007). Financial aid: A broken bridge to college access? *Harvard Educational Review, 77*(1).

17. Saunders, K. (2015). *Barriers to success: Unmet financial need for low-income students of color in community colleges*. Washington, DC: Center for Postsecondary and Educational Success. Retrieved from http://www.clasp.org/resources-and-publications/publication-1/Barriers-to-Success-Unmet-Financial-Need-for-Low-Income-Students-of-Color.pdf.

18. Hossler, D., Ziskin, M., Sooyeon, K., Cekic, O., & Gross, J. P. K. (2008). Student aid and its role in encouraging persistence. In S. Baum, M. McPherson, & P. Steele (Eds.), *The effectiveness of student aid policies: What the research tells us* (pp. 101–116). Washington, DC: College Board. Retrieved from https://www.researchgate.net/profile/Sandy_Baum/publication/265183135_The_Effectiveness_of_Student_Aid_Policies/links/54748a5b0cf245eb436de4cd.pdf?inViewer=0&pdfJsDownload=0&origin=publication_detail.

19. Deming, D., & Dynarski, S. (2009). *Into college, out of poverty? Policies to increase the postsecondary attainment of the poor* (NBER Working Paper No. 15387). Cambridge, MA: National Bureau of Economic Research.

20. Dynarski, S., & Scott-Clayton, J. (2013). Financial aid policy: Lessons from research. *Future of Children, 23*(1), 67–91.

21. Long, B. T. (June 2006). *The contributions of economics to the study of college access and success*. New York, NY: Social Science Research Council.

22. Long, B. T. (2010). Making college affordable by improving aid policy. *Issues in Science and Technology*. Retrieved from http://issues.org/26-4/long-2/.

23. Kelchen, R. (2015). Analyzing trends in Pell Grant recipients and expenditures. Washington, DC: Brookings Institution. Retrieved from https://www.brookings.edu/blog/brown-center-chalkboard/2015/07/28/analyzing-trends-in-pell-grant-recipients-and-expenditures/.

24. Leslie, L., & Brinkman, P. (1987). Student price response in higher education. *Journal of Higher Education, 58*, 181–204.

25. Elliott, W., & Rauscher, E. (2016). *When does my future begin? Student debt and intragenerational mobility* (AEDI Working Paper 03-16). Lawrence, KS: Center on Assets, Education, and Inclusion.

26. Burman, L. E., Maag, E., Orszag, P., Rohaly, J., & O'Hare, J. (2005). *The distributional consequences of federal assistance for higher education: The intersection of tax and spending programs* (Discussion Paper No. 26). Washington, DC: Urban Institute.

27. Reschovsky, A. (2008). Higher education tax policies. In S. Baum, M. McPherson, & P. Steele (Eds), *The effectiveness of student aid policies: What the research tells us*. Washington, DC: College Board.

28. Delisle, J., & Dancy, K. (2015). *A new look at tuition tax benefits*. Washington, DC: New America. Retrieved from https://static.newamerica.org/attachments/10416-a-new-look-at-tuition-tax-benefits/TaxCredits11.2.277d3f7daa014d5a8632090f97641cee.pdf.

29. Bulman, G. B., & Hoxby, C. M. (2015). The returns to the federal tax credits for higher education. *Tax Policy and the Economy, 29*(1), 13–88. doi:10.1086/683364

30. Long, B. T. (2004). The impact of federal tax credits for higher education expenses. In C. Hoxby (Ed.), *College choices: The economics of which college, when college, and how to pay for it* (pp. 101–167). Chicago: University of Chicago Press and the National Bureau of Economic Research.

31. O'Sullivan, R., & Setzer, R. (2014). *A federal work study reform agenda to better serve low-income students*. Washington, DC: Young Invincibles. Retrieved from http://younginvincibles.org/wp-content/uploads/2014/09/Federal-Work-Study-Reform-Agenda-Sept-181.pdf.

32. Scott-Clayton, J., & Minaya, V. (2016). Should student employment be subsidized? Conditional counterfactuals and the outcomes of work-study participation. *Economics of Education Review, 52*, 1–18.

33. Cohodes, S. R., & Goodman, J. S. (2014). Merit aid, college quality, and college completion: Massachusetts' Adams scholarship as an in-kind subsidy. *American Economic Journal: Applied Economics, 6*(4), 251–285.

34. Mundel, D. (2008). What do we know about the impact of grants to college students? In S. Baum, M. McPherson, & P. Steele (Eds.), *The effectiveness of student aid policies: What the research tells us* (pp. 9–38). Washington, DC: College Board.

35. Kane, T. J. (2001, June). *College-going and inequality: A literature review*. New York, NY: Russell Sage Foundation.

36. Mundel, D. S., with Coles, A. S. (2004, November). *An exploration of what we know about the formation and impact of perceptions of college prices, student aid, and the affordability of college-going*. Boston, MA: Education Resources Institute.

37. Hartle, T., & Nellum, C. (2015, November 25). *Where have all the low-income students gone?* Washington, DC: American Council on Education. Retrieved from http://higheredtoday. org/2015/11/25/where-have-all-the-low-income-students-gone/.

38. Mundel, D. S. (2005, May). A preliminary assessment of the distributional impacts of the college price discounting 1995/1996 to 2003/2004—analyzing the impact of institutional grants (Unpublished manuscript).

39. Boatman, A., Evans, B., & Soliz, A. (2017). Understanding loan aversion in education: Evidence from high school seniors, community college students, and adults. *AERA Open, 3*(1), 1–16.

40. Burdman, P. (2005). *The student debt dilemma: Debt aversion as a barrier to college access* (CSHE.13.05). Berkeley: Center for Studies in Higher Education, University of California. Retrieved from http://www.cshe.berkeley.edu/sites/default/files/shared/publications/ docs/ROP.Burdman.13.05.pdf.

41. Caetano, G. S., Palacios, M., & Patrinos, H. A. (2011). *Measuring aversion to debt: An experiment among student loan candidates* (World Bank Working Paper). Washington, DC: World Bank.

42. Baker, D. & Doyle, W. R. (2017). Impact of community college student debt levels on credit accumulation. *ANNALS, American Academy of Political and Social Sciences, 671*, 132–153.

43. Cofer, J., & Somers, P. (2000). A comparison of the influence of debt load on the persistence of students at public and private colleges. *Journal of Student Financial Aid, 30*(2), 39–58.

44. McKinney, L., & Burridge, A. B. (2015). Helping or hindering? The effects of loans on community college student persistence. *Research in Higher Education, 56*(4), 299–324.

45. Robb, C.A., Moody, B., & Abdel-Ghany, M. (2011-2012). College student persistence to degree: The burden of debt. *Journal of College Student Retention, 13*(4), 431–456.

46. Heller, D. E. (2008). The impact of student loans on college access. In S. Baum, M. McPherson, & P. Steele (Eds.), *The effectiveness of student aid policies: What the research tells us* (pp. 39–67). New York, NY: College Board.

47. Chen, J., & Hossler, J. (2017). The effects of financial aid on college success of two-year beginning nontraditional students. *Research in Higher Education, 58*, 40–76.

48. Elliott, W., & Sherraden, M. S. (2013). Institutional facilitation and CSA effects. In W. Elliott (Ed.), *Building expectations, delivering results: Asset-based financial aid and the*

future of higher education, Biannual report on the assets and education field (pp. 30–49). Lawrence, KS: Center on Assets, Education, and Inclusion.

49. Grodsky, E., & Jones, M. T. (2007). Real and imagined barriers to college entry: Perceptions of cost. *Social Science Research, 36*(2), 745–766.

50. Kane, T. J., & Avery, C. (2004). Student perceptions of college opportunities: The Boston COACH program. In C. Hoxby (Ed.), *College decisions: The new economics of choosing, attending and completing college* (pp. 355–394). Chicago: University of Chicago Press and National Bureau of Economic Research.

51. Perez-Pena, R. (2014, April 9). What you don't know about financial aid (but should). *The New York Times.* Retrieved from https://www.nytimes.com/2014/04/13/education/edlife/what-you-dont-know-about-financial-aid-but-should.html?_r=0.

52. Lobosco, K. (2016, April 13). How to read your ridiculously confusing financial aid letter. *CNN Money.* Retrieved from http://money.cnn.com/2016/04/13/pf/college/college-financial-aid-award/.

53. Wang, M. (2012). How financial aid letters often leave students confused and misinformed. ProPublica. Retrieved from https://www.propublica.org/article/how-financial-aid-letters-often-leave-students-confused-and-misinformed.

54. Dynarski, S., & Scott-Clayton, J. (2006). The cost of complexity in federal student aid: Lessons from optimal tax theory and behavioral economics. *National Tax Journal, 59*(2), 319–356.

55. Maag, E., & Rohaly, J. (2007, March). Who benefits from the hope and lifetime learning credit? Paper presented at the American Education Finance Association's 32nd Annual Conference, Baltimore, MD.

56. Bettinger, E. P., Long, B. T., Oreopoulos, P., & Sanbonmatsu, L. (2012). The role of application assistance and information in college decisions: Results from the H&R Block Experiment. *The Quarterly Journal of Economics, 127*(3), 1205–1242. https://doi.org/10.1093/qje/qjs017.

57. Woo, J., & Choy, S. (2011). *Merit aid for undergraduates: Trends from 1995–96 to 2007–8.* Washington, DC: National Center for Education Statistics.

58. Burd, S. (2013). *Undermining Pell: How colleges compete for wealthy students and leave the low-income behind.* Washington, DC: New America Foundation, Education Policy Program. Retrieved from https://s3.amazonaws.com/new-america-composer/attachments_archive/Merit_Aid%20Final.pdf.

59. Van der Klaauw, W. (2002). Estimating the effects of financial aid offers on college enrollment: A regression discontinuity approach. *International Economic Review, 43*(4), 1249–1287.

60. Davis, J. S. (2003, Summer). Unintended consequences. National Crosstalk. Retrieved from http://www.highereducation.org/crosstalk/ct0303/voices0303-consequences.shtml.

61. Singell, L. D., & Stone, J. A. (2002). The good, the poor and the wealthy: Who responds most to college financial aid? *Bulletin of Economic Research, 54*(4), 393–407.

62. Dynarski, S. (2000). Hope for whom? Financial aid for the middle class and its impact on college attendance. *National Tax Journal, 53*(3), 629–661.

63. Center on Budget and Policy Priorities. (2016). *State-by-state fact sheets: Higher education cuts jeopardize students' and states' economic future.* Washington, DC: Author. Retrieved from http://www.cbpp.org/research/state-by-state-fact-sheets-higher-education-cuts-jeopardize-students-and-states-economic.

64. Reich, D., & Debot, B. (2015). House Budget Committee plan cuts Pell Grants deeply, reducing access to higher education. Washington, DC: Center on Budget and Policy Priorities. Retrieved from http://www.cbpp.org/research/house-budget-committee-plan-cuts-pell-grants-deeply-reducing-access-to-higher-education.

65. Fain, P. (2017, March 29). White House calls for more cuts to Pell. *Inside Higher Ed*. Retrieved from https://www.insidehighered.com/quicktakes/2017/03/29/white-house-calls-more-cuts-pell.

66. Bombardieri, M., Flores, A., Miller, B., & Garcia, S. (2017, March 17). Trump's higher education budget robs more than $5 billion from low-income students. Washington, DC: Center for American Progress. Retrieved from https://www.americanprogress.org/issues/education/news/2017/03/17/428554/trumps-higher-education-budget-robs-5-billion-low-income-students/.

67. Douglas-Gabriel, D. (2017, March 28). Trump budget cuts could hit research universities hard, Moody's warns. *The Washington Post*. Retrieved from https://www.washingtonpost.com/news/grade-point/wp/2017/03/28/trump-budget-cuts-could-hit-research-universities-hard-moodys-warns/?utm_term=.4fb81cf92b01.

68. Dynarski, S., & Scott-Clayton, J. (2008). Complexity and targeting in federal student aid: A quantitative analysis. *Tax Policy and the Economy, 22*(1), 109–150. Dynarski, S. & Scott-Clayton, J. (2013). Financial aid policy: Lessons from research. *Future of Children,* 23(1), 67–91.

69. Mizala, A., & Torche, F. (2010). Bringing the schools back in: The stratification of educational achievement in the Chilean voucher system. *International Journal of Educational Development.* doi:10.1016/j.ijedudev.2010.09.004

70. Organisation for Economic Co-operation and Development. (2012). *Public and private schools: How management and funding relate to their socio-economic profile.* Retrieved from http://dx.doi.org/10.1787/9789264175006-en.

71. Valenzuela, J. P.; Bellei, C.; & de los Ríos, D. (2014). Socioeconomic school segregation in a market-oriented educational system: The case of Chile. *Journal of Education Policy,* 29(2), 217–241.

72. Giancola, J., & Kahlenberg, R. (2016). *True merit: Ensuring our brightest students have access to our best colleges and universities.* Lansdowne, VA: Jack Kent Cooke Foundation. Retrieved from http://www.jkcf.org/assets/1/7/JKCF_True_Merit_Report.pdf.

73. Kolodner, M. (2015). Black students are drastically underrepresented at top public colleges, data show. *Hechinger News.* Retrieved from http://hechingerreport.org/black-students-are-drastically-underrepresented-at-top-public-colleges-data-show/.

74. Faricy, C. (2017, March 15). Donald Trump's tax plan would mean huge breaks for millionaires like Trump. *The Washington Post.* Retrieved from https://www.washingtonpost.com/posteverything/wp/2017/03/15/donald-trumps-tax-plan-would-mean-huge-breaks-for-millionaires-like-trump/?utm_term=.7796db6fd1fc.

75. Kamenetz, A. (2017, March 16). Trump's budget blueprint pinches pennies for education. *NPR News.* Retrieved from http://www.npr.org/sections/ed/2017/03/16/520261978/trumps-budget-blueprint-pinches-pennies-for-education.

76. Lauter, D. (2017). Trump wants more money for school vouchers, cuts elsewhere. *San Diego Union-Tribune.* Retrieved from http://www.sandiegouniontribune.com/la-essential-education-updates-southern-trump-wants-more-money-for-vouchers-1489674823-htmlstory.html.

77. Bergeron, D. A., & Van Ostern, T. (2013). *A comprehensive look at the student loan interest-rate changes that are being considered by Congress.* Washington, DC: Center for American Progress. Retrieved from https://www.americanprogress.org/issues/education/reports/2013/06/27/68237/a-comprehensive-analysis-of-the-student-loan-interest-rate-changes-that-are-being-considered-by-congress/.

78. Camera, L. (2016, August 12). Education Department experiments with student loan counseling. *U.S. News & World Report.* Retrieved from https://www.usnews.com/news/articles/2016-08-12/education-department-experiments-with-student-loan-counseling.

79. Huelsman, M. (2015). *The debt divide: The racial and class bias behind the "new normal" of student borrowing.* Washington, DC: Demos. Retrieved from http://www.demos.org/publication/debt-divideracial-and-class-bias-behind-new-normal-student-borrowing.

80. Elliott, W., Lewis, M., & Johnson, P. (2014). *Unequal outcomes: Student loan effects on young adults' net worth accumulation.* Lawrence, KS: Center on Assets, Education, and Inclusion.

81. Grinstein-Weiss, M., Covington, M., Clancy, M. M., & Sherraden, M. (2016). *A savings account for every child born in Israel: Recommendations for program implementation* (CSD Policy Brief 16-11). Retrieved from https://csd.wustl.edu/Publications/Documents/PB16-11.pdf.

82. Baylor, E. (2016). *Closed doors: Black and Latino students are excluded from top public universities.* Washington, DC: Center for American Progress. Retrieved from https://www.americanprogress.org/issues/education/reports/2016/10/13/145098/closed-doors-black-and-latino-students-are-excluded-from-top-public-universities/.

83. Scott-Clayton, J., & Li, J. (2016). *Black-White disparity in student loan debt more than triples after graduation.* Washington, DC: Brookings Institution. Retrieved from https://www.brookings.edu/research/black-white-disparity-in-student-loan-debt-more-than-triples-after-graduation/.

84. Addo, F. R., Houle, J., & Simon, D. (2016). Young, Black, and (still) in the red: Parental wealth, race, and student loan debt. *Journal of Race and Social Problems, 8*(1), 64–76.

85. McKernan, S. M., Ratcliffe, C., Steuerle, C. E., Kalish, E., & Quakenbush, C. (2015). *Nine Charts about wealth inequality in America.* Washington, DC: Urban Institute. Retrieved from http://apps.urban.org/features/wealth-inequality-charts/.

86. U.S. Census Bureau. (2015). Educational attainment in the United States. Retrieved from https://www.census.gov/hhes/socdemo/education/data/cps/2015/tables.html.

87. Brown, M., & Caldwell, S. (2013, April 17). Young adult student loan borrowers retreat from housing and auto markets. *Liberty Street Economics.* Retrieved from http://libertystreeteconomics.newyorkfed.org/2013/04/young-student-loan-borrowers-retreat-from-housing-and-auto-markets.html.

88. Dynarski, S. (2016). *The dividing line between haves and have-nots in home ownership: Education, not student debt* (Evidence Speaks Reports, Vol. 1, #17). Washington, DC: Brookings Institution. Retrieved from https://www.brookings.edu/research/the-dividing-line-between-haves-and-have-nots-in-home-ownership-education-not-student-debt/.

89. Stone, C., Van Horn, C., & Zukin, C. (2012). *Chasing the American dream: Recent college graduates and the great recession.* New Brunswick, NJ: Center for Workforce Development. Retrieved from http://www.heldrich.rutgers.edu/sites/default/files/content/Chasing_American_Dream_Report.pdf.

90. Houle, J., & Berger, L. (2014). *Is student loan debt discouraging home buying among young adults?* Washington, DC: Association for Public Policy and Management. Retrieved

from http://www.appam.org/assets/1/7/Is_Student_Loan_Debt_Discouraging_Home_Buying_Among_Young_Adults.pdf.

91. Shand, J. M. (2007). *The impact of early-life debt on the homeownership rates of young households: An empirical investigation*. Washington, DC: Federal Deposit Insurance Corporation Center for Financial Research. Retrieved from http://www.fdic.gov/bank/analvtical/cfr/2008/ian/CFRSS2008Shand.pdf.

92. Rose, S. (2013). The value of a college degree. *Change: The Magazine of Higher Learning* (November–December).

93. Bennett, W. J., & Wilezol, D. (2013). *Is college worth it?: A former United States Secretary of Education and a liberal arts graduate expose the broken promise of higher education.* New York, NY: Thomas Nelson.

94. Bidwell, A. (2015, February 10). College grads question how much a degree is worth. *U.S. News & World Reports*. Retrieved from http://www.usnews.com/news/articles/2015/02/10/college-grads-question-the-return-on-investment-of-todays-degrees.

95. Touryalai, H. (2013). Student loan problems: One third of millennials regret going to college. *Forbes*. Retrieved from https://www.forbes.com/sites/halahtouryalai/2013/05/22/student-loan-problems-one-third-of-millennials-regret-going-to-college/#318e38937797.

96. Vien, C. L. (2015, July 1). 68% of Americans with student loans are unhappy with how they financed college. *Journal of Accountancy*. Retrieved from https://www.journalofaccountancy.com/issues/2015/jul/college-financing-student-loans.html.

97. Akers, B., & Chingos, M. M. (2014). *Is a student loan crisis on the horizon?* Washington, DC: Brookings Institution.

98. Government Accountability Office. (2016). *Education needs to improve its income-driven repayment plan budget estimates* (GAO-17-22). Washington, DC: Author. Retrieved from http://www.gao.gov/assets/690/681064.pdf.

99. U.S. Government Accountability Office. (2003). *Student financial aid: Monitoring aid greater than federally defined need could help address student loan indebtedness* (GAO–03–508). Washington, DC: U.S. Government Printing Office.

100. Cunningham, A. F., & Kienzl, G. S. (2011). *Delinquency: The untold story of student loan borrowing*. Washington, DC: Institute for Higher Education Policy. Retrieved from http://www.ihep.org/assets/files/publications/a-f/delinquency-the_untold_story_final_march_2011.pdf.

101. Brown, M., Haughwout, A., Donghoon, L., Scally, J., & van der Klaauw, W. (2015, February 19). Looking at student loan defaults through a larger window. *Liberty Street Economics*. Retrieved from http://libertystreeteconomics.newyorkfed.org/2015/02/looking_at_student_loan_defaults_through_a_larger_window.html#.VpVJeStGmKz.

102. Delisle, J. (2013). Beware savvy borrowers using income-based repayment. Washington, DC: New America. Retrieved from https://www.newamerica.org/education-policy/edcentral/beware-savvy-borrowers-using-income-based-repayment/.

103. Pew Charitable Trusts. (2014). *A new financial reality: The balance sheets and economic mobility of Generation X*. Washington, DC: Author. Retrieved from http://www.pewtrusts.org/~/media/assets/2014/09/pew_generation_x_report.pdf.

104. Emmons, W. R., & Noeth, B. J. (2015). *Why didn't higher education protect Hispanic and Black wealth?* (In the Balance, Issue 12). St. Louis, MO: Federal Reserve Bank of St. Louis. Retrieved from https://www.stlouisfed.org/publications/in-the-balance/issue12-2015/why-didnt-higher-education-protect-hispanic-and-black-wealth.

105. Emmons, W. R., & Ricketts, L. R. (2017). College is not enough: Higher education does not eliminate racial and ethnic wealth gaps. *Federal Reserve Bank of St. Louis Review, 99*(1), 7–40. https://dx.doi.org/10.20955/r.2017.7-39

106. Hershbein, B. (2016, February 19). A college degree is worth less if you are raised poor. *Brookings Social Mobility Memos*. Washington, DC: The Brookings Institution. Retrieved from http://www.brookings.edu/blogs/social-mobility-memos/posts/2016/02/19-college-degree-worth-less-raised-poor-hershbein.

107. Education Commission of the States. (2017). Free college and adult student populations [Interactive Dashboard]. Retrieved from http://www.ecs.org/free-college-and-adult-student-populations/.

108. Schramm, M. (2015). Bernie Sanders issues bill to make 4-year colleges tuition-free. *USA Today*. Retrieved from http://college.usatoday.com/2015/05/19/bernie-sanders-issues-bill-to-make-4-year-colleges-tuition-free/.

109. Glum, J. (2017, April 11). Free tuition plans could spread among states as Sanders Pushes Congress for "college for all." *Newsweek*. Retrieved from http://www.newsweek.com/free-college-tuition-new-york-bernie-sanders-582345.

110. Lobosco, K. (2017, August 4). Tuition-free college is getting bigger. Here's where it's offered. *CNN Money*. Retrieved from http://money.cnn.com/2017/05/16/pf/college/states-tuition-free-college/index.html.

111. Zinshteyn, M. (2017). Who benefits from New York's free college plan? *Hechinger News*. Retrieved from http://hechingerreport.org/benefits-new-yorks-free-college-plan/.

112. Poutre, A., Rorrison, J., & Voight, M. (2017). *Limited means, limited options*. Washington, DC: Institute for Higher Education Policy.

113. Butler, S. (2015, January 20). Obama's SOTU free college plan is bad for poor Americans [Op-Ed]. Washington, DC: Brookings Institution. Retrieved from http://www.brookings.edu/research/opinions/2015/01/20-obama-free-community-college-bad-idea-sotu-butler.

114. Phillips, M. (2013). The high price of a free college education in Sweden. *The Atlantic*. Retrieved from https://www.theatlantic.com/international/archive/2013/05/the...sweden/276428/.

115. Hamilton, D., Darity W. Jr., Price, A. E., Shridharan, V., & Tippett, R. (2015). *Umbrellas don't make it rain: Why studying and working hard is not enough for Black Americans*. Report produced by The New School, Duke University Center for Social Equity, and Insight Center for Community Economic Development. Retrieved from http://www.insightcced.org/wp-content/uploads/2015/08/Umbrellas_Dont_Make_It_Rain_Final.pdf.

116. Traub, A., Sullivan, L., Meschede, T., & Shapiro, T. (2017). The asset value of Whiteness: Understanding the racial wealth gap. Washington, DC: Demos and IASP. Retrieved from http://www.demos.org/publication/asset-value-whiteness-understanding-racial-wealth-gap.

117. Rauscher, E. (2016). Passing it on: Parent-to-adult child financial transfers for school and socioeconomic attainment. *The Russell Sage Foundation Journal of the Social Sciences, 2*(6), 172–196.

118. Annie E. Casey Foundation. (2016). *Investing in tomorrow: Helping families build savings and assets*. Retrieved from http://www.aecf.org/m/resourcedoc/aecf-investingintomorrow-2016.pdf.

119. Center on Assets, Education, and Inclusion. (2013). *Building expectations, delivering results: Asset-based financial aid and the future of higher education*. Biannual report on the assets and education field. Lawrence, KS: Center on Assets, Education, and Inclusion.

120. Butler, S., Beach, W. W., & Winfree, P. L. (2008). *Pathways to economic mobility: Key indicators*. Washington, DC: Economic Mobility Project, an Initiative of the Pew Charitable Trusts. Retrieved from http://www.pewtrusts.org/~/media/legacy/uploadedfiles/ wwwpewtrustsorg/reports/economic_mobility/pewempchartbook12pdf.pdf.

121. Friedline, T., Johnson, P., & Hughes, R. (2014). Toward healthy balance sheets: Are savings accounts a gateway to young adults' asset diversification and accumulation? *Federal Reserve Bank of St. Louis Review, 96*(4), 359–389. Retrieved from https://files. stlouisfed.org/files/htdocs/publications/review/2014/q4/friedline.pdf.

122. Cramer, R., O'Brien, R., Cooper, D., & Luengo-Prado, M. (2009). *A penny saved is mobility earned: Advancing economic mobility through savings*. Washington, DC: Economic Mobility Project, an initiative of the Pew Charitable Trusts. Retrieved from http://www.pewtrusts.org/~/media/legacy/uploadedfiles/pcs_assets/2009/ empsavingsreportpdf.pdf.

123. Sherraden, M. (1991). *Assets and the poor: A new American welfare policy*. Armonk, NY: M. E. Sharpe.

124. Elliott, W. (2013). *Can a college-saver identity help resolve the college expectation-attainment paradox?* St. Louis, MO: Center for Social Development. Retrieved from https://csd.wustl.edu/Publications/Documents/FS13-30.pdf.

125. Reardon, S. F. (2013). The widening income achievement gap. *Educational Leadership, 70*(8), 10–16.

126. Elliott, W. III, & Lewis, M. (2014). Child development accounts (CSAs). In *The Encyclopedia of Social Work*. Retrieved from http://socialwork.oxfordre.com/view/ 10.1093/acrefore/9780199975839.001.0001/acrefore-9780199975839-e-871.

127. Sallie Mae. (2016). *How America pays for college*. Washington, DC: Author. Retrieved from http://news.salliemae.com/files/doc_library/file/ HowAmericaPaysforCollege2016FNL.pdf.

128. Goldberg, F. (2005). The universal piggy bank: Designing and implementing a system of savings accounts for children. In M. Sherraden (Ed.), *Inclusion in the American dream: Assets, poverty, and public policy* (pp. 303–322). New York, NY: Oxford University Press.

129. Loya, R. M., Garber, J., & Santos, J. (2017). *Levers for success: Key features and outcomes of Children's Savings Account programs*. Waltham, MA: Institute on Assets and Social Policy.

130. Cook, N. (2015, June 20). Confirmed: Millennials' top financial concern is student-loan debt. *The Atlantic*. Retrieved from https://www.theatlantic.com/business/archive/2015/ 06/millennials-student-loan-debt-money/396275/.

131. Fottrell, Q. (2015, August 5). Most Americans say their children will be worse off. *MarketWatch*. Retrieved from http://www.marketwatch.com/story/ most-americans-say-their-children-will-be-worse-off-2015-08-05.

132. Elliott, W. (2013). Small-dollar children's savings accounts and children's college outcomes. *Children and Youth Services Review, 35*(3), 572–585. doi:10.1016/ j.childyouth.2012.12.015

133. Elliott, W., Kite, B., O'Brien, M., Lewis, M., & Palmer, A. (2016). *Initial elementary education finding from Promise Indiana's Children's Savings Account program* (AEDI Working Paper 04-16). Lawrence: Center on Assets, Education, and Inclusion.

134. Elliott, W., & Beverly, S. (2011). The role of savings and wealth in reducing "wilt" between expectations and college attendance. *Journal of Children and Poverty, 17*(2), 165–185. doi:10.1080/10796126.2011.538375

135. Elliott, W., Song, H. A., & Nam, I. (2013). Small-dollar children's saving accounts and children's college outcomes by income level. *Children and Youth Services Review, 35*(3), 560–571. doi:10.1016/j.childyouth.2012.12.003

136. Prosperity Now. (2016). *State of the children's savings field 2016.* Washington, DC: Author. Retrieved from https://prosperitynow.org/resources/state-childrens-savings-field-2016.

137. Harold Alfond Foundation. (2013). *HAF 2012 grant report.* Portland, ME: Author. Retrieved from http://haroldalfondfoundation.org/pdf/announcements/2012GrantReport_000.pdf.

138. Markoff, S., & Debigny, D. (2015). *Investing in dreams: A blueprint for designing Children's Savings Account programs.* Washington, DC: Prosperity Now. Retrieved from https://prosperitynow.org/resources/investing-dreams-blueprint-designing-childrens-savings-account-programs.

139. Lewis, M., & Elliott, W. (2015). *A regional approach to Children's Savings Account development: The case of New England.* Lawrence, KS: Center on Assets, Education, and Inclusion.

140. Elliott, W., & Levere, A. (2016, June). Promise models and CSAs: How college savings can bolster the early financial aid commitment. Paper presented at the Designing Sustainable Funding for College Promise Initiatives meeting. Retrieved from http://collegepromise.org/wp-content/uploads/2016/10/DSF_Children_Savings_Paper_ETS_2016_0227_PromiseNet-1.pdf.

141. Totten, K. (2014). State treasurer: $50 college-savings fund for every Nevada kindergartner. *Las Vegas Review-Journal.* Retrieved from https://www.reviewjournal.com/news/state-treasurer-50-college-savings-fund-for-every-nevada-kindergartner/.

142. Johnson, M. (2014). *Innovative arrears and economic stability initiatives.* Webinar for Western Interstate Child Support Enforcement Council. Retrieved from http://www.wicsec.org/wp-content/uploads/2014/09/W-35-Innovative-Arrears-and-Economic-Stability-Initiatives-Melissa-Johnson-David-Johnson-Asaph-Glosser-Cynthia-Osborne.pdf.

143. Clancy, M., & Lassar, T. (2010). *College savings plan account at birth: Maine's statewide program.* St. Louis, MO: Center for Social Development. Retrieved from https://csd.wustl.edu/Publications/Documents/PB10-16.pdf.

144. Powell, G. (2014). *Remarks to the Portland Regional Chamber of Commerce and announcement of "automatic enrollment" for the Harold Alfond College Challenge.* Retrieved from http://www.haroldalfondfoundation.org/pdf/announcements/EggsIssues3.4.14FINAL_000.pdf.

145. Clancy, M., & Sherraden, M. (2014). *Automatic deposits for all at birth: Maine's Harold Alfond College challenge.* Retrieved from http://csd.wustl.edu/Publications/Documents/Maine%E2%80%99sHaroldAlfondCollegeChallenge.pdf.

146. Bevans, J. S. (2013). *Children's education savings accounts: A case study of San Francisco's Kindergarten to College Program.* San Francisco, CA: EARN Research Institute. Retrieved from https://www.earn.org/wp-content/uploads/2015/03/130619-K2C-Practitioners-Report-Final.pdf.

147. Coté, J. (2010, October 5). S.F. 1st U.S. city to start college savings plan. *SFGate.* Retrieved from http://www.sfgate.com/education/article/S-F-1st-U-S-city-to-start-college-savings-plan-3171940.php.

148. Elliott, W., Lewis, M., Poore, A., & Clark, B. (2015). *Toward an agenda for CSA delivery systems.* Boston, MA: Federal Reserve Bank of Boston.

149. O'Brien, M., Lewis, M., Jung, E. J., & Elliott, W. (2017). *Harold Alfond College Challenge (HACC) 2017 savings report for households who opted in to the program from 2008 to 2013.* Ann Arbor, MI: Center on Assets, Education, and Inclusion. Retrieved from http://aedi.ssw.umich.edu/sites/default/files/publications/Harold-alfond-college-challenge-2017-savings-report_0.pdf.

150. John, D. C. (2010). Perspective from the right: Building a cross-ideological consensus for child development accounts. *Children and Youth Services Review, 32*(11), 1601–1604.

151. Yadama, G. N., & Sherraden. M. (1996). Effects of assets on attitudes and behaviors: Advance test of a social policy proposal. *Social Work Research, 20*(1), 3–11. https://doi.org/10.1093/swr/20.1.3

152. Kim, Y., Sherraden, M., Huang, J., & Clancy, M. (2015). Child development accounts and parental educational expectations for young children: Early evidence from a statewide social experiment. *Social Service Review, 89*(1), 99–137.

153. Elliott, W. (2015). *Building college-saver identities among Latino immigrants: A two-generation Prosperity Kids account pilot program* (AEDI Report 06-2015). Lawrence, KS: Center on Assets, Education, and Inclusion.

154. Oyserman, D. (2015). *Pathways to success through identity-based motivation.* New York, NY: Oxford University Press.

155. Oyserman, D., Bybee, D., & Terry, K. (2006). Possible selves and academic outcomes: How and when possible selves impel action. *Journal of Personality and Social Psychology, 91*(1), 188–204.

156. Oyserman, D. (2007). Social identity and self-regulation. In A. Kruglanski & T. Higgins (Eds.), *Handbook of social psychology* (2nd ed., pp. 432–453). New York, NY: Guilford Press.

157. Oyserman, D., & Destin, M. (2010). Identity-based motivation: Implications for intervention. *The Counseling Psychologist, 38*(7), 1001–1043. doi:10.1177/0011000010374775

158. Fisher, O., & Oyserman, D. (2017). Assessing interpretations of experienced ease and difficulty as motivational constructs. *Motivation Science, 17*, 1–31.

CHAPTER 5

1. Heller, D. E. (2008). The impact of student loans on college access. In S. Baum, M. McPherson, & P. Steele (Eds.), *The effectiveness of student aid policies: What the research tells us* (pp. 39–67). New York, NY: College Board.

2. Nam, Y., Kim, Y., Clancy, M. M., Zager, R., & Sherraden, M. (2013). Do Child Development Accounts promote account holding, saving, and asset accumulation for children's future? Evidence from a statewide randomized experiment. *Journal of Policy Analysis and Management, 32*(1), 6–33.

3. Burke, A. (2015, November 20). *Eight big ideas for reforming college in the U.S.* Washington, DC: The Brookings Institution. Retrieved from http://www.brookings.edu/blogs/brookings-now/posts/2015/11/8-big-ideas-for-reforming-college-in-the-us.

4. Bandura, A. (1997). *Self-efficacy: The exercise of control.* New York, NY: W. H. Freeman.

5. Cunha, F., & Heckman, J. J. (2008). Formulating, identifying and estimating the technology of cognitive and noncognitive skill formation. *Journal of Human Resources, 43*(4), 738–782.

6. McClelland, M. M., Morrison, F. J., & Holmes, D. L. (2000). Children at risk for early academic problems: The role of learning-related social skills. *Early Childhood Research Quarterly, 15*(3), 307–329.

7. Blair, C., & Diamond, A. (2008). Biological processes in prevention and intervention: The promotion of self-regulation as a means of preventing school failure. *Developmental Psychopathology, 20*(3), 899–911.

8. Denham, S. A. (2006). Social-emotional competence as support for school readiness: What is it and how do we assess it? *Early Education and Development, 17*(1), 57–89.

9. Raver, C. C. (2002). Emotions matter: Making the case for the role of young children's emotional development for early school readiness. *Social Policy Report, 16*(3), 3–18.

10. Snow, K. L. (2007). Integrative views of the domains of child function. In R. C. Pianta, M. J. Cox, & K. L. Snow (Eds.), *School readiness and the transition to kindergarten in the era of accountability* (pp. 197–216). Baltimore, MD: Paul H. Brookes.

11. Vandivere, S., Pitzer, L., Halle, T., & Hair, E. (2004). Indicators of early school success and child well-being. In *Ready schools reference guide*. Battle Creek, MI: W. K. Kellogg Foundation. Retrieved from http://www.wkkf.org/default.aspx?tabid=101&CID=3&CatID=3&ItemID=5000284&NID=20&LanguageID=0

12. Merrell, C., & Bailey, K. (2008, September). Predicting achievement in the early years: How influential is personal, social and emotional development? Paper presented at the International Association for Educational Assessment conference. Cambridge, UK. Retrieved from http://www.iaea.info/documents/paper_2b715b7.pdf.

13. Shala, M. (2013). The impact of preschool social-emotional development on academic success of elementary school students. *Psychology, 4*(11), 787–791.

14. Durlak, J. A., Weissberg, R. P., Dymnicki, A.B., Taylor, R. D., & Schellinger, K. B. (2011). The impact of enhancing students' social and emotional learning: A meta-analysis of school-based universal interventions. *Child Development, 82*(1), 474–501.

15. Whitehurst, R. (2016). *Hard thinking on soft skills*. Washington, DC: Brookings Institution. Retrieved from https://www.brookings.edu/wp-content/uploads/2016/07/Download-the-paper2.pdf.

16. McMunn, A. M., Nazroo, J. Y., Marmot, M. G., Boreham, R., & Goodman, R. (2001). Children's emotional and behavioural well-being and the family environment: Findings from the Health Survey for England. *Social Science and Medicine, 53*(4), 423–440.

17. Sheffield Morris, A., Silk, J. S., Steinberg, L., Myers, S. S., & Robinson, L. R. (2007). The role of the family context in the development of emotional regulation. *Social Development, 16*(2), 361–388.

18. Winer, A. C. & Thompson, R. (n.d.). *How poverty and depression impact a child's social and emotional competence*. Davis: University of California-Davis, Center for Poverty Research. Retrieved from http://poverty.ucdavis.edu/sites/main/files/file-attachments/policy_brief_thompson_risk_print.pdf.

19. Huang, J., Sherraden, M., Kim, Y., & Clancy, M. (2014). Effects of Child Development Accounts on early social-emotional development an experimental test. *Journal of American Medical Association Pediatrics, 168*(3), 265–271.

20. Votruba-Drzal, E. (2006). Economic disparities in middle childhood development: Does income matter? *Developmental Psychology, 42*(6), 1154–1167.

21. Cummings, E. M., & Davies, P. T. (1994). Maternal depression and child development. *Journal of Child Psychology and Psychiatry, 35*(1), 73–122.

22. Kiernan, K. E., & Huerta, M. C. (2008). Economic deprivation, maternal depression, parenting and children's cognitive and emotional development in early childhood. *The British Journal of Sociology, 59*(4), 783–806.

23. Essex, M. J., Klein, M. H., Cho, E., & Kalin, N. H. (2002). Maternal stress beginning in infancy may sensitize children to later stress exposure: Effects on cortisol and behavior. *Biological Psychiatry, 52*(8), 776–784.

24. Kahn, R. S.; Brandt, D., & Whitaker, R. C. (2004). Combined effect of mothers' and fathers' mental health symptoms on children's behavioral and emotional well-being. *Archives of Pediatric Adolescent Medicine, 158*(8), 721–729.

25. Huang, J., Sherraden, M., & Purnell, J. Q. (2014). Impacts of Child Development Accounts on maternal depressive symptoms: Evidence from a randomized statewide policy experiment. *Social Science & Medicine, 112,* 30–38. doi:10.1016/j.socscimed.2014.04.023

26. Golden, O., Loprest, P., & Mills, G. (2012). *Economic security for extremely vulnerable families: Themes and options for workforce development and asset strategies.* Washington, DC: Urban Institute. Retrieved from http://www.urban.org/research/publication/economic-security-extremely-vulnerable-families-themes-and-options-workforce-development-and-asset-strategies.

27. National Research Council and Institute of Medicine. (2009). *Depression in parents, parenting, and children: Opportunities to improve identification, treatment, and prevention.* Washington, DC: National Academies Press.

28. Rost, K., Smith, J., & Dickinson, M. (2004). The effect of improving primary care depression management on employee absenteeism and productivity. A randomized trial. *Medical Care, 42*(12), 1202–1210.

29. Schoenbaum, M., Unutzer, J., McCaffey, D., Duan, N., Sherbourne, C., & Wells, K. (2002). The effects of primary care depression treatment on patients' clinical status and employment. *Health Services Research, 37*(5), 1145–1458.

30. Huang, J., Kim, Y., & Sherraden, M. (2016). Mateial hardship and children's social-emotional development: Testing mitigating effects of Child Development Accounts in a randomized experiment. *Child: Care, Health and Development, 43,* 89–96. doi:10.1111/cch.12385

31. Huang, J., Kim, Y., Sherraden, M., & Clancy, M. (2017). Unmarried mothers and children's social-emotional development: The role of Child Development Accounts. *Journal of Child and Family Studies, 26,* 234–247.

32. Conger, R. D., Conger, K. J., & Elder, G. H. Jr. (1997). Family economic hardship and adolescent adjustment: Mediating and moderating processes. In G. J. Duncan & J. Brooks-Gunn (Eds.), *Consequences of growing up poor* (pp. 288–310). New York, NY: Russell Sage Foundation.

33. McLanahan, S., Tach, L., & Schneider, D. (2013). The causal effects of father absence. *Annual Review of Sociology, 39,* 399–427. doi:10.1146/annurev-soc-071312-145704

34. Pew Research Center. (2012). *Most parents expect their children to attend college.* Washington, DC: Author. Retrieved from http://www.pewresearch.org/daily-number/most-parents-expect-their-children-to-attend-college/.

35. Howard, K., & Reeves, R. (2014). *Vague hopes and active aspirations, Part I.* Washington, DC: Brookings Institution. Retrieved from https://www.brookings.edu/blog/social-mobility-memos/2014/04/15/vague-hopes-and-active-aspirations-part-1/.

36. Zhan, M., & Sherraden, M. (2011). Assets and liabilities, educational expectations, and children's college degree attainment. *Children and Youth Services Review, 33*(6), 846–854.

37. Sherraden, M. (1991). *Assets and the poor: A new American welfare policy.* Armonk, NY: M. E. Sharpe.

38. Kim, Y., Huang, J., Sherraden, M., & Clancy, M. (2017). Child Development Accounts, parental savings, and parental educational expectations: A path model. *Children and Youth Services Review, 79,* 20–28.

39. Mistry, R. S., White, E. S., Benner, A. D., & Huynh, V. W. (2009). A longitudinal study of the simultaneous influence of mothers' and teachers' educational expectations on low-income youth's academic achievement. *Journal of Youth and Adolescence, 38*(6), 826–838.

40. Sallie Mae, & Gallup. (2015). *How America saves for college: Sallie Mae's national study of parents with children under age 18*. Washington, DC: Author. Retrieved from http://news.salliemae.com/sites/salliemae.newshq.businesswire.com/files/doc_library/file/HowAmericaSaves2015_FINAL.pdf.

41. Kim, Y., Sherraden, M., & Clancy, M. (2013). Do mothers' educational expectations differ by race and ethnicity, or socioeconomic status? *Economics of Education Review, 33*, 82–94. http://dx.doi.org/10.1016/j.econedurev.2012.09.007

42. Sandefur, G. D., Meier, A. M., & Campbell, M. E. (2006). Family resources, social capital, and college attendance. *Social Science Research, 35*(2), 525–553.

43. Singh, K., Beckley, P., Trivette, P., Keith, T. Z., Keith, P., & Anderson, E. (1995). The effects of four components of parental involvement on eighth-grade student achievement: Structural analysis of NELS-88 data. *School Psychology Review, 24*(2), 299–317.

44. Hess, R. D., Holloway, S. D., Dickson, W. P., & Price, G. G. (1984). Maternal variables as predictors of children's school readiness and later achievement in vocabulary and mathematics in sixth grade. *Child Development, 55*(5), 1902–1912.

45. Davis-Kean, P. D. (2005). The influence of parent education and family income on child achievement: The indirect role of parental expectations and the home environment. *Journal of Family Psychology, 19*(2), 294–304.

46. Englund, M. M., Luckner, A. E., Whaley, G. J. L., & Egeland, B. (2004). Children's achievement in early elementary school: Longitudinal effects of parental involvement, expectations, and quality of assistance. *Journal of Educational Psychology, 96*, 723–730.

47. Pearce, R. R. (2006). Effects of cultural and social structural factors on the achievement of White and Chinese American students at school transition points. *American Educational Research Journal, 43*(1), 75–101.

48. Vartanian, T. P., Karen, D., Buck, P. W., & Cadge, W. (2007). Early factors leading to college graduation for Asians and non-Asians in the United States. *The Sociological Quarterly, 48*(2), 165–197.

49. Zhang, Y., Haddad, E., Torres, B., & Chen, C. (2011). The reciprocal relationships among parents' expectations, adolescents' expectations, and adolescents' achievement: A two-wave longitudinal analysis of the NELS data. *Journal of Youth and Adolescence, 40*, 479–489.

50. Entwisle, D. R., Alexander, K. L., & Olson, L. S. (2005). First grade and educational attainment by age 22: A new story. *American Journal of Sociology, 110*(5), 1458–1502.

51. Gill, S., & Reynolds, A. J. (1999). Educational expectations and school achievement of urban African American children. *Journal of School Psychology, 37*(4), 403–424. http://dx.doi.org/10.1016/S0022-4405(99)00027-8

52. Chamberland, C., Lacharité, C., Clément, M.-È., & Lessard, D. (2015). Predictors of development of vulnerable children receiving child welfare services. *Journal of Child and Family Studies, 24*(10), 2975–2988.

53. McCoy, D. C., Connors, M. C., Morris, P. A., Yoshikawa, H., & Friedman-Krauss, A. H. (2015). Neighborhood economic disadvantage and children's cognitive and social-emotional development: Exploring Head Start classroom quality as a mediating mechanism. *Early Childhood Research Quarterly, 32*, 150–159.

54. Augustine, J. M., Cavanagh, S. E., & Crosnoe, R. (2009). Maternal education, early child care and the reproduction of advantage. *Social Forces, 88*(1), 1–29.

55. Furstenberg, F. F., Cook, T. D., Eccles, J., & Elder, G. H. (1999). *Managing to make it: Urban families and adolescent success*. Chicago, IL: University of Chicago Press.

56. Grogan, K. E. (2012). Parents' choice of pre-kindergarten: The interaction of parent, child, and contextual factors. *Early Child Development and Care, 182*(10), 1265–1287.

57. Magnuson, K. (2007). Maternal education and children's academic achievement during middle childhood. *Developmental Psychology, 43*(6), 1497–512.

58. Morrissey, T. W. (2008). Familial factors associated with the use of multiple child-care arrangements. *Journal of Marriage and Family, 70*, 549–563.

59. Elliott, W., & Harrington, K. (2015). *Identifying short term outcome metrics for evaluating whether Children's Savings Accounts programs are on track.* Boston, MA: Federal Reserve Bank of Boston. Retrieved from https://www.bostonfed.org/commdev/issue-briefs/2016/cdbrief12016.htm.

60. Beal, S. J., & Crockett, L. J. (2010). Adolescents' occupational and educational aspirations and expectations: Links to high school activities and adult educational attainment. *Developmental Psychology, 46*(1), 258–265.

61. Cook, T. D., Church, M. B., Ajanaku, S., Shadish, W. R., Kim, J. R., & Cohen, R. (1996). The development of occupational aspirations and expectations among inner-city boys. *Child Development, 67*(6), 3368–3385.

62. Marjoribanks, K. (1984). Ethnicity, family environment and adolescents' aspirations: A follow-up study. *Journal of Educational Research, 77*(3), 166–171.

63. Ou, S.-R., & Reynolds, A. J. (2008). Predictors of educational attainment in the Chicago Longitudinal Study. *School Psychology Quarterly, 23*, 199–229.

64. Uno, M., Mortimer, J. T., Kim, M., & Vuolo, M. (2010). Holding on or coming to terms with educational underachievement: A longitudinal study of ambition and attainment. In S. Shulman& J. E. Nurmi (Eds.), *The role of goals in navigating individual lives during emerging adulthood* (pp. 41–56). (New Directions for Child and Adolescent Development 130). New York, NY: John Wiley.

65. Oyserman, D. (2013). Not just any path: Implications of identity-based motivation for school outcome disparities. *Economics of Education Review, 33*(1), 179–190.

66. Elliott, W., Choi, E. H., Destin, M., & Kim, K. (2011). The age old question, which comes first? A simultaneous test of young adult's savings and expectations. *Children and Youth Services Review, 33*(7), 1101–1111.

67. Elliott, W., & Friedline, T. (2013). You pay your share, we'll pay our share. *Economics of Education Review, 33*(1), 134–153.

68. Flint, T. A. (1997). Intergenerational effects of paying for college. *Research in Higher Education, 38*(3), 313–344.

69. Powell, B., & Steelman, L. C. (1995). Feeling the pinch: Child spacing and constraints on parental economic investments in children. *Social Forces, 73*, 1465–1486.

70. Lesnick, J., Goerge, R., Smithgall, C., & Gwynne, J. (2010). *A longitudinal analysis of third-grade students in Chicago in 1996–97 and their educational outcomes.* Chicago, IL: Chapin Hall Center for Children at the University of Chicago.

71. Whitney, S. (2005). Reading by Grade 3: Reading First and NCLB. Wrights Law. Retrieved from http://www.wrightslaw.com/nclb/reading.grade3.htm.

72. Lloyd, K. E. (1978). Behavior analysis and technology in higher education. In A. D. Catania & T. A. Brigham (Eds.), *Handbook of applied behavior analysis: Social and instructional processes* (pp. 482–521). New York, NY: Irvington.

73. Hernandez, D. J. (2011). *Double jeopardy: How third-grade reading skills and poverty influence high school graduation.* Baltimore, MD: Annie E. Casey Foundation. Retrieved from http://www.aecf.org/m/resourcedoc/AECF-DoubleJeopardy-2012-Full.pdf.

74. Lee, J. (2012). College for all: Gaps between desirable and actual P–12 math achievement trajectories for college readiness. *Educational Researcher, 41*(2), 43–55.

75. Cabrera, A. F., & La Nasa, S. M. (2000). Understanding the college-choice process. *New Directions for Institutional Research, 107,* 5–22.

76. Hallinan, M. T. (1996). Track mobility in secondary school. *Social Forces, 74,* 983–1002.

77. Klasik, D. (2012). The college application gauntlet: A systematic analysis of the steps to four-year college enrollment. *Research in Higher Education, 53,* 506–549.

78. Long, M. C., Conger, D., & Iatarola, P. (2012). Effects of high school course-taking on secondary and postsecondary success. *American Educational Research Journal, 49,* 285–322.

79. Lucas, S. R., & Berends, M. (2002). Sociodemographic diversity, correlated achievement, and de facto tracking. *Sociology of Education, 75,* 328–348.

80. Feister, L. (2013). *Early warning confirmed: A research update on third-grade reading.* Baltimore, MD: Annie E. Casey Foundation. Retrieved from http://www.aecf.org/resources/early-warning-confirmed/.

81. Jussim, L, Eccles, J., & Madon, S.J. (1996). Social perception, social stereotypes, and teacher expectations: Accuracy and the quest for the powerful self-fulfilling prophecy. *Advances in Experimental Social Psychology, 29,* 281–388.

82. Kuklinski, M. R., & Weinstein, R. S. (2001), Classroom and developmental differences in a path model of teacher expectancy effects. *Child Development, 72,* 1554–1578. doi:10.1111/1467-8624.00365

83. Madon, S. J., Jussim, L., & Eccles, J. (1997). In search of the powerful self-fulfilling prophecy. *Journal of Personality and Social Psychology, 72,* 791–809.

84. Rist, R. C. (2001). On understanding the processes of schooling: The contributions of labeling theory. In A. R. Sadovnik, P. W. Cookson, & S. F. Semel, (Eds.), *Exploring education* (2nd ed., pp. 149–157). Boston, MA: Allyn & Bacon. (Original work published 1977)

85. Seginer, R. (1983). Parents' educational expectations and children's academic achievements: A literature review. *Merrill-Palmer Quarterly, 29*(1), 1–23.

86. Duncan, G., Dowsett, C. J., Claessens, A., Magnuson, K., Huston, A. C., Klebanov, P., & Japel, C. (2007). School readiness and later achievement. *Developmental Psychology, 43*(6), 1428–1446.

87. Bodovski, K., & Youn, M. J. (2011). The long term effects of early acquired skills and behaviors on young children's achievement in literacy and mathematics. *Journal of Early Childhood Research, 9*(1), 4–19.

88. Ansari, A., & Lopez, M. (2015). *Preparing low-income Latino children for kindergarten and beyond: How children in Miami's publicly funded preschool programs fare* (Publication No. 2015-40). Bethesda, MD: National Research Center on Hispanic Children and Families. Retrieved from http://www.childtrends.org/wp-content/uploads/2015/09/Hispanic-Center-MSRP-Brief-FINAL.pdf.

89. Brooks-Gunn, J., Burchinal, M. R., Espinosa, L. M., Gormley, W. T., Ludwig, J., Magnuson, K. A. & Zaslow, M. J. (2013). *Investing in our future: The evidence base on preschool education* (Vol. 9). Washington. DC: Society for Research in Child Development and Foundation for Child Development.

90. Child & Family Policy Center. (2013). *Preschool participation and third-grade reading proficiency.* Des Moines, IA: Author. Retrieved from http://www.cfpciowa.org/documents/filelibrary/issues/early_care_and_education/PRESCHOOL_PARTICIPATION_AND_THIRD_G_1BEC3D3D09E13.pdf.

91. Elliott, W. (2009). Children's college aspirations and expectations: The potential role of college development accounts (CDAs). *Children and Youth Services Review, 31*(2), 274–283.

92. Huang, J., Guo, B., Kim, Y., & Sherraden, M. (2010). Parental income, assets, borrowing constraints and children's post-secondary education. *Children and Youth Services Review, 32*(4), 585–594. doi:10.1016/j.childyouth.2009.12.005

93. Elliott, W., Jung, H., & Friedline, T. (2010). Math achievement and children's savings: Implications for Child Development Accounts. *Journal of Family and Economic Issues, 31*(2), 171–184.

94. Elliott, W., Kim, K. H., Jung, H., & Zhan, M. (2010). Asset holding and educational attainment among African American youth. *Children and Youth Services Review, 32*(11), 1497–1507.

95. Elliott, W., Kite, B., O'Brien, M., Lewis, M., & Palmer, A. (2016). *Initial elementary education finding from Promise Indiana's Children's Savings Account program* (AEDI Working Paper 04-16). Lawrence: Center on Assets, Education, and Inclusion.

96. Lopez, L. (2015, October 13). America's student debt nightmare actually started in the 1980s. *Business Insider.* Retrieved from http://www.businessinsider.com/student-debt-crisis-started-in-the-1980s-2015-10.

97. Elliott, W., Song, H. A., & Nam, I. (2013). Small-dollar children's saving accounts and children's college outcomes by income level. *Children and Youth Services Review, 35*(3), 560–571. doi:10.1016/j.childyouth.2012.12.003

98. Elliott, W., & Beverly, S. (2011). The role of savings and wealth in reducing "wilt" between expectations and college attendance. *Journal of Children and Poverty, 17*(2), 165–185. doi:10.1080/10796126.2011.538375

99. Castleman, B. L., & Page, L. C. (2014). *Summer melt: Supporting low-income students through the transition to college.* Cambridge, MA: Harvard University Press.

100. Belkin, D. (2017, August 11). College Admissions officers won't just "chill" about summer melt. *The Wall Street Journal.* Retrieved from https://www.wsj.com/articles/college-admissions-officers-wont-just-chill-about-summer-melt-1502468367.

101. Elliott, W. (2013). *Can a college-saver identity help resolve the college expectation-attainment paradox?* St. Louis, MO: Center for Social Development. Retrieved from https://csd.wustl.edu/Publications/Documents/FS13-30.pdf.

102. Elliott, W. (2013). Small-dollar Children's Savings Accounts and children's college outcomes. *Children and Youth Services Review, 35*(3), 572–585. doi:10.1016/j.childyouth.2012.12.015

103. Elliott, W., Constance-Huggins, M., & Song, H. (2013). Improving college progress among low- to moderate-income (LMI) young adults: The role of assets. *Journal of Family and Economic Issues, 34*(4), 382–399.

104. Mettler, S. (2014). *Degrees of inequality: How the politics of higher education sabotaged the American dream.* New York, NY: Basic Books.

105. Pfeffer, F. (2016). *Growing wealth gaps in education.* Ann Arbor, MI: National Poverty Center. Retrieved from http://npc.umich.edu/publications/u/2016-06-npc-working-paper.pdf.

106. Swail, W. S., with Redd, K. E., & Perna, L. W. (2003). *Retaining minority students in higher education: A framework for success* (ASHE-ERIC Higher Education Report No. 2). Washington, DC: George Washington University, School of Education and Human Development.

107. Alliance for Excellent Education. (2011). *Saving now and saving later: How high school reform can reduce the nation's wasted remediation dollars.* Washington,

DC: Author. Retrieved from http://all4ed.org/wp-content/uploads/2013/06/Saving-NowSavingLaterRemediation.pdf.

108. Armstrong, J., & Zaback, K. (2014). *College completion rates and remedial education outcomes for institutions in Appalachian states.* Washington, DC: Appalachian Regional Commission. Retrieved from http://www.arc.gov/assets/research_reports/CollegeCompletion-RatesandRemedialOutcomesforAppalachianStates.pdfS.

109. Stewart, S., Lim, D. H., & Kim, J. (2005). Factors influencing college persistence for first-time students. *Journal of Developmental Education, 38*(3), 12–20. Retrieved from http://files.eric.ed.gov/fulltext/EJ1092649.pdf.

110. Tross, S. A., Harper, J. P., Osher, L. W., & Kneidinger, L. M. (2000). Not just the usual cast of characteristics: Using personality to predict college performance and retention. *Journal of College Student Development, 41*, 323–334.

111. Adelman, C. (1999). *Answers in the toolbox: Academic intensity, attendance patterns, and bachelor's degree attainment.* Washington, DC: U.S. Department of Education, Office of Educational Research and Improvement.

112. Adelman, C. (2000, January). Participation in outreach programs prior to high school graduation: Socioeconomic status by race. Paper presented at the ConnectED Conference, San Diego, CA.

113. Nunez, A., & Cuccaro-Alamin, S. (1998). *First-generation students: Undergraduates whose parents never enrolled in postsecondary education* (NCES 98-082). Washington, DC: National Center for Education Statistics, U.S. Government Printing Office.

114. Swail, W. S., Cabrera, A. F., Lee, C., & Williams, A. (2005). *Latino students and the educational pipelines: A three-part series. Part III: Pathways to the bachelor's degree for Latino students.* Stafford, VA: Education Policy Institute.

115. Hamrick, F. A., & Stage, F. K. (2004). College predisposition at high-minority enrollment, low-income schools. *The Review of Higher Education, 27*(2), 151–168.

116. Tierney, W. G., Corwin, Z. B., & Colyar, J. E. (Eds.). (2004). *Preparing for college: Nine elements for effective outreach.* Albany: State University of New York Press.

117. Dynarski, S. (2015, June 2). For the poor, the graduation gap is even wider than the enrollment gap. *The New York Times.* Retrieved from https://www.nytimes.com/2015/06/02/upshot/for-the-poor-the-graduation-gap-is-even-wider-than-the-enrollment-gap.html.

118. Pew Charitable Trusts. (2015). How do families cope with financial shocks? Washington, DC: Author. Retrieved from http://www.pewtrusts.org/en/research-and-analysis/issue-briefs/2015/10/the-role-of-emergency-savings-in-family-financial-security-how-do-families.

119. Ashby, J., Schoon, I., & Webley, P. (2011). Save now, save later? Linkages between saving behavior in adolescence and adulthood. *European Psychologist, 16*(3), 227–237. Advance online publication. doi:10.1027/1016-9040/a00006

120. Elliott, W., Rifenbark, G., Webley, P., Friedline, T., & Nam, I. (2012). *It is not just families; Institutions play a role in reducing wealth inequality: Long-term effects of youth savings accounts on adult saving behaviors* (AEDI Working Papers No. 01-2012). Lawrence, KS: Center on Assets, Education, and Inclusion.

121. McCormick, M.H. (2009). The effectiveness of youth financial education: A review of the literature. *Journal of Financial Counseling and Planning, 20*(1), 70–83.

122. Mandell, L., & Klein, L. S. (2009). The impact of financial literacy education on subsequent financial behavior. *Journal of Financial Counseling and Planning, 20*(1), 15–24.

123. Sawady, E. R. & Tescher, J. (2008). *Financial decision making processes of low-income individuals.* Cambridge, MA: Harvard University, Joint Center for Housing Studies. Retrieved from http://www.jchs.harvard.edu/sites/jchs.harvard.edu/files/ucc08-2_sawady_tescher.pdf.

124. Elliott, W., Webley, P., & Friedline, T. (2011). *Two accounts for why adolescent savings is predictive of young adult savings: An economic socialization perspective and an institutional perspective* (CSD Working Papers No. 11-34). St. Louis, MO: Center for Social Development. Retrieved from https://csd.wustl.edu/Publications/Documents/WP11-34.pdf.

125. Webley, P., & Nyhus, E. K. (2006). Parents' influence on children's future orientation and saving. *Journal of Economic Psychology, 27*(1), 140–164. doi:10.1016/j.joep.2005.06.016

126. Friedline, T., & Elliott, W. (2013). Connections with banking institutions and diverse asset portfolios in young adulthood: Children as potential future investors. *Children and Youth Services Review, 35*(6), 994–1006.

127. Friedline, T., Johnson, P., & Hughes, R. (2014). Toward healthy balance sheets: Are savings accounts a gateway to young adults' asset diversification and accumulation? *Federal Reserve Bank of St. Louis Review, 96*(4), 359–389. Retrieved from https://files.stlouisfed.org/files/htdocs/publications/review/2014/q4/friedline.pdf.

CHAPTER 6

1. Elliott, W. (2013). Small-dollar Children's Savings Accounts and children's college outcomes. *Children and Youth Services Review, 35*(3), 572–585. doi:10.1016/j.childyouth.2012.12.015

2. Kingdon, J.W. (2010). *Agendas, alternatives, and public policies* (2nd ed.). New York, NY: Pearson.

3. Davis, T., & Harper, E. (2007, September 28). Clinton floats $5,000 baby bond. *ABC News.* Retrieved from http://abcnews.go.com/Politics/story?id=3668781&page=1.

4. Edwards, C. (2007, October 4). Clinton's $5,000 baby giveaway. Washington, DC: Cato Institute. Retrieved from https://www.cato.org/blog/clintons-5000-baby-giveaway.

5. John, D. C. (2010). Perspective from the right: Building a cross-ideological consensus for child development accounts. *Children and Youth Services Review, 32*(11), 1601–1604.

6. Cramer, R., & Newville, D. (2009). *Children's savings accounts: The case for creating a lifelong savings platform at birth as a foundation for a "save-and-invest" economy.* Washington, DC: New America Foundation.

7. Loya, R. M., Garber, J., & Santos, J. (2017). *Levers for success: Key features and outcomes of Children's Savings Account programs.* Waltham, MA: Institute on Assets and Social Policy.

8. King, J. (2016, November). Understanding the context CSA programs fit into: CSA legislation in the 114th Congress. Paper presented at the CSA Symposium, Center on Assets, Education, and Inclusion, Lawrence, KS.

9. Government Accountability Office. (2012). *A small percentage of families save in 529 Plans* (GAO-13-64). Washington, DC: Author. Retrieved from http://www.gao.gov/assets/660/650759.pdf

10. Barr, A. (2010). The GOP's no-compromise pledge. *Politico.* Retrieved from http://www.politico.com/story/2010/10/the-gops-no-compromise-pledge-044311.

11. Kuhn, T. S. (1962). *The structure of scientific revolutions.* Chicago, IL: University of Chicago Press.

12. Kennedy, J. F. (1962). *Test of President John Kennedy's Rice stadium moon speech*. Retrieved from https://er.jsc.nasa.gov/seh/ricetalk.htm.

13. Sherraden, M. (1991). *Assets and the poor: A new American welfare policy*. Armonk, NY: M. E. Sharpe.

14. Vien, C. L. (2015, July 1). 68% of Americans with student loans are unhappy with how they financed college. *Journal of Accountancy*. Retrieved from https://www.journalofaccountancy.com/issues/2015/jul/college-financing-student-loans.html.

15. Newport, F. (2015). Americans continue to say U.S. wealth distribution is unfair. Washington, DC: Gallup. Retrieved from http://www.gallup.com/poll/182987/americans-continue-say-wealth-distribution-unfair.aspx.

16. Bernstein, J. (2005). Critical questions in asset-based policy. In M. Sherraden (Ed.), *Inclusion in the American dream: Assets, poverty, and public policy* (pp. 351–359). New York, NY: Oxford University Press.

17. Mettler, S. (2007). *Soldiers to citizens: The G.I. Bill and the making of the greatest generation*. New York, NY: Oxford University Press.

18. Subcommittee on Education and Health. (1988). *A cost-benefit analysis of government investment in post-secondary education under the World War II GI Bill*. Retrieved from http://www.jec.senate.gov/reports/100th%20Congress/Improving%20Access%20to%20Preschool%20and%20Postsecondary%20Education%20%281480%29.pdf.

19. Hamilton, D.; & Darity, W. A. Jr. (2010). Can "baby bonds" eliminate the racial wealth gap in putative post-racial America? *Review of Black Political Economy, 37*(3-4), 207–216.

20. Fisher, O., & Oyserman, D. (2017). Assessing interpretations of experienced ease and difficulty as motivational constructs. *Motivation Science, 17*, 1–31.

21. Sullivan, L, Meschede, T., Shapiro, T., Asante-Muhammed, D., & Nieves, E. (2016). *Equitable investments in the next generation: Designing policies to close the racial wealth gap*. Waltham, MA: Institute on Assets and Social Policy and CFED. Retrieved from https://iasp.brandeis.edu/pdfs/2016/EquitableInvestments.pdf.

22. O'Brien, M., Lewis, M., Jung, E. J., & Elliott, W. (2017). *Harold Alfond College Challenge (HACC) savings report for households who opted in, from 2008–2013*. Ann Arbor, MI: Center on Assets, Education, and Inclusion.

23. O'Brien, M., Lewis, M., Jung, E. J., & Elliott, W. (2017). *Savings behavior and asset accumulation in New Mexico's prosperity kids Children's Savings Account (CSA) program*. Ann Arbor, MI: Center on Assets, Education, and Inclusion.

24. O'Brien, M., Lewis, M., Jung, E. J., & Elliott, W. (2017). *Savings patterns and asset accumulation in the Promise Indiana Children's Savings Account (CSA) program: 2017 Update*. Ann Arbor, MI: Center on Assets, Education, and Inclusion.

25. Gray, K., Clancy, M. M., Sherraden, M. S., Wagner, K., & Miller-Cribbs, J. (2012). *Interviews with mothers of young children in the SEED for Oklahoma Kids college savings experiment* (CSD Research Report No. 12-53). St. Louis, MO: Washington University, Center for Social Development. Retrieved from http://csd.wustl.edu/Publications/Documents/RP12-53.pdf.

26. West, S., Banerjee, M., Phipps, B., & Friedline, T. (2017). Coming up short: Family composition, income, and household savings. *Journal of the Society for Social Work and Research, 8*(3), 355–377.

27. Elliott, W. (2017). *Policy response to existing challenges in CSA programs*. Ann Arbor, MI: Center on Assets, Education, and Inclusion.

28. Lewis, M., & Elliott, W. (2014). *Lessons to learn: Canadian insights for U.S. Children's Savings Account (CSA) policy.* Lawrence, KS: Center on Assets, Education, and Inclusion.

29. Grinstein-Weiss, M., Covington, M., Clancy, M. M., & Sherraden, M. (2016). *A savings account for every child born in Israel: Recommendations for program implementation* (CSD Policy Brief 16-11). Retrieved from https://csd.wustl.edu/Publications/Documents/PB16-11.pdf.

30. Lewis, M., Elliott, W., O'Brien, M., Jung, E., Harrington, K., & Jones-Layman, A. (2016). Saving and educational asset-building within a community-driven CSA program: The case of Promise Indiana. Lawrence: University of Kansas, Center on Assets, Education, and Inclusion.

31. Lewis, M., O'Brien, M., & Elliott, W. (2017). Immigrant Latina families saving in Children's Savings Account program against great odds: The case of Prosperity Kids. *Race and Social Problems, 9*(3), 192–206.

32. Government Accountability Office. (2016). *Education needs to improve its income-driven repayment plan budget estimates* (GAO-17-22). Washington, DC: Author. Retrieved from http://www.gao.gov/assets/690/681064.pdf.

33. Dynarski, S., & Scott-Clayton, J. (2016). Tax benefits for college attendance (Working Paper 22127). Cambridge, MA: National Bureau of Economic Research. Retrieved from http://www.nber.org/papers/w22127.

34. Reeves, R. (2017). *Dream hoarders: How the American upper middle class is leaving everyone else in the dust, why that is a problem, and what to do about it.* Washington, DC: Brookings Institution Press.

35. Bulman, G. B., & Hoxby, C. M. (2015). The returns to the federal tax credits for higher education. *Tax Policy and the Economy, 29*(1), 13–88. doi:10.1086/683364

36. Bulman, G. B., & Hoxby, C. M. (2015). The returns to the federal tax credits for higher education. *Tax Policy and the Economy, 29*(1), 13–88. doi:10.1086/683364

37. Long, B. T. (2004). The impact of federal tax credits for higher education expenses. In C. Hoxby (Ed.), *College choices: The economics of which college, when college, and how to pay for it* (pp. 101–167). Chicago: University of Chicago Press and National Bureau of Economic Research.

38. Burd, S. (2015). *Out-of-state student arms race: How public universities use merit aid to recruit nonresident students.* Washington, DC: New America, Education Policy Program. Retrieved from https://www.newamerica.org/education-policy/policy-papers/out-of-state-student-arms-race/.

39. Greer, J., & Levin, E. (2014). *Upside down: Tax incentives to save and build wealth* (CFED Federal Policy Brief). Retrieved from http://preview.cfed.org/assets/pdfs/Policy_Brief_-_Tax_Incentives.pdf.

40. McCall, L. (2013). *The undeserving rich: American beliefs about inequality, opportunity, and redistribution.* New York, NY: Cambridge University Press.

41. Cole, A., & Greenburg, S. (2016). *Details and analysis of Senator Bernie Sanders's tax plan.* Washington, DC: Tax Foundation. Retrieved from http://taxfoundation.org/sites/taxfoundation.org/files/docs/TaxFoundation-FF498.pdf.

42. Galston, W.A. (2017, April 14). Polling spotlight: America's shifting attitudes on taxes. Washington, DC: Brookings Institution. https://www.brookings.edu/blog/fixgov/2017/04/14/polling-spotlight-americas-shifting-attitudes-on-taxes/.

43. Huang, J., Beverly, S., Clancy, M., Lassar, T., & Sherraden, M. (2013). Early program enrollment in a statewide Child Development Account program. *Journal of Policy Practice, 12*(1), 62–81.

44. CFED (Prod.). (2016, May 20). Lessons learned from statewide CSA programs. [Webinar]. Retrieved from http://cfed.org/knowledge_center/events/upcoming/webinar_lessons_learned_from_statewide_csa_programs/

45. Beverly, S. G., & Sherraden, M. (1999). Institutional determinants of saving: Implications for low-income households and public policy. *Journal of Socio-Economics, 28*(4), 457–473.

46. Dworak-Fisher, K. (2008). *Encouraging participation in 401(k) plans: Reconsidering the employer match.* Washington, DC: Bureau of Labor Statistics. Retrieved from https://www.bls.gov/osmr/pdf/ec080060.pdf.

47. Beverly, S., Clancy, M., & Sherraden, M. (2015). *The early positive impacts of Child Development Accounts.* St. Louis, MO: Washington University.

48. Elliott, W., Lewis, M., Poore, A., & Clark, B. (2015). *Toward an agenda for CSA delivery systems.* Boston, MA: Federal Reserve Bank of Boston.

49. Powell, G. (2014). *Remarks to the Portland Regional Chamber of Commerce and announcement of "Automatic Enrollment" for the Harold Alfond College Challenge.* Retrieved from http://www.haroldalfondfoundation.org/pdf/announcements/EggsIssues3.4.14FINAL_000.pdf.

50. Friedline, T. (2014). The independent effects of savings accounts in children's names on their savings outcomes in young adulthood. *Journal of Financial Counseling and Planning, 25*(1), 69–89.

51. Huang, J., Sherraden, M., Kim, Y., & Clancy, M. (2014). Effects of Child Development Accounts on early social-emotional development an experimental test. *Journal of American Medical Association Pediatrics, 168*(3), 265–271.

52. Richards, K. V., & Thyer, B. A. (2011). Does Individual Development Account participation help the poor? A review. *Research on Social Work Practice, 21*(3), 348–362.

53. Eugenios, J. (2015). How low-income families have saved $1M for college. *CNN Money.* Retrieved from http://money.cnn.com/2015/05/20/news/economy/kindergarten-to-college-1-million/index.html.

54. Sallie Mae. (2013). *How America saves for college.* Washington, DC: Author. Retrieved from http://news.salliemae.com/sites/salliemae.newshq.businesswire.com/files/publication/file/HowAmericaSaves_Report2013_1.pdf.

55. Schreiner, M., & Sherraden, M. (2006). *Can the poor save? Saving and asset building in Individual Development Accounts.* New York, NY: Transaction.

56. Elliott, W., Lewis, M., O'Brien, M., LiCalsi, C., Rickles, J., Brown, L., & Sorensen, N. (2017). *Kindergarten to college Children's Savings Account Program.* Ann Arbor, MI: Center on Assets, Education, and Inclusion and American Institutes for Research.

57. Mason, L. R., Nam, Y., Clancy, M., Kim, Y., & Loke, V. (2010). Child Development Accounts and saving for children's future: Do financial incentives matter? *Children and Youth Services Review, 32*(11), 1570–1576. doi:10.1016/j.childyouth.2010.04.007

58. Elliott, W., Lewis, M., O'Brien, M., LiCalsi, C., Brown, L., Tucker, N., & Sorensen, N. (2017). *Contribution activity and asset accumulation in a universal Children's Savings Account program.* Ann Arbor, MI: Center on Assets, Education, and Inclusion and American Institutes for Research.

59. Lewis, M., Elliott, W., O'Brien, M., Jung, E., Harrington, K., & Jones-Layman, A. (2016). *Saving and educational asset-building within a community-driven CSA program: The case of Promise Indiana.* Lawrence: Center on Assets, Education, and Inclusion.

60. Duflo, E., Gale, W., Liebman, J., Orszag, P., & Saez, E. (2006). Saving incentives for low- and middle-income families: Evidence from a field experiment with H&R Block. *Quarterly Journal of Economics, 121*(4), 1311–1346.

61. John, D. C. (2010). Perspective from the right: Building a cross-ideological consensus for child development accounts. *Children and Youth Services Review 32*(11), 1601–1604.

62. Trump, D. (2011). *Time to get tough: Make America great again!* New York, NY: Regnery Publishing.

63. Dowd, M. (1999, November 28). Liberties; Trump shrugged. *The New York Times*. Retrieved from http://www.nytimes.com/1999/11/28/opinion/liberties-trump-shrugged.html.

64. Keyes, S. (2012, October 12). GOP congressional nominee derides poor people for "slothfulness and laziness" at fundraiser. Think Progress. Retrieved from https://thinkprogress.org/gop-congressional-nominee-derides-poor-people-for-slothfulness-and-laziness-at-fundraiser-b2e0e2db8943#.fgfqcl6vu.

65. Shapiro, T. (2017). *Toxic inequality: How America's wealth gap destroys mobility, deepens the racial divide, and threatens our future.* New York, NY: Basic Books.

66. Walsh, J. (2012, January 5). Rick Santorum flip-flops on Black people. *Salon*. Retrieved from http://www.salon.com/2012/01/05/rick_santorum_flip_flops_on_black_people/.

67. Blake, A. (2017, March 31). Republicans' views of Blacks' intelligence, work ethic lag behind Democrats at a record clip. *The Washington Post*. Retrieved from https://www.washingtonpost.com/news/the-fix/wp/2017/03/31/the-gap-between-republicans-and-democrats-views-of-african-americans-just-hit-a-new-high/.

68. Swanson, E., & Delaney, A. (2014). Americans think people are poor because of bad breaks, not because they're losers: Poll. *Huffington Post*. Retrieved from http://www.huffingtonpost.com/2014/04/17/poverty-poll_n_5167460.html?utm_hp_ref=politics.

69. Kuttner, R. (2008). *Obama's challenge: America's economic crisis and the power of a transformative presidency.* White River Junction, VT: Chelsea Green.

70. Paul, R. (2014, January 28). Tea Party response to the 2014 State of the Union address. Retrieved from https://www.paul.senate.gov/news/press/sen-paul-delivers-response-to-state-of-the-union-address.

71. Lesniewski, N. (2015, January 20). *Rand Paul to quote MLK, John Lewis in SOTU response.* Roll Call. Retrieved from http://www.rollcall.com/news/home/paul-to-quote-king-lewis-in-sotu-response.

72. Carson, B. (2012). *America the beautiful: Rediscovering what made this nation great.* Grand Rapids, MI: Zondervan.

73. Pew Research Center. (2014). *The rising cost of not going to college.* Washington, DC: Author. Retrieved from http://www.pewsocialtrends.org/files/2014/02/SDT-higher-ed-FINAL-02-11-2014.pdf.

74. Peter D. Hart Research Associates, Inc. (2007). *Memorandum re: public support for Children's Savings Accounts.* Washington, DC: CFED. Retrieved from http://cfed.org/assets/documents/seed/hart_public_support_memo.pdf.

75. Goldberg, F., Friedman, B., & Boshara, R. (2010). CDA legislative challenges and opportunities. *Children and Youth Services Review, 32*, 1609–1616.

76. Malloy, D. P. (2014, February 6). State of the State Address. Retrieved from http://www.governor.ct.gov/malloy/cwp/view.asp?A=11&Q=539440.

77. Mason, L. R., Nam, Y., Clancy, M., Loke, V., & Kim, Y. (2009). *SEED account monitoring research: Participants, savings, and accumulation.* St. Louis, MO: Washington University, Center for Social Development.

78. Beverly, S. G., Clancy, M. M., Huang, J., & Sherraden, M. (2015). *The SEED for Oklahoma Kids Child Development Account experiment: Accounts, assets, earnings, and savings*

(CSD Research Brief No. 15-29). St. Louis, MO: Washington University, Center for Social Development. Retrieved from http://csd.wustl.edu/Publications/Documents/RB15-29.pdf.

79. O'Connor, L. (2015, Feburary 4). America's most expensive city just got even more expensive. *Huffington Post.* Retrieved from http://www.huffingtonpost.com/2015/02/03/san-francisco-rent-2015-most-expensive-city_n_6609396.html.

80. Clancy, M., Sherraden, M., & Beverly, S. (2015). *College savings plans: A platform for inclusive and progressive child development accounts* (CSD Policy Brief 15-07). St. Louis, MO: Washington University, Center for Social Development.

81. Steverman, B. (2014). Why 97% of people don't use 529 college saving plans. *Bloomberg.* Retrieved from http://www.bloomberg.com/news/articles/2014-09-09/why-97-of-people-don-t-use-529-college-savings-plans.

82. Elliott, W. (2015). *Building college-saver identities among Latino immigrants: A two-generation Prosperity Kids account pilot program* (AEDI Report 06-2015). Lawrence, KS: Center on Assets, Education, and Inclusion.

83. Stoesz, D. (2016). *The excluded: An estimate of the consequences of denying Social Security to agricultural and domestic workers.* St. Louis, MO: Center for Social Development. Retrieved from https://csd.wustl.edu/Publications/Documents/WP16-17.pdf.

84. Thomas, H., Meschede, T., Mann, A., Boguslaw, J., & Shapiro, T. (2014). *The web of wealth: Resiliency and opportunity or driver of inequality?* Waltham, MA: Institute on Assets and Social Policy. Retrieved from https://iasp.brandeis.edu/pdfs/2014/Web.pdf.

85. Despard, M., & Friedline, T. (2017). *Do metropolitan areas have equal access to banking? A geographic investigation of financial services availability.* Lawrence: Center on Assets, Education, and Inclusion.

86. Elliott, W., Lewis, M., Poore, A., & Clark, B. (2015). *Toward an agenda for CSA delivery systems.* Boston, MA: Federal Reserve Bank of Boston.

87. Loke, V., & Sherraden, M. (2009). Building assets from birth: A global comparison of Child Development Account policies. *International Journal of Social Welfare, 18,* 119–129.

88. Lieber, R. (2017, November 8). The private school tax-break in the middle-class tax bill. *The New York Times.* Retrieved from https://www.nytimes.com/2017/11/08/your-money/the-private-school-tax-break-in-the-middle-class-tax-bill.html?_r=0.

89. Stokes, B. (2013). *The U.S.'s high income gap is met with relatively low public concern.* Washington, DC: Pew Research Center. Retrieved from http://www.pewresearch.org/fact-tank/2013/12/06/the-u-s-s-high-income-gap-is-met-with-relatively-low-public-concern/.

90. Elliott, W., Chan, M., & Poore, A. (2015). Counterbalancing student debt with "asset empowerment" and economic mobility. *The New England Journal of Higher Education.* Retrieved from http://www.nebhe.org/thejournal/counterbalancing-student-debt-with-asset-empowerment-and-economic-mobility/.

91. Cramer, R., O'Brien, R., Cooper, D., & Luengo-Prado, M. (2009). *A penny saved is mobility earned: Advancing economic mobility through savings.* Washington, DC: Economic Mobility Project, an initiative of The Pew Charitable Trusts. Retrieved from http://www.pewtrusts.org/~/media/legacy/uploadedfiles/pcs_assets/2009/empsavingsreportpdf.pdf.

92. Elliott, W., & Lewis, M. (2014). *Harnessing assets to build an economic mobility system: Reimagining the American welfare system.* Lawrence, KS: Center on Assets, Education, and Inclusion.

93. Bivens, J., & Mishel, L. (2015). *Understanding the historic divergence between productivity and a typical worker's pay: Why it matters and why it's real* (Briefing Paper #406). Washington, DC: Economic Policy Institute. Retrieved from http://www.epi.org/publication/understanding-the-historic-divergence-between-productivity-and-a-typical-workers-pay-why-it-matters-and-why-its-real/.

94. Pfeffer, F. (2016). *Growing wealth gaps in education.* Ann Arbor, MI: National Poverty Center. Retrieved from http://npc.umich.edu/publications/u/2016-06-npc-working-paper.pdf.

95. Pew Charitable Trusts. (2015). *How do families cope with financial shocks?* Washington, DC: Author. Retrieved from http://www.pewtrusts.org/en/research-and-analysis/issue-briefs/2015/10/the-role-of-emergency-savings-in-family-financial-security-how-do-families.

96. Annie E. Casey Foundation. (2016). *Investing in tomorrow: Helping families build savings and assets.* Retrieved from http://www.aecf.org/m/resourcedoc/aecf-investingintomorrow-2016.pdf.

97. Bartels, L. (2002). *Economic inequality and political representation.* New York, NY: Russell Sage Foundation. Retrieved from http://www.russellsage.org/sites/all/files/u4/Bartels_Economic%20Inequality%20%26%20Political%20Representation.pdf.

98. Reich, R. (2016). *Saving capitalism: For the many, not the few.* New York, NY: Vintage.

99. Sitaraman, G. (2017). *The crisis of the middle-class constitution: Why economic inequality threatens our republic.* New York, NY: Knopf.

100. Bradley, R., & Corwyn. R. (2004). *Socioeconomic status and child development.* Weinheim: Wiley-VCH.

101. Latimer, M. (2017). RIP U.S. Senate: 1789–2017. *Politico.* Retrieved from http://www.politico.com/magazine/story/2017/04/gorsuch-fillibuster-us-senate-214992.

102. Bidwell, A. (2014, August 21). Parents worry about student debt burden too. *U.S. News.* Retrieved from https://www.usnews.com/news/blogs/data-mine/2014/08/21/parents-worry-about-student-debt-burden-too.

CHAPTER 7

1. Pathe, S. (2014). Why half of U.S. adults no longer believe in the American dream. *PBS Newshour.* Retrieved from http://www.pbs.org/newshour/making-sense/why-half-of-u-s-adults-no-longer-believe-in-the-american-dream/.

2. Chetty, R., Grusky, D., Hell, M., Hendren, N., Manduca, R., & Narang, J. (2016). *The fading American dream: Trends in absolute income mobility since 1940* (NBER Working Paper No. 22910). Cambridge, MA: National Bureau of Economic Research. Retrieved from http://www.nber.org/papers/w22910.pdf.

3. Case, A., & Deaton, A. (2017, March). Mortality and morbidity in the 21st century (Brookings Papers on Economic Activity). Paper prepared for the Brookings Panel on Economic Activity. Washington, DC: Brookings Institution. Retrieved from https://www.brookings.edu/wp-content/uploads/2017/03/6_casedeaton.pdf.

4. Bayles, M. (2015, October 10). How the world perceives the new American dream. *The Atlantic.* Retrieved from https://www.theatlantic.com/international/archive/2015/10/american-dream-world-diplomacy/410080/.

5. Constable, P., & Clement, S. (2014, January 31). Hispanics often lead the way in their faith in the American dream, poll finds. *The Washington Post.* Retrieved from https://www.washingtonpost.com/local/hispanics-often-lead-the-way-in-their-faith-in-the-american-dream-poll-finds/2014/01/30/c9d4d498-6c2a-11e3-b405-7e360f7e9fd2_story.html?utm_term=.8345edb9af6d.

6. Vasilogambros, M. (2016, March 8). The ethnic groups that still believe in the American dream. *The Atlantic*. Retrieved from https://www.theatlantic.com/business/archive/2016/03/the-ethnic-groups-that-still-believe-in-the-american-dream/472776/.

7. Bick, A., Bruggemann, B., & Fuchs-Schundeln, N. (2016). *Hours worked in Europe and the U.S.: New data, new answers* (IZA Discussion Paper No. 10179). Bonn, Germany: Institute for the Study of Labor. Retrieved from http://ftp.iza.org/dp10179.pdf.

8. Bivens, J., & Mishel, L. (2015). *Understanding the historic divergence between productivity and a typical worker's pay: Why it matters and why it's real* (Briefing Paper #406). Washington, DC: Economic Policy Institute. Retrieved from http://www.epi.org/publication/understanding-the-historic-divergence-between-productivity-and-a-typical-workers-pay-why-it-matters-and-why-its-real/.

9. Piketty, T. (2014). *Capital in the twenty-first century*. Translated by Arthur Goldhammer. Boston, MA. Belknap Press.

10. Asante-Muhammed, D., & Collins, C. (2016). *America's racial wealth divide is nothing short of shocking*. Washington, DC: Institute for Policy Studies. Retrieved from http://www.ips-dc.org/americas-racial-wealth-divide-nothing-short-shocking/.

11. Saez, E., & Zucman, G. (2016). Wealth inequality in the United States since 1913: Evidence from capitalized income tax data. *The Quarterly Journal of Economics, 131*(2), 519–578.

12. Shapiro, T. (2017). *Toxic inequality: How America's wealth gap destroys mobility, deepens the racial divide, and threatens our future*. New York, NY: Basic Books.

13. Tozzi, J. (2015). More proof that the richer you are, the healthier you'll be. *Bloomberg News*. Retrieved from https://www.bloomberg.com/news/articles/2015-04-13/more-proof-that-the-richer-you-are-the-healthier-you-ll-be.

14. Pfeffer, F. (2016). Growing wealth gaps in education. Ann Arbor, MI: National Poverty Center. Retrieved from http://npc.umich.edu/publications/u/2016-06-npc-working-paper.pdf.

15. Parker, K. (2012). *Yes, the rich are different*. Washington, DC: Pew Research Center. Retrieved from http://www.pewsocialtrends.org/2012/08/27/yes-the-rich-are-different/.

16. Graham, C. (2015, February 19). The high cost of being poor in America: Stress, pain, and worry. *Brookings Social Mobility Memos*. Retrieved from https://www.brookings.edu/blog/social-mobility-memos/2015/02/19/the-high-costs-of-being-poor-in-america-stress-pain-and-worry/.

17. Graham, C. (2016, February 10). The rich even have a better kind of stress than the poor. *Brookings Social Mobility Memos*. Retrieved from https://www.brookings.edu/research/the-rich-even-have-a-better-kind-of-stress-than-the-poor/.

18. Cingano, F. (2014). *Trends in income inequality and its impact on economic growth* (OECD Social, Employment and Migration Working Papers No. 163). Paris: OECD Publishing. http://dx.doi.org/10.1787/5jxrjncwxv6j-en.

19. Sitaraman, G. (2017). *The crisis of the middle-class constitution: Why economic inequality threatens our republic*. New York, NY: Knopf.

20. Sherraden, M., Clancy, M. M., Nam, Y., Huang, J., Kim, Y., Beverly, S. G., & Purnell, J. Q. (2015). Universal accounts at birth: Building knowledge to inform policy. *Journal of the Society for Social Work and Research, 6*, 541–564.

21. Huang, J., Kim, Y., Sherraden, M., & Clancy, M. (2017). Unmarried mothers and children's social-emotional development: The role of Child Development Accounts. *Journal of Child and Family Studies, 26*, 234–247.

22. Gray, K., Clancy, M. M., Sherraden, M. S., Wagner, K., & Miller-Cribbs, J. (2012). *Interviews with mothers of young children in the SEED for Oklahoma Kids college savings experiment* (CSD Research Report No. 12-53). St. Louis, MO: Washington University, Center for Social Development. Retrieved from http://csd.wustl.edu/Publications/Documents/RP12-53.pdf.

23. Hershbein, B. (2016, February 19). A college degree is worth less if you are raised poor. *Brookings Social Mobility Memos*. Washington, DC: The Brookings Institution. Retrieved from http://www.brookings.edu/blogs/social-mobility-memos/posts/2016/02/19-college-degree-worth-less-raised-poor-hershbein.

24. Collins, C. (2013, May 29). Wealthy parents, inherited advantage, and declining mobility. Retrieved from http://inequality.org/wealthy-parents-inherited-advantage-declining-mobility/.

25. National Bureau of Labor Statistics. (2015). Earnings and unemployment rates by educational attainment. Washington, DC: Author. Retrieved from https://www.bls.gov/emp/ep_chart_001.htm.

26. Pew Charitable Trusts. (2016). *Who's in, who's out*. Washington, DC: Author. Retrieved from http://www.pewtrusts.org/~/media/assets/2016/01/retirement_savings_report_jan16.pdf.

27. Walsemann, K. M., Bell, B. A., & Hummer, R. A. (2012). Effects of timing and level of degree attained on depressive symptoms and self-rated health at midlife. *American Journal of Public Health, 102*(3), 557–563.

28. Dynarski, S. (2016). *The dividing line between haves and have-nots in home ownership: Education, not student debt* (Evidence Speaks Reports, Vol. 1, #17). Washington, DC: Brookings Institution. Retrieved from https://www.brookings.edu/research/the-dividing-line-between-haves-and-have-nots-in-home-ownership-education-not-student-debt/.

29. Emmons, W. R., & Noeth, B. J. (2015). *Why didn't higher education protect Hispanic and Black wealth?* (In the Balance, Issue 12). St. Louis, MO: Federal Reserve Bank of St. Louis. Retrieved from https://www.stlouisfed.org/publications/in-the-balance/issue12-2015/why-didnt-higher-education-protect-hispanic-and-black-wealth.

30. Hamilton, D., Darity, W. Jr., Price, A. E., Shridharan, V., & Tippett, R. (2015). *Umbrellas don't make it rain: Why studying and working hard is not enough for Black Americans*. Report produced by The New School, Duke University Center for Social Equity, and Insight Center for Community Economic Development. Retrieved from http://www.insightcced.org/wp-content/uploads/2015/08/Umbrellas_Dont_Make_It_Rain_Final.pdf.

31. Urahn, S. K., Currier, E., Elliott, D., Wechsler, L., Wilson, D., & Colbert, D. (2012). *Pursuing the American dream: Economic mobility across generations* (Economic Mobility Project, the Pew Charitable Trusts). Washington, DC: Pew Charitable Trusts. Retrieved from http://www.pewtrusts.org/~/media/legacy/uploadedfiles/wwwpewtrustsorg/reports/economic_mobility/pursuingamericandreampdf.pdf

32. Baker, B. D., Farrie, D., & Sciarra, D. G. (2016). Mind the gap: 20 years of progress and retrenchment in school funding and achievement gaps. *ETS Research Report Series, 1*, 1–37. doi:10.1002/ets2.12098

33. Campbell, F. A., Wasik, B. H., Pungello, E., Burchinal, M., Barbarin, O., Kainz, K., & Ramey, C. T. (2008). Young adult outcomes of the Abecedarian and CARE early childhood educational interventions. *Early Childhood Research Quarterly, 23*(4), 452–466.

34. Heckman, J. J., Malofeeva, L., Pinto, R., & Savelyev, P. (2013). Understanding the mechanisms through which an influential early childhood program boosted adult outcomes (Unpublished manuscript). Department of Economics, University of Chicago.

35. Schweinhart, L. J., Barnes, H. V., & Weikart, D. P. (1993). *Significant benefits: The High/Scope Perry Preschool Study through age 27.* Ypsilanti, MI: High/Scope Press.

36. Huang, J., Sherraden, M., Kim, Y., & Clancy, M. (2014). Effects of Child Development Accounts on early social-emotional development an experimental test. *Journal of American Medical Association Pediatrics, 168*(3), 265–271.

37. Kim, Y., Huang, J., Sherraden, M., & Clancy, M. (2017). Child Development Accounts, parental savings, and parental educational expectations: A path model. *Children and Youth Services Review, 79,* 20–28.

38. Kim, Y., Sherraden, M., Huang, J., & Clancy, M. (2015). Child development accounts and parental educational expectations for young children: Early evidence from a statewide social experiment. *Social Service Review, 89*(1), 99–137.

39. Elliott, W., & Lewis, M. (2015). *The real college debt crisis: How student borrowing threatens financial well-being and erodes the American dream.* Santa Barbara, CA: ABC-CLIO.

40. Huelsman, M. (2015). The debt divide: The racial and class bias behind the "new normal" of student borrowing. Washington, DC: Demos. Retrieved from http://www.demos.org/publication/debt-divideracial-and-class-bias-behind-new-normal-student-borrowing.

41. Bulman, G. B., & Hoxby, C. M. (2015). The returns to the federal tax credits for higher education. *Tax Policy and the Economy, 29*(1), 13–88. doi:10.1086/683364

42. Long, B. T. (2004). The impact of federal tax credits for higher education expenses. In C. Hoxby (Ed.), *College choices: The economics of which college, when college, and how to pay for it* (pp. 101–167). Chicago: University of Chicago Press and the National Bureau of Economic Research.

43. Levin, E., Greer, J., & Rademacher, I. (2014). *From upside down to right-side up: Redeploying $540 billion in federal spending to help all families save, invest, and build wealth.* Washington, DC: CFED. Retrieved from http://cfed.org/assets/pdfs/Upside_Down_to_Right-Side_Up_2014.pdf.

44. Khazan, O. (2014). How being poor makes you sick. *The Atlantic.* Retrieved from https://www.theatlantic.com/health/archive/2014/05/poverty-makes-you-sick/371241/.

45. Hu, L., Kaestner, R., Mazumder, B., Miller, S., & Wong, A. (2016). *The effect of the Patient Protection and Affordable Care Act Medicaid expansions on financial well-being* (NBER Working Paper No. 22170). Cambridge, MA: National Bureau of Economic Research. Retrieved from http://www.nber.org/papers/w22170.pdf.

46. McKernan, M.-S., Brown, S., & Kenney, G. M. (2017). *Past-due medical debt a problem, especially for Black Americans.* Washington, DC: Urban Institute. Retrieved from http://www.urban.org/urban-wire/past-due-medical-debt-problem-especially-black-americans.

47. Hamel, L., Norton, M., Pollitz, K., Levitt, L., Claxton, G., & Brodie, M. (2016). *The burden of medical debt: Results from the Kaiser Family Foundation/New York Times Medical Bills Survey.* Menlo Park, CA: Kaiser Family Foundation. Retrieved from https://kaiserfamilyfoundation.files.wordpress.com/2016/01/8806-the-burden-of-medical-debt-results-from-the-kaiser-family-foundation-new-york-times-medical-bills-survey.pdf.

48. Vallas, R., & Valenti, J. (2014). *Asset limits are a barrier to economic security and mobility.* Washington, DC: Center for American Progress. Retrieved from https://www.americanprogress.org/issues/poverty/reports/2014/09/10/96754/asset-limits-are-a-barrier-to-economic-security-and-mobility/.

49. O'Brien, M., Lewis, M., Jung, E. J., & Elliott, W. (2017). *Harold Alfond College Challenge (HACC) savings report for households who opted in, from 2008–2013.* Ann Arbor, MI: Center on Assets, Education, and Inclusion.

50. Pew Charitable Trusts. (2015). *Americans' financial security: perception and reality.* Washington, DC: Author. Retrieved from http://www.pewtrusts.org/~/media/assets/2015/02/fsm-poll-results-issue-brief_artfinal_v3.pdf.

51. Matias Cortes, G., Jaimovich, N., & Siu, H.E. (2016). *Disappearing routine jobs: Who, how, and why?* Cambridge, MA: National Bureau of Economic Research. Retrieved from http://www.nber.org/papers/w22918.

52. Holmes, T. (2011). *The case of the disappearing large-employer manufacturing plants: Not much of a mystery after all* (Economic Policy Paper 11-4). Minneapolis, MN: The Federal Reserve Bank. Retrieved from https://www.minneapolisfed.org/research/economic-policy-papers/the-case-of-the-disappearing-largeemployer-manufacturing-plants-not-much-of-a-mystery-after-all.

53. Kim, Q. (2016, September 24). As our jobs are automated, some say we'll need a guaranteed basic income. *NPR News.* Retrieved from http://www.npr.org/2016/09/24/495186758/as-our-jobs-are-automated-some-say-well-need-a-guaranteed-basic-income.

54. Gould, E. (2014). *Why America's workers need faster wage growth—and what we can do about it* (Briefing Paper #382). Washington, DC: Economic Policy Institute. Retrieved from http://www.epi.org/files/2014/why-americas-workers-need-faster-wage-growth-final.pdf.

55. Rosenberg, J. (2013). *Measuring income for distributional analysis.* Washington, DC: Tax Policy Center, Urban Institute, and Brookings Institution.

56. Widerquist, K., & Lewis, M. A. (2006). An efficiency argument for the basic income guarantee. *International Journal of the Environment, Workplace, and Employment, 2*(1), 21–43.

57. Acemoglu, D., & Restrepo, P. (2017). *Robots and jobs: Evidence from US labor markets* (NBER Working Paper No. w23285). Cambridge: MA: National Bureau of Economic Research. Retrieved from http://www.nber.org/papers/w23285.pdf.

58. Parkin, A. (2016). *Family savings for post-secondary education.* Toronto: Omega Foundation. Retrieved from http://www.theomegafoundation.ca/documents/Family-Savings-for-Post-Secondary-Education.pdf.

59. Lewis, M., & Elliott, W. (2014). Lessons to learn: Canadian insights for U.S. Children's Savings Account (CSA) policy. Lawrence, KS: Center on Assets, Education, and Inclusion.

60. Grinstein-Weiss, M., Covington, M., Clancy, M. M., & Sherraden, M. (2016). *A savings account for every child born in Israel: Recommendations for program implementation* (CSD Policy Brief 16-11). Retrieved from https://csd.wustl.edu/Publications/Documents/PB16-11.pdf.

61. Harris, D., & Shaefer, H. L. (2017). Fighting poverty with a universal child allowance. *The American Prospect.* Retrieved from http://prospect.org/article/fighting-child-poverty-universal-child-allowance.

62. Gordon, N. (2014, August 6). A conservative case for a guaranteed basic income. *The Atlantic.* Retrieved from https://www.theatlantic.com/politics/archive/2014/08/why-arent-reformicons-pushing-a-guaranteed-basic-income/375600/.

63. Murray, C. (2006). *In our hands: A plan to replace the welfare state.* Washington, DC: American Enterprise Institute Press.

64. Lewis, M., Elliott, W., O'Brien, M., Jung, E., Harrington, K., & Jones-Layman, A. (2016). *Saving and educational asset-building within a community-driven CSA program: The case of Promise Indiana.* Lawrence: Center on Assets, Education, and Inclusion.

65. Lewis, M., O'Brien, M., Elliott, W., Harrington, K., & Crawford, M. (2016). *Immigrant Latina families saving in Children's Savings Account program against great odds: The case of Prosperity Kids.* Lawrence: Center on Assets, Education, and Inclusion.

66. Center on Budget and Policy Priorities. (2016). *Policy basics: The Earned Income Tax Credit.* Washington, DC: Author. Retrieved from http://www.cbpp.org/research/federal-tax/policy-basics-the-earned-income-tax-credit.

67. Grinstein-Weiss, M., Perantie, D. C., Russell, B. D., Comer, K., Taylor, S. H., Luo, L., . . . Ariely, D. (2015). *Refund to savings 2013: Comprehensive report on a large-scale tax-time saving program.* St. Louis, MO: Center for Social Development. Retrieved from https://www.brookings.edu/wp-content/uploads/2016/06/taxtime_savings.pdf.

68. Biggs, A. (2016, December 23). Middle class retirement accounts at record levels; Low-income households still saving little [Opinion]. *Forbes.* Retrieved from http://www.forbes.com/sites/andrewbiggs/2016/12/23/middle-class-retirement-accounts-at-record-levels-low-income-households-still-saving-little/#2c32294d113f.

69. Kim, C., & Tamborini, C. (2016, August 23). Disadvantages of the less educated: Education and contributory pensions at work. Paper presented to the American Sociological Association's 111th annual meeting. Seattle, WA.

70. Morrissey, M. (2016). *The state of American retirement: How 401(k)s have failed most American workers.* Washington, DC: Economic Policy Institute. Retrieved from http://www.epi.org/publication/retirement-in-america/.

71. Freeman, A., & Quercia, R. G. (2014). *Low- and moderate-income homeownership and wealth creation* (Working Paper). Chapel Hill, NC: UNC Center for Community Capital. Retrieved from https://ccc.unc.edu/files/2014/04/HomeownershipandWealth.pdf.

72. Sullivan, L., Meschede, T., Dietrich, L., Shapiro, T., Traub, A., Ruetschlin, C. & Draut, T. (2015). *The racial wealth gap: Why policy matters.* Waltham, MA: IASP/Demos. Retrieved from http://www.demos.org/sites/default/files/publications/RacialWealthGap_2.pdf.

73. Rothstein, R. (2017). *The color of law: A forgotten history of how our government segregated America.* New York, NY: Liveright.

74. Shapiro, T. M. (2006). Race, homeownership and wealth. *Washington University Journal of Law & Policy, 20*(53). Retrieved from http://openscholarship.wustl.edu/law_journal_law_policy/vol20/iss1/4.

75. Beverly, S. G., & Sherraden, M. (1999). Institutional determinants of saving: Implications for low-income households and public policy. *Journal of Socio-Economics, 28*(4), 457–473.

76. Beverly, S. G., Elliott, W. III, & Sherraden, M. (2013). *Child Development Accounts and college success: Accounts, assets, expectations, and achievements* (CSD Perspective No. 13-27). St. Louis, MO: Center for Social Development. Retrieved from http://csd.wustl.edu/publications/documents/p13-27.pdf.

77. Sherraden, M. (1991). *Assets and the poor: A new American welfare policy.* Armonk, NY: M. E. Sharpe.

78. Friedline, T., Despard, M., & West, S. (2017). *Investing in the future: A geographic investigation of brick-and-mortar financial services and households' financial health.* Lawrence: Center on Assets, Education, and Inclusion.

79. Despard, M., & Friedline, T. (2017). *Do metropolitan areas have equal access to banking? A geographic investigation of financial services availability.* Lawrence: Center on Assets, Education, and Inclusion.

80. Barr, M. (2007, March). Financial services for low- and moderate-income households. Paper delivered at a National Poverty Center conference: "Access, Assets, and Poverty." Ann Arbor, MI. Retrieved from http://www.npc.umich.edu/news/events/access_assets_agenda/barr.pdf.

81. Traub, A., Sullivan, L., Meschede, T., & Shapiro, T. (2017). The asset value of Whiteness: Understanding the racial wealth gap. Washington, DC: Demos and IASP. Retrieved from http://www.demos.org/publication/asset-value-whiteness-understanding-racial-wealth-gap.

82. Lynch, R., & Oakford, P. (2013). *The economic effects of granting legal status and citizenship to undocumented immigrants*. Washington, DC: Center for American Progress. Retrieved from https://www.americanprogress.org/issues/immigration/reports/2013/03/20/57351/the-economic-effects-of-granting-legal-status-and-citizenship-to-undocumented-immigrants/.

83. Terry, S. (2016, September 15). Citizenship, an essential step to building wealth. *Huffington Post*. Retrieved from http://www.huffingtonpost.com/sabrina-terry-/citizenship-an-essential-_b_11996952.html.

84. Holmberg, S. (2017). *Boiling points: The inextricable links between inequality and climate change*. New York, NY: Roosevelt Institute. Retrieved from http://rooseveltinstitute.org/boiling-points/.

85. Reeves, R. (2017). *Dream hoarders: How the American upper middle class is leaving everyone else in the dust, why that is a problem, and what to do about it*. Washington, DC: Brookings Institution Press.

86. Bankman, J., & Shaviro, D. (2015). Piketty in America: A tale of two literatures. *Tax Law Review, 68*, 453–516.

87. Sawhill, I., & Rodrigue, E. (2015). Wealth, inheritance, and social mobility. *Social Mobility Memos*. Washington, DC: Brookings Institution. Retrieved from https://www.brookings.edu/blog/social-mobility-memos/2015/01/30/wealth-inheritance-and-social-mobility/.

Index

Tables are indicated by an italic *t* following the page number.